Indian Asceticism

by

M. G. BHAGAT

D1497382

Munshiram Manoharlal Publishers Pvt. Ltd.

Ref
BL
2015
.A8
B48
1976
Cop. 1

First published 1976
© 1976, **Bhagat,** Dr. Mansukh Ghelabhai (b. 1922)
Published by
Munshiram Manoharlal
Publishers Pvt. Ltd.
54, Rani Jhansi Road,
New Delhi-110055

Printed in India by
Radiant Printers
20/26, West Patel Nagar,
New Delhi-110008

To

the ever-cherished memory

of

my father

Contents

Abbreviations

AV.	Atharvaveda
Ang. Nik.	Aṅguttara Nikāya
Ap. DS.	Āpastaṁba Dharmasūtra
Acar.	Ācārańga Sūtra
AB.	Aītareya Brāhmaṇa
AIOC.	All India Oriental Conference
Aup.	Aupapātika Sūtra
BG.	Bhagavadgītā
BS.	Brahmasūtra
Brhad. Up.	Bṛhadāraṇyaka Upaniṣad
Baudh. DS.	Baudhāyana Dharmasūtra
Bhag.	Bhagavat
Chand. Up.	Chāṅdogya Upaniṣad
Comm.	Commentary
CHI.	Cambridge History of India
CSUP.	Constructive Survey of Upaniṣadic Philosophy
Digha. Nik.	Dīgha Nikāya
DS.	Dharmasūtras
DP.	Dhammapada
Dasa.	Dasāsuyakkhandha
Dsv.	Dasaveyāliya
Divya.	Divyāvadāna
DOB.	Dialogues of the Buddha
ESD.	English Sanskrit Dictionary
Epi. Car.	Epigraphia Carnatica
Epi. Ind.	Epigraphia Indica
EB.	Encylopaedia Britannica
EBM.	Early Buddhist Monachism
ERE.	Encyclopaedia of Religion and Ethics
FDOB.	Further Dialogues of the Buddha
Gaut. DS.	Gautama Dharmasūtra
GB.	Gaupatha Brāhmaṇa

HOS.	Harvard Oriental Series
HIP.	History of Indian Philosophy
HDS.	History of Dharmaśāstra
HSL.	History of Sanskrit Literature
HIL.	History of Indian Literature
HJM.	History of Jaina Monachism
IP.	Indian Philosophy
IA.	Indian Antiquary
JBU.	Journal of the Bombay University
JAOS.	Journal of the American Oriental Society
JRAS.	Journal of the Royal Asiatic Society
JBORS.	Journal of the Bihar and Orissa Research Society
JASB.	Journal of the Asiatic Society of Bengal
JDL.	Journal of Department of Letters
JOI.	Journal of the Oriental Institute
JS.	Jaina Sūtras
JA.	Jaina Antiquary
Jat.	Jātaka
JMJ.	Jaina Monastic Jurisprudence
Kau. Up.	Kauśītaki Upaniṣad
KS.	Kathā Saṁhitā
Kalpa.	Kappasūtta
Kau. Br.	Kauśītaki Brāhmaṇa
Mbh.	Mahābhārata
Man. Up.	Maṇdukya Upaniṣad
Mund. Up.	Muṇḍaka Upaniṣad
MU.	Minor Upaniṣads
Mul.	Mulācāra
Maj. Nik.	Majjhima Nikāya
Maha. Up.	Mahānārāyaṇopaniṣad
Manu.	Manusmṛiti
Naya	Nāyādhammakahāö
OST.	Original Sanskrit Texts
OIP.	Outline of Indian Philosophy
POU.	Philosophy of the Upaniṣads
PU.	Principal Upaniṣads
P.	Pāli
PTS.	Pāli Text Society
q. b.	Quoted by
ṚV.	Ṛgveda

RPU.	Religion and Philosophy of the Upaniṣads
Rayap.	Rāyapaseniya
Ram.	Rāmāyaṇa
Śveta. Up.	Śvetāśvatara Upaniṣad
SB.	Śankar's Commentary on the BS
SBE.	Sacred Books of the East
Sk.	Saṅskṛit
SV.	Sāmaveda
Sam. Nik.	Saṁyutta Nikāya
Sum. Vil.	Sumangala Vilāsini
Suyagad.	Suyagaḍanaga
Stkr.	Sutrakṛtāṅga
Smv.	Saṃvāyaṅga
SED.	Saṅskṛit English Dictionary (Macdonell)
SB.	Śatapatha Brāhmaṇa
Tait. Up.	Taittirīya Upaniṣad
Than.	Thānaṅga
TS.	Taittirīya Saṁhitā
TPU.	Thirteen Principal Upaniṣads
Theri.	Therigāthā
Thera.	Theragāthā
Tattva.	Tattvārthasūtra
TB.	Taittirīya Brāhmaṇa
Up.	Upaniṣad
Uttar.	Uttarajjhāyana
Vinay.	Vinaya Texts
Vas DS.	Vasiṣṭha Dharmasūtra
VS.	Vājasaneyi Saṁhitā
Vis.	Viṣṇu Dharmasūtra
YV.	Yajurveda
Yaj.	Yājñavalkya Smṛti

Preface

In August 1957 in the Lok Sabha a Sadhu Bill urging the registration of nearly six lakhs of Sādhus and Saṁnyāsis was moved. The intention of the mover of the Bill was "to purge the increasing number of imposters and blacksheep robed in saintly saffron guise from committing unsocial acts." After an animated discussion the Bill was defeated as the Government found it difficult to implement it. The reasons were two-fold. Firstly, the law could not drag the nuns—Budhist, Jaina and Christian, who had renounced the world to line up with the Sādhus at a registration office. The very idea of registration was mundane to those who had left all social conventions. Secondly, the basic question was to define the terms 'Sādhu' and 'Saṁnyāsi' in the terms of law. It was found an impossible task; for once a saṁnyāsi or monk took the vow of saṁnyāsa or renunciation, he or she ceased to have any antecedents.

The discussion emphasised three salient points. Firstly, the Bill was an attack on the spiritual heritage of India. Secondly, this ancient institution had rendered yeoman services to the society by bringing about a healthy blending of material prosperity and spiritual requirement of the people. Thirdly, the ascetic in ancient India was known by many names. Rishis and munis, Yogis and mystics, Sages and saṁnyāsis all alike basked under the holy banyan tree of asceticism.

The fake elements in the holy institution of Sadhus and Saṁnyāsis and their being involved in anti-social acts is not peculiar to modern times. The Kautilya Arthaśāstra, echoes the state of ascetic institution of those times and how it was viewed as a force which disrupted society. Even the Buddhist Vinaya Laws and Jaina Monastic jurisprudence partly reflect the anxiety of the Buddha and Mahāvīra to keep their orders pure in harmony with the social conscience. However, that is only the other side of the picture.

It is also true that no one can study India's ancient history and culture without being struck with the splendid heights and dignity of the aims of the ascetic movement and the seriousness of the men and women who were inspired by it. When the movement first made its appearance, it was the greatest intellectual and religious force of the time. It captured the noblest minds and ruled them. It produced the finest flowers of the human spirit of whom many known and unknown seers of the Upanishads, the Buddha and Mahāvīra were representatives. For many centuries, thereafter, the highest spiritual life of the land found for itself in its discipline, a sufficient and a satisfying expression. Only high ideals most earnestly pursued could have produced the lofty literature of asceticism and monastic ideals. The present thesis attempts to capture some glimpses of that movement, trace its genesis and evaluate its contributions to social, religious, intellectual, ethical and other spheres of life of the people. It is a vast panorama of ancient India that the study seeks to capture —right from its earliest dawn to the beginning of the Christian era. The vastness of the subject and its deeper philosophical ramifications permit us, however, to attempt only the main outlines of the problem.

The work is divided into eleven chapters. The sources utilised are Indian and foreign. In main literary sources of the Vedic texts, Buddhist and Jaina writings, the Epics (the *Mahābhārata*, the *Gītā* and the Rāmāyaṇa), Arthaśāstra, Dharmasūtras and Yogasūtras are utilised for the purpose of investigation. The foreign sources consist of the impressions recorded by the Greeks and the Romans before and after the invasion of Alexander.

The method followed is two-fold. Firstly, the progressive development of asceticism is divided into various periods so as to enable us to have a full picture of each age and see how far the position of ascetic institution went on changing in response to the varying conditions and human needs of the society. Secondly, with a view to have a synthetic picture of the ascetic institution, a connected narrative of the different ideas and aspects of asceticism viz. *Tapas*, *Vairāgya*, *Saṁnyāsa* and *Yoga* is given while discussing the concept of asceticism. Each one of the four facets assume different forms of processes and disciplines of Indian asceticism at different times. Each aspect is separately treated with a view to show how each was closely related with the other to form a composit concept of asceticism. The evolution of ascetic institution as a socio-religious institution can be perceived here clearly in its various strands and stages.

With regard to the origin of asceticism, an attempt is made to study the problem from a perspective of human psychology besides that of theology and philosophy of religion. It is also endeavoured to assess the impact of primitive religions on the ascetic beliefs and practices and the possible contributions of the pre-Āryans to the evolution of asceticism.

I am greatly beholden to all the scholars, Western and Eastern, whose works I have studied and utilised for the purpose of investigation. I am indebted to my guide Dr. L.B. Keny for the personal and persistent interest he has taken in the progress of my work at every stage. My thanks are also due to my innumerable friends, who have given me the benefit of their suggestions and advice from time to time.

This work, which has since been revised, was presented as a thesis to the Bombay University for which I was awarded the degree of Doctor of Philosophy.

In the meanwhile, all constructive and valuable suggestions for the improvement of this work will be welcome.

M. G. Bhagat

Bombay
24 April 1976

Chapter 1

Introductory

It is the legacy of the European scholars, who in their attempt to understand and interpret Indian inheritance, have described the 'East as passive, tranquil and dreamy as opposed to the active, busy and practical West.'[1] India is symbolic of 'the brooding East' and it is very characteristic of her ancient wisdom that she has always appeared to them antique and mystic. It is due to this reason, it is often said that it is in the East that wisdom dawned earlier.[2] This is also borne out by ancient India's speculative activity. When it was the beginning of philosophy in Greece, India had already made considerable progress in philosophy. And it has been rightly noted by a great scholar that the highest wisdom of Greece was 'to Know Ourselves'; the highest wisdom of India is 'to Know Our Self.'[3] It is this wisdom and thought with their bewildering variety and mosaic pattern have drawn, not only in the past but even now to India's bosom, many a traveller in the quest of her rich and precious treasures. The journey might not have taken them to the goal of complete unfoldment of her ancient heritage, but the attempt must have been amply rewarding in the enrichment of the heart and mind of those who undertook this fascinating and eventful though arduous journey.

In the long line of such travellers was Max Muller who endeavoured to plumb the depths of the heart and mind of India. He took a lofty view of her art, sciences, literature and philosophy. Says he: 'Whatever sphere of the human mind you may select for

[1]The brooding East, Arnold. India, dreamy India, Philosophical, Unpractical and hopelessly unsuccessful in the maintenance of her political freedom...... Zimmer, *Philosophies of India*, p. 65. India favours passivity more than activity—Urquhart, *The Vedanta and Modern Thought*, p. 4. The West is more practical, the East more mystical—Crook, S., *EB*., Art. 'Jesus Christ.' Oman, *The Mystics, Ascetics and Saints of India*, p. 270.

[2]Brunton, *The Hidden Teaching beyond Yoga*, pp. 165, 320, 321; 'All that we value most has come to us from the East...' Muller, *What Can India Teach Us*? p. 32; From the East comes the light, from the West law—A Latin Proverb.

[3]Slater, *The higher Hinduism in Relation to Christianity*, p. 78.

your special study, whether it be language, or religion, or mythology or philosophy, whether it be laws or customs, primitive art or primitive sciences, everywhere you have to go to India, whether you like it or not, because some of the most valuable and most instructive materials in the history of man are treasured up in India and in India only.'[1] The word 'materials' means the sources viz. archaeology, sculpture, painting, literature and coins which unfold manifold aspects of India's cultural history.

Out of the many others, most worthy of mention are Goethe, Schopenhauer, Rolland and Toynbee. Goethe is said to have danced with joy over the German translation of the *Śākuntala* by Kalidās. Schopenhauer eloquently expressed his faith in the Upanishads: 'It has been the solace of my life; it will be the solace of my death.' Rolland, who interpreted Gandhi, Vivekananda and Ramakrishna Paramhamsa to the Western world said: 'If there is one place on the face of the earth where all the dreams of living men have found a home from the very earliest days when men began their dream of existence, it is India.' In very recent memory, Toynbee, as if to flatter us declared : 'In India there is an attitude towards life and an approach to the needs of the present situation in the world as a whole,' and exhorted her 'to go on giving the world Indian examples of the spiritual fight that makes man human.'[2]

There is another type of travellers, who in their readiness to criticise, has only discovered the lower elements of Indian culture and thus failed to do justice to its higher aspects. In their endeavour to analyse its essential strength and weakness, their vision and judgement fall an easy prey to hasty generalisations that accentuate only the weakness of Indian culture. Representatives of this class are a legion.

Oman believes that 'It is the ascetic profession that time out of mind has been of pre-eminent dignity in the eyes of the Indian people.' Quite oblivious of the fact that they have also eminent regard for the heroic tradition, he adds : 'The only possible state of a religious (holy) life is one involving asceticism.'[3] Renou considers Hinduism as 'the very type of a religion of renunciation.' He labels this observation as 'a global characterization of Hinduism.'[4]

[1]Muller, op. cit., p. 15.
[2]Toynbee, *One World and India*, pp. 41, 63.
[3]Oman, op. cit., pp. 271-272.
[4]Renou, *Hinduism*, Introduction, p. 5.

Schweitzer brands Indian religion, thought and culture as 'life-negating.'[1] McKenzie finds Indian asceticism 'full of abhorrent ideas, anti-social and not spiritual enough and as defended by philosophic thought does not partake of the nature of ethical activity.'[2] Ronaldshay finds that 'Pessimism infects the whole physical and intellectual life of India and that the Indian philosophers have never been able to paint any positive picture of bliss.'[3] Koestler mocks at our Indian way of life, especially the Yoga tradition as a physical or spiritual discipline. To him *Samādhi* is 'pure imagination without thought.'[4] He feels that Indians are not as contemplative as they are reputed to be and concludes that he had 'never encountered a people as uncontemplative as the nation of Yogis.'[5] He is not merely a biased observer but a hostile witness. Many Western scholars unduly harp on the note of pessimism in Indian asceticism and characterize Indian thought as wholly pessimistic and other-worldly.

To the research worker of history who has to discover and assess factual reality in its varied aspects from many divergent as well as harmonious views, both the sets of views are equally important and deserve careful examination.

It becomes necessary for the research worker, therefore, to be very careful in his interpretation of Indian culture. He has to view every cultural phenomenon or reality dispassionately, with a sense of historical proportion and perspective. Tradition is respected but not as a blind adoration of the past. The sentimental approach has to be discarded, inasmuch as tradition is examined in the context of its cultural setting to yield its essential strength as also its weakness. It is this approach that is intended to be followed to investigate the problem of asceticism in ancient India, its origin and development and its contribution to Indian culture as a whole.

Importance of the Subject

India is one of the few countries where ascetic ideal has been

[1]Schweitzer, *Indian thought and its development*, Preface. Also q. b. Basham, *The Wonder that was India*, p. 9.

[2]McKenzie, *Hindu Ethics*, p. 240, also q.b. Hopkins, *Ethics of India*, Preface, pp. x-xi; Kane refutes this allegation, *HDS.*, Vol. II, Pt. I, pp. 3-4.

[3]Ronaldshay, *India—a Bird's eye-view*, p. 313.

[4]Koestler, *The Lotus and the Robot*, pp. 125-132. Walker defends Yoga against Koestler's criticism and proves the fallacy of his observations. *The Conscious Mind*, pp. 117-122.

[5]ibid.

fondly upheld and ascetic practices have been widely followed from very ancient times. Its roots seem to be lost in the mist of the pre-Āryan civilization. 'It is a tribute to the high metaphysical capacity of the Indian people,' says Deussen,[1] 'that the phenomenon of asceticism made its appearance among them earlier and occupied a larger place than among any other known people.'

Throughout the history of Hinduism, ascetic ideals have maintained a stronghold on the minds of the people. To the mind of the Hindu, the life of the *Sannyāsī* who has freed himself from all human ties and given up all physical comfort and well-being for a spiritual existence, has always seemed to be the highest. Even today its appeal to the masses as a symbol of holy life is considerable. For ancient Indian culture is dominated by religion. And the assertion is not without truth that 'the Hindus are the most religious people in the world, that is, the greatest slaves to the bondage of tradition.'[2]

The reason for the perpetuation of such a tradition can be traced to the role which the ascetic group of seers and *ṛishis*, saints and sannyāsis, mystics and yogis played in moulding the religious history of India through the ages. The Vedas were revealed according to the orthodox tradition to *ṛishis* like Atri, Vaśiṣṭha and Viśwāmitra and many others. Yājñavalkya, Śānḍilya, Manu, Vālmiki and Veda Vyās, most of the thinkers of the Upanishads, Buddha and Mahāvira, belonged to the ancient family of seers, munis and ascetics. The six systems of philosophical thought, the *Darśānas*, are symbolic of India's moral and spiritual values. These were also originated or promulgated by the *ṛishis* or ascetics.[3] Ascetics and saints have played an important role in ancient India.[4] Even today holy men hold a real fascination for almost all the classes in India. And a Western scholar has rightly observed: 'In Indiano religious

[1]Deussen, *The Philosophy of the Upaniṣhads*, p. 65.

[2]Williams, *Brahmanism & Hinduism*, Introduction, p. vii.

[3]Ghurye, *Indian Sadhus*, p. 255; Mahadevan, *Ten Saints of India*, p. 1.

[4]Dutt, *Early Buddhist Monachism*, Preface, p. ix; Radhakrishnan, *Eastern Religion and Western Thought*, p. 35. Dutt writes: 'It is to the ascetics that India owes largely all that is valuable and enduring in her cultural and spiritual life.' Radhakrishnan observes: 'From the beginning of her history India has adored and idealised not soldiers and statesmen, not men of science and leaders of industry, not even poets and philosophers but those rarer and chastened spirits......time has discredited heroes as easily as it has forgotten every one else but the saints remain.'

teacher can expect a hearing unless he begins by renouncing the world.'[1] Dutt elaborates : 'One who has need to sway the group-mind whether a religious preacher, a social reformer or even a political leader—finds it to his purpose to appear in *sannyāsī's* likeness in this country, for in that semblance he is able to command the highest respect and the readiest following.'[2] This suggests how the Indian mind still perceives in him a symbolic relation to the moral and spiritual values the *Bhikṣu* or the *Sannyāsin* embodied in himself in ancient India.

The ascetic in ancient India had peculiar beliefs and practices which evoked considerable curiosity and admiration. The power born of his austerities and self-mortification which came to be known as *Tapas*, was a great force which could achieve extraordinary results. It was a method of achieving highest goal of power, happiness, wisdom or emancipation.[3] One can attain *Brahmaloka* or go to heaven through *tapas*.[4] The efficacy of *tapas* is so great that even venerable Gods like Viṣṇu are described as practising *tapas* to achieve soul-force before embarking on momentous undertaking.[5] Even Prajāpati is said to have practised *tapas* prior to each act of creation.[6] Tapas was also one of the ways of self-realisation, the search for truth : *tapasā brahmā vijijñāsva*.[7] Through *tapas* the ascetic could reach out for perfection. His life of *tapas* was an eloquent testimony to the supremacy of the spiritual over the material splendour. Agrawala observes : '*Tapas* is the soul of *Sādhanā* aspect of Indian culture. It is the backbone of our culture. Strength and charm have been added to our thinking solely through *tapas*. Its beauty alone illumines the lives of Shiva, Buddha, Tirthankara, Nara-Nārāyana, Pārvati, Bhagiratha and Arjuna. The attraction of their images lies in their devotion to *tapas* which leads us towards the goal.'[8]

[1] Elliot, *Hinduism & Buddhism*, I, Introduction, p. XVI.
[2] *Buddhist Monks and Monasteries of India*, p. 44.
[3] cf. Dasgupta, *Hindu Mysticism*, p. 91.
[4] *Ram.*, III. 5. 28; IV. 13-19.
[5] *Ram.*, I. 29. 3.
[6] *SB.*, X. 4. 42; *Bṛhad. Up.*, I, 26; *TU.*, II. 6.1.
[7] *Mund. Up.*, III 1-2-3 Also *Śveta. Up.*, I. 15-16; *Maitri Up.*, 4.4.
[8] Agrawala, *Kala aur Sanskriti*, p. 199.
भारतीय संस्कृति का जो साधना-पक्ष है तप उसका प्राण है। तप हमारी संस्कृति का मेरुदंड है। तप की शक्ति के बिना भारतीय संस्कृति में जो कुछ ज्ञान है वह फीका रह जाता है। तप से

It was a unique phenomenon that *tapas* came to occupy such a vital significance in the life and culture of ancient India and influenced its history of religious and philosophical thought. How *tapas* came to be regarded as a significant part of asceticism, an aspect of *Sādhanā* and a backbone of our culture becomes relevant to our investigation.

All this is not intended to exalt ascetic institution or the ascetic ideal as the most sublime. Nor it is desired to convey an impression that the ascetic life was the best and the only ideal life in ancient India. The main aim of almost all the *Darśanas* was to show the way to salvation and they represented the life of renunciation (*Saṁnyāsa*) as an ideal for everyone. But it will be an error to hold that they represent the whole life of every Indian. It must be noted that not even one out of ten thousands took to renunciation.[1] Although a life of renunciation was considered necessary for salvation, there is also abundant evidence in ancient India, as we shall see in the sequel, of a vigorous reaction to the challenges and attractions of mundane life. It also meets with disapproval as in Buddhism, *Arthaśāstra* and the *Gītā*. But the fact remains that the ascetic life came to be regarded as holy and essential for salvation at certain times and later on found a place as the fourth *aśrama* as *Saṁnyāsāśrama*. How did asceticism or *tapas* and renunciation (*Saṁnyāsa*) come to play such a vital role in ancient India, form the theme of this study.

Purpose of the Study

The problem of Indian asceticism in its modern form has been studied and investigated by Oman[2] and Farquhar.[3] With regard to its ancient form, Sharma[4] has made some contributions. Ghurye in his work has also presented 'the rise, history, work and present

ही यहां का चिन्तन सशक्त और रसमय बना है। शिव, बुद्ध, तीर्थंकर, नर-नारायण, पार्वती, भागीरथ आदि के जीवन में तप का ही सौंदर्य है। लक्ष्य तक पहुँचने के लिए तप की साधना उनके स्वरूप का आकर्षण है।

[1]cf. Raju & Radhakrishnan, *The Concept of Man*, p. 207.

[2]Oman, *Mystics, Saints and Ascetics of India*, London, 1920.

[3]Farquhar, *JRAS.*, 1925, pp. 479-81. *The Organisation of the Samnyāsis of Vedānta.*

[4]Sharma, *Contributions to the History of Brāhmanical Asceticism (Samnyāsa)*, Poona, 1939.

organization of Hindu asceticism and ascetics.'[1] The work takes a rapid survey of asceticism during the course of its development over four millennia. Though in the later part of the book, it succeeds in its object of furnishing the details of the extant various orders and sects and sub-sects *ad infinitum*, and the rules of each order or sect supposed to govern the conduct and mode of life of its members, it does not adequately trace the origins of asceticism and its influence over the monastic orders of the Buddha and Mahavira, whose contribution to asceticism also does not receive deserving treatment.

In his concluding chapter, Ghurye remarks that, 'it has not been possible to make a statistically satisfying survey of the reasons and motives that impel individuals to renounce ordinary life in favour of asceticism.'[2] Thus for the modern as well as the ancient period, the motives and desires which also form the basis for the origins of asceticism, remain to be surveyed. We are, however, concerned only with the ancient period.

Moreover, with regard to ascetic origins, Ghurye traces them to our sacred literature and not the minds of men. He discusses asceticism as 'a complex of a number of traits viz. celibacy, austerity, concentration and ecstasy.'[3] Now a 'complex' has the meaning of 'group' or 'combination' but it also has a psychological connotation when it suggests a state of mind which is not normal. The normal human tendency seeks material progress in and through society. What were the factors that turned the normal tendency away from society and drove men to run away from normal life? What were the psychological or other needs to prompt such tendencies? We do not have satisfactory answers to these questions which demand an insight into the psychology of religious phenomena with reference to the conditions that preceded and accompanied them. Most of the writers on asceticism have either ignored or not paid due attention to this psychological basis. The result is that the interpretation of asceticism in terms of theology and philosophy alone has led to the misrepresentation of this universal phenomenon. Eliade has also done exhaustive research on Yoga—one of the facets of Indian asceticism.[4] However, all this

[1]Ghurye, *Indian Sadhus*, Bombay, 1953, Preface.
[2]ibid, p. 251.
[3]ibid, pp. 17-19.
[4]Eliade, *Yoga, Immortality and Freedom*, London, 1958.

leads us to affirm that though Sharma, Ghurye and Eliade have dealt with some of its aspects, the problem of asceticism in its whole range has not so far been submitted to scientific investigation. The present work attempts to do this and thus reveals a neglected chapter in India's social history with a special emphasis on the genesis of asceticism.

Extent of the Work

The study is confined to the period from the Indus Valley Civilisation (*c.* 2500 BC) to the advent of the Christian era.

Sources

The sources and materials available for the present work naturally divide themselves into two classes : (1) Indian and (2) Foreign.

Indian Sources

The archaeological sources of ancient India available at present are meagre. We have, therefore, to rely solely upon tradition as recorded in our sacred and secular literature. Thus literature on the *Saṁhitās*, *Brāhmaṇas*, *Āraṇyakas*, *Upaniṣads*, *Epics*, *Buddhist* and *Jaina* texts, *Arthaśāstra*, *Dharmasūtras* and *Yogasūtras* is explored, and evidence adduced therefrom, for the purpose of investigation.

Foreign Sources

These will merely consist of the impressions recorded by foreigners, especially the Greeks and the Romans, in their writings on India before and after the invasion of Alexander. The writers on whose accounts we will rely are Herodotus (484-431 BC), Tertullian, Aristoxenus of Toranto (3rd Century BC), Strabo (60 BC-AD 19), Arrian (200 AD) and Megasthenes who was the ambassador of the Graeco-Persian King Seleukes at the court of Chandragupta Maurya from 311 to 302 BC. Despite certain inaccuracies and mutual contradictions they have their own value as they throw considerable light on the ascetic practices and beliefs of the Indian ascetics of the times.

Chapter 2

The Concept of Asceticism

From very early times asceticism has been a curious phenomenon in India. The ascetics have always exercised considerable influence, capturing the imagination of a great number of population of India, literate and illiterate alike. The strange beliefs, practices and pretentions of these ascetics have always exercised interest of many foreigners who came to India at different times from Strabo in the fourth century BC[1] to Oman,[2] Brunton,[3] Rutledge,[4] Marshall[5] and Ouspensky[6] in our own times.

The ascetic ideal which the institution of asceticism fosters has been the outcome of a slow and long evolution through many centuries. With this ideal many ancient elements and ideas, beliefs and practices so mingle that it becomes essential for us to have a clear idea of the different aspects which have gone to constitute the whole concept of asceticism.

The word 'asceticism' is derived from the Greek word *askesis* which meant exercise and training for the purpose of strength, skill and mastery in the athletic games.[7]

The Webster's dictionary (1962) defines an ascetic as 'one who

[1]We have the records of the Romans and the Greeks before and after the invasion of Alexander, Vide Chapter IX.

[2]*Mystics, Saints and Ascetics of India*, Chapter VI. Oman describes the impressions of some European visitors to India and of the Sadhus they had met.

[3]Brunton's *A Search in Secret India*, is a record of the *Sadhus* or ascetics he had met in India.

[4]Rutledge's *In Search of A Yogi* is an enquiry into the supernatural powers acquired by the Yogis of India.

[5]Marshall's *Hunting the Guru in India*, is an account of the holy men, the religious teachers belonging to the ascetic institution whom she has encountered. This, however, is not to say, she discovered the 'mysterious East' and miracles in India. What she found is summed up in the preface: 'Of all the nations of the world, only India knows how to nourish the soul.'

[6]In his *In Search of the Miraculous*, Ouspensky describes how man can achieve immortality through the ways of the fakir, the monk and the Yogi and deals with the Indian tradition.

[7]*ERE.*, II, p. 63.

lives a life of contemplation and rigorous self-denial for religious purposes,' or 'any one who lives with strict self-discipline and abstinence.'

In the same dictionary we find asceticism defined as (a) 'the practice or way of life of an ascetic, systematic self-denial for some ideal.' (b) 'the religious doctrine that we can reach a higher spiritual state by rigorous self-discipline and self-denial.'

The ascetic in ancient India was known by many terms : *Vānaprasthin*, *Tapasvin*, *Yogin*, *Tāpas*, *Yatin*, *Vairāgin*, *Vairāṅgika*, *Muni*, *Parikāñṣin*, *Saṁnyāsin* and *Vaikhānasa*. All these terms connoted only relative attitudes of varied conducts of the ascetics detached existence.

Vānaprasthin is a forest dweller, a hermit, (*Araṇyavāsi*, *Vanavāsi*, *Vanasthāyi*, *Vanastha*), a Brahmin in the third stage of life.[1] He is often called a *Vaikhānasa*.[2]

Yogin is one who is engaged in *Yoga* or meditation (from *Vyuj*, to join, to direct, to employ, to unite).[3]

Tāpasa is one who practises *tapas* (from *tap*, to be heated, to burn, hence austerity).[4] He is the one who is habituated to austerities : *tapaḥ śilamasya*.[5] He is also called tapasvin : *tapasvibhyo adhiko yogi*.[6]

Yatin is one who has controlled his passions (from *yam* and *yat*, to restraint, to subdue, to control; to strive, to exert oneself). In the Vedic and later Brahmanical literature, a Yati is one who has brought all his passions and feelings under restraint.[7] The term

[1] *SED.*, p. 299.

[2] *Tait. Ar.*, (I. 13.3) describes them as one of the Ṛṣis who were born of Prajāpati: Yenakhāḥ tevaikhānasāḥ yevālāḥ tevālakhilyāḥ. Manu (vi. 21) refers to the institutes of *Vaikhānasa* when he prescribes rules for the *Vānaprasthas*. Medhatithi comments: Vaikhānasaṁ nāma śāstraṁ yatravānaprastha dharmāvihitāsteṣāṁ mate sthitaḥ. There is also a work called *Vaikhānasasmārtasūtra* which can be dated in the fourth century AD but which contains far earlier material.

[3] *Śvetā. Up.*, II. 12: Yogagune pravṛtte yogāgnimayaṁ śariraṁ. *BG.*, VI. 46: Karmbhya ca adhiko Yogi.

[4] *AV.*, xiii.2.25; *Brhad. Up.*, IV.3.22; *Sankh. Br.*, XIV.6,8,10; *Uttar.*, *SBE.*, XLV, p. 140, 418 n2; *Manu*, vi.27: tāpaseṣveva vipreṣu yātrikaṁ bhaikṣamāharet.

[5] *Shabdakalpadrum*, tapo'syastiti tapoyuktaḥ tāpasaḥ cf. tapati tapate ayaṁ ātmanepadinyanye, p. 587.

[6] *BG.*, VI.46; *AV.*, XIII.2.25.

[7] *Taitt. Sam.*, iii.4.9.2; *Ait. Br.*, VII.28; *Tandya Br.*, VIII.1.4, XIII.8-17; *Mund Up.*, III.2.6; Saṁnyāsayogādyatayaḥ. *Manu*-VI.55-59; *BG.*, V. 25: yatātmanaḥ.

Yatin always means a *Saṁnyāsin* i.e. a person in the last of the four *āśramas*.[1] The word is also used synonymously to denote a *muni*, a *parivrājaka* and a *bhikṣu*. All these terms denote the fourth stage of an Aryan's life.[2] The Jaina monk is often called the *Yati*.[3] *Yama* meaning control is the first among the eight elements (*aṅgas*) of classical Yoga.[4]

Vairāgin is one who has subdued or freed himself from all earthly desires. The word comes from *Vi*, meaning apart, away without *raga* meaning desire or attachment, *virāgasya bhāvaḥ*.[5]

Vairāṅgik is one who is free from all worldly desires due to acquiring *vairāgya*.[6]

Muni is originally one who has taken the vow of silence, *mauneya*[7] also *man*, to think (*mananāt muniḥ*).[8] The Ṛigvedic muni is *deveṣito* and *unmaditā maunayena*, 'inspired' or 'moved by the spirit' and 'mad with silence.'[9] He is also the one who knows the Brahman.[10] He is variously styled as *Yati*, *Parivrājaka*, *Bhikṣu* or *Saṁnyāsin* synonymous with the fourth *āśrama*.[11] The Jaina monk is also called the *muni*.[12] The word acquired a general meaning in Buddhism and is applied by the Buddha to any man attaining perfection in self-restraint and insight.[13]

Pārikāñṣin is a contemplative Brāhmin in the fourth stage of his life. He is the same as the *Saṁnyāsin*.[14] The word also means an ascetic who devotes himself to abstract meditation or a contempla-

[1] *Taitt. Sam.*, vi.2.7.5, *Ait. Br.*, vii, 28.1; *Kau. Up.*, iii.1; *Manu*, vi.87, 96; *Vas DS.*, xi.34.

[2] *Ap. DS.*, II.9.21.1: mauna-atha parivrājaḥ; *Vas. DS.*, II.6.17.

[3] Stevenson, *The Heart of Jainism*, p. 233.

[4] *YS.*, II.29.

[5] *SED.*, p. 301; *ESD.*, p. 1025.

[6] *ESD.*, p. 27; *SED.*, p. 300.

[7] *Chand. Up.*, viii.5.2; cf. Moneyya or Mona (Pali) Munis are called *mounis*: *Mbh.*I.91.8.

[8] cf. *Unādisūtras*, IV.122: *man-in-ucca*, manyate jānāti iti munir Vaśiṣṭhādiḥ fr man=impulse, eagerness cf. *ṚV.*, VII.56.8; *Brhad. Up.*, iii.5.1.

[9] *ṚV.*, X.136.2-3, cf. *SED.*, p. 231.

[10] *Bṛhad. Up.*, IV.4.22 cf. *Munāti* in Pali means 'fathoming,' 'recognising,' 'knowing'; *Petavatthu*, 163. cf. *Uttar.*, *SBE.*, XLV, p. 140.

[11] *Mund. Up.*, III.2.6; *Baudh DS.*, II.10.17; *Gaut. DS.*, III.2.11; *Vis DS.*, X.1; *Manu*, VI.11, 54, 56, 69, 86.

[12] Stevenson, op. cit., p. 65.

[13] *DP.*, 268-269; Also attahitañ ca parahitañ ca munāti jānāti ti muni: *Petavatthu*, 163.

[14] *ESD.*, p. 620.

tive saint.[1]

Saṁnyāsī is one who lays down or renounces the world, a Brāhmin in the fourth *āśrama.*[2] The word *saṁnyāsa* is derived from *sam+ni+ās*, to place or put down, deposit, give up, abandon or quit : *Kāmyānāṁ karmaṇāṁ nyāsaṁ saṁnyāsāṁ.*[3] It also means *sam+nyās, samyag prakāreṇa*, completely laying aside or down *nyāsa*, abandonment of all worldly concerns.[4]

Saṁnyāsin is the most common term applied to an ascetic, the one who completely renounces the world and its attachments.[5] The term also means in the *Gītā*, to make, to deliver, entrust or commit to the care of: *mayi sarvāṇi karmāṇi saṁnyasādhyatmacetasā.*[6] As to the question what he renounces, apart from the world, there are different answers. According to the *Saṁnyāsa Upanishad*, it is a fire meaning the Vedic sacrifices.[7] In the Vedanta it is the renunciation of false values and attachment.[8] This is explained and reiterated in the *Gītā*, according to which it is the renunciation of actions done with some fruit or purpose in view, *Karmaphalatyāgaṁ.*[9]

According to the *Vaikhānasadharmapraśna* the Brahmins alone were allowed to become *saṁnyāsis.*[10] However, this privilege, according to Manu was extended to the higher-castes (*dvijāti*).[11] The *śūdra* was not only not allowed to take to *saṁnyāsa* but also forbidden to practise austerities.[12] A *saṁnyāsī* was also called a *Pārikāñṣik.*[13]

[1] *SED* (Apte), p. 1012.

[2] *ESD.*, p. 1148.

[3] *BG.*, XVIII. 2.

[4] *Maha. Up.*, 62, 11.

[5] *SED.*, (Apte), p. 1625; *Manu*, vii.94; Vedāntaṁ vividhacśrutva saṁnyāsedanṛṇo dvijaḥ. *Bhartṛhari*, III.192; Saṁdaśya kṣaṇabhaṅguraṁ tad khilaṁ dhanyastu saṁanyasti.

[6] *BG*, III.30.

[7] *MU*, p. 20.

[8] Sankar in *Bhāgavatpāda*: dehanyāso hi saṁnyāso naiva kāsāyavāsasā, nāhaṁ deho' hamātmeti niscayo nyāsalakṣaṇam. Also nityānityavastu-viveka.

[9] *BG.*, XVIII.2.

[10] I.10-13: brāhmaṇasyāśramascatvāraḥ kṣatriyāsyādyastrayaḥ vaiṣyasyādyau tadāśramiṇascatvāro brahmacāri gṛhastho vānaprastho bhikṣuriti. Also IX-8: brāhmaṇānāṁ cāturaśramyaṁ kṣatriyāṇāṁ tryāśramyaṁ vaiṣyāṇāṁ dvayāśramyaṁ vihitam.

[11] *Manu*, VI.87, V.137; cf. *Jabala. Up.*, IV. VI.2.42.

[12] Rama kills Śaṁbuka, a *śūdra* practising penance (*Ram.* VII-76 f.). Also Mātaṅga, a *cāṇḍāla* practising austerities is looked upon with disfavour (*Mbh.*, xiii.27).

[13] *ESD.*, p. 27.

There are other terms viz. *Parivrājaka*, *Bhikṣu* and *Śramaṇa* which were also used to denote the ascetic or the *saṁnyāsi*. Though these are purely Sanskrit terms they were originally Prākrit words describing the Buddhist and Jaina monks but subsequently incorporated in Sanskrit literature by the Vedic authors. All these terms viz. *Pabajjaka* (P), and *Bhikkhu* (P) and *Samaṇa* (P) were used to denote that mode of life described in the Pali literature as 'passing from the household to the homeless state': *Agārasma anagāriyam pabajjati.*[1] 'The same idea is conveyed in Jainism by the phrase: *Agārāo anagāriam pavvayai.*'[2] The Buddhist *Piṭakas* and Jaina *Aṅgas* are full of references to the existence of a numerous community of men who were called world-forsakers and who lived outside society. The terms are used to refer to a wandering community of homeless men.

It may be remembered that the Buddhist and Jaina monks and nuns were not homeless but they were persons without a family life. They had the *saṅghas* of brothers and sisters and led a monastic life at different places and cannot be truly described as a wandering community. In contrast a Brahmanic wanderer (*parivrājaka*) had no shelter at all, having left home and possessions: *paritajya sarvaṁ gācchati* or *vrajati iti parivrājakaḥ.*[3]

Tapas

The scholars, Western as well as Indian, have translated the term 'asceticism' as *tapas* or austerity or renunciation.[4] It is also used to mean *Vairāgya.*[5] It is to be noted that though asceticism is rendered as *tapas*, *tapas* is one of the facets of asceticism. *Tapas* has a wider connotation than what is conveyed by the word 'austerity.' It is used sometimes to comprehend all forms of the pursuit of self-control.[6]

The word 'austerity' implies severity.[7] Life denied of comforts and pleasures becomes austere and painful. The austere life is one

[1] *Digha Nik.*, I.60, I.240, III.55.

[2] *Acar.*, II.2.1.

[3] *Bhaṭṭojidikṣita.*

[4] Radhakrishnan, *PU.*, pp. 109-110; Winternitz, *HIL.*, I, p. 220; *ESD.*, p. 27; Eliot, *Hinduism & Buddhism*, I, p. 71.

[5] *ESD.*, p. 27.

[6] *Chand. Up.*, II.23.1. cf. Radhakrishnan, *The Principal Upaniṣads*, p. 375.

[7] Sanskrit terms for austerity are: kārkaśyaṁ, kāṭhiṇyaṁ, ugratā, kathinatā, niṣṭhuratā, kathoratā, kaṭutā.

that is given to abstinence, severe discipline hence, *tapas*. This sense is often conveyed by the use of the word, *ugram*. Ṛṣi Agastya engaged in *tapas* is called *ṛṣir ugraḥ*.[1] The *tāpasas* or *tapasvis* are called, *ugratapas*.[2] When the term 'austerity' is used to mean *tapas*, it stands for physical endurance or harsh treatment of the body by fasts or wanton avoidance of pleasure or comfort of life. Hence it is used in the ascetic literature to convey self-torture or self-mortification.[3]

Sometimes an attempt is made to distinguish 'austerity,' from 'asceticism' both of which are rendered by the Sanskrit term '*tapas*.' To Radhakrishnan, *tapas* is 'severe self-discipline undertaken for spiritual ends.'[4] Farquhar, on the other hand, points out that austerity is 'the endurance of pain to gain some material end, whereas asceticism aims at moral or spiritual ends.'[5] This difference, however, is not absolute and has little practical significance, as *tapas* is used for both the terms *austerity* and *asceticism* to denote the *tapasvin's* ascetic effort. Moreover, *tapas* is employed not only for spiritual ends but for various motives where the ends are not purely material but also not moral. For instance, Ravana who carried off Sītā had acquired his power by *tapas* which enabled him to extort a boon from Brahmā.[6]

The Sanskrt term *tapas* is derived from the root *tap* and means 'to be hot or heated,' 'to burn.'[7] *Tapas*, signifies, therefore, in the first instance warmth, fervour or heat and means that which generates heat. Various practices were capable of generating 'fervour,' 'heat' or 'warmth' in the literal sense viz. sitting near the fire or in the sun, consumption of intoxicating and narcotic substances, internal heating and ecstasy.[8] The condition of internal heat can be caused by fasting or holding the breath.[9] The Vedic as well as the Buddhist

[1] *ṚV*, I.179.6.

[2] *Ram.*, I.63-18, I.63.15 & 24; *Mbh.*, I.8.36, I.223-35, I.123.26, IX.5.19, 48.3, XII.324.26; cf *Manu*, VI.75 tapascaranaiścangrahai sādhyanti tatpadam.

[3] cf. *ERE.*, II. p. 87.

[4] op. cit., pp. 109-110.

[5] *The Crown of Hinduism*, p. 247; cf. *ERE.*, II, pp. 225-235.

[6] *Ram.*, I.16.4-5. Such examples can be multiplied: The powerful *ṛṣis* cursed to make one's life miserable, even to extinction: *Ram.*, I.25.12-13; I.64.15; I.58.10; I.59.18; VII.5.16.

[7] *ṚV.*, 6.5.4, 7.34.19, 4.5.4.

[8] cf. Renou, *Vedic India*, p. 125.

[9] *Jaiminī*, iii.3.1; *Kau. Br.*, XXIII.5; *Baud. DS.*, IV.1.24.

texts refer to the heat obtained by holding the breath.[1] The Buddha is described as burning : *tapati tejasā.*[2] He is called 'burning' as he practices 'tapas.' It also means its effect as 'shining' or 'glowing' with lustre.[3] Ahalya, practising austerities, is described as magnificent, flaming in ascetic energy.[4] *Tapas* was thus extended to the feelings or sensations usually painful experienced as a result of 'heat' or 'fervour'; and thus pain or suffering in general, especially the pain which is voluntary and self-inflicted as in austerities, ascetic practices. The term, therefore, came to be applied in particular to religious penance, austerity, devotion and to connote the merit which such devotion was supposed to assure.[4] The ascetics (*tāpasas, tapasvis*) are described as highly effulgent by virtue of austerities, ascetic practices (*mahatejāḥ, mahātapāḥ*)[5] whose wealth is austerities (*tapodhanam*),[6] of great austerities (*param-tapāḥ*).[7]

Tapas is often translated as penance but the idea of sin and its expiation is not always present behind the austerities of most ascetics. However, in some cases the penance is performed as in the case of Viśvāmitra, not only to atone for moral lapses but also to transmute his lower nature of lust and passions into a higher state of perfection. Vanquished by Vaśiṣṭha many a time Viśvāmitra realised that a warrior's strength was nothing as compared with that of a Brahmin. He resolved to achieve this lofty pinnacle by the might of his austerities. He engaged himself in *tapas* of the most rigid (*ugra*) and awe-inspiring kind. Roots and fruits were his only food. After Menakā's seduction he added to his *tapas* the vow of chastity and to bring his senses under control. Raṁbhā came to lead him astray from the path of virtue and rob him of all that he gained. But this time he resisted the temptation and cursed Raṁbhā, giving vent to anger which deprived him of a great deal of accumulated ascetic merit. He started observing *maunavrata.* His *tapas* grew more fierce: he never opened his mouth, never spoke, never ate and held even his breath for all the time. He was in

[1]*AV.*, XV.15; *Maj. Nik.*, I.244.

[2]*DP.*, 387.

[3]In Pali *tapati* means shines, *tappati* is tormental, 'oppressed.'

[4]*Ram.*, I 49.17: paritāṅgi dhumenāpi diptāmagniśikhamiva durāgarṣam diptām sūryaprabhāmiva.

[5]*Ram.*, I.32.1, I.51.27.

[6]*Ram.*, I.29.12, III.12.5.

[7]*Ram.*, III.12.24.

a *samādhi* for a very long time. He was satisfied only when he could subjugate lust, greed, anger and all kinds of passions and lower propensities of his nature. As the result of his unparalleled *tapas* he became a *Brahmarṣi*, not only a Brāhmin by caste but also gaining all the moral virtues required of an ideal Brāhmin. He came to be known to every age as the greatest of all ascetics, asceticism incarnate. He affords an excellent example how *tapas* elevates a mere mortal to the highest state of perfection.[1]

Sankaracarya explains *tapas* as *kṛchra* a noun from the root *kṛs* (Sk) which means 'to draw together,' 'obtain,' 'master' and implying exertion, retention etc.[2] This word has a merit of explicitly conveying the idea of 'harnessing' or 'mastering' the lower tendencies of man for a higher life, spiritual training. It thus brings out the idea of control, hence self-discipline.

Let us now see how the concept of *tapas* has evolved from very early times. As this aspect is exhaustively dealt with in the subsequent chapters, only a brief account is given here so as to obtain a connected picture.

The Āryan conquest of India was the most important event in the history of India. With their entry began a new era: the first literary document of the Āryan world, the Ṛgveda marked its dawn. Though the original habitat of the Āryans is still a subject of speculation and controversy, the scholars believe that they destroyed the Mohenjodaro settlements of the pre-Āryan settlers. The latter knew agriculture and trade but were not good warriors like the Āryans. They worshipped a *three-faced deity and Mother Goddess* and also knew some sort of meditation.[3] It is natural to surmise that the Āryan religion in which nature worship was predominant, borrowed some forms of religious beliefs and practices when it came into contact with the pre-Āryans.[4]

Let us first turn to the Ṛgveda. The Vedic hymns declare that the prayers and worship are the best means for gaining the favour of the gods. Later scholarship has often made the claim that every Vedic hymn is the condensed expression of a triple feeling: an overt prayer for material prosperity, a homage to the gods and

[1] *Ram.*, I.51-55, 57-66, *Mbh.*, I.177.
[2] Comm. on *Taitt. Up.*, I.9.
[3] Vide Chapter IV.
[4] ibid, III.

a veiled allegorical notation of a profound philosophical intuition.[1] No doubt, the philosophical insight as manifested in *ekaṁ sad vipra bahudhā vadanti*[2] finds its fuller development in the Upaniṣads. The Ṛgvedic Āryans frankly accepted the world and life as we find them living a full, vigorous and simple life propitiating the different gods through prayers, poetic homages and yajña or sacrifice.

We find *tapas* used in its primary sense of heat or burning.[3] Its meaning is extended to zeal or fervour of doing things. It becomes the unflagging, unsparing effort in the achievement of things worthwhile.[4] It is hence conceived as a mighty power from which spring all great things. *Satya* and *Rita*, Truth and Order, are said to be born at the beginning out of *tapas*.[5] Gods and sages perform noble things through *tapas*.[6] *Tapas* turns Manyu into a mighty warrior.[7] Indra is said to have conquered heaven by *tapas*.[8] It is emphasised that it led the ṛṣis engaged in *tapas* to heaven.[9] The creation hymn depicts the Primal Being as practising *tapas* before the creation of the world.[10] *Kāma* (desire) is said to be born out of *tapas*.[11] The power of *tapas* is so miraculous that it enables the long-haired *Muni* to wander about the earth, fly through the air and divine the thoughts of others.[12] In the Ṛgveda, *tapas* is thus used to mean: the heating, the burning of sun and fire; to consume by fire and heat, evil or enemies; in the psychological sense to give pain or to make to suffer, self-inflicted heat and pain i.e. *ascetic* practices resulting into magical powers. Tapas also means devotion.

In the *Atharvaveda* we find that a Vedic student had to undergo certain physical and mental disciplines to acquire fitness for the knowledge of Brahman. His life of *tapas* comes to be associated with celibacy or *brahmacarya*. Much stress is laid on the control

[1]Sampurnananda, *Evolution of the Hindu Pantheon*, pp. 6ff; Chaitanya, *A New History of Sanskrit Literature*, p. 52.

[2]*ṚV.*, I.164, 46; X.114.5.

[3]*ṚV.*, 7, 34.19; X.89.12; VI.5.4, III.18.2; X.83.3.

[4]Bose, *The Call of the Vedas*, p. 56.

[5]*ṚV.*, X.169.2.

[6]*ṚV.*, X.83.3.

[7]*ṚV.*, X.167.1.

[8]*ṚV.*, I.109.4; X.154.4.

[9]*ṚV.*, X.129.3.

[10]*ṚV.*, X.129.4.

[11]ibid.

[12]*ṚV.*, X.136.2-7.

and sublimation of sex energy which is to be turned into spiritual power. It is said that 'animated by this creative vigour the four quarters live.'[1] It is said that through *tapas* of *Brahmacarya* the king protected his kingdom, the teacher desired his pupil, the girl received a youthful husband, the gods turned away death and Indra brought heavenly lustre to the gods.[2] The glorification of the Brahmacārī is extended to all these to emphasize the idea that *Brahmacarya* should precede as a necessary condition to the knowledge of Brahman. It is said that Agastya who wished offspring and strength practised both *Brahmacarya* as well as *Gārhasthya*.[3] It is also emphasised that he practised *tapas* while living a chaste life of a householder.[4] *Brahmacarya* thus becomes a part of *Tapas*.

The great virtue ascribed to *Brahmacarya* is further illustrated by the *Taittirīya Brāhmaṇa* which speaks of Brahmacarya in the sense of studying the Vedas with due self-control. Bhāradvāja, who practised Brahmacarya for one whole life which was as long as three lives, is approached by Indra, who finding him, decayed and old said: 'Bhāradvāja, if I were to give you a fourth life, what would you do with it?' He answered: 'I would use it in practising *Brahmacarya*.'[5] Here by *Brahmacarya* is meant a life of *tapas* which signifies the exertion of mental energy for the Brahma-knowledge and for the endurance of privations of all kinds, of heat, cold and the like.[6]

Brahmacarya as an integral part of a life of *tapas* acquires increasing significance in the institution of Naiṣṭhika Brahmacārīs in the Upaniṣadic times.[7] In Buddhism and Jainism it found a place amongst the five great vows of monastic conduct.[8] In Patañjali's Yoga discipline it is recognised as one of the moral virtues (*yamas*) to be cultivated.[9] Though it is said that purity is godliness and physical as well as mental purity in offering prayers to God is

[1] *AV.*, XI.5.12 : brahmacārī siricati sānau retaḥ pṛthivyāṁ tena jivanti pradiśas catasraḥ.

[2] *AV.*, XI.5.17-19.

[3] *ṚV.*, I.179.6: ubhau varṇau pupoṣa.

[4] *ṚV.*, I.179.2.

[5] *TB.*, iii.10.11.3.

[6] cf. *BG.*, VI.7, II.14, II.38, VI.7; Also Manu I.26, VI.81: *dvandai sukhadukhādibhiḥ sarvadvaṅda vinimukto brahmanyevāvatiṣṭhate.*

[7] *Chand. Up.*, II.23.1.

[8] Rhys Davids, *Buddhism*, p. 139.

[9] *YS.*, II.30.

emphasised,[1] it seems that the tremendous power generated by Brahmacarya is not fully appreciated as it ought to be. That it radiated spiritual energy is clearly denoted by the Vedic Brahmacārī and the example of Bhāradvāja.

The association of the sublimation of sex-energy with spiritual power is understood in fuller detail in modern times than it was before, owing to the new light thrown on the subject of psycho-analysis led by Freud. Sorokin, examining the effects of sex upon health and longevity, shows how among the Christian saints, majority of whom were the ascetics, continence was an important life-prolonging factor.[2] He commends *Brahmacarya* as a strong force for spiritual and moral growth and explains how religious creators and great moral leaders have been either ascetics, like most of the monastics or became continent or semi-continent after the beginning of their religious and ethical activity.[3] He cites the examples of the Buddha, Al Ghazzali, Gandhi and Aurobindo as also many spiritual teachers of the East and the West. It was not a chance matter, therefore, that Brahmacarya was viewed as an essential condition for ascetic conduct and monastic life by Hinduism, Budhism and Jainism. Sorokin observes: 'Most of the spiritual leaders require chastity not for the purpose of torturing the body or securing salvation for the soul, but as a condition necessary for the attainment of the highest spirituality.'[4]

The ancient Indian thinkers were aware of the great potentiality of *Brahmacarya* as a creative power. They believed that the seed within man and woman was intended for the purpose of creating a body by which another soul may come into physical embodiment. When this is controlled Brahmacarya helped creative work of every kind. It transformed the *tapasvin's* vital energy into 'special power called *Ojas*.'[5] In the Vedic literature we come across many prayers for strength (*savas*),[6] valour (*virya*),[7] manliness (*nrimna*),[8]

[1] *ṚV.*, VII.95-7, VIII.44.21.
[2] *Sane, Sex-Order*, pp. 50ff.
[3] ibid, pp. 61-63.
[4] ibid, p. 62.
[5] Gonda, *Ancient Indian Ojas*, p. 36.
[6] *ṚV.*, X.148.4; I.11.2., cf. *Sam.*, V.828.
[7] *ṚV.*, IX.110.7.
[8] *SV.*, 231.

conquering power (*sāhas*),[1] wrath (*manyu*),[2] fearlessness (*abhaya*),[3] vigour (*bala*)[4] and other qualities of heroic power. *Ojas* is one of them.[5] It stands for soul-force or spiritual power.[6] Swami Vivekananda according to whom *ojas* literally means 'the illuminating or bright' defines it as 'the highest form of energy attained by a constant practice of continence and purity.' He holds that every man possesses a certain measure of *ojas* in his brain. This measure may be increased by chastity, strict chastity even in word and thought, for even impure words and thoughts disperse that energy which if preserved, is transformed into *ojas*. 'The more the *ojas* in a man's head,' says he, 'the more powerful he is, the more intellectual, the more spiritually strong will that man be.'[7] In this connection Gonda remarks that the Indians 'have always been aware of the mighty energy of a great personality.'[8] For the Indians a great personality is that 'from which *ojas* is set free and imparts to those who approach a sensation of vitality, soul-force and authority, of the heroic, the impetuous and the wonderful.'[9] We are thus led to believe that behind the *tapas* of many an ascetic, lay the idea of the acquisition of *Ojas* through *Brahmacarya.*

We find now an increasing tendency of *tapas* to travel from the external physical plane inwards. The Ṛgvedic *muni* was in an ecstatic trance, described as '*mauneya unmadā.*'[10] *Mauneya* also implies silence. Solitude can be gained only when there is a mental withdrawal from the world outside. It is conducive to concentration (*ekāgratā*). To this is added Brahmacarya and inwardness. The Āraṇyakas pass from the fruit or flesh of the sacrifices to their spiritual interpretation, and explain the efficacy of the inner or mental sacrifice. It is said that a man should perform the *Brahman* sacrifice in his body, which is purified and should constantly brood on the Ātman by means of *tapas*, *brahmacarya* and fasting.[11]

1*YV.*, 19.9.
2ibid.
3*AV.*, XIX.15.6, *ṚV.*, VIII.4.7.
4*ṚV.*, III.53.18.
5*ṚV.*, III.62.5, *SV.*, 372, *AV.*, VII.21.1.
6cf. Bose, op. cit., p. 81.
7*Rajayoga*, p. 252.
8op. cit., p. 37 note 6.
9ibid, p. 42.
10*ṚV.*, X.136.3.
11*SA.*, XV.1.

Breathing exercises are more and more emphasised: he who chants the *Gāyatrastotra* should not breathe.[1] The idea of *Upāsanā* or internal worship to gain *Brahmavidyā* develops. We meet with the institution of the *Vānaprastha*, the hermits who retire to the woods to study the inner meaning of the sacrificial rites and formulas. From the moment when meditation on the ritual becomes more important than the rite itself, the ascetic becomes more important than the priest and the inner way of enlightenment and perfection more important than the ritual order.[2] *Tapas* has, in the *Āraṇyakas*, come to be associated with meditative worship.

In the Upaniṣads where the *Upāsanas* are prescribed we find meditation and knowledge gaining an increasing importance along with sacrifice. Not that the sacrifices are totally discarded but their efficacy is only partially accepted. Some of the best minds turned away from them and sought peace and salvation in true knowledge which led to the infinite bliss by the absorption of the individual Atman in the Universal Brahman. The Upaniṣad says: 'There is joy in the infinite; there is no joy in the finite.'[3] It is at this precise point that the Upaniṣadic ṛṣis seemed to have met with the ascetics and yogins. Some yogic methods were employed as preliminary exercises in purification and contemplation. The *Śvetāśvatara Upaniṣad* not only describes all the conditions that are required for perfection in Yoga but also the early mystical experiences, the vision of the Self and the ultimate identity of Self with God. It is said that the Yogin by the Self is able to reach the Brahman.[4] Side by side it is now accepted that the magical value of the sacrifices could be attained also by *tapas*, involving meditation and self-imposed sufferings and mortifications.[5] It is regarded as a great force which could achieve extraordinary results. Thus it is said that the Great Being, Brahman performed *tapas* and having done so created all the world.[6] Śaṅkara means by tapas, knowledge: The Supreme reflected on the form of the world to be created. He willed, he thought and he created.[7] *Tapas* is the creative moulding

[1] *Jaimini Br.*, III.3.1; *Kau. Br.*, xxiii.5.
[2] cf. Dawson, *Religion And Culture*, p. 179.
[3] *Chand. Up.*, VII. Sec. 23.
[4] *Sveta. Up.*, II. 8-14: Yadātmatattvena tu Brahmatatvam.
[5] Dasgupta, *Indian Idealism*, p. 8.
[6] *Tait. Up.*, II. 6.
[7] Tapa iti jñānam ucyate tapaḥ paryālocanam Srjyamāna-jagad-racanādi-viṣayam ālocanām akarod ātmety arthaḥ.

power, concentrated thinking.[1] In a number of passages *tapas* is identified with Brahman (*tapo Brahmā*) and it is also emphasised that Brahman performed *tapas*.[2] Even the thought of Brahman is regarded as his *tapas*: (*Yasya jñānamayaṁ tapaḥ*).[3] It is stated that Brahman is nurtured by *tapas* and yet asserted that for the real knower, knowledge is *tapas*.[4] *Tapas* comprehends all forms of the pursuit of self-control.[5] *Tapas* reveals the nature of the reality[6] and is considered indispensable as a means of knowing the Ātman.[7] *Tapas* thus stands for energy or self-effort, thought, self-control or study and a means to enlightenment or self-knowledge.

The Buddha, having practised the most vigorous *tapas* or self-torture himself almost to the point of death for six long years to attain the highest wisdom, condemned self-mortification as painful, unworthy and unprofitable. He preached a middle path which avoided the two extremes of over-indulgence and self-mortification and led to peace of mind, to the higher wisdom, to full enlightenment and to *Nirvāṇa*. To reach this goal one has to follow the eight-fold path.[8] His sole emphasis was on leading a good life—life of right conduct and right meditation.

Tapas in Jainism is of two kinds: physical or external and mental or internal. Physical austerity is of six types: fasting, decreased diet, collecting alms, giving of delicious diet and mortification of the flesh. Similarly, mental austerity consists of expiation, humility, service, study, renunciation of the body and meditation.[9] The six forms of physical austerity practised in a right manner are said to result in non-attachment, lightness of the body, conquest of the senses, protection of self-discipline and annihilation of *Karmic* matter.[10] The Jains emphasise external *tapas* not as the end in itself but for the sake of a higher life. They hold that physical mortification is essential for a successul self-control. It is

[1]See *Bṛhad. Up.*, I. 4. 10-11, *Maitri. Up.*, VI. 17 which assume that consciousness is at the source of manifestation.

[2]*Tait. Up.*, III. 2 f.

[3]*Mund. Up.*, I.1.9.

[4]ibid, I. 1. 8-9.

[5]*Chand. Up.*, II. 23.1.

[6]*Tait. Up.*, 3.2, *Katha Up.*, 1.2.15.

[7]*Maitri Up.*, 4.3.

[8]*Mahaparinibbana Sutta*, 1-4.

[9]*Uttar*, xxx. 8, 30.

[10]*Tattva*, ix. 19.

desirable so long as it serves the cause of self-discipline. No kind of *tapas* can be of any good until the mind is purified.

The idea of *tapas* as severe ascetic practises or self-mortification is carried on in the Epics. In the *Rāmāyaṇa* the phrase *ugraṁ tapas* is of frequent occurrence indicating its severity. *Tapas* is called *ugra*,[1] *ghoraṁ*.[2] *Ugra tapas* is also called *durādharṣam*.[3] The performance of *tapas* was the sole objective that led the anchorites—the *ṛṣis*, *munis* and hermits to seek the calm solitude of the forest. Their *tapas* involved abstinence, mortification, meditation and self-restraint. The epic gives an exhaustively rich picture of *vanavāsa*, the life in the hermitages (*āśramas*) against idyllic surroundings. Not only the hermits but the Āryan lay men and women, Rākṣasas and Yakṣas practise austerities for various ends. It was common to perform austerities for progeny.[4] Viśvāmitra becomes Rājarṣi through severe *tapas* but vanquished by Vasiṣṭha again undertakes *tapas* to attain Brāhmanhood.[5] Rākṣasas Rāvaṇa and Virādha performed *tapas* to attain a divine boon from Brahmā which made them superior to mortals.[6] Viśvāmitra practised more and more rigorous *tapas* with a view to subjugate his temper and passions.[7] He had attained such extraordinary powers through *tapas* that he started creating another Brahmā and a rival universe. He had gone as far as the creation of new constellations but was prevailed upon to stop it by the entreaties of the alarmed gods.[8]

As in the *Rāmāyaṇa*, the practice of austerities is not the sole privilege of the ascetics in the *Mahābhārata*. Even the kings and *asuras* practise *tapas* for variety of motives but broadly either to gain power or some material end. Women perform austerities to get husbands. Some of them have taken to the life of *Naiṣṭhika Brahmacarya*. We find detailed descriptions of the ascetics engaged in *tapas* and who have become immune to their environment and physical needs. Ascetic practices are called ugra.[9] Durvāsā is called

[1] *Ram.*, I. 63.18.
[2] *Ram.*, I. 15.24.
[3] *Ram.*, I. 65.17, 61.4; 3.5.28, III. 7.13.
[4] *Ram.*, I. 8.1-3, I. 25.5, I. 4.46.2.
[5] *Ram.*, I. 56.24, I. 57.8.
[6] *Ram.*, I. 16.4-5, III. 3.6.
[7] *Ram.*, I. 64.16-19.
[8] *Ram.*, I. 60f.
[9] *Mbh.*, xii. 217.14.

ugra, *saṁśitavrata*.[1] Many examples describe what sort of *tapas* was practised and with what motives.[2] By *ugram tapas* one can win, satisfy and influence even great gods and force them to grant one's heart's desire,[3] to obtain Brāhmanhood,[4] to kill demons[5] and to gain divine or spiritual vision.[6] The epic eulogises the power and efficacy of *tapas*. There is nothing superior to it and by its miraculous might great results can be achieved. Śakri could convert a king into a cannibal.[7] Cyavana could control all the activities of a whole army.[8] Vasiṣṭha was no less powerful who could defeat Viśvāmitra a number of times.[9] However, it should be noted that there are various meanings of the word *tapas* suggested in the epic: fast, the religious observance to be performed during the acquirement of the Vedas, any particular practice, acquiring the knowledge of Ātman, the act of giving, austerity control of senses, *jñāna* etc.[10]

Let us now turn our attention to the *Gītā*. It fully recognises the part which nature has to play in the spiritual development of man. It says: all beings follow their nature; what can repression do? Nature, therefore, is neither to be indulged nor suppressed.[11] Suppression of the natural appetites and desires of the flesh would do more harm than good. Hence it advocates the middle path of wise guidance. It says that Yoga is not for him who eats too much or eats too little but for him who is temperate in all habits.[12] 'Eating' should be understood as to include all sense enjoyments. It speaks of the nourishing kinds of food that are liked by the wise and the

[1] I. 67.132.
[2] I. 123.26; IX. 5.19, 48.3, XII. 324.26.
[3] I. 223.35, II. 14.65, III. 138.8.
[4] IX. 40.29.
[5] XII. 74.9.
[6] XII. 271.36, 300.27; XIII. 26.96.
[7] I. 178.
[8] III. 122.
[9] I. 179.
[10] *Mbh.*, XII. 228 (Kṛsnamacarya and Vyasacarya, Bombay, 1907 edition pakṣamāsopavasādin manyate ve tapodhanā vedavratādini tapa apare vedapāragāḥ yathāvihitamācārastapaḥ sarvaṁ vrataṁ gatāḥ ātmavidyāvidhānaṁ yattapaḥ parikirtitaṁ tyāgastapastathā saṅtistapaḥ indriyanigraḥ brahmacaryaṁ tapaḥ proktamāhurevaṁ dvijātayaḥ jñānātmakaṁ tapaḥ śabdaṁ ye vadanti viniścitāḥ.
[11] *BG.*, III. 33-34.
[12] *BG.*, VI. 16-17.

good.[1] Religious life is to be based on temperate habits which avoid the excesses of indulgence and repression. We are advised neither to avoid the desires prompted by the objects of the senses nor to be carried away by them.[2] True *tapas* consists in the control of the natural man and not in his eradication. The limitations of fasting and other forms of self-restraint are shown.[3] The *Rājasa* and *Tāmasa* austerity are condemned.[4] The *Gītā* also denounces all kinds of penances and practices which involve the torture of the flesh.[5] It is only immature religious teaching that advocates extreme asceticism. True *tapas* involves the discipline of the body, speech and mind.[6] *Tapas* is not dwelling in a cave, giving up food or the affairs of the world or tormenting the body. Its secret lies in what the *Gītā* calls *Bhāvasaṁśuddhi*—purification of attitudes and emotions.[7] It is a discipline by which instincts and urges are sublimated by purifying the body and mind.

Tapas in the *Dharmasūtras* covers vows and rites both purifactory and expiatory. The first is three-fold: *kṛcchra*, *atikṛcchra* and *kṛcchrati-kṛcchra*.[8] The expiatory ones are called *prāyaścitta*.[9] As the three *kṛcchras* differ only in point of a degree of severity of fasting, they naturally came to be regarded as *tapas*.[10] Gautama regards the three *kṛcchras* as the greatest of all expiations,[11] thus showing that *tapas* and *prāyaścitta* become almost co-extensive in meaning. Moreover, *tapas* stands for moral virtues and strict abstinence from pleasures, comforts and luxuries. Gautama says that *tapas* consists in celibacy, truthfulness, baths in three Savans, wearing wet-garments, using ground as bed and fasting.[12] Apastamba means by *tapas* rules of etiquette a Brahmacārin has to

[1]*BG.*, XVII. 8-10.
[2]*BG.*, II. 70.
[3]*BG.*, II. 59.
[4]*BG.*, XVII. 18-19.
[5]*BG.*, XVII. 5-6.
[6]*BG.*, XVII. 14-16.
[7]*BG.*, XVII. 15.
[8]*Gaut.*, xxvi. 1-11, xix. 20, xxvii. 2; xxv. 1-17, xxvi. 20. *Ap.*, I. 25.8, 27.6.8, 20, 28, I. 27.7; *Baud.*, I. 12, 12, II. 2, 37/38, 42-45, IV. 5-7, II. 2, 41, IV. 5-9-10; *Vas.* XXI. 20, XXIV. 3, XXII. 16; *Yaj.*, XXII. 42-43. XXIV. 4-5. *Samvidhana*, I. 2. I.
[9]*Samvidhana*, I. 5.8.
[10]ibid. i. 22, 3; cf. *Manu*, ix. 211, Hardatta on *Gautama*, xix. 15.
[11]*Gaut.* xix. 20.
[12]ibid, xix. 15.

observe.[1] Thus *tapas* signifies not only bodily mortifications but also some definite virtues and practices. Fasting is regarded as the greatest *tapas* and becomes its constant factor.[2] But the highest value is attached to the moral qualities of the soul.[3]

We find in the *Dharamasūtras* that some of the duties and regulations prescribed for the *Vānaprasthas* are practically the same as those for *saṁnyāsis*.[4] But the *vānaprastha* had to concentrate upon *tapas*, subject himself to privations, severe austerities and self-mortifications, while the *saṁnyāsin* was concerned mainly with *saṁyama*, restraint and contemplation of the highest reality.[5] Manu makes *tapas* and sacred learning as the distinct mark of a Brāhmin.[6] He also uses the word *tapas* by analogy, for the special duty or merit of each of the four castes.[7]

Tapas in the Yoga system of Patañjali has come to acquire a special shade of meaning. 'Yoga' means union. *Tapas*, as we have seen in its primary sense, means that which generates heat or energy. *Tapas* now becomes the practice of conserving energy and directing it towards the goal of Yoga, toward union with the Ātman.[8] The object is to tame the bodily and mental habits and make the body fit for any hardships.[9] As such, it finds a place in the Niyama and in the practice of kriyayoga: *tapas*, *svādhyāya* and *Īshwar Praṇidhāna*.[10] According to Patañjali, *tapas* does not mean self-mortification or injury to the body. It means body conditioning for the removal of impurities and the perfection of the physical and mental powers.[11] This means that *tapas* results in perfect bodily vigour, endurance, agility, immunity from illness,

[1] *Ap.*, i. 5.1.

[2] *Gaut.*, xix. 15.

[3] *Ap.*, *DS*. (I. 8.23.3-6) calls upon all *āśramas* to eradicate faults that tend to destruction and to cultivate the opposite virtues. This shows that in the scale of values mere performance of sacrifices and purificatory and other religious ceremonies ranked, according to the law-givers, very low.

[4] *Manu, vi.* 25-29, 38, 43-44.

[5] *Ap.*, II. 9.18, 21, 18, II. 9.23.2.

[6] *Manu*, xii. 104.

[7] ibid, xi. 235 f.

[8] Prabhavananda, *The Spiritual Heritage of India*, p. 241.

[9] Bhat, *Yogic Powers and God Realisation*, pp. 9-10.

[10] *YS.*, II, 32.

[11] *YS.*, II, 43, 45.

besides beauty and brightness.[1] Patañjali says that yogic powers (*siddhis*) are either a gift from birth or acquired by medicines (*auṣadhi*), repetition of the sacred mantras, *tapas* and *samādhi*.[2] Except the last one *samādhi*, he does not dilate upon the first four sources. The reason is that he calls them 'obstacles' in the spiritual path. These are exploited usually for selfish purposes. Patañjali and all the representatives of classic yoga considered these *siddhis* of no value towards deliverance. No doubt their exhibition has always made a deep impression on the Indian people. Tantricism does not reject them; it even regards them as direct proof of man's gaining divinity. But the *siddhis* play no part in the *Gītā*.

Let us take a resumê of the evolution of the concept of *tapas*. It can be clearly seen that the idea of tapas has taken on a new meaning from time to time. From its basic sense of 'heat,' it came to be associated with 'heat' or 'fervour' caused by harsh treatment of the body or physical endurance extended to self-torture or self-mortification. The term *tapas* came to be used for austerities or ascetic practices. With the growth of religious and philosophical ideas in the Vedic age, austerities came to be very much valued. *Tapas* and *Brahmacarya* were regarded as great virtues and considered as being productive of the highest power. Gradually it assimilated within its fold abstinence, meditation, self-restraint and moral qualities till it finally emerged as an inward discipline. From its mere physical plane, thus it came to be understood as a mental discipline and a moral factor until it was assimilated by the Yoga system. During its long span, it came to be practised with various ends in view: material, moral, religious and spiritual.

From our above discussion we will not be wrong to conclude that *tapas* had two aspects. One was the negative aspect of self-torture and the other, the positive aspect of self-training. Thus there were some thinkers in ancient India who favoured the perverse cult of fanatical self-punishment whereas there were others who held the view that there was no need for the torture of the body for the discipline of the mind. The teachings of the Buddha, the *Gītā* and the *Yogasūtras* by Patañjali favour the latter view. They emphasised the quiet and sane self-control which is the joyful positive aspect of *tapas*.

[1] *Sveta. Up*. (II. 12-14) mentions the physical and spiritual results of the yoga in identical terms.

[2] *YS*., IV. 1.

Vairāgya

The extinction of desires is for Indian philosophy, the indispensable ethical desideratum for all spiritual achievement,'[1] says Dasgupta. Whether it is the Hindu, Buddhist or Jaina scheme of life, the emphasis is always on the attainment of freedom from the attractions of the world, mundane desires and possessions and conquering the flesh in order to qualify for self-liberation. In other words, it is emphasised that self-conquest leads to self-liberation. What is implied in self-conquest is the conquering of the sensuous self. This is possible only when the mind is totally withdrawn from the world. As such this is the main idea behind *vairāgya* which is known by various terms: indifference, non-attachment, detachment, dispassion, desirelessness, passionlessness, freedom from or absence of desire and renunciation.

The word *vairāgya* (Sk.) comes from vi, apart, away, without *raga*, attachment, desire. One who has attachments or desires is called *Ragī*, *Anurāgī*. One who is the opposite is *Vairāgī*. The ascetic, the *saṁnyāsin* is, therefore, called a *vairāgī*, a *Bairāgī*, one who has not only given up the world but also all the desires that bind him or attach him to the world which has ceased to be of any attraction to him. He has acquired a state of mind which has made him indifferent to all that is worldly. He is thus a *Vairāṅgika*: 'One who is free from all worldly desires or one who has subdued all earthly desires.'[2] *Vairāgya*, thus implies 'aversion, disgust or indifference to worldly objects or weariness of life.'[3] It stands for freedom from all worldly desires, indifference to the worldly objects of life.

Though the term asceticism is used to mean both '*Vairāgya*' and '*saṁnyāsa*' (*tyāga*),[4] there is a difference between the two. *Vairāgya* is an essential condition leading to *tyāga*, withdrawal from worldly life, *saṁnyāsa*. This withdrawal to be complete has to be necessarily a total withdrawal, physical as well as mental. The physical *tyāga* must go together with *tyāga* on the mental plane. This mental withdrawal from the world is *vairāgya*. It presupposes a training, a discipline, which prepares the mind to be detached from worldly life. Hence it is the pre-requisite of a *saṁnyāsī*:

[1] *Hindu Mysticism*, p. 96.
[2] *ESD.*, p. 27.
[3] ibid, p. 301.
[4] ibid, p. 27.

saṁnyāsahetu vairāgyaṁ.[1] The *Jābālopanishad* makes *vairāgya* the only alternative condition for entering *saṁnyāsa.* Having first emphasised that a man should pass through the first three *āśramas* in their proper order, it says that he may take to *saṁnyāsa* the very day he is free from attachments.[2] Thus vairāgya is the spirit behind renunciation.

What constitutes *Vairāgya* is well illustrated by the *Maitri* Upanishad. It refers to the king Brihadratha who performs a severe *tapas* for a thousand days with the aim of gaining the knowledge of Ātman. Before retiring to the forest it is clearly stated that he had acquired indifference to objects (*vairāgya*) reflecting the body as impermanent (*aśāśvataṁ*).[3] The same source lays down elsewhere that when indifference towards all objects (*vairāgya*) arises in the mind, a learned person may take up *Saṁnyāsa.*[4] In other words, *Vairāgya* lies in the realisation of the transitoriness of all worldly objects and desires. It is the state of mind which has found out that worldly possessions like wealth, wife, children and other things were not likely to give permanent happiness. Happiness lay not in earthly goods but in something else. It was a thing of inner life, an aspiration for higher things of the spirit. So we read in the *Bṛhadāraṇyaka Upaniṣad*:

'The wise of old did not desire for progeny. For they thought: What shall we do with children? To us the entire world is our own self. So they gave up the desire for sons, for riches and for worlds and wandered about begging.'[5]

It should be noted here that no special emphasis is given in the Upaniṣads to the sex-desire or the desire for a son for being called *kāma*, whatever was the desire for a son was the same as the desire for wealth and the desire for wealth was the same as any other

[1] *Jivanmuktiviveka*, 1-3.

[2] Jabala, 4: *Yad āhāra eva virajet, tad āhāra eva pravrajet.*

[3] *Maitri. Up.*, I. 1-7.

[4] ibid, II. 3-10: Yadā manasi vairāgyaṁ jātaṁ sarveṣu vastuṣu tadaiva saṁnyāsetvidvāna. In order to generate *vairāgya* and to curb his senses, an ascetic should make his mind dwell upon the body as liable to disease and old age and as packed full of impurities. He should resolve in his mind the impermanence of all mundane things, the trouble one has to undergo in body and mind from conception to death, the incessant round of births and deaths. *Manu*, VI. 76-77; *Yaj.*, III. 63-64; *Vis. DS.*, 96. 25-42.

[5] *Bṛhad. Up.*, IV. 4.22.

worldly desire. Hence sex-desire stands on the same plane as any other desire.[1]

Such a state as described above characterizes the Indian Mind 'which has realised the self which is the self within all beings'[2] and has risen above the desire for mundane things. It is said that one who has attained this state of self-realisation 'transcends hunger and thirst, grief, delusion, decay and death.'[3] He verily crosses over the ocean of suffering: *Tarati śokam ātmavit*.[4] It was thus a worthy goal for the Upaniṣadic thinkers to strive after and achieve. Here we find the supreme aspiration of the Indian mind to seek salvation through knowledge which was termed *para-vidyā*. It was the higher knowledge which led to the Supreme Self, the Imperishable Brahman.[5] To the seers of the Upanisads no knowledge had any value if it did not seek the salvation of man. 'Save for that nothing is worth knowing,' declares the *Śvetāśvara Upaniṣad*.[6] All else was therefore considered useless. 'Everything else was of evil: *ato'nyad ārtaṁ*.[7] All obstacles that distract from the path leading to salvation were, therefore, to be crossed over, subdued. And what are these obstacles? On the one hand they are the attachments and desires of the human heart which bind man to the world and as a result of which he clings to the world and its wealth and attractions. On the other these desires are accompanied by fear, hatred, possessiveness, vanity and pride etc. which constitute his lower nature. With regard to the first aspect of desires *Kathā Upaniṣad* says: 'When all the bonds of the heart are broken in

[1] cf. Dasgupta, *HIP*., I, p. 57.

[2] *Bṛhad. Up.*, III. 5.1 *Ya ātma sarvāntarstaṁ me vyācakṣvetyeṣa ta ātma sarvāṅtaraḥ.*

[3] ibid. This Vairāgya is called *jñānagarbha* vairāgya by Śaṅkarācārya. According to him *vairāgya* is of two kinds: *Nairvaidya* and *Jñānagarbha*. *Nairvaidya* arises out of the unhappiness resulting from the craving for home, friend, son, wealth etc. *Jñānagarbha* is born as the result of jñāna or divine knowledge. In this case the mind feels the apathy for worldly things as for the sight of vomitted food. In a similar manner for one who has controlled the mind, his Saṁnyāsa (*parivrājya*) is two fold: first he gives up home and possessions and then he renounces the "I-ness" of this body. (*Śataśloki, 14*).

[4] *Chand. Up.*, VII. 1.3.

[5] *Mund. Up.*, I. 4-5.

[6] *Sveta. Up.*, I. 12. Bhoja commenting on a text of the *Yoga-sutras* (iv-22) also says that any knowledge whose object is not deliverance is valueless.

[7] *Bṛhad. Up.*, III. 5.1.

this life[1] or all the desires cherished in the heart cease, then one knows the Brahman and attains immortality.'[2] This is further elaborated by the *Gītā* which also shows how the second aspect of refining man's lower nature and raising it to the higher level through the restraint of passions and urges is possible of attainment through *Vairāgya*.

It is obvious that both these aspects of the removal of obstacles implies a training and a discipline through which man can attain a mental and moral development for spiritual life. It signifies as Aurobindo says 'the self-denial and self-conquest by which man represses his lower impulses and rises to greater heights of his nature.'[3] Though both Vedic thoughts and the *Gītā* emphasise *Vairāgya* as a valuable process towards self-perfection, they differed mainly on one point. Whereas the former prepared the seeker of truth through *Vairāgya* to leave the world, the *Gītā* shows how this attainment for spiritual life is possible even when living a worldly life.

Let us now examine how the idea of *Vairāgya* has developed right from the earliest Vedic times onwards until it becomes an essential condition for *saṁnyāsa* and a worthy objective towards the attainment of self-perfection or preparation for a spiritual life even when leading a worldly life.

We do not come across the word *Vairāgya* in the Vedas and the ten principal Upaniṣads. We find that the majority of the Āryans accepted life with all its blessings and joys and there seemed to be no need to deny it as all the worldly desires and even heaven were within their reach through a righteous life lived according to the Vedic rituals. However, *Brahma-jñāna* and its value were emphasised and commended by the Upaniṣadic thinkers and mystics who formed but a minority, we do come across the terms '*nirveda*' and the like together with *tapas*, faith, *brahmacarya* and *satya* as the essential qualifications of a seeker after self-realisation.[4] The words '*nirveda*' which means 'freedom from desire,'[5] '*vitarāgāḥ*' 'tranquil' and *praśāntāḥ*, 'free from passions' are to be met with.[6]

[1]cf. *DP* (211) also speaks of breaking the bonds or knots: *ganthā tesaṁ na vijjanti*.

[2]*Katha Up.*, VI. 14-15; cf. *Maitri. Up.*, VI. 34.

[3]*The Foundations of Indian Culture*, p. 85.

[4]*Chand. Up.*, 8.5.3.5; *Mund. Up.*, 3.1.5; *Prasna Up.*, 1-2.

[5]*Mund. Up.*, I. 2.12.

[6]ibid, III. 2.5.

These terms are used to qualify the seers who have found the self in all and therefore enter into everything. They describe the perfect state of tranquillity when the sages have realized the self.[1] It is only by implication that it is suggested that these virtues were necessary to reach Him. The principal Upaniṣads do not seem to dwell upon *vairāgya* as an essential condition or training for self-realisation. Even the later Upaniṣads take it for granted and address themselves to the seekers of truth as if they have already undergone the training and acquired the necessary moral fitness.[2] It is only in the *Gītā* and Śaṅkarācārya's exposition of the *Vedānta* philosophy that the idea of *vairāgya* finds its full development.

However, the *Kathā Upaniṣad* points out the conflict between what is good (*śreyas*) and what is pleasant (*preyas*). The path of *preyas* leads only to transitory pleasures whereas that of *śreyas* to Brahma-knowledge. The ideal pilgrim on the path of *śreyas* is Nachiketas who refuses to be chained in the life of pleasures and like a true *vairāgī* and seeker after truth spurns all wealth, heavenly as well as earthly. The Upaniṣad says that it is only one of the thousands that turn to the path of *śreyas*.[3]

But the stage is now slowly set for *vairāgya* as illustrated by the story of the king Bṛhadratha. Having been disgusted with worldly pleasures and having renounced his kingdom he has practised severe penance (*tapas*) in the forest. When asked by the sage Śākāyana, the knower of the self, to choose a boon, the king requested the sage to instruct him in self-knowledge but the sage tried to pursuade him to return to worldly pleasures. But full of pessimism the king said: 'What good can there be in the enjoyment of pleasures in this useless body, which is but a mass of bones, skin and other things; which is again assailed by passions and over-powered with hunger, thirst, grief and other evils like old age, disease and death?' 'Moreover', the king continued, 'we see that all that exists is perishable: the plant world and the animal world, the warriors and emperors, the demigods and gods, die. The oceans dry up, the mountains fall, the pole-star moves, the

[1]*Katha Up.*, II. 3.18: *brahmaprāpto virajo'bhud.*

[2]cf. Sharma, *The Upanishads—An Anthology*, p. 27.

[3]*Katha Up.*, I. 2 ff. The *Dhammapada* in the canto of the Pleasant (xvi) dwells upon the path of the *preyas* which hinders the path of the higher knowledge,

earth is submerged under water and the gods depart. What is the use of pleasures in such an uncertain world as this?'[1] Here we find a contempt of the body and its pleasures. The King's *vairāgya* has taken a form of aversion, a loathing towards worldly objects and the world itself. He has realized the impermanence of everything and seeks only the Ātman.

The idea of *Vairāgya* gains further importance with the rise and development of the doctrine of transmigration (*saṁsāra*) and law of *Karma*. The Karma theory says: 'A person consists of desire and as is his desire, so is his will. As is his will, so is his deed; and whatever deed he does, that he will reap.'[2] According to *Saṁsāra* and *Karma* doctrines, the destiny of man moves in an endless chain of births and rebirths. Man is born again and again due to the fact that he is full of desires and for their fulfilment he performs actions out of attachments, passions and antipathies. He enjoys or suffers the fruits of his actions in this or in subsequent births. So if the successive chain of births is to be stopped, the accumulation of the fruits of *Karma* must be stopped. Toward this end, desire must be rooted out. Extinction of desires, therefore, becomes of primary importance. This position is accepted by the Brahmanic, Buddhist and Jaina schemes of life though called differently as *Vairāgya*, *tṛṣṇākṣaya* and *nirjarā*. All of them aim at the total annihilation of desires.

It is necessary to consider here the Buddhist attitude towards desire as revealed by the teachings of the Buddha.

The essential truths to which the Buddha attained are known as the Four Noble Truths. They are:

(1) Life is suffering,
(2) Cause of the suffering is thirst or attachment (*tanhā*, *tṛṣṇā*) which leads to rebirth,
(3) Suffering ceases with the cessation of *tanhā*, and,
(4) For this one must tread the Eight-fold Path.[3]

It follows from the above that the origin of suffering is human passions, cravings. It results from desire (*kāma*), thirst (*tanhā, tṛṣṇā*). Until *tanhā* is destroyed, it leads to continued transmigration and the return of suffering. It is said that from *tanhā* arises attachment

[1] *Maitri. Up.*, I. 2-4.
[2] *Brhad. Up.*, IV. 4.5.
[3] *Mahaparinibbana Sutta*, II. 2; *Digha Nik.*, 1.119.

to worldly objects. This leads to continued 'becoming' (*bhāva*), an infinite series of new existence. These finally are the causes of birth, old age and death, pain, sorrow, suffering and despair.[1]

We read in one of the earliest Buddhist scriptures that the craving for existence is rooted out through the noble conduct of life, the noble earnestness of meditation, the noble kind of wisdom and the noble salvation of freedom.[2] The Buddha also recommends the Middle Path which avoids the two extremes of self-indulgence and self-mortification—a path which leads to peace of mind and to *Nirvāṇa.* What is that Middle Path? It is the noble Eight-fold Path: right view, right aspiration, right speech, right conduct, right livelihood, right effort, right mindfulness and right contemplation.[3]

The *Dhammapada* declares Nirvana as the highest happiness (*nibbānaṁ param sukhaṁ*).[4] *Nibbāna* is described in many ways. The basic idea leading to it, however, remains the same: the extinction of *tanhā.* The stopping of becoming (*bhāva*) is *nibbāna.*[5] It is called *Nibbāna* because of the removal of craving (*tanhā*).[6] It is said that the monk of wisdom devoid of desire and passion, attains to deathlessness, peace, the unchanging state of *Nibbāna.*[7] *Nirvāṇa* is also described as the calm of all the impulses, the casting out of all 'basis,' the extinction of craving, dispassion, stopping.[8] Dispassion is called the Way. It is said: 'through dispassion is one fried' yet in meaning all these words: stopping, renunciation, surrender, release, lack of clinging are synonyms for *Nirvāṇa.*[9]

The *Dhammapada* in the canto of craving (*tanhā*) not only narrates the havoc *tanhā* plays in the life of a worldly man and a Bhikkhu but also the entire mankind. It is described as base and poisonous, difficult to be conquered.[10] It is likened to the deeply rooted, luxuriantly growing Birana grass and a great flood crushing reeds. It is like an evergrowing tree, which although cut never

[1] *Mahavagga*, I. 1.2.
[2] *Mahaparinibbana Sutta*, IV. 2.
[3] ibid, I-4.
[4] *DP.*, 204.
[5] *Sam. Nik.*, II. 117.
[6] ibid, I. 39.
[7] *Suttanipata*, 204.
[8] *Ang. Nik.*, V. 322.
[9] *Visuddhimagga*, pp. 507-09.
[10] *DP.*, 335-36.

withers, unless it is rooted out, root, trunk, branch and all.[1] Man in the clutches of *tanhā* is no better than grass or a reed. It is said that mankind surrounded by *tanhā* circles round and round as a hare entangled in the net of a hunter.[2] One who has to go forth and retire from the world has to break fetters stronger than wood or iron. Thus it is said that 'the love for jewels and ornaments and intense longing for sons and wife are the strongest bonds. For they drag men down and although loose, are difficult to break. Men have to cut asunder even such bonds, abandon sense pleasures, having become indifferent to them and go forth, retiring from the world.'[3] Freedom from craving and attachment is one of the qualifications of a great sage (*mahāpuriso*).[4] The *Bhikkhu* is exhorted to banish his craving and be free from passion and lust.[5] He is called tranquil when he is quiet in body, peaceful in speech, regulated in thought and has entirely renounced the material delights of the world.[6]

Freedom from *tanhā* is verily an ornament of a Brāhmin. The Buddha says that there exists no craving in a Brāhmin.[7] He is without worldly belongings, free from every attachment,[8] all fetters, who has transcended all ties and is absolutely unshackled.[9] Not only he has left behind all human attachments such as love of life or sensual pleasures but also transcended heavenly attachments, thus detaching himself from all ties.[10] He owns nothing, possesses nothing and is attached to nothing.[11] It is declared that extinction of *tanhā* conquers all suffering.[12]

Jainism

The words *Jaina* and *Jainism* are derived from the *saṅskṛt* root *ji*, which means to conquer. A *Jina* is one who believes in conquering

1 *DP.*, 335, 337, 338.
2 *DP.*, 343.
3 *DP.*, 345-46.
4 *DP.*, 352.
5 *DP.*, 343, 369.
6 *DP.*, 378.
7 *DP.*, 411, 416, 422.
8 *DP.*, 369.
9 *DP.*, 397, 410.
10 *DP.*, 417.
11 *DP.*, 421.
12 *DP.*, 355.

the flesh in order to attain that supreme purity which leads to infinite knowledge, infinite happiness and infinite power—the same conquering the flesh and the same self-liberation that all other religions have taught.[1] Mahavira and his followers were called the 'Nigganthas' (*Nirganthas*) which means 'free from fetters.' The designation stood for one who had forsaken all the bonds of this worldly life and thus achieved a high state of *Vairāgya.* The whole apparatus of the monastic conduct, the importance the Jains assign to the institution of *tapas* in its external and internal form, the art of fasting developed by the Jaina *Sādhus* in which they have acquired a remarkable proficiency and carried to the extent of religious suicide, the practice of nudity by the *Digaṁbaras* as a vindication of their vow of *aparigraha* and *brahmacarya*, pulling out the hair with one's own hands (*loya*)—all these speak of their utter indifference not only for the physical frame but also the world, their effort to free the mind from the bondage of sensual attractions, worldly care and attachment.[2]

The monks have reached a high level of *Vairāgya* for they are described as 'free from all worldly occupation, ever engrossed in four kinds of devotion (*darśana, jñāna, caritra, tapaḥ*) without worldly ties, without delusion.'[3] The spiritual journey of a man from *saṁsāra* is also described in identical terms: 'The soul exists (in *saṁsāra*) in combination with *Karma*. To reach the end of *loka*, the soul is to be purified of the dirt of *karmic* matter. Thus desirous of quiescence, the soul shall not submit to the slightest attachment to anything. Having thus became free from attachment, it crosses the ocean of *saṁsāra*.'[4] Complete dispassion or detachment is essential to break the chain of *saṁsāra*.

Jaina yoga which also aims at *Vairāgya* is quite different from the traditional Hindu yoga of Patañjali or even of the Buddhists.[5] An aspirant to *dhyāna* has to achieve an equilibrium of mind and become unattached to all things, adopt equality to all beings, become disinclined to all worldly enjoyments. Then he gets rid of all passions with a mind full of peace.[6] The resulting indifference

[1]Prabhavananda, *The Spiritual Heritage of India*, p. 155.
[2]Vide Chapter on Jainism.
[3]*Niyam-sara*, p. 75.
[4]*Panchastikayagatha*, V. 27-28, 179.
[5]Dasgupta, *HIP.*, I, p. 203.
[6]ibid, pp. 202-203.

to the world is the same as *Vairāgya* described in the *Yoga-sūtras*.[1]

Epics

The *Mahābhārata* enjoins *Vairāgya* to destroy all desire (*vāsanā*) which is at the root of attachment. Attachment is the root of all mental agonies: it is attachment that makes every creature miserable and brings on every kind of woe. It is the root of all misery and of all fear. It produces joy and grief of every kind. From it spring all worldly desires and the love of worldly goods. Both of these are evils but the first is worse than the second.[2]

Desire, the epic says, is also linked up with the *Karma* theory. The fulfilment of a desire leads to another desire and so on in unending series of desires which in consequence create karmas. Man is never satisfied as it is said: Contentment does not come from an acquisition of the objects of desire. The thirst for acquisition is only further thrown into it.[3] It is further stated: Desires are not fulfilled by their gratification; the more they are gratified the more they are intensified.[4] The most effective way to end the life of Karmas is, therefore, to destroy all desire. It is thus said: 'Liberation from the cycle of births and deaths and its accompanying happiness and sorrow can be achieved when there is no more *Karma*. To attain this end all desire must be killed.'[5] Towards this end, *mokṣa* is the highest object of pursuit for all classes. It is attainable by renunciation (*tyāgaḥ*) of all worldly possessions and of desire for them. When the knowledge of identity with the one eternal Atman is gained then only no trace of *Karma* will be left behind.[6]

Let us now turn our attention to the *Gītā* wherein the idea of *Vairāgya* finds a full development.

The *Gītā* speaks of *Vairāgya* as detachment from all affections like son, wife or home.[7] It is also called dispassion towards the

[1]Dasgupta, *HIP*, I, p. 203. *YS.*, I. 12: abhyāsavairāgyābhyaṁ taṅ nirodhaḥ.

[2]*Mbh.*, III. 2. 26-28.

[3]ibid, XIII. 174-48.

[4]ibid, cf. *Manu*, II. 94.

[5]ibid, XII. 174, 45 ff.

[6]ibid, XII. 181 ff. bhaktirbhāve maraṇajanmamayaṁ hṛdisthaṁ sneho na bandhuṣu na manmathajā vikārāḥ saṁsargadoṣarahitā vijanā vanāntā vairāgyamasti kimataḥ paramārthaniyaṁ (Vairāgyaśatakam 72).

[7]*BG.*, XIII. 10.

objects of the senses (*indriyārtheṣu vairāgyaṁ*).[1] The word *indriya* is used to include the passions, as in *indriyanigraha* or *indriya-damana*. *Vairāgya* thus connotes freedom from worldly attachments, desires as well as freedom from the lust of the senses.[2] This state of mind, the *Gītā* says, is not to be achieved by repressions and inhibitions which are condemned.[3] The emphasis here is on the subdual of the senses or restraint of the passions. It is said: 'A man who curbs the organs of action but allows to dwell on the sense-objects is a hypocrite. The truly admirable man controls his senses by the power of his will.'[4] Self-imposed physical restraint is a condition precedent to mental restraint. The mind and body should be made to accord well. The passions and desires should be regulated for this purpose, which demands self-control. The *Gītā*, with this end in view, repeatedly lays stress on mental discipline: 'Yoga is hard to be attained by one of uncontrolled self.' Hence Yoga is called '*samatvam*.'[5] It means balance or equilibrium which is not possible of attainment without mental discipline. Thus *Vairāgya* becomes a method of self-control (*ātmavinigraha*).[6] Self-control is also called self-harmony.[7] It is a beautiful word which not only describes the process of self-control but also its total effect on the individual which is one of harmonious adjustment or integration of personality.

The *Gītā* shows how this self-control is to be achieved through *Vairāgya*. The *Gītā* is called the *Yogaśāstra* and Lord Kṛṣṇa the *Yogeśwara*. The *Gītā* is also called a scripture of God-realisation. With this end in view Kṛṣṇa exhorts Arjuna: 'Do thou become a yogi'—*yogi bhava*.'[8] The Yogi is one who has mastered himself (*yatātmanaḥ*).[9] To become a yogi is the central teaching of the *Gītā*. This means that one should realize the ideal of a perfect man: the *sthitapragna*. One of the essential qualifications of a *sthitapragna* is to have a mind which has attained balance, equalibility, equilibrium

[1]*BG.*, XIII.8.
[2]Mascaro, *The Bhagavad Gita*, p. 99.
[3]*BG.*, III. 6-7.
[4]ibid.
[5]*BG.*, II. 48.
[6]*BG.*, XIII. 8, XVII. 16.
[7]Mascaro, op. cit., p. 99.
[8]*BG.*, VI. 46.
[9]*BG.*, V. 25.

(*samatva*).[1] Now the mind is the instrument of perception. If it is disturbed, we are disturbed. So long as it is unsteady and unstable, we cannot perceive a thing. Nor can a restless mind have the possibility for realising the ultimate truth. Mind in Indian thought, Hindu and Buddhist is said to be fickle and difficult to control.[2] The question arises: how can the mind which wanders at will, become stable and obedient? The *Gītā* admits that it is a difficult proposition but says: 'The mind can be held in check by constant practice (*abhyāsa*) and dispassion (*vairāgya*).[3] *Vairāgya* is interpreted here as 'apathy' or absence of desire'[4] and 'mastery over the mind.'[5] However, the basic idea remains the same; the mind must be trained and controlled so as to attain the state of dispassion or detachment.

Now to control and train the turbulent mind it is not enough that we withdraw it from the senses and sense-objects. It must be diverted to some higher purpose, the life of the spirit. In other words it must be directed to God, to become God-minded. To use a beautiful simile the mind is a *Kalpavṛkṣa*. Standing under this *Kalpavṛkṣa* whatever we think, we so become.[6] If we train the mind to dwell on God, through *abhyāsa* it will indwell Him. We will become God-minded. According to the *Gītā* this is the easiest way to achieve self-control. For it says: It is the disciplined and the self-controlled *Yogis* who see Him seated in self, with the eye of the spirit: those without self-control do not see Him, in spite of all endeavours.[7] It is no wonder that the *Gītā* calls for the unwavering and all exclusive devotion to Him; 'Abandon all duties and come to Me, the only refuge.'[8] Thus *Vairāgya* through *abhyāsa* aims at educating the restless mind to cultivate non-attachment to pleasures of the senses and worldly desires and to think of the Supreme.

The *Gītā* carries the idea of *Vairāgya* still further. It says that complete detachment towards the world and sense-objects is not possible unless one rises above the pairs of opposites—above cold

1 *BG.*, II. 56-57.
2 *BG.*, VI. 35 also *DP.*, 33, 35.
3 *BG.*, VI. 35.
4 Tilak, *Gita Rahasya*, II, p. 1000, Index, p. 98.
5 *BG.*, VI, 36: Vaśyātmanā tu yatatā sakyovāptumupāyatah.
6 Agrawala, *Veda-Vidya*, pp. 52-53.
7 *BG.*, XV. 11.
8 *BG.*, XVIII. 66.

and heat, pleasure and pain, honour and dishonour, victory and defeat etc.[1] This implies rising above the planes of body, mind and feelings. In other words, we should learn to move amidst the sense-objects and the world with an easy self-mastery neither attracted nor repelled by them. As the *Gītā* says: 'The disciplined soul moves along the objects of sense with the senses fully under control and free from likes and dislikes.'[2] Thus *Vairāgya* or *virāga* meaning without *Rāga* or attachments—signifies not only detachment from all affections but also from all aversions. It neither accepts nor rejects: neither seeks nor rejects. This is the ideal of serenity and detachment which is implied in *Vairāgya*. It is real equanimity which teaches: 'to be moved but not to be swept away.' Such a state of detachment enables one to look at life in all its aspects and evenly.[3] *Vairāgya* thus becomes a state of higher indifference which can be described thus: 'Vāiragya is not running away from the world or callousness towards men and matters or going through the routine of life disliking it. It is the capacity to face the realities of existence and evaluate men, things and events at their true worth, without letting ourselves be affected by any of them.'[4] Throughout, the *Gītā* stress is laid on the cultivation of this higher indifference.[5]

It should be pointed out that the concept of *Vairāgya* as elaborated by the *Gītā* is applicable to all the worldly as well as the *renouncers of worldly life*. But the fact that since the *Gītā* does not support *saṁnyāsa* in the sense of leaving the world, its teaching was of not much value to the *saṁnyāsis*. If they were to practise *vairāgya* as taught by the *Gītā*, there would have been no need for them to renounce worldly life. By the time *Gītā* was preached, the institution of asceticism was well established. In the Brahmanic school, *Vairāgya* remained the essential condition as also the precedent of *Saṁnyāsa*.

There seems to be another reason why the teachings of the *Gītā* did not have enough and even far-reaching influence on Indian asceticism. In this connection, Dawson, a Western critic of the *Gītā* writes: 'The *Gītā* in spite of its immense popularity and in-

[1]*BG.*, II. 15, 38, 48; cf. *Manu*, VI. 75, 81.
[2]*BG.*, II. 64.
[3]Mahadeva Desai, *Gita According to Gandhi*, p. 53.
[4]*Theosophic Movement*, Vol. XXIX (March 1959), p. 176.
[5]*BG.*, V. 19-22, VI. 9.

fluence has not changed the religious ideal of India. Arjuna, the happy warrior, the hero of the *Gītā*, who attains salvation by the performance of his duty in battle has never displaced the figure of the world-renouncing ascetic and contemplative as the pattern of Indian sanctity.'[1]

Like Dawson, such a thought might have disturbed many a mind. The reason is not far to seek. We cannot do better than quote Panikkar who is of the view that the teachings of the *Gītā* lay hidden for a thousand years until the *Gītā* was rediscovered in the nineteenth century. He gives two reasons for it. First was the dominance of the renunciatory creed of which Sankar was the champion. Secondly, the earlier religious thinkers only used the *Gītā* to support their own previously enunciated religious doctrines and paid no attention to the social ethics of Lord Kṛṣṇa's teachings.[2]

To us this is not all surprising. For we find that Arjuna, a mere mortal like us, having heard the Lord's Celestial song once, had already forgotten what the Lord had taught him. The Gracious Lord must have smiled within, not without some amusement, that even mankind would likewise err and forget His gospel—that also, too soon. However, He repeats all over again whatever he had taught, in the *Anugītā* for the benefit of Arjuna. If Arjuna could afford to forget, so could mankind. But having rediscovered and heard this 'Song of Spiritual Life' once again, its music reverberates in the soul. We begin to live in the work of the moment, which becomes a humble offering to Him, as if it were a beautiful flower. And we are for ever grateful.

Yogasūtras

Yoga deals with the means by which we control the mind: *citta-vaśikāro upāyah.*[3] In the language of the *Gītā*, Patañjali uses the same two words, steady practice (*abhyāsa*) and detachment, non-attachment (*vairāgya*) as the two disciplines, along with the others, to control the activities (*nirodha*) of the mind (*citta*).[4] *Abhyāsa* is explained as the continuous effort to keep the mind's activities

[1] *Religion and Culture*, p. 189 f.
[2] Panikkar, *The Foundations of New India*, p. 43.
[3] *YS.*, II. 29.
[4] *YS.*, I. 12.

under control.[1] *Vairāgya* means the deliberate renunciation of all objects of enjoyment, either *seen or heard*.[2]

We are told, we have to start with the training of the mind to concentrate, but Patañjali warns us that the practice of concentration must be accompanied by detachment, *Vairāgya*. If we try to concentrate while remaining attached to things of the world, we shall either fail miserably or our newly acquired powers will bring us into great danger, because we shall be tempted to use them for selfish unspiritual ends.

What is the simplest way to acquire detachment? We must begin by cultivating attachment to the highest object we can conceive of, to God Himself. The more we love and thirst for the union with Him, the more we detest the fleeting pleasures. It means we have 'to convert the natural yearnings for things of the flesh into a consuming passion for things of the spirit.'[3] Like the *Gītā*, Patañjali recommends to us devotion to God (*iśwarpraṇidhān*).[4] When higher ideals and values are rooted in the mind then lesser bodily pleasures lose their attraction. What is important is that we must exercise self-discipline. We must control our physical appetites and passions. Towards this end *Yamas* and *Niyamas* are prescribed.[5]

The aspirant has to practice the eight disciplines and along with it he must sow the seed of *vairāgya* in *his heart*. In fact *abhyāsa* and *vairāgya* must go together. *Vairāgya* reaches its climax when the seeker has attained self-knowledge or self-realisation.[6] In contrast with this stage, the whole world naturally pales into insignificance.

From our study of the development of the concept of *Vairāgya* from the early Vedic times to the time of Patañjali, it can be seen that not only it had guided the destiny of the Brahmanic ascetic institution but it also had an important place in the *Buddhist* and *Jaina* schools of thought besides the *Gītā* and the *Yogasūtras*. It was an essential condition for renouncing the world (*saṁnyāsa*) and a

[1] *YS*., I. 13.

[2] *YS*., I. 15; An absolutely literal translation of the word '*Vairāgya*' is 'uncolouredness.' It well expresses the idea that one must not let one's emotions be coloured by the various things and ideas which come up: Wood, *Yoga*, p. 76.

[3] Desai, op. cit., p. 239, Commentary on VI. 35.

[4] *YS*., II. 1.

[5] *YS*., II. 30, 32.

[6] *YS*., I. 16.

worthy objective towards the attainment of self-perfection or preparation for a spiritual life even when leading a worldly life. In its aspect of extinction of *tṛṣṇā* or desire as an essential state or process leading to salvation, it has been accepted by all schools of thought including Brahmanism, Buddhism and Jainism. About its influence on Indian life and culture, Max Müller says:

'It is interesting to see how deeply this idea of *Vairāgya* must have entered into the daily life of Hindus. It is constantly mentioned as the highest excellence not for ascetics only but for everybody. It signifies the highest unworldliness and a complete surrender of all selfish desires.'[1]

Saṁnyāsa

The word *saṁnyāsa*, however, is derived from *sam+nyāsa*: *samyaga prākareṇa* (completely) *nyāsa* (pulling away, deposit, laying aside, resignation or abandonment).[2] The word *saṁnyāsa* also means 'to make or deliver over,' 'entrust,' 'commit to the care of,'[3] 'to resign the world, discard all worldly ties and attachments,'[4] hence a *saṁnyāsi* is one who abandons or gives up,'[5] complete renunciation of the world and its attachments.[6] Thus *saṁnyāsa* connotes abandonment of worldly possessions and the concentration of thought and devotion on the Supreme.

Monier Williams defines the *saṁnyāsi* thus: 'One who abandons or resigns worldly affairs, an ascetic devotee, who has renounced all earthly concerns and devotes himself to meditation and the study of the Āraṇyakas or Upaniṣads, a Brāhmaṇa in the fourth *āśrama* or stage of life, a religious mendicant.[7] The definition brings out different aspects of the ascetic's life according to Brāhmaṇism. He has become indifferent to the worldly affairs. He has retired from the world and having done so, subsists on begging. He is in the

[1] *Six Systems of Indian Philosophy*, p. 339.

[2] *BG.*, VIII. 2: kāmyānāṁ karmaṇāṁ nyāsamsanyāsaṁ kavayo viduḥ; Also *Manu.*, I. 114. *Ram.* 2. 115. 14. etad rājyaṁ mama bhrātrā dattaṁ saṁnyāsamuttamaṁ.

[3] *BG.*, III. 30: mayi sarvāṇi karmaṇi saṁnyāsyadhyātmacetasā.

[4] *Manu.*, VII. 94: vedāntaṁ vividhacśṛtvā saṁnyāsedanṛṇo dvijaḥ.

[5] *BG.*, VI. 4: sarvasaṁkalpa saṁnyasi yogāṛdhastadacyate., *BG.*, V. III jñeyaḥ sa nityasaṁnyāsi yo na dveşti na kāṇşti.

[6] *BG.*, III. 4: na ca saṁnyasanādeva siddhiṁ samadhigacchati.

[7] *ESD.*, p. 1148.

last *āśrama* and devotes himself to the study of the Āraṇyakas or Upaniṣads.

In the Vedic times the Saṁnyāsa mode of life is suggested in the *Bṛhadāraṇyaka Upaniṣad* which points to a class of men who are world-forsakers and almsmen: 'Men, knowing Brahman, give up the desire for sons, wealth and prosperity and become almsmen (*Bhikṣācaryaṁ caranti*).'[1] The *Muṇḍaka Upanishad* mentions *saṁnyās* and refers to such men 'those who live in the forest purified by austerities, those who know *brahmā* and were learned become almsmen.'[2] The stage of those transcending the triple mode of life—*atyāśramin* and *brahma-saṁstha*) seem to stand for the life of *saṁnyāsa*.[3]

In the Pāli texts, this mode of life is described as 'passing from the household to the homeless state': *Agārasma anāgariyaṁ pabajjati*.[4] The same idea is conveyed in Jainism by the phrase: *Agārāo anāgariam pavvayai*.[5] It should be remembered, however, that in Buddhism, the object and purpose of world-forsaking and becoming almsmen is said to be nothing more than *Brahmacarya* (the higher life). The Buddha exhorts his followers: 'Go along in accordance with what has been enjoined, having realized . . . .the Supreme goal of *Brahmacarya*, for the sake of which family men go forth from home into homelessness.'[6] The ideas of self-mortification (*tapas*) and *nyāsa* (renunciation) are not associated with *Brahmacarya*. According to the Buddha, the attachment to household life must be discarded not because, there is any special virtue in the mere rejection of it, but because worldly attachments are hindrances to a life of *Brahmacarya*.

The *Mahābhārata* describes the four stages of life. The modes of life of the hermit (*vānaprastha*) and of the *saṁnyāsi* (*parivrājaka*) are depicted in detail.[7] It is stated that when a householder (*gṛhastha*) finds his body wrinkled and hair grey and children born to his children, he should retire into the forest. He may live with his wife and practise severe austerities.[8] His daily life consists of

[1] *Brhad. Up.*, IV. 4. 22; III. 5. 1.
[2] *Mund. Up.*, I. 2. 11, III. 2. 6 (Saṁnyāsayogādyatayaḥ).
[3] *Sveta., Up.*, VI. 21. *Chand. Up.*, II. 23 : 1 cf. Vide Chapter V.
[4] *Digha. Nik.*, I. 60, I. 240, III. 55.
[5] *Acar.*, II. 2. 1.
[6] *Mahavagga*, I. 11. 1.
[7] *Mbh*, xii. 191 f. xii. 243 ff, xii. 278.
[8] *Mbh.*, xii. 191 f.

postures (*virāsana*), yogic postures (*maṇḍuka-yoga*) ritual and vows. (*purṇamāsya* and *chaturmāsya*).[1] Passing into the last stage of life of *saṁnyāsa*, he should leave off Vedic study and the sacred thread. He should regard neither life nor death with joy. He should purify his heart and mind of all shortcomings, purge himself of all sins. He abstains from injury, regards all creatures with impartiality and is devoted to truth. Having controlled all his senses, he has become free from all attachments. He has nothing which he calls his own. Leading a lonely life, he seeks only the knowledge of the self.[2]

The *Mahābhārata* mentions Agastya and the seven Ṛṣis—Madhucchandās, Aghamarśana, Sāṅkriti, Sudivātaṇdi, Ahoviryya, Kavya, Tāndya and adds the names of Medhātithi, Karmanirvaka and Śunyapāla to the list of those who were the authors of *Saṁnyāsāśrama*. The epic states that these ṛṣis have all gone to heaven practising the course of duties pertaining to *Saṁnyāsa*.[3] Many who observed the vows of *Saṁnyāsa* are referred to as living in a sacred asylum in the Himavat.[4]

Both the trends of thought—one favouring the path of renunciation emphasising *saṁnyāsa* and the other favouring the path of action emphasising *gārhasthya*, are discussed in the *Mahābhārata*. It looks upon the scheme of the four stages (*āśramas*) of life as providing a proper balancing of the four aims of life viz. *artha*, *kāmā*, *dharma* and *mokṣa*. Adopting the first three aims as the incentives for all the worldly activities, it emphasises that these motives should lead one to the ultimate realisation of the inner spirituality which is the aim of human life.[5] But it is the heroic aspect of human life that the epic eulogises. Its message is to cultivate *samatva*, equability, harmony and balance. It asks man to face the battle of life like a warrior, however hopeless it might be, to fight it out and not run away like an ascetic.[6]

It is this very heroic theme which is elaborated in the *Gītā* which is an integral part of the *Mahābhārata*. The *Gītā* does not favour a life of renunciation (*saṁnyāsa*). It defines *saṁnyāsa* as 'the

[1] *Mbh.*, xiii. 141, 110-15.
[2] *Mbh.*, xii. 243 ff.
[3] *Mbh.*, xii. 244. 16-18.
[4] *Mbh.*, xiii. 10. 10.
[5] *Mbh.*, xii. 167 f.
[6] *Mbh.*, xii. 12. 12; cf., Chapter viii.

renunciation of actions springing from selfish desires' and the abandonment of the fruit of all actions, *tyaga.*[1] It explains that this giving up of the desire for fruit must be *sāttvika.* Even austerity, sacrifice and charity which are a means of purification have to be pursued without desire for fruit and without attachment.[2] It exhorts one and all: 'Do not be attached to actionlessness'—*ma te saṅgo astu akarmāṇi.*[3] It gives us the call of *Niṣkāmakarma* or action without personal desire or attachment. It tells us: 'Thy business is with the action only, never with its fruits.'—*Karmaṇyeva adhikāraste māphaleṣu kadācana.*[4] The *Gītā* adds lustre to the *gṛhasthāśrama* by favouring the *pravṛttimārga* and its philosophy of *niṣkāmakarma-yoga*—and *lokasaṁgraha.* The ideal of renunciation (*saṁnyāsa*) is made a part of the active life, *gṛhasthāśrama.*

The *Rāmāyana* does not explicitly mention *Saṁnyāsa* or depict it as a mode of life-stage. All the while we meet the *ṛṣis*, *munis* and hermits who are *vānaprasthas*, living the Vedic mode of life and thought. However, we come across the words *bhikṣu* and *parivrājaka.*[5] We cannot definitely say whether a *parivrājaka* or a *bhikṣu* was the same as a *saṁnyāsin.* It is also not certain whether the final stage of life of *saṁnyāsa* followed that of *vānaprastha* or could be resorted to even earlier. The epic does not shed any light on this point. But it is the *gṛhasthāśrama* which is upheld as the highest ideal wherein the righteous *gṛhastha* can fulfil all worldly and other-worldly obligations. The *Rāmāyaṇa* itself is an epic *par excellence* of this stage of Indian life.

The *Arthaśāstra* describes the rules of the four *āśramas*—that of a *gṛhastha*, *brahmacārī*, *vānaprastha* and the *ascetic* (*parivrājaka*). The ascetic is described as having 'complete control of the organs of sense, abstaining from all kinds of work, disowning money, keeping away from society, begging in many places, dwelling in forests and purity both internal and external.'[6] The *Arthaśāstra* reflects the social mind which is fully aware of the anti-social and disintegrating influence of the ascetic institution especially on the realisa-

[1]Kāmyānāṁ karmaṇāṁ nyāsaṁ saṁnyāsaṁ kāvayo viduḥ Sarvakarmphalatyāgaṁ prāhustyāgaṁ vichakṣaṇāḥ; *BG.*, xviii. 2.

[2]Yagno dānaṁ tapaschaiva pāvanāni maniṣiṇāṁ Etānyapi tu karmāṇi sangaṁ tyaktvā phalāṇi cha; *BG.*, xviii. 5-6.

[3]*BG.*, ii. 47.

[4]*BG.*, ii. 47.

[5]*Ram.*, iii. 46, 3; IV. 3. 2. 23.

[6]I. 3. 9-12.

tion and protection of the *artha* ideal of the society. It, therefore, lays down various restrictions and conditions for both the sexes before they embraced asceticism.[1] It values asceticism primarily for its usefulness in espionage and intelligence activities.[2]

The law-books elaborately deal with the four stages of life and prescribe duties for each of them.[3] However, the law-givers differ in their sequence. Āpastamba describes the four *āśramas* as *gārhasthya*, *ācāryakulaṁ*, *muni* and *vānaprastha*.[4] Gautama enumerates them as *Brahmacarya*, *Gārhasthya*, *Bhikṣu* and *Vaikhānasa*.[5] Vasiṣṭha and Baudhāyana name the first two stages after Gautama but the last two as *Vānaprastha* and *Parivrājaka*.[6] Manu follows the order naming the last as that of *Yati* and *saṁnsāsin*.[7] All the law-givers praise *Gṛhasthāśrama* as the most excellent and the highest *āśrama*.[8] They also frown upon people taking to asceticism without passing through the first three stages in their proper order. Many of them look upon *saṁnyāsa* not only as an anti-Vedic custom but also regard it outside the normal scheme of Āryan life.[9]

Saṁnyāsa thus as an institution arose in the Vedic times and was known before the advent of the Buddha and Mahāvira. With the emergence of the four *āśramas*, *saṁnyāsa* became a worthy aspect of an Āryan's life which was to be realised through the progressive stages, after one had discharged one's obligations to the family and society.[10] It came to be known in the later times as *nivṛtti-mārga*, a pathway of life and world-negation as opposed to *pravṛtti-mārga*, that of life and world affirmation. Some of the later Upaniṣads assigned to the *Saṁnyāsāśrama* the highest position.

[1]II. 1. 29; II. 1. 32.

[2]I. 11. 12, I. 10. 7-8, IV. 5, V. 1. 19, XI. 1. 40-41, XIII. 2.

[3]*AP. DS.*, II. 21. 23, 2-17; *Gaut. DS.*, III. 26-35, III. 11-25; *Baudh. DS.*, II. ii. 14-15 and III. 18 ff.; II. 11, 16-26; 17. 1-18, 27; *VAS.*, *DS.*, VI. 19-20 and IX; *Manu*, VI. 87, 96.

[4]*AP. DS.*, II. 9, 21. 1.

[5]*Gaut. DS.*, III. 2.

[6]*Vas. DS.*, VII. 1-2; *Baudh. DS.*, II. 6. 17.

[7]*Manu*. IV. 1, V. 169, VI. 33, 87, 96.

[8]*Gaut*. III. 1 & 35, *Baudh.*, II. 6. 29 f; *Manu*, III. 77-80, VI. 87, 89, 90.

[9]*Baudh. DS.*, II. 6. 29-31.

[10]*Jabala Up*. 4, *Manu*. VI. 33, *Maitri*. *Up*. IV. 3; *Kathasruti*. *Up*. 31; *Narada Up*. pp-131-132; *Maha. Up*. I. 91, XII. 61 ff, 191 ff, 242 ff, 269, 278; XIII. 141 f; XIV. 46. *Viṣṇu*, 96. 1; *Baudh. DS.*, II. 10. 17. 6.

As a reaction to the Brāhmanical Saṁnyāsa and monastic movement started by the Buddha and Mahāvira, the *Gītā's* gospel of activistic teachings of *Niṣkāmakarma* and *Lokasaṁgraha* prevented the social order of those times from disruption. Side by side, the *Mahābhārata*, the *Rāmāyaṇa* and the *Dharmasūtras* praised *Gṛhasthāśrama* as the best of all *āśramas* and even a necessary training ground for the final spiritual journey. In the *Arthaśāstra* and the law-books we hear many voices of dissent against *saṁnyāsa*. The theory of the four *āśramas* was never practised fully in the ancient times. Though theoretically laid down for the whole society, it was followed by the few particularly the *dvijāti*.

Yoga

From the very early times in India, yogic practices were known in the esoteric circles of ascetics and mystics. There are ample literary evidences that describe them as concentrating their minds on particular objects and thereby stopping the movement of their minds and senses and achieving wonderful miraculous powers. Patañjali collected and classified the ascetic practises and contemplative formulas that were extant in his times and were known to the yogis from time immemorial. He was thus not the founder or originator but the editor of the yoga. But it is to his credit that in the process the yoga techniques have preserved and purified some of the oldest psychical introspections known to ancient India. He gave a philosophical basis to the whole system and demonstrated for the first time how yoga may be utilised for the emancipation of man from the bondage of his mind, senses and ignorance. He prescribed yoga practices for the spiritual enlightenment, the ultimate and asolute freedom of man.

Hopkins, who has investigated the problem of yoga-technique in the *Māhābhārata* states: 'Asceticism, devout meditation, speculation, magical power, hallucination as means of salvation are factors of yoga. Their combination into a formal system represents a late stage of Hindu thought.'[1] It becomes clear from this observation that yoga has close and definite association with asceticism. As Garbe says: 'The concept of the *yoga* is developed out of *tapas*.'[2]

The representation of a three-faced nude male deity with the soles of his feet touching each other, his hands resting on his knees and

[1] *JOAS.*, Vol. XXII, 1901, p. 333.
[2] *ERE.*, XII, p. 833.

seated like the yogi and the bust of the priest-king with his eyes half-closed and looking at the tip of the nose indicate that the practice of meditation was also known in the Indus Valley. It also suggests existence of ascetic practices in India as early as 2500 BC.[1] Yoga thus seems to have had antique roots.

The Ṛgvedic Muni is described as in a state of ecstasy or maddened with silence (*unmaditā mauneya*), and mounted on the winds and whose bodies the mortals cannot see. He flies through the air and is a friend of the gods. He roams at will in different regions and paths and divines secret desires or thoughts of men.[2] Here we find the root of the later idea of miraculous powers arising out of *tapas*, which in the course of time came to be associated with the yogic tradition.

In the *Artharvaveda*, Ekavrātya as Isāna is described as having seven *Prāṇas*, seven *Apānaś* and seven *Vyānaś*.[3] *Prāṇa*, *Apāna* and *Vyāna* are three kinds of breaths which along with seven others form the ten vital energies. They are located in particular arteries which together form the subtle body in the fully developed yoga system. Of these, *Prāṇa* and *Apāna* are considered to be the most important. This leads us to believe that some kind of breath-control was known and practised at the time. In *tapas*, the inner 'heat' was caused by retention of breath. There is no doubt that rhythmically regulated breathing was the result of certain experiments directed towards increasing inner heat leading to ecstasy.

The practice of continence (*Brahmacarya*) is an important element in yoga. The *Brahmacarya-sūkta* of the Atharvaveda praises the power of continence. It asserts that with the aid of *brahmacarya* and *tapas* the gods were able to conquer death.[4] Here is demonstrated the efficacy of discipline, austerities and sex-control. In the later developed theory and practice of Yoga, great stress is laid upon the cultivation of the status of *urdhvaretas*—one who succeeds in transforming his lower sensual energy into higher spiritual power. The eulogy of the *Atharvaveda* in praise of the power of Brahmacarya indicates that the germs of the later ideas of yogic mysticism were prevalent at that time.

In the Upanishads when the *jñāna-mārga* is given a preference,

[1] Vide Chapter IV.
[2] *ṚV.*, X. 136, 1-7.
[3] *AV.*, XV. 15. 1-2.
[4] *AV.*, XI. 5-19.

meditation requiring control of sense and thought is emphasised. The *Bṛhadarāṇyakopaniṣad* lays down the means of knowing Brahman: Veda-study (*vedānuvacan*), sacrifice (*yajña*), gifts (*dana*), austerity (*tapas*) and fasting (*anāśakena*).'[1] According to *Kena Upaniṣad*, penance (*tapaḥ*), self-control (*damaḥ*) and works (*karma*) are the support of the secret relating to Brahman.[2] In the *Kathā Upaniṣad* we find references to *adhyātma-yoga* and yoga as 'a firm grip on the senses' (*sthira indriyadhāraṇā*) which shows an earlier concept of Yoga-discipline.[3] *Muṇḍaka Upaniṣad* mentions the yoga of renunciation (*saṁnyāsa-yoga*). It says: 'Having well ascertained the object of the knowledge of Vedānta and having purified their minds by *saṁnyāsa-yoga*, these ascetics (*yatayaḥ*) enjoy the highest immortality, become free in the worlds of Brahma at the time of death.'[4] In the *Maitri Upaniṣad*, pranayam as a part of six-fold yoga is mentioned.[5] Here *yama* and *Niyama* of the Yoga system are only omitted. The theistic *Śvetāśvatra Upaniṣad* states that a man becomes one with Iśwara, the Lord of the Universe by meditation.[6] Elsewhere it emphasises the results of Yoga: 'When the five-fold quality of Yoga is produced, arising from earth, water, fire, air and ether—then there is no longer any sickness, no old age or death for him who has obtained a body produced by the fire of yoga (*Yogāgnimayaṁ Śariram*).'[7]

It seems that the later yogin relies on *āsana*, the older Muni on *upāsanā*. This and the doctrine of sleep-union with Brahman,[8] the breath and the concommittant vein-theory[9] belongs to that background of yoga afterwards worked out into a system. Besides knowledge of Ātman and of Karman, the 'secret doctrines' (*guhya ādeśaḥ*) of the Muni contained much that was included into the

[1]*Bṛhad. Up.*, IV. 4. 22.

[2]*Kena.*, IV. 8: tasya tapo damaḥ karmeti pratiṣṭhā vedāḥ sarvāngaṁ satyamāyatanam.

[3]*Katha Up.*, VI. 11,18.

[4]*Mund. Up.*, iii. 2. 6; cf. *Tait. Ar.*, X. 10.

[5]*Maitri Up.*, VI. 18; cf. *Amritbindu* 6: tathā tatprayogakalpaḥ prāṇāyāmaḥ pratyāhāro dhyānaṁ dhāraṇā tarkaḥ samādhīḥ saḍanga ity ucyate yogaḥ.

[6]*Svetā Up.*, I. 11: tasyābhidhyānā tritiyaṁ dehbhede viśvaiṣvarayaṁ keval āptakāmaḥ.

[7]Ibid, II. 12: prithvyāptejonilakhe samuthite pancātmake yogagune pravṛtte na tasya rogo na jarā na mṛtyuḥ yogāgnimayaṁ śariraṁ.

[8]*Man. Up.*, 7 & 12.

[9]*Mbh.*, xii. 51, 6, 185. 14-16; Hopkins, *The Great Epic of India*, pp. 36 ff, 172.

subsequent system of the later Upaniṣads and Yogasūtras. For example, the yoga teaching in regard to the limited sphere of the breath, one *pradeṣa* from the mouth.[1] The rigorous discipline which we associate with the yoga system was probably known but the technical nomenclature was still undeveloped.

The Buddhist texts speak of four magical powers of translation (*gaman*), the first being the ability to fly like a bird.[2] In the early Buddhist literature Sariputta, Mogalana and Nanda are described as adepts in *dhyāna*. Anuruddha, Revata and Subhuti are also experts in *dhyāna*.[3] The fact that the exercise of Yoga imparts magical powers is recognised in early Buddhist books but the attainment of such powers was lightly set aside by the Buddha himself as not conducive to perfection.[4] In later Buddhist literature we find fully developed Yoga-technique.[5]

In the *Mahābhārata* Vasiṣṭha appears as the expositor of *Yoga-kṛtya*: 'The wisdom-knowing men declare that meditation is two-fold (*dhyānaṁ-dvividhaṁ*); meditation being the highest power of yogins.'[6] It is then stated: 'Concentration of mind and restraint of breath (are the two): restraint of breath is (meditation) with characeristics, mental (restraint) is without characeristics.'[7] After declaring that the *yoga* system is identical with the *Sāṅkhya*, Yājña-valkya teaches the special Yoga-practices depending on the breaths (*rudrapradhanā*).[8] It seems that the term *Yoga* applied to the *āsana* or posture of the regular Yoga practice, had also absorbed the meaning of *tapas* so that any austerity, whether in *prāṇāyama* exercise or not, was called Yoga. Austerity is thus caused by Yoga.[9] Both are the sign of *nivṛtti* or renunciation for the sake of the soul of him who is *yukto yogam prati sadā prati sāṁkhyānam eva ca*,[10] whether he be an ascetic, now at the foot of a tree, now

[1] *Aitareya Ar.*, i. 2. 4. 21: pradeşamātra etāvatā vai prāṇaḥ sammitāḥ.

[2] *Viśuddhimāgga*, p. 396.

[3] *Theri*, CCLVI. 3. 1, *Thera*, 263, p. 382.

[4] *DOB.*, I. p. 278, *Digha Nik.*, I. 16-20.

[5] *Viśuddhimāgga* (iii. 105) contains a standard list of forty subjects of meditation. Also Thomas, *History of Buddhist Thought*, pp. 44 ff; Conze, *Buddhist Meditation*, pp. 11-41.

[6] *Mbh.*, xii. 307.

[7] ibid, xii, 307.8: ekāgrātā ca manasaḥ prāṇāyāmas tathāi'va ca prāṇāyāmas tu saguṇo nirguṇo manasas tathā.

[8] ibid, xii, 317.5 f.

[9] *Mbh.*, xii. 153.36.

[10] *Mbh.*, xiii. 141.83.

lying on the ground, now wandering about or engaged in the *Virāśayyā* etc. Those recognised as Yogins thus include ascetics of every sort, though they have formal divisions viz. *muktāḥ* and *yūktāḥ*, *kuṭicaka* and *bahūdaka*, *haṅsa* and *paramahaṅsa*.[1] The discipline of Yoga is explained as fixing the spirit on different parts of the body and then in dieting, in chastity and in renouncing sensual pleasures of all kinds.[2] The yoga-powers are alluded to as *aṣṭagunam aiśvaryam*[3] and are called, in general, *bhutis*, *vibhutis*, *aiśvarya* or *Yogeśvaratva*, powers or masteries and are grouped as *animālaghimāprāptiḥ*.[4] They are attributes of God. Austerities alone are also said to give mastery (*aiśvaryaṁ*).[5] The powers of Yoga are also described viz. becoming the size of an atom and entering a lotus stalk,[6] entering the body of another,[7] exercising hypnotic power[8] and knowing another's thoughts.[9] The yoga-practice of Vidura is that of an ascetic. With unkempt hair, naked (*digvāsāḥ*) he wanders through the woods, eating air and holding a stone in his mouth[10] by which means of asceticism (*tapobala*) as well as by mental discipline (*yogadharma*)[11] he won success (*siddhi*).[12] What a yogin can do is done by an ascetic and upto a certain point the two are one. But posture (*āsana*) seems to be a chief concern of the Yogin and not the Muni. In many a tale, the Muni is described as either standing or hanging himself upside down to acquire not only power but highest bliss.[13] It can be seen from the above that there are three epic groups, old tapas tales and teaching, void of yoga, tales and teaching in which tapas and yoga are synonymous and both are directed towards the achievement of physical and

[1]*Mbh.*, xiii. 141.89.

[2]*Mbh.*, xii. 301. pp. 30-37, 39 ff. xii. 195.10, xiii. 141.8.

[3]*Mbh.*, xii. 340.55.

[4]*Mbh.*, xii. 303.16.

[5]*Mbh.*, xii.161.5 : āiśvaryam ṛṣayaḥ prāptās tapasāi'va.

[6]*Mbh.*, xii.343.42 : āiśvaryayogād aṇumātro bhūtvā.

[7]*Mbh.*, xv.26.26-29, xii.285. 175, 290.12 : xiii.40 ff, xiii.55.19, 53.68, 54.15; cf. *YS.*, iii.38 : cittasya paraśariraveśaḥ.

Mbh., xiii.40.46, 47, 50-51, 58; 41.13, 18.

[9]*Mbh.*, xii. 343.48.

[10]*Mbh.*, xv. 26.17; 37.12: Vitāmukhaḥ vitam mukhe samādhāya.

[11]*Mbh.*, xv. 26.30; 28.16 : dhāraṇān manasā dhyānād yaṁ dharmaṁ kavayo viduḥ.

[12]*Mbh.*, xv. 35.3.

[13]*Mbh.*, i.13, 40.25, 41.4; 43.8; 73.25. iii.187.4 ff, V.63.9 ff.

mental powers; tales and didactic passages in which is found an elaborated systematic yoga philosophy.

Fixing the mind by looking only at the nose and gradually withdrawing the breath is alluded to in the *Gītā*.[1] The state where thought is suppressed is also indicated.[2] Yoga is called *rājavidyā rājaguhyaṁ*.[3] Lord Kṛṣṇa is called *mahāyogeśvara*[4] and *yogācārya*.[5] The art of meditation is described in a simple manner[6] but no difficult postures and ascetic discipline are prescribed.[7] But yoga is not merely thought-control as in the technical *yoga-śāstra* but the whole of spiritual life which aims at union with the Supreme. The yoga in *Gītā* is equanimity (*samatva*),[8] the discipline of restraining the mind at all levels and all circumstances.

In the *Rāmāyaṇa* the ṛṣis, munis and hermits have been described as acquiring through tapas many miraculous powers akin to yogic *siddhis*. They could know the intent of others[9] and were credited with intuitive vision by which they could divine unseen things.[10] The sage Gautama detected the crime of adultery committed by Indra and his wife Ahalya.[11] Through yogic powers it was possible to be gifted with divine vision (*jñāna dṛṣti*, *jñāna cakṣu*). Aided by his *dharma-virya*, Vālmiki is said to have visualised the past, present and future incidents in Rama's life.[12] During the period of austerities, the ascetics were required to keep their senses under control, remain absorbed in meditation and observe purity of conduct.[13] *Virāsana* was a generally adopted posture during their meditation.[14]

1 *BG*., V.27, VI.13, viii. 10.

2 *BG*., VI. 20-23 : yatroparamate cittaṁ nirudhaṁ yogasevayā tam vidyād duḥkhasaṁyogaviyogaṁ yogasaṁjnitaṁ.

3 *BG*., ix.2.

4 *BG*., II.9.

5 *BG*., XVI.4.26.

6 *BG*., VI.10-13.

7 *BG*., VI.16-17 : nātyaśnatastu yogo'sti na caikāntamanśnataḥ na cātisvapnaśilasya jāgṛto naivacārjuna yuktāhāravihārasya yuktacceṣṭasya karmasu yuktasvapnāvabudhasya yogo bhavati duḥkhahā.

8 ibid, II.48 : siddhayasiddayoḥ samo bhūtvā samatvaṁ yoga ucyate.

9 *Ram*., VII.9.19.

10 *Ram*., VII. 49.6 : *tapasā labhdhacakṣumān*.

11 *Ram*., I.84.

12 *Ram*., I.3.4.6.7.

13 *Ram*., VII.9.39; 10.3; III.10.5-6.

14 *Ram*., VII.10.4.

The *Yoga-sūtras* describes yoga as consisting of eight limbs (*aṅgas*): the various forms of abstention from evil doing (*yama*), the various observances (*niyama*), posture (*āsana*), control of the breath (*prāṇāyam*), withdrawal of the mind from sense-objects (*pratyāhāra*), concentration (*dharma*), meditation (*dhyāna*) and absorption in the Purusha (*samādhi*).[1] The last three *dhāraṇā, dhyāna* and *samādhi* when practised with regard to one object is called *saṁyama*.[2]

The first two *Yama* and *Niyama* indicate the preliminary ethical preparation necessary for a spiritual aspirant. They emphasise good conduct and purity without which there can be no meditation. Niyamas comprise (i) *Shoucha* (bodily and mental purity), (ii) *Santosha* (contentment), (iii) *Tapas* (ascetic practices to tame the bodily and mental habits), (iv) *Svādhyāya* (study of the sacred books) and (v) *Iśwar Praṇidhāna* (total dedication to God.[3] Yamas are five: (i) *Ahiṁsā* (non-violence), (ii) *Satya* (veracity), (iii) *Asteya* (non-covetousness), (iv) *Brahamacarya* (continence) and (v) *Aparigraha* (frugal living).[4] The Yamas are basic rules of conduct for the Hindu *saṁnyāsis*, Buddhist *Bhikkhus* and Jaina *Yatis* in their ascetic life or monastic conduct. In Jainism these five great vows were called *pānca mahāvayyas* or *mahānubratas*.[5] The Buddhists also had eight precepts (*atthangaśila*) of which the first five (*pañcśila*) agree with the five *mahāvayyas* of the Jains.[6] The ideal of *aparigraha* was common to Brahmanism, Buddhism and Jainism. The Nigantha was not only free from all worldly ties and bonds but he was the one who had discarded even clothing as its visible symbol. The *Digaṁbaras* even today practise nudity as a vindication of their vow of non-possession (*aparigraha*).[7]

Thus we find that certain Yogic practices were current and allied with ascetic practices from very early times and that the ascetics or monks of various orders derived the theoretical and practical knowledge from their preceptors. The concept of Yoga seems to

[1]*YS.*, II.28-29.

[2]*YS.*, III.4.

[3]*YS.*, II.32.

[4]*YS.*, II.30.

[5]Deo, *JMJ*, p. 10.

[6]Rhys Davids, *Buddhism*, p. 139.

[7]According to Jainism, celibacy and nudity are closely related from the point of view of controlling the senses and non-attachment to bodily pleasures and external needs.

have developed out of that of *tapas* as a *tapasvi* had often some kind of knowledge in the method of meditation and was familiar with certain respiratory discipline. With the increasing emphasis in the times of the Upaniṣads on the attainment of Supreme wisdom (*jñāna*) for liberation, the value of Yoga for spiritual enlightenment and a means of emancipation came to be recognised. In its early periods of development, Yoga was resorted to for exhilaration and enhancement of physical and mental powers. In the later phase, it became a technique of intellectual illumination and a system of philosophy.

Asceticism as a Cultural Phenomenon

When we talk of a 'cultural phenomenon,' what we mean by 'culture' is 'the sum-total of the way of living built up by groups of human beings and transmitted from one generation to another.'[1] But we must be clear in our minds about its difference from 'civilisation.' Civilisation is 'the sum-total of social heritage projected on the social plane' while culture 'is the same heritage focussed on the individual plane.'[2] 'Civilisation is what we have and culture is what we are.'

Sorokin's is perhaps the most complete attempt to assemble and analyse the various complex cultures of the world into a few thematic patterns.[3] He begins with examining cultural phenomena in two aspects: internal and external. The first belongs to the realm of the mind and its inner experience, the latter to those external manifestations of its internal aspect. Sorokin places asceticism as a cultural phenomenon as in its *internal* aspect of value, meaning, inner experience pertaining to the realm of the mind.[4]

Sorokin then divides the world cultures in two broad categories —*ideational* and *sensate*. Between these two extremes the varied cultures of the world, according to him, could lie—the different degrees constituting not only a quantitative but a qualitative problem.

In *ideational* culture, reality is perceived as non-sensate and non-material, everlasting being, its needs and ends being mainly spiritual. The *sensate* culture views reality as only that which is presented

[1]Rajagopalachari, *Our Culture*, p. 9.
[2]Ghurye, *Culture and Society*, p. 3.
[3]Sorokin, *Social & Cultural Dynamics*, Vol. I, pp. 55-83.
[4]ibid, p. 55.

to the sense organs and its needs and aims are mainly physical. Whereas *ideational* mentality fulfils the spiritual needs and ends by self-imposed minimization or elimination of the physical needs, the *sensate* culture seeks to realize its aims mainly physical by exploitation of the external world. In brief, the *sensate* culture is the opposite of the *ideational* culture.[1]

Sorokin then assigns ascetic mentality to *ideational* culture as demonstrated in the asceticism of Hindus, Buddhists, Taoists, Early Christians, Jains and Sufis and the numberless ascetics affiliated with smaller sects.[2]

As a sharp contrast to this *ideational* culture wherein the ascetic mentality is dominant, Sorokin views *sensate* culture thus and observes: This type of mentality is quite familiar to us. It pervades our contemporary culture, and emphasises that, 'the character of most of the Oriental, especially the Hindu and conspicuously Sensate culture of most of the contemporary Western societies is indubitable and remains probably the fundamental difference between them.'[3] This view is out of date now. But it is this difference which is meant when we often contrast Indian spirituality which belongs to *Ideational* culture, in opposition to the materialism of the West, which is called the *Sensate* culture by Sorokin. In *Sensate* culture the primacy is laid on sensuous enjoyment of life as the sole reality of existence. This would correspond to *Artha* and *Kāma*, two of the four ends of human life recognised in Indian thought. The *Cārvāka* Philosophy of materialism also properly belongs to the *Sensate* culture.

All the other culture mentalities in Sorokin's view represent a mixture of the *Ideational* and *Sensate* forms in various combinations and proportions. This he calls *Mixed culture* mentality.

While discussing the Hindu and Buddhist systems which according to Sorokin contain the highest ascetic mentality, he cites these four elements as the essence of this highest mentality:

(1) Ultimate reality is spiritual, towards which one must strive by throwing off the illusion of personality and by being absorbed in the Ultimate
(2) Needs are purely spiritual
(3) The extent of their satisfaction is maximum

[1]Sorokin, *Social & Cultural Dynamics*, Vol. I, pp. 73 ff.
[2]ibid, pp. 83 ff.
[3]ibid, p. 74. f.

(4) The method of satisfaction consists in a complete mastery of all sensate needs, even to the point of annihilation of their very source, that is, a complete modification (dissolution) of self, social, psychological and biological.[1]

Sorokin very rightly observes that for the masses this highest form of mentality and conduct is impossible. Only those types which are closer to the *Sensate* can be achieved by them.[2] This explains why Indian asceticism which demands a strenuous path of self-discipline, a life of contemplation and *tyāga* (renunciation) was not for all. The path, which is for the few, is likened to a razor's edge and hard to cross : *kṣurasya dhārā niśitā duratyayā.*[3] However, it may be noted that in the light of the scheme of four *āśramas*, *saṁnyāsa* was meant for all, excepting the Śudras after they have fulfilled their responsibility of life.[4]

It will be pertinent to state that though Indian thought recognises the four ends of human life (*puruṣārtha*) and the last aim of *mokṣa* is exhorted for an individual for attainment by all the systems of Indian philosophy, every individual cannot aspire and much less struggle to achieve it in practice. Śaṅkarācārya points out that even the desire for *mokṣa* is to be rarely found in all persons: *durlabhaṁ manuṣyatvaṁ mumukṣutvaṁ.*[5] And mere desire is not enough. As the eye naturally demands light and colour as the body desires food and drink, so the soul cherishes a natural desire to know God's truth and free itself from falsehood. This is the passion for *mokṣa* which requires to be backed up through a ceaseless effort through many paths suited to different temparaments. These paths were and still recognised as the pathways of *Jñāna*, *Karma* and *Bhakti.* Each one of these demands certain basic requirements, intellectual, idealistic or emotional equipment leading towards the goal. These paths are only the means towards an end, which is *mokṣa* or

[1]Sorokin, *Social & Cultural Dynamics,* Vol. I, pp. 119-120.

[2]ibid, p. 121.

[3]*Katha Up.*, III.14.

[4]*Vaikhānasdharmapraśna,* I.10.13, IX.8.

[5]Śaṅkara says : Only through God's Grace we obtain the three rarest advantages : human birth, the longing for liberation (*mumukṣatva*) and discipleship of an illumined teacher. *Vivekacudāmani*, 3.

cf. manuṣyāṇāṁ sahasreṣu kaścidyatati siddhaye yatatāmapi siddhānāṁ kaścinmāṁ vetti tattvataḥ *BG.*, VII.3.

cf. Kiccho manussapatilābho kicchaṁ maccāna jīvitaṁ kicchaṁ saddhammasavaṇaṁ kiccho buddhānamuppādo *DP.*, 182.

release, described variously by Brāhmanism, Buddhism and Jainism in their systems, as also in the *Darśaṇas*. Even asceticism was also a means towards the very end, though it was erroneously considered as the end itself by some in the times when the Buddha appeared on the scene. It was he who condemned asceticism which had assumed fanatical proportions and was practised for its own sake and recommended a Middle Path.

Reverting to Sorokin's view that asceticism was not for the masses, it will be interesting to affirm how the ancient thinkers realised this fact too well. Bringing out their typical and realistic attitude towards the institution, Vaidya observes: 'The wise Ṛṣis of the Upaniṣadic period had prudently ordained that it was not every man who could be an ascetic. Frail humanity required to be chastened and softened before a man could aspire to be an ascetic. The renunciation of the world required as much a preparation and a regular course of training for it as the proper and successful enjoyment of life required previous education.'[1] If one has to learn how to enjoy all that this world has to offer, it becomes equally important, if not more, to learn how to discard all that the world has already offered by way of pleasures and joys family and property for a higher life of *tyāga* or renunciation. Thus it becomes vital that a person acquires necessary training and becomes fit through the earlier three stages.

Not only premature life of *saṁnyāsa* was frowned upon but it was also considered anti-social in practice is the view which could be supported by much evidence. A legend describes how on the Buddha's first preaching mission in Magadha, there was an outcry against him and a propaganda that he intended to 'make families sonless and women widows and to cut off the line of succession.'[2] It was against this anti-social tendency of ascetic institution which threatened to disrupt the social order that the *Gītā* raised a voice of disapproval and condemned it, preaching the gospel of *niṣkāma-karma*. Even the Brāhmanical law-codes give it a tardy and unwilling recognition, for it is the condition of the pious householder that is exalted in their socio-religious scheme of life.[3] One hears

[1] *Epic India*, p. 362.

[2] *Mahaparinirvana Sutta*, I.24.5.

[3] *Manu* III.77-80, VI.89-90, *Gautama Ch.* II. *Vasiṣṭha* VIII.14-17 *Viṣhnu* 59.29 *Vyāsa* IV.2.

the voices of dissent against *saṁnyāsa* in the *Mahābhārata*.[1] In the *Arthaśāstra* it is looked upon with disfavour.[2] And Manu clearly laid down that one should enter *saṁnyāsa* when one's hair turned grey and that too having passed through the three stages or *āśramas* in their respective order.[3]

Sorokin has examined the elements which according to him constitute the highest mentality in Hindu and Buddhist systems.[4] Its fulfilment through a complete mastery of all sensate needs, even to the point of annihilation of personality, can be achieved through asceticism which presents several aspects viz.

(a) fasting or at least reducing the intake of food,
(b) abstention from meat and drink and pleasures of sense,
(c) total absence of sexual gratification and suppression of the sexual emotion,
(d) Vow of silence, and
(e) sleeping on bare ground, nakedness or making use of minimum clothing, contempt for the world and its riches.[5]

Asceticism in the several forms indicated above became afterwards more or less a feature common to all religions. The Hindu scriptures, however, do not enjoin self-infliction of pain or flagellation that was indulged in by monks in the early centuries of Christianity.

To the common inheritance of ascetic philosophy of mankind which as an ideal has guided the life and thought of ascetics all the world over, the Buddha's and the *Gītā's* contributions stand out in bold relief. Both commend moderation and avoidance of extremes of self-indulgence and self-restraint.[6]

From our examination of the several aspects of asceticism, the idea behind this mode of existence becomes very clear. It is the cultivation of complete indifference to the needs of the body, disgust or aversion to worldly joys and things with a view to discipline the mind for higher life of the spirit. This is the doctrine of *Vairāgya*. It answers to what Sorokin calls the *Ideational* culture or mentality which fulfils the spiritual needs by self-imposed

[1]Vide Chapter VIII.
[2]Vide Chapter IX.
[3]*Manu.*, VI.33.
[4]op. cit., pp. 119-120.
[5]Kane, *HDS.*, Vol. II, Pt. I, p. 975.
[6]*Mahāparinibbāna Sutta* I.4; *BG.*, VI.16-17.

minimisation or elimination of the physical needs. It is carried to such an extent that the body emaciates through fasts and austerities and even ends by religious suicide as in Jainism.[1] The ideal of *aparigraha* is common to *Brahmanism*, *Buddhism* and *Jainism* and is recommended by Patañjali to the aspirant of his Yoga system.[2] Celibacy which is considered at the top of all vows by Jainism,[3] is equally considered necessary for spiritual endeavour by them. According to Jainism celibacy and nudity are closely related from the point of view of controlling the senses and non-attachment to bodily pleasures and external needs. All this is a part of the doctrine of *Vairāgya*.

In Indian Philosophy the ideal of detachment or *Vairāgya* according to Jayachamaraja Wadiyar characterises 'one who delights in decreasing his wants.' In its successful application to modern living, this ideal can save the modern man from falling a victim to what Sorokin has called the *Sensate Culture*. That is the only way by which the modern world, he says, can be made to see the 'beauty of holiness' and abandon its poverty and vacuity of spirit which is leading it to the brink of destruction.[4]

We may conclude Sorokin's classification and our examination of it with regard to Indian asceticism. All the systems Brahmanism, Buddhism and Jainism which belong to ascetic cultural mentality, set forth *Ascetic Ideationalism* as their sublime and supreme form. But realising that it is attainable only by the few, they admit for the mass of their adherents either the *Active Ideationalist* or the *Idealistic* or a *Mixed* mentality of a less *Sensate* sort.[5] These may broadly correspond to the main pathways to reach God viz. *Jñāna*, *Karma* and *Bhakti* as accepted by the Indian philosophical thought as suitable to different temperaments.

Summing Up

The concept of Indian asceticism had four dimensions: *Tapas*, *Vairāgya*, *Saṁnyāsa* and *Yoga*.

Tapas or austerity had two aspects. In its negative aspect it was

[1]*ERE.*, Vol.12, p. 34; Also vide Chapter VII.
[2]Rhys Davids, *Buddhism*, p. 139; *YS.*, II.30; *Baudh DS.*, II.10.18.
[3]*Suyagada* 1, 6, 23.
[4]Jaya Chamaraja Wadiyar, Art: Is Indian Philosophy applicable to modern living?—*Sunday Standard* (June 25, 1961).
[5]Sorokin, op. cit., p. 112.

self-mortification or self-torture. In its positive aspect it was self-control through self-training or self-discipline. Vairagya was an essential condition to cultivate non-attachment to worldly pleasures and interests leading to renunciation, *tyāga*, or *saṁnyāsa*. It was a worthy path towards the attainment of self-perfection or preparation for a spiritual life even when leading a worldly life. All schools of thought including Brāhmanism, Buddhism and Jainism viewed extinction of desire (*tṛṣṇā*) as an essential state or discipline leading to the path of emancipation. *Saṁnyāsa* was an unsocial, resourceless and detached existence when all earthly ties were broken and all worldly desires given up for the final quest of the Ātman. Yoga was an art of meditation which was closely connected with *tapas* for achievement of physical and mental powers. When Yoga was accepted as a system of philosophy, certain basic rules of ascetic practices and behaviour viz. observance of *Ahiṁsā*, *Satya*, *Asteya*, *Brahmacarya* and *Aparigraha* came to be included in it. They formed a standard of holiness to be observed by Hindu *Saṁnyāsis*. Buddhist *Bhikkhus* and Jaina *Samaṇas*. Yoga became a technique of intellectual illumination and a means of spiritual enlightenment.

The exhaustive evidences quoted prove the necessity of *Tapas*, *Vairāgya*, *Saṁnyāsa* and *Yoga* as specific forms of processes and disciplines of Indian asceticism. It is very interesting to note, as reflected in different sources like the *Gītā*, the *Arthaśāstra* for example, that the concept of these four disciplines and therefore of asceticism itself, have changed from time to time. Such changes clearly reflect the changing social needs of the times as discussed. Asceticism as a socio-religious institution was a barometer of social changes and needs of ancient India.

Chapter 3

The Origin of Asceticism

The genesis of asceticism is shrouded in the mists of a remote antiquity. The task of its discovery poses not only a difficult but also a complex problem. The reasons are two-fold.

Firstly, asceticism had so greatly influenced life in ancient India and contributed so largely to the religious and philosophical thought of the times that the subject assumes a peculiar character. It has a long history of evolution and development which involves varied interpretations of the various elements, traits and concepts which go to form its main content. Secondly, we have not only to deal with the mass of people of a time immemorially remote but also with their inner world of ideas and sentiments, yearnings and aspirations, desires and motives, whose echoes are recorded and preserved in the sacred and secular literature handed down to us through the past four millennia or more.

Before we start our enquiry to search out the roots of asceticism, it will be both convenient and necessary to clearly state and confine ourselves to the particular aspect we have to investigate by asceticism. As discussed in the previous chapter, it is a composite concept. We would include under the term asceticism, not merely the monastic system but also all efforts to withdraw from the world in order to cultivate a high degree of sanctity.[1] Asceticism originated in India as an individual phenomenon and concerned primarily with individual conduct.[2] It gradually developed into a movement. We have to understand the problem from two angles: as a life of austerity or *tapas* and as a complete withdrawal from the world, a life of renunciation, *saṁnyāsa*. In other words, we have to trace the basic ideas or motives behind the ascetic practices or *tapas* and the abandonment of worldly life and its interests, *saṁnyāsa*.

Asceticism has been a persistent feature of ancient Indian civili-

[1]Leckey, *History of European Morals*, Vol. I, p. 130.
[2]Ghurye, *Indian Sadhus*, p. 1.

zation. Ever since the Indian religious and philosophical thoughts drew European scholars to their study, it has not failed to excite its due share of curiosity and interest. Its origin and growth have been subjects of speculations and enquiry. Surprisingly enough, the opinions of these scholars have varied a great deal with regard to the origin. Some scholars like Hardy[1] and Kern[2] traced the origin of the ascetic to the Vedic Brahmachāri, Max Müller[3] and Jacobi[4] ascribed it to Brāhmaṇa Parivrājaka, while others like Keith,[5] Griswold[6] and Griffith[7] thought that the *Śramaṇa* (ascetic) was the descendent of the Vedic Muni or the pre-Vedic Yogi as suggested by Marshall.[8] All these views have been examined by Durgā Bhāgvat and proved to be incomplete.[9]

Let us assess the attempts of all these scholars. An inherent defects of the approach of the Western scholars has been their consideration of asceticism as *primarily* a life of a wandering religious mendicant with disregard to the basic ideas underlying that particular institution viz. the manifestation of the otherworldly spirit, non-acquisition or detachment which led to the concept of *Vairāgya* and turning away from the world. The reasons and responsibilities of motives underlying the ascetic institution were not examined. They also did not consider other forces at work which gave rise to and developed ascetic tendencies. All of them attempt to explain 'when' rather than 'how' various factors or forces of the times conspired to generate that state of mind of withdrawal from the society. They pinpoint the *human agents* rather than the *ideas* responsible for driving them to the ascetic life. Durgā Bhāgvat provides a corrective by examining certain traits which gradually developed Indian monachism. She traces the origin of asceticism to the Brāhmaṇas,[10] but does not adequately deal with the motives or ideas of this period which led an individual to prefer a life of

[1]*Eastern Monachism*, p. 74.
[2]*Mannual of Buddism*, p. 73.
[3]Hibbert Lectures, p. 351.
[4]*Jain Sutras*, I, pp. xxiv-xxxii.
[5]*Vedic Index*, II, p. 164.
[6]*Ṛigvedic India*, pp. 338-39.
[7]*Sāmveda*, p. 50.
[8]*Mohenjodaro and Ancient Indus Civilization*, I, p. 49.
[9]Art. '*Origin of Indian Monachism*,' *J.B.U.* Vol. VIII, Pt., 2. September 1939, pp. 104-30.
[10]Bhagvat, *loc. cit*, p. 29.

asceticism. The 'ascetic' philosophy of the Upaniṣads does not receive due treatment and the epics are not included at all in the discussion. Moreover, she follows Sāyaṇa and accepts the Ṛgvedic Muni of the *Muni-sūkta* as a seer (*ṛiṣhi*). Contrary to this view, we have evidence to prove in the sequel that he is like a *Shaman* of a primitive, tribal society and thus the ascetic institution should be reasonably traced to him.

Some of our Indian scholars like Barua, Das, Sharma and Ghurye have also examined the problem of asceticism. Barua does not seek to go to the roots of it and though he refers to the wanderers as the sophist movement he merely remains content saying: 'The early history of the wanderers has yet to be written.'[1] Das traces the origin to the Vedic Muni[2] and thus follows the line of Keith and others. Sharma opines that 'Saṁnyāsa was originally the doctrine of the dissenters from the orthodox ritualism of the ancient Āryans.' According to him, 'the institution of *Saṁnyāsa* arose out of the recognition of the transitoriness of all worldly objects.'[3] He does not, however, explain the reasons why the orthodox ritualism of the ancients found disfavour with some Āryans. Nor does he try to depict the various forces at work or the conditions behind the emergence of that 'state of mind' which realised that all worldly objects were transitory. Ghurye traces the ascetic origins to the Ṛgvedic Munis who are 'some kind of ascetics.'[4] Though he traces the development of traits like celibacy, austerity, concentration and ecstasy[5] which form the main content of asceticism, he does not explain how these constitute 'a whole complex' of it. In other words no reasons and motives or conditions influencing the formation of the ascetic 'complex' are indicated and examined. Instead of an analytic and objective approach which the problem demands, what we find is a traditional explanation. As a result he touches only the fringes of the problem.

A common name to designate the wandering community of a religious mendicant whether Brāhmanic, Buddhist or Jaina was Śramaṇa or Parivrājaka. Hence *śramaṇism* is the word used for

[1]Barua, *A History of Pre-Buddhistic Indian Philosophy*, p. 130.
[2]Das, *Rigvedic India*, p. 11.
[3]Sharma, *Contributions to the History of Brahmanical Asceticism* (Saṁnyas), p. 11f.
[4]Ghurye, *Indian Sadhus*, p. 12.
[5]ibid, pp. 17ff.

by some scholars. Attempts are also made by scholars like Dutt,[1] Upadhye[2] and Deo[3] to trace the origin of the *Śramaṇas*. The gist of their theories is that 'Śramaṇism seems to have developed out of the non-Āryan east Indian indigenous element which did not see eye to eye with the Western Āryans who were not very favourable to monastic life.'[4] Dutt traces the origin of the Śramaṇas to 'a class of men answering to the Brāhmaṇas in Āryan society.'[5] Taking a compromising view of all the views Deo sums up: 'Śramaṇism was the outcome of the blending of all these elements—indigenous and borrowed.'[6] Dutt despite his efforts to solve the problem says: 'The (Vedic) legends point to almsmanship as something customary among the people. It seems probable that the philosophy of the Upaniṣads idealized a condition of life that already existed and was in practice, filling it with a spiritual content and idealistic purpose.'[7] How the almsmanship arose still remained a mystery. He, however, admits that it 'is a baffling question to which there can be only a theocratic, a speculative approach.'[8]

We thus find that various scholars, European and Indian, have from time to time made attempts to trace the origin of religious mendicancy, which is but a phase in the development of asceticism. As emphasised earlier, we look at this problem from a different angle. We endeavour to trace the ideas, reasons or motives and conditions which were responsible for this institution to arise. We have, therefore, to have an insight into the working of the heart and mind of the ancient Indians, the reasons and motives behind their adoption of the ascetic life which gradually crystallized into belief and practice until it received the sanction and sanctity of the Vedic religion and emerged as an ideal to inspire and influence to certain extent the Jaina and Buddhist monastic life. As thought takes its imprint and character from the age in which it is born, it will be necessary to examine the conditions and circumstances of those times when the cult of renunciation arose and spread. The

[1]Dutt, *Early Buddhist Monachism.*
[2]Upadhye, *Pravacansara*, Preface.
[3]Deo, *History of Jaina Monachism*, p. 56.
[4]cf. Deo, ibid, p. 54.
[5]Dutt, op. cit., pp. 54-55.
[6]Deo, op. cit., p. 56.
[7]*Buddhist Monks a d Monasteries in India*, p. 45.
[8]ibid, p. 42.

traditional approach to interpret ascetic thought in terms of theology or the philosophy of religion alone, as has been done by most of the scholars, will not serve the purpose. The psychological basis, therefore, holds the key to the proper understanding and investigation of the problem. Viewed thus, it demands a psychological enquiry of the custom and practice, the spirit and aspiration for taking to a life away from the world as influenced by the geographical, political, social, religious and economic conditions prevalent in ancient India.

Non-Āryan Influence

Though most of the scholars in the West and the East hold the view that the Āryans have come in India from outside, whatever their original home may be. Some Indian scholars have recently maintained that the Āryans were indigenous to India.[1] The view does not appear likely to become generally accepted. It was inevitable for the earliest Āryan settlers to come in contact with the native people as they spread over to different parts of India. Though numerically inferior, the Āryans had certain advantages over these indigenous people of the land. They had better methods of transport like the horse and the horse-drawn chariots and also fighting weapons which gave them certain superiority. They were quick in adopting the material culture of the land and gradually imposed some of their own beliefs and practices on the people in the process. This process was not a violent one and they did not attempt to exterminate the local culture. The result was the blending of the Āryan culture with the multitude of indigenous elements. It was thus natural that the Āryans were influenced by and borrowed many beliefs and practices of the indigenous people who have been as hitherto believed to be not so civilised.

Evidence is not wanting to show that the contact between these people known as the Dravidians led the Āryan conquerers to borrow elements of their culture. Radhakrishnan says: 'Hinduism accepted the multiplicity of aborginal gods and others which originated, most of them outside the Āryan tradition and fulfilled them all. The Āryans also accepted image worship which was a striking feature of the Dravidian faith.'[2] Suniti Kumar Chatterjee goes further and holds the view that no less than three-fourths of Indian

[1]Majumdar ed., *The Vedic Age*, pp. 215-217.
[2]*Hindu View of Life*, pp. 37-38, 41.

culture as it grew up through ages and as we find it today is non-Āryan.[1] It seems thus clear that the Drāvidians lent their beliefs to the conquering Āryans and in turn imbibed their culture.

There is at present a gap between the Indus Valley culture and the earliest beginnings of the Āryan civilisation in the Ṛgveda. But the above views not only indicate the assimilative character of the Āryan religion, so characteristic of Hinduism, but also the non-Āryan influence on the earliest Vedic thought. This becomes obvious if we try to explain the existence of the ascetic beliefs and practices in the Ṛgveda. We have here the picture of a society that takes keen pleasure in material prosperity, living a full life of zest and vigour. There is no evidence of an ascetic *weltanshauung* so that the inference naturally follows that such an outlook was derived from the Drāvidians.[2] This makes Oldenberg to believe that 'the practice of *tapas* which lies in the midst of the Vedic ritual is a relic of bygone days.[3] J. Van Troy who calls *tapas* 'a non-Ṛgvedic practice' holds a similar view. He says: 'the word *tapas* came to be used for a practice already existing with all its basic characteristics before it was assumed in Ṛgvedic Society.'[4] This practice, as we will see, was a trait associated with the medicine man called the *Shaman*, by the primitive peoples. According to Schweitzer, the Ṛgvedic Muni was the *Shaman* and medicine man later called the Yogin.[5] There is no difficulty, therefore, to associate the origin of ascetic (*Śraman*) or the Yogi to the primitive *Shaman* or the medicine man.

Primitive Culture

Dawson believes that the ascetic element is prominent in primitive culture and both in primitive as well as advanced religions. But there is one difference in primitive culture; the law of life is the law of sacrifice and discipline.[6] This means that the necessity of maintaining the common life is so great that a continuous effort

[1]q.b. Bhattacharya, Art: The Background of Buddhist Philosophy, *Indo-Asian Culture*, July 1952, p. 66.

[2]cf. Geden, *ERE.*, II, p. 88. Also Bouquet, *Hinduism*, p. 33. Brandon, *Man and His Destiny in the Great Religions*, p. 301.

[3]*Ancient India, its Language and Religions*, p. 83.

[4]Art. The Origin of Asceticism and of the Āśrama Dharma, *Bharati*, VIII, Pt. I, pp. 6-10.

[5]*Indian Thought and its Development*, p. 22.

[6]*Religion and Culture*, pp. 56-62.

of individual and social discipline becomes vital. He explains, for instance, if the hunter is to capture his prey, if the warrior is to overcome his enemies, if the cultivator is to receive the fruits of the earth, he must give as well as take. This giving, according to Dawson, is viewed by the tribal people in religious terms as sacrifice and penance and ritual acts are paid to the powers above. The individuals thus for the tribal welfare make it possible to ward off the forces of evil and death and gain life and good fortune and prosperity. Here we have an indication as to how the primitive man thought of practising various kinds of austerities.

Similarly some kind of physical austerities combined with magic or witchcraft were practised to keep the evil spirits away or to ward off danger from forces of nature. This gave rise to customs in which ascetic practices were to an extent a part.[1] A famine was viewed by primitive man as a direct infliction of the demons. To keep this danger away, self-inflicted periods of hunger i.e. fasting were the natural remedy. The demons were, it was, believed conciliated. In course of time this became a religious custom. There was no ascetic motive until this custom was viewed as a means of self-discipline, and a way to propitiate the gods. Such customs often accompanied by austerities marked the social and religious life of the primitive people.

In the collective life of a tribe these austerities were adopted as a necessity. They were often enjoined by tribal custom to serve as ordeals and methods of discipline for purposes of forming a stern and hardy race, capable of facing the most heroic tasks for the welfare of the tribe.[2] For example, if a boy was to become a good warrior and serve his people well, he had to undergo at some stage of his youth a painful initiation into the corporate life of the tribe. As the tribe and the god of tribe were closely identified this voluntary suffering took a religious meaning. Thus natural sacrifice and self-inflicted pain, when sanctioned by the tribal custom, gained in importance and significance.

In pre-historic and even early historic times problems both of the body and of the soul were ministered by the same persons: priests, *Shamans*, medicine men.[3] According to Lowie, who has studied the role of *Shamans* in primitive religion, they were known as capable

[1]Hall, *ERE.*, pp. 63-65.

[2]Rufus Jones, *New Studies in Mystical Religion*, p. 59.

[3]Mowrer, *Mental Health and Hindu Psychology*, Introduction, p. IX.

of establishing direct communion with the spirit world.[1] In the primitive society, they occupied an important status as magicians. The technique the *Shaman* employed as a magician's art is described by Chattopadhyaya:

'He worked himself up to a point of delirious frenzy and ecstasy. He had to feel a super-normal power within himself with the aid of which alone he could hope to bring the force of nature under his control. Such a super-normal power could not be a material reality; it had to be a psychological one. The primitive magician had to feel that he possessed it. He tried various techniques to acquire a sense of the most stupendous power which included fasting, various physical exercises, the control of breath, abstinence, withdrawal into solitude, self-torture, narcotics. By these means he excited within himself ecstatic conditions, induced morbid nervous and cerebral exaltation and sometimes even a cataleptic rigidity and insensibility.'[2]

It would seem natural that strange powers were attributed to the *Shaman*. The society attached the greatest importance to the super-normal psychic experiences of dream and vision, trance and ecstasy. The *Shaman* who possessed such experiences was the religious leader of the community.

The role of the *Shaman* in the primitive societies is exhaustively dealt with by Dawson and Eliade. The Shaman is both a diviner and a seer. He is also an ascetic and a holy man who has acquired by training the mastery of spiritual techniques. His figure is frequently associated with psychic abnormality. He is a highly neurotic type. He attains his professional status after a profound psychic crisis. He loses his interest in ordinary affairs and ceases to share in the work or talk of his fellows. He goes out into the wilderness where he lies in trance and hears the voices of the spirit. The highly individualistic character of his vision and his spiritual power involves possibilities of social conflict. In fact no figure is more feared by primitive society than the evil *Shaman* or magician who uses his relations with the spiritual world for his private advantage against the interests of the society. But it is also believed that as he has transcended society and acquired superhuman powers, he is best able to help his fellow men in their spiritual necessities.[3]

[1]Lowie, *Primitive Religion*, p. 350.

[2]*Lokayata*, pp. 444-445; cf. Oldenberg, op. cit., p. 108.

[3]Dawson, op. cit., pp. 69-70, 177-179; Eliade, *Yoga, Immortality and Freedom*, pp. 320-341; Also Thomas, *Incredible India*, pp. 18-20.

Against this background the question arises: Has this *Shaman* of the primitive cultures a counterpart in the hoary pre-Āryan tribal society? Let us turn our attention to the Āryans in the earliest epoch of their existence and attempt to find out how their minds turned to ascetic beliefs and practices.

Sacrifice was a persistent feature of Vedic religion. Its importance could be seen right from the Ṛgveda onwards. In the Brāhmaṇas sacrifices became all important and they multiplied in number and variety without end. The Brahmin priests who had the exclusive privilege of the knowledge of sacrifices became more powerful than the gods. Even the gods were described as owing their divine position or the very existence and attaining immortality to sacrifice. As a result, the priestly class as the depository of sacrificial ritualism came to be exalted. It was believed that if the sacrifices were correctly performed they were bound to produce desired results. We thus find that magical value came to be attached to the sacrifices which were raised to the level of extreme glorification.[1] The religion, as Edgerton says, was a pure magical ritualism.[2] Even the whole world was supposed to be permeated by a mysterious principle which could be known and subdued by the science of the sacrificing priests.[3] This primeval principle described as neither *sat* nor *asat* was believed to have sprung from *tapas;* similarly the *ṛta* and *satya* in the beginning of creation.[4]

In the earlier period of the Ṛgveda, it was believed that human desires were granted by the gods when they were propitiated by the ritual of sacrifice and praise. The hymns were used as having peculiar magic property, in relation to the particular operations of the sacrifices by virtue of which the sacrificer could attain his ends when in need of any special favour from the gods to whom the hymns were dedicated.[5]

The Atharvaveda partly reflects earlier practices and beliefs of the more primitive pre-Āryan people. Several Atharva hymns deal with magic charms and incantatious intended to accompany a mass of simple rites and ceremonies. It was believed that every conceivable human need and aspiration could be fulfilled through magic

[1]cf. Chapter 5.
[2]*Beginnings of Indian Philosophy*, p. 17.
[3]cf. Charles Eliot, *Hinduism and Buddhism*, I, p. 71.
[4]*RV.*, X.190.1; X.129.3.
[5]cf. Dasgupta, *Indian Idealism*, p. 1.

spells. Their religious basis seems to have been simple animism and their method of operation was simple magic. All creatures, things, powers and even abstract principles were animated by spirits which were sought to be controlled by incantatious and magic rites.[1] It is clear that many classes of the society resorted to magic practices which probably had their beginnings in pre-Vedic magical beliefs and practices of the Vedic people.

This process is indicated by the change in the meaning of the world 'Brahman.' The world in the Ṛgvedic period meant 'a simple prayer.'[2] Owing to the contact and fusion of two opposite racial cultures of the invading Āryans and the original pre-Āryan inhabitants, the word 'Brahman' in the *Atharvaveda* period signified 'magical formula.'[3] In the *Atharvaveda*, as a whole, the word stands for the magical act or the mysterious power which arises out of that act in the priest and which pervades the man and universe.[4] That pre-Vedic religion was surcharged with magic is also proved by the Atharvavedic hymns which throw light on the lore of the *Vratyas* regarding exorcism, magic, serpent-worship and tree-worship.[5] Oldenberg rightly says: 'The religion and cult of the Veda point on the one hand to the past of the savage religion; on the other hand, they point forward.'[6]

The above evidences indicate the association of the Āryan sacrifices with the pre-Āryan magical rites. Pai observes: 'The practice of magic, sorcery and witchcraft, the belief in the efficacy of charms, spells and incantations and the belief that men could obtain power over nature and even gods paved the way for asceticism to set in.'[7] The ancient Indian literature is replete with instances of ascetics engaged in severe austerities such as sitting in the midst of fire, standing on one leg, holding up arms, staring at the sun, hanging upside down from a tree etc.

It is in this light that the Ṛgvedic Muni's experience which is

[1]cf. Edgerton, op. cit., p. 18.
[2]cf. Belvalkar and Ranade *HOIP*., Vol. II, pp. 10-14.
[3]Belvalkar, q.b. Shende, 'The Brahman in the *AV*', Principal Karmarkar Commemoration Volume.
[4]Shende, ibid, p. 216.
[5]*AV*., XV.
[6]Oldenberg, op. cit., p. 83.
[7]Pai, *Monograph on the Religious Sects in India Among the Hindus*, p. 2.

comparable to 'shamanic ecstasy' is to be understood.[1] The Ṛgvedic *Muni*, abandoning his body, divining the thoughts of others, flying in air, roaming at will in different regions and inhabiting the two seas, seems to reflect the impact of pre-Āryan primitive magician. The Ṛgvedic Muni's magical powers (*siddhis*) were very probably the direct descendants of the primitive magic practices of the *Shaman* or the medicine man.

Besides the association of the primitive magic with asceticism, some scholars have even suggested the importance of other aspects of asceticism and put forward certain theories to explain the origin of ascetic practices.

Theories

Oman[2] and Rufus Jones,[3] for example, suggest the importance of the Dualistic theory. The gist of the theory is that 'ascetic practices by conquering the evil tendencies of matter—that is, the flesh—purify the imprisoned spirit and render it fit for re-union with God.'

This theory views matter, by its essential nature, as evil. Hence the body with all its propensities is evil and defiling. The very act of propagating life is assumed to be sinful for it dooms another spirit to enter the prison-house of gross flesh and compels it to be subjected to constant contact with it. Celibacy is, therefore, enjoined. Through the self-inflicted tortures the power of the soul over matter grows more effective.

This Dualistic theory, ine ssence, is akin to *Śāṅkhya-Yoga* philosophy. According to this philosophy the universe is a duality of *puruṣa*, spirit and *prakṛti* matter. The spirit is immersed in and identified with the phenomenal world and, therefore, unable to realize itself. It suffers because it is obscured by all that is matter. Peace can only be attained when it comes to a true knowledge of itself and escapes from the prison house of the empirical life. This release comes about when man discriminates between *puruṣa* and *prakṛti* and destroys the wall of ignorance, *avidyā*, due to which he identifies *puruṣa*, the self with *prakṛti*, the non-self. As Patañjali

[1]cf. Eliade, says: 'The essential and defining element of Shamanism is ecstasy—the *Shaman* is a specialist in the sacred, able to abandon his body and undertake cosmic journeys in the spirit in trance.' *Yoga, Immortality and Freedom*, p. 320.

[2]Oman, op. cit., pp. 19-20.

[3]Rufus Jones, op. cit., pp. 63-64.

says: 'The obstacles to enlightenment—the cause of man's sufferings are ignorance, egoism, attachment, aversion and the desire to cling to life. To regard the non-eternal as pleasant and the non-self as the Puruṣa, that is ignorance.'[1] The Yogin, through the technique of meditation, destroys this avidya and attains to the vision of the Puruṣa, in Samadhi. This state of liberation is called *Kaivalya*, derived from '*keval*,' '*sole*,' 'only' thus implying the separation or detachment of the *Puruṣa* from *Prakṛti*.[2]

The theory explains the true goal of *Yoga* rather than the purpose behind the ascetic practices. The state of liberation (*Kaivalya*) which is the true goal of *Yoga* is something far beyond the stage marked by the attainment of supernormal powers (siddhis). The ascetic practices were known and practised much before the art of meditation evolved. The theory, at best, only emphasises the need of ascetic practices to make the body subservient to one's will and does not trace their origin.

Another theory responsible for the acetic practices according to Rufus Jones is that of the Majestic Sovereign. The gist of the theory is that God grants mercy and favours only to those who conform to the stern conditions of the Majestic Sovereign of the universe, only to those who satisfy His sense of 'justice,' in fact, those who accumulate sufficient 'merit' to deserve attention.[3]

The theory views God as imperial, severe, cold, hard and authoritative. He listens only to those who have attained humility setting aside all pride, self-assertion and human claims. To the Indian mind, this is a 'perverted' image of God who is considered all-merciful, compassionate and always ready to help His devotee who has only to offer Him in the words of the *Gītā*, 'a leaf, a flower, a fruit or a drop of water with devotion.'[4] Such a devotee is very dear to Lord Krishna who only demands self-surrender. For he declares: 'Abandon all duties and come to Me the only refuge I will release the from all sins; grieve not'![5] The Vedic conception of God

[1] *YS.*, II, 3.5: Samādhibhavanārthaḥ kleṣatanūkaraṇārthaśya anityāśuciduḥkhātmasu nityaśucisukhātmakhyātirvidyā.

[2] *Sankhya-Kārika*, p. 56.

[3] op. cit., pp. 68-69.

[4] *BG.*, IX, 26: patraṁ puṣpaṁ phalaṁ toyaṁ yo me bhaktyā prayacchati tadahaṁ bhaktyupahṛtamaṣnāmi prayatātmanaḥ.

[5] *BG.*, XVIII. 66: sarvadhārmān parityajya māmekaṁ śaraṇaṁ vraja ahaṁ tvā sarvapāpebhyo mokṣayisyami ma śucaḥ.

is not that of Father and Mother combined but also that of all affectionate relationships.[1] Nowhere in the entire range of Indian thought there is any reference to the severe cold and hard Majestic Sovereign. Such a concept of God is quite alien to it.

The Concept of Ojas

Ojas is, according to Gonda, one of the key-words of Indian culture.[2] The word is usually rendered by 'bodily strength,' 'vigour,' 'energy,' 'ability,' 'power' and 'might.' It is according to him synonyms with the Latin word '*augustus*' from '*augus.*' He has made an enquiry as to what sort of energy or power was really meant by the ancient Indians when they used the word '*ojas.*' He has deduced from the Vedas, the Epics, the *Kāvyas* and medical literature[3] and shows that the general idea expressed by the word is 'that of power or power-substance of a vital and magnetic energy present in beings in phenomena or things.'[4] There we come across *ojas* very often associated with *tejas*, *jyotis*, *balam*, *viryam*, *sahas*, *varcas*, *nṛmnam*. It is often used with the word *ugra*. 'Words are said to be *ugra* when they possess magical, mysterious, occult or incomprehensible power and in motion.'[5]

Gonda opines that *Ojas* originally implied 'an experience that is primarily of the perceptual order, a frame of mind in which this special type or manifestation of power is principally sensed.'[6] *Tapas* which is the physical and religious ardour of the ascetic is also a very potent creative power. By accumulating it by fervent ascetic practices, the ascetic performs supernormal activities such as seeing, creating what is beyond human powers and which being discharged is automatically and irrevocably effective.'[7] Hence according to Gonda, the word *ugra* is the right word to express this very potent creative power of *tapas*. According to the *Mahābhārata* it is the most effective means of achieving all purposes; the creator himself resorted to it in order to create the universe, plants grow by it, etc.[8]

[1] *ṚV.*, X. 7-3. VI. 47-11, *AV.*, VII. 86.1, *YV.*, 20.50., *SV.*, 333.
[2] Gonda, *Ancient Indian Ojas, Latin Angos and the Indo-European nouns in es-os*, p. 1.
[3] ibid, pp. 4-37 and 44-46.
[4] ibid.
[5] ibid, p. 26.
[6] ibid.
[7] ibid, p. 25.
[8] *Mbh.*, 12.9. 161.

In ancient Javanese literature, *ugra* is used to qualify 'asceticism,' the heat of the sun, the powers of a warrior, the intellectual abilities of a scholar, an inauspicious constellation, fierce words.' There is another shade of meaning: holy, a holy man, a man who devotes himself to religion and asceticism.[1]

That the word *ojas* stands for vital energy is proved by Gonda through our medical literature, especially the Atharvaveda and Caraksamhitā. In the Vedic literature *brahamacarya* finds an important place along with *satya*, *tapas* and right knowledge for the attainment of the self.[2] The illustration of Bhāradvaja who would spend even his fourth life in the practice of *brahamacarya* suggests the great virtue ascribed to the sublimation of sex-energy as the fittest preparation for the *Brahma*-knowledge.[3] We thus find that *brahamacarya* occupied a significant role in the life of *tapas* directed towards self-realisation. It enabled the *tapasvin* 'to possess the special power or vital energy called *ojas*.'[4] It is also stated that *ojas* is generated by *tapas*.[5]

It is interesting to note that *brahmacarya* was an important element in the ascetic life of a *Samnyāsin* or the monastic conduct of a Buddhist *Bhikkhu* or a Jaina *Yati* or *Samaṇa*. It was one of their vows of personal behaviour.[6] Patañjali strongly advises the aspirants to the *Yoga-sadhana* to make it their creed if they wish to achieve the maximum of spiritual and moral growth. He includes it in the *Niyamas* or regulations for the *Yoga* Students.[7] Thus it seems quite reasonable to believe that behind the *tapas* of many an ascetic in which *brahmacarya* was an important factor, the idea to achieve *ojas* was dominant which was a necessary condition for the attainment of the highest spirituality or self-realisation.

Precedents of Asceticism (Renunciation)

It is a truism that man is a social animal. He is born and bred in society; he moves and lives and has his being in it. It is in his nature to crave for worldly possessions like home, wife, children,

[1]Gonda, op. cit., p. 36.
[2]*Mund. Up.*, 3.1.5.
[3]*TB.*, iii. 10.11.3.
[4]Gonda, op. cit., p. 36.
[5]*Tait. S.*, 5.7.4.3. *Tait. A.*, 3.11.9.
[6]Vide Chapter II and XI.
[7]*YS.*, II. 32.

kith and kin, wealth, status, honour and comfort. He is bound by these things and this attachment to these things of the world induces in him material ambitions for his own welfare and prosperity. The path of asceticism requires that he should turn his face away from these worldly possessions and material ambitions. Normally he remains attached with his heart and mind to the world and its concerns. 'Unless he begins to feel the interest in life waning for him, he does not see the necessity for harbouring the ascetic virtues,' says Ranade.[1] This means that due to some reasons he has begun to lose interest in life and worldly things. Where there was attachment, there is now a sense of pessimism or weariness or indifference. As Laxman Shastri observes: 'Time is eternal and so is this universe. Against these, the thoughtful are likely to feel that this life is momentary and hence of no consequence. Moreover, it is doubtful whether the self exists or not after death. Such thoughts may make them pessimistic.'[2] Or there is a vague realisation that worldly possessions do not give true and lasting happiness. On the contrary misery and unhappiness are more to be met with than happiness. The *Gītā* affirms: *anityaṁ asukhaṁ lokaṁ* (IX. 33). In a struggle to solve this problem but not knowing how, a mood is born to escape from the world of misery and unhappiness. But the mind that has tasted the pleasures of the world and known the pursuit of earthly pleasures does not easily forsake them. The world continues to lure and the flesh also keeps on tempting. Turning away from the world involves the renunciation of worldly pleasures and things. Only by love of God we become detached from worldly temptations: *anurāgāt virāgaḥ.* We meet with such a frame of mind in the quest of the Brahman. For we read in the Bṛihadāraṇyaka Upaniṣad: 'The wise of old did not desire for progeny. For they thought: What shall we do with children? To us the entire world is our own Self. So they gave up the desire for sons, for riches and for worlds, and wandered about begging.'[3]

[1]*CSUP.*, p. 295.

[2]Charvak, *Itihas ani tatvajñan*, Preface, p. 14.
जीवित हें क्षणभगुंर आहे व मरणोत्तर आत्मास्तित्व नाहीं, या विचारानें कांहीं माणसें निवृत्तिवादीहि बनूं शकतील। अनंतकालाच्या व अनंत विश्वाच्या विस्तारांत अत्यंत क्षुद्र दिसणारें हें क्षणभगुंर जीवित पाहून विचारवंताला या जीविताबद्धल औदासिन्य उत्पन्न होऊं शकतें।

[3]*Bṛhad. Up.*, IV.4.22: etad sma vai tatpūrve vidvāṁsaḥ prajāṁ na kāmayante kiṁ prajayā kariṣyāmo yeṣam no' yaṁ ātma yaṁ loka iti te ha sma Putraiṣṇāyāsca vittaiṣaṇāyāsca lokaiṣāṇāyaśca vyutthāyātha bhikṣācaryaṁ caranti.

Such a state of mind torn away from the alluring world and temptations of the flesh in pursuit of a spiritual ideal, implies a radical change in habit, thought and life. To bring about these changes many influences are at work within a man and without. Let us analyse these influences or conditions working upon man and inducing him to adopt the ascetic mode of living. These spring from man's environment, its effect upon him and his power to react to it. Broadly speaking, these may be enumerated as physical conditions which influence him from without and internal states like sorrow, frustration pessimism, pleasure, intellectual craving, spiritual urge etc., which work within him and his attempt to satisfy them, pacify them or overcome them. These factors have to be assessed in the context of the social, religious and economic conditions prevalent in ancient India.

Climatic Conditions

It is an interesting question whether the physical climate of India has affected the course of asceticism. Brunton writes: 'A fiercely hot and depressingly humid country whose climate causes everyone to shun physical effort, led man naturally to search for part of his satisfaction in contemplative thought and inward life.'[1] Oman also observes that the hot and extreme type of climate prompts and favours this thoughtful, sobre and philosophical bent of mind.[2] The views of Brunton and Oman suggest that the effect of climate was two-fold. On the one hand it made the physical labour unattractive and on the other it prompted a philosophical bent of mind. It has also been argued that the great heat and humidity which prevails in much of India has produced in its inhabitants a general lassitude of spirit which predisposes to pessimism and the adoption of a world-denying attitude.[3] Climatic environment has been thus singled out as the devisive factor for pessimism and asceticism. This is not wholly true.

It has to be pointed out that like most other countries in the world the history of India has been profoundly influenced by its geographical features. These have affected the lives and habits of the people. At the same time, India is a region indeed full of contrast in physical features and in climate. Every variety of climate

[1]*Indian Philosophy and Modern Culture*, p. 11.
[2]Oman, op. cit., p. 13.
[3]cf. Brandon, op. cit., p. 301.

from extreme cold to extreme heat is to be found in the country. There are regions like Rajputānā where there is minimum rainfall and places like Cherapunjī in Assam where the monsoon is the heaviest. However, the enervating effect of the climate in those parts where it is hot and humid cannot be disproved but should not be exaggerated.

A different view has been suggested by Basham: 'The climate of India produced in its people a kind of alternating rhythm of reaction between a sensuous appreciation of the delights of the world and an austere rejection of even the simplest comforts.'[1] This seems to be a proper view of the impact of climate on the people. Albig, however, indicates different proportion of the effect of environment on climate: 'In the simpler cultures geographic influences although place some limits upon the quantity and quality of man's thought, the possible range of the products of thought outside of these limits is almost infinite.'[2] Even modern philosophers like Vivekananda hold the same view. To the question: 'Is there any connection between the idea of super consciousness and the heat of India?' Vivekananda replies: 'No, because all this philosophy might have been thought out fifteen thousand feet above the sea-level among the Himalayas in an almost Arctic temperature.'[3] And he adds that it is practicable to attain success in Yoga in a cold climate.[4]

There is no doubt that man is a product of heredity and environment. The effect of climatic environment, therefore, cannot be ruled out. There is some truth in the view that climate, as one of the factors, tended to produce in the Aryans both a philosophical bent of mind and a general lassitude of spirit. It seems to have influenced their religious expression as has been rightly pointed out by Urquhart who says: 'The character of the gods a people worship is to some extent determined by climatic conditions.'[5] Buckle, who shares the same view, is more emphatic: 'The majestic natural scenery of India overwhelmed the Hindu mind and courage and inclined it to superstition and worship; the simpler scenery of Europe left man uncowed and permitted the growth of a disposition to control nature

[1]Basham, A.L., *The Wonder that was India*, pp. 3-4, 9.
[2]Albig, *Modern Public Opinion*, p. 61.
[3]Vivekananda, *Vedanta Philosophy*, p. 27.
[4]ibid, p. 28.
[5]Urquhart, *Pantheism and the Value of life*, p. 161.

instead of worshipping it.'[1] The impressive phases of nature were taken as the objects of religious worship by the Ṛgvedic people who were nomads in the land of the Punjab then called *Saptasindhu.* Theirs was a cheerful worship, a religion of light and glandness and was determined by the kind of life they had been living. When they migrated to the East towards the land of Gangetic Valley where some of them became engaged in philosophical speculations of the Brahman-Ātman, the tropical climate of the region was partly responsible for their contemplative bent of mind.

Climate thus cannot be considered as the only factor leading to pessimism and asceticism. But it will not be an exaggeration to suggest that it was one of the impoıtant factors shaping the religious thought of the people in ancient India

Intellectual Craving

An intense intellectual craving for something higher than the material existence and to risk all the earthly joys for such a pursuit has been a singular and perhaps the most prominent trait of Indian asceticism.[2] In their spiritual urge to attain salvation, the Upaniṣadic thinkers came to realize that all worldly possessions and desires are not only transitory but also distracting. The *Bṛhadāraṇyakopaniṣad* declares: 'Him the Brāhmins desire to know through sacrifice, through gifts, through austerity of fasting. Having known Him one becomes an ascetic (*muni*), sage, wise one. Desiring Him only as their world, mendicants (*pravrājino*) leave their homes. It is because they knew this that the sages of old did not wish for offspring, they said—we who have attained this Self, this world? And they, having risen above the desire for sons, the desire for wealth, the desire for worlds, wander about as mendicants (*bhikṣācaryaṁ caranti*). For the desire for sons is the desire for wealth, and the desire for wealth is the desire for worlds. Both these are indeed desires only.[3] Thus a

[1]Buckle, *Introduction to the History of Civilisation*, Vol. I, p. 593.

[2]Durga Bhagwat, loc. cit., p. 107.

[3]*Brhad.* IV. 4.22 cf. III. 5.1: Tam etaṁ vedānuvacanena brāhmaṇā vividiṣanti, yajñena, dānena, tapasānāśakena; etaṁeva viditvā munirbhavati, etaṁeva pravrājino lokaṁ icchantaḥ pravrajanti, etaddha sma vai tat pūrve vidvaṁsaḥ prajāṁ na kāṁayante: kiṁ prajayā kariṣyāmaḥ; yeṣām no'yam ātmāyaṁ loka iti. te ha sma putraiṣaṇayas ca vittaiṣaṇayas ca lokaiṣaṇayas ca vyutthāya, atha bhikṣā-caryaṁ caranti; ya hyeva putraiṣaṇā sa vittaiṣaṇā (Ya vittaiṣaṇa) sa lokaiṣaṇa; ubhe hyete esane eva bhavataḥ sa. cf. *Jivanmuktviveka* 12: *prāhu jñānāya jijñāsonyāsaṁ*, Sankar, comments on III. 5.1: *ātmajñanaṁ sasaṁnyāsaṁ amṛtatvasādhanam.*

will to give up home, possessions and all the normal joys of life, a life of complete withdrawal from worldly attractions and concerns was considered essential for self-realization. *Saṁnyāsa* was a natural outcome as a means to the knowledge of the *Ātman* and the attainment of *mokṣa.*

Pessimism

Western scholars single out this pessimistic note in Indian monachism when they say: 'By the Indians, life has ever been regarded as essentially evil and relief from burden and sorrow from existence as the chief and final aim.'[1] The pessimism of India, in the words of Brandon, is to be sought in 'its evolution of life in this present world of space and time as something essentially deceptive and therefore, evil and from which final release must be increasingly sought.'[2] This seems to be a fair assessment of the Indian attitude towards pessimism in ancient India.

What are the forces responsible for pessimism? Bloomfield observes: 'India herself, through her climate, her nature and her economic conditions, furnishes reasonable ground for pessimism.'[3] The effect of climate as discussed earlier was not the only condition and a conclusive proof for the mood of pessimism to set in. The same thing can be said about the economic conditions. The valleys of the big rivers like the Indus, the Ganges and their tributaries offered easy means of cheap livelihood and communication and were the sources of India's wealth and happiness. As a result we find that on the one hand people became fond of ease and luxury devoted to the ideals and pursuits of peace and on the other less hardy and preserving than their opponents facing the hardship of nature and a keen struggle for existence. We are thus led to examine India's nature as revealed in her religious and philosophical thought to trace the causes of pessimism.

It has often been argued that early monastic Buddhism preached 'a gospel of unalloyed pessimism.' The theme is: 'All earthly existence is full of sorrow and the only deliverance from sorrow is in renunciation of the world and eternal rest.'[4] Some writers like Urquhart have pointed out that this pessimism is the old Indian

[1]*ERE.*, Vol. VIII, p. 803.

[2]Brandon, op. cit., p. 301.

[3]Bloomfield, *Religion of the Vedas*, p. 264.

[4]Oldenberg, *Buddha*, p. 1.

tendency manifest in the Ṛgveda. According to him though the Vedic religion is one of light and gladness, these are 'somewhat superficial.' 'The joy' is not the assured result of struggle. It is rather the happiness of innocence, possible only through an avoidance of the truly spiritual quest.' He further argues that 'the logical outcome of certain tendencies of Vedic thought was a growing sense of the helplessness of the individual and of the poverty and wretchedness of his life in the presence of universal forces.'[1]

The Ṛgvedic Āryans were 'essentially an active, energetic, warrior people, engaged in struggles with the aborignes and even among themselves but in the main prosperous and contented with their life.'[2] As discussed elsewhere, their life was simple, fresh and full of vigour and was inspired by a healthy appreciation of the good things of the world and an endeavour to seek its pleasures. The prevalent atmosphere was one of optimism.[3] Urquhart concedes that their religion was one of light and gladness but the joy was 'somewhat superficial' because of an avoidance of the truly spiritual quest. But the evidence from the Ṛgveda itself goes against this view. If philosophy springs from wonder, if the impulse to it is in scepticism, we find the beginnings of doubt in the hymns to Indra: 'Of whom they ask, where is he? There is no Indra, who has ever seen him? To whom are we to direct the song of praise?'[4] Even the philosophical idea about the nature of different gods who are but a manifestation of a higher spirit is to be found in the Ṛgvedic statement: *ekam sad viprā bahudhā vadanti.*[5] The tenth *maṇḍala* of the Ṛgveda contains many hymns of a philosophic nature and the scholars have not failed to notice this fact. However, the latest research in this direction goes even further. Scholars like Sampurnananda have suggested that even if the whole of the tenth *maṇḍala* were to be excluded, there are passages all over the rest of the Ṛgveda and many parts of the Atharvaveda which 'refer to deeper, more esoteric things, including spiritual experience, the experience of the Yogi.'[6] These philosophical layers of thought do not justify Urquhart's contention that there was an avoidance of the spiritual quest. His view

[1]Urquhart, op. cit., pp. 79-83.
[2]cf. Keith, *RPV.*, I, p. 243.
[3]cf. Chapter V.
[4]*ṚV.*, II.12; VIII, 100.3 ff.
[5]*ṚV.*, I. 164.46; cf. X.114.5 : *ekaṁ santaṁ bahudhā kalpayanti.* Also, I.79-10.
[6]Sampurnananda, *Evolution of the Hindu Pantheon*, pp. 8-38.

that 'life did not lend to much searching of soul or to any serious attempt to penetrate beneath the surface'[1] is not tenable.

Urquhart then refers to 'a growing sense of the helplessness of the individual and of the poverty and wretchedness of his life in the presence of universal forces.' This, according to him, was 'a natural development of thought aided perhaps by the persistence of magical ideas drawn from lower and more primitive religions.'[2] If it was so, the optimistic outlook of the Ṛgvedic Āryans on life does not in any way suggest that theirs was a hopeless and helpless existence. Urquhart states further: 'As thought proceeds from polytheism in the direction of pantheism, the insignificance of the individual life becomes more apparent.'[3] It would be correct to describe this thought process as one of monotheism, more properly, as that of monism found in the Upaniṣadic philosophy. But it is not right to conclude that the individual life became insignificant. It would be wrong to suggest that because of this, the entire Āryan society was engulfed by pessimism. As discussed elsewhere, the common man still believed that minor gods did exist and one could go to heaven by the performance of sacrifices.[4] The highest philosophy of the Upaniṣads by its very nature was meant for the few. Hence Urquhart's view that pessimism was the old Indian tendency manifest in the Ṛgveda seems to be too sweeping a generalisation unsupported by any evidence.

As we proceed from the Vedas to the Upaniṣads we find that there is a gradual but definite change in the religious thought of the people. Slowly sacrifices rose so much in importance and became so complex and varied that in the age of the Brāhmaṇas, sacrificial religion of a mechanical and soulless kind began to prevail. The belief in the great magical value of the meticulous performance of the sacrifices resulted into the priestly class becoming all-powerful and supreme. The masses found the bloody sacrifices of innocent animals gruesome and shocking. To the illiterate, this ritualistic religion was inuntelligible and uninspiring and to the literate extravagant and meaningless. The result was a general unrest and discontent with the Brahmanic cult.[5] Thus began a reactionary movement of

[1]Urquhart, op. cit., p. 79.
[2]ibid, p. 83.
[3]ibid.
[4]cf. Chapter V.
[5]ibid.

the intelligentia emphasising the acquisition of divine knowledge (*jāñna*) over the performance of rites and ceremonies, which came to be known as the *jñāna-marga*. The sacrifices came to be considered as 'leaky boats' (*plavā ādṛḍhā yajñarupā*) incapable of taking men beyond the sea of existence.[1]

The movement saw the spiritual awakening and the philosophical activity on the part of the Upaniṣadic seers and thinkers engaged in the quest of the ultimate reality, the *Brahman*. The gods receded into the background, the priests were subordinated, contemplation took the place of worship and *Jñāna* that of *Yajña*. The seers of the Upaniṣad said: 'What shall we do with offspring—we who have this Self and this world of *Brahman*?' They realised that the ever-lasting happiness of man consisted not in the possession of this world but in the possession of the soul. They taught that sacrifices led only to a temporary heaven after death whereas true knowledge led to immortal bliss even on this earth.[2] The absolute Brahman was identified with *Ātman*.

With the emergence of the doctrine of Brahman-Ātman which is the main theme of the Upaniṣadic philosophy, the knowledge of the Self came to be given more prominence. All else became of no value. Sorrows and sufferings and miseries of life, it was emphasised, could be removed by knowing the *Ātman*: *tarati śokaṁ Ātmavit*.[3] Whatever was beside Him was full of sorrow: *ato anyad ārtaṁ*.[4] The cause of suffering is indicated here. The eternal was bliss and the transient painful. Deliverance from sorrow lay in the knowledge of the Ātman. In the Katha Upaniṣad there are repeated suggestions that the state we are to flee from was one of misery.[5] In the contemplation of this world of finite experience, there is nothing but pain. And the reason of this pessimistic attitude is hinted at over and over again. It was the fleeting and unsatisfying character of human experience: 'There is no joy in anything finite.'[6] All pleasures come to an end; this knowledge poisons their enjoyment and after they are gone their remembrance makes life doubly

[1] *Mund. Up.*, I.2.7.

[2] *Bṛhad. Up.*, VI.2.1; IV.4.7: atha maṛtyomṛto bhavatyatra brahma samaśnuta iti.

[3] *Chand. Up.*, VII. 2-3.

[4] *Bṛhad. Up.*, III.4.2.

[5] *Katha. Up.*, II.4, II.6.7.

[6] *Chand. Up.*, VII. 25-1.

bitter. Death is an unavoidable misery. No human is free from disease, old age, separation from loved ones and other ills. The fleeting pleasures of life by no means compensate for all these evils. In short, life is fundamentally bad (*duḥkha*, misery). But it is said: 'He who sees this (the Self) does not see death nor illness nor pain.'[1] The *Ātman* was all real, everything beside it of no consequence. If the *Ātman* was real, it followed that existence otherwise must be bad (*duḥkha*) illusory and evil. In the language of the Vedantic philosophy, it was emptiness, vanity (*avam*) it was mirage (*māyā*). To think otherwise was the supreme error and the source of all further error and sin. On the other hand, to realise this truth was wisdom and salvation. As contrasted with the changeless bliss of the Ātman, the world was evil, worthless and deceptive. *Saṁsāra* was full of misery and ruled by *Karma* resulted into an eternal cycle of birth and death. The minds of men were filled with the fear of present ills and future rebirths. Deliverance from sorrow was their main concern. In the words of Radhakrishnan, 'In the Upaniṣads, we do not have appeals to the Vedic gods, who were the sources of material prosperity for increase of happiness but only prayers for deliverance from sorrow.'[2] Here we meet with a serious and gloomy aspect of Upaniṣadic philosophy.

Another factor which turned the earlier outlook into a pessimistic one was the total inadequacy of *tapas* for self-realisation as described in the Maitri Upaniṣad. We are told that king Bṛhadratha had obtained freedom from all desires (*vairāgya*) considering his body as transient (*aśāṣvataṁ*). He had performed the highest penance, standing with uplifted arms and looking up to the sun. At the end of a thousand days, he realized that *tapas* was futile as it could not lead him to the knowledge of the self.[3] Even Yājñavalkya proclaims disbelief in *tapas* and its futility for Brahma-realisation. He tells Gārgi that a thousand years of *tapas* without the knowledge of *Brahma* is of no avail.[4]

The king was so much overcome by the pessimistic mood at the failure of *tapas* that he says: 'In this evil-smelling, pithless body,

[1]*Chand. Up.*, VII. 26. 2: *na paśyo mṛtyuṁ paśyati na rogaṁ nota dukhatāṁ sarvaṁ ha paśyaḥ paśyati sarvamāpnoti sarvaśa iti.*

Also, VII.26.2: *Satyāngākāmān teṣām sarveṣu lokeṣu kāmacāro bhavati.*

[2]Radhakrishnan, S., *IP.*, I, p. 146.

[3]*Maitri. Up.*, I.2.

[4]*Bṛhad. Up.*, III.8.10: Yo vā etadaksaraṁ Gārgyaviditvāsmin loke juhoti, yajate, tapastapyate, bahūni varṣāsahasraṇy antavadevāsya tadbhavati.

what is the use of the enjoyment of pleasures? How can one enjoy pleasures in this body which is assailed by lust, hatred, greed, delusion, fear, anguish, jealousy, separation from what is loved, union with what is not loved, hunger, thirst, old age, death, illness, grief and other evils?'[1] Here we find a sense of disgust for worldly pleasures and towards the human body which is viewed as an abode of evil.

The king continues: 'We see that all this is perishable, as these flies, gnats and other insects, as herbs and trees, growing and decaying. And what of these? There are the great ones, mighty wielders of bows, rulers of empires, and kings and others, who before the eyes of their whole family surrendered the greatest happiness and passed on from this world to that. There are other great ones. We have seen the destruction of supernatural beings, demons and demigods, ghosts and goblins snakes and vampires. There is the drying up of the great oceans, the falling of the mountains, the moving of the pole-star, the cutting of the wind-ropes (that hold the stars), the emergence of the earth and the departure of the gods from their place.' He ends by bowing before the sage Sakayana and entreating him: 'In this world, I am like a frog in a dry well. Please, therefore, take me out.'[2] A feeling of the futility, impermanence and misery of all finite things is expressed here. Not only the human body decays and the pleasures are rejected but also the rejection of the whole world is thought desirable. Here we find a radical questioning and negation of the whole social-cultural scale of values. It is a statement of the fundamental psychological attitude that inspired the movement of world renunciation and world transcendence.

The attitude of king Bṛhadratha, according to Ranade, was the logical outcome only carried to an excess of the anti-hedonistic tendency suggested in the Kaṭhopaniṣad and which now has degenerated into utter pessimism.[3] Nachiketas was the symbol of this anti-hedonistic tendency. We are reminded of the exaltation of a life of spirit (*śreyas*) to attain the spiritual wisdom and Nachiketas asking in a pessimistic vein: 'What decaying mortal here below would delight in a life of the contemplation of the pleasures, of beauty and love, when once he (a seeker of truth) has come to

[1]*Maitri. Up.*, I-3.
[2]*Maitri. Up.*, I-4.
[3]Ranade, *CSUP.*, p. 294.

taste of the kind of life enjoyed by the unageing immortals?'[1] The anti-hedonistic tendency now asserts itself behind the destruction of desire which brings in its wake an attitude of contempt towards the human body. This is only a prelude to the state of *vairāgya* which came to be accepted as an essential condition of renunciation.[2]

The growth of the doctrines of transmigration (*saṁsāra*) and Karma gave momentum to the forces of pessimism. In the context of the doctrine of *saṁsāra*, death was always terrible and the prospect of having to die innumerable times was painful. Life, even in the absence of major sorrows, was found to be inadequate and drab while the eternal cycle of birth and rebirth seemed monotonous and boring. Rebirth in heaven was not enough.[3] A way had to be found not only to escape the evil of an unhappy and miserable world but also the unending bondage of birth and rebirth, as *saṁsāra* was ruled by *Karma*. According to the *Karma* theory, the journey of the soul from life to life was determined by man's conduct here for his status thereafter. Everything depended on *Karma*. But it was believed that *Karma* was bound up with desire which was solely responsible for the continuation of the cycle of birth and rebirth.[4] Desire was the root of empirical existence (*saṁsāra-mūla*). Not only this but the freedom from desire was considered essential for self-realization.[5] The problem was, therefore, the destruction of all desire for worldly things which chained a man to the eternal cycle of birth and rebirth and hence suffering.

The best minds of the times were thus engaged in finding out a solution to this problem. Some thought of a life of complete meditation in pursuit of self-knowledge. This was possible only if they could at all be free from all the worldly desires and earthly ties in a distracting world. Others thought of stopping the operation of

[1]*Katha. Up.*, I. 1.28.

[2]Vide Chapter 2.

[3]*Mund. Up.*, I.2.10: istāpurtaṁ manyamānā variṣṭhaṃ nānyacchreyo vedayante pramūdhāḥ nākasya pṛṣṭhe te sukṛte'nubhūtvemaṁ lokaṁ hinataraṁ vā viṣanti. *Bṛhad. Up.*, VI.2.16: *Chan. Up.*, III.10; *Kau. Up.*, I: Give different versions of the two ways after death—*Deva-yāna* and *Pitṛ-yāna* but they all agree that there is repeated return to birth determined by *Karma*.

[4]*Bṛhad. Up.*, IV. 4.6.

[5]*Katha. Up.*, VI.14-15; *Bṛhad. Up.*, IV.4.7.

Yadā serve pramucyante kāma ye'sya hṛdi śṛitaḥ atha martyo'mṛto bhavati, atra brahma samaśnute Yadā sarve prabhidyante hṛdayasyeha granthayaḥ atha martyo'mrto bhavati, etāvad anuśāsanam.

Karma theory. If in some way, they thought, the accumulation of *Karma* is stopped, the chain of *Karma* would be broken as there would be no *Karma* either to be carried over or to be credited to one's account. This meant all cessation of activity, a life of complete retirement, *nivṛtti*, of no Karma. As a result some thought man would discontinue creating new *Karma* and thus might stop creating new chains of Karma for himself. But *nivṛtti*, by itself did not mean cessation of desires or their destruction. For out of desires came the actions and their fruits and out of actions and the enjoyment or suffering of their fruits of pleasures or sorrows came further desires and so on. The bondage of *Karma* seemed perpetual. It was necessary, therefore, to gain freedom from all the desires and ties of the mundane life towards this end. Thus arose the ideal of giving up or renouncing home, possessions, family and all that stimulated desire. This meant rejection of ordinary human aims, freedom from all the ties of the earth, the casting off from oneself (*saṁnyāsa*) of all that bound man to the duties and responsibilities of the worldly life, its attractions and its concerns. It implied dying to the world and passing beyond the pale of society, community and nation.

Psychological Insecurity

Behind the growth of pessimism and asceticism lay, according to Basham, a deep psychological uneasiness and a deep feeling of insecurity. He observes: 'It was a time of great social change, when old tribal units were breaking up. The feeling of group solidarity, which the tribe gave, was removed and men stood face to face with the world, with no refuge in their kinsmen. Chieftains were overthrown, their courts dispersed, their lands and tribesmen absorbed in greater kingdom. A new order was coming into being (as described by the king Bṛhadrath). Despite the great growth of material civilization at this time, the hearts of many were failing them for fear of what should come to pass upon earth.[1]

This is to be found in the Maitri Upaniṣad, probably the latest of all the classical Upaniṣads. This Upaniṣad was probably written at about the same time that Buddhism and Jainism came into existence.[2] Between the Bṛhadāraṇyaka Upaṇiṣad, one of the earliest

[1]Basham. op. cit., pp. 41, 246-247.

[2]cf. Zaehner, *Hinduism*, pp. 82-83; Max Muller ascribes this Upanisad an anti-Pāninean period. *SBE.*, Vol. XV, p. 6.

principal Upaniṣads and Maitri Upaniṣad, the evolution of ascetic thought is notable. Transitoriness of the world and its objects leading to mendicacy is suggested in the two passages of the Bṛhadāraṇyaka Upaniṣad. In one it is said that the mendicants (*pravājino*) leave their homes (*bhikṣācaryaṁ caranti*) as a natural consequence of the knowledge of the Ātman, in the other it is made the most efficacious means by which it was hoped to attain that knowledge.[1] Secondly *Vairāgya* was taken for granted which by the time of the Maitri Upaniṣad had reached its logical conclusion in the anti-hedonistic attitude. Impermanence of the world and its pleasures, the fear of present ills and future births have brought about a pessimistic outlook of life, a loathsome attitude towards the human body. The endless prolongation of life, *sāṁsāra* was now deemed to be the evil from which salvation (*mokṣa*) was sought.[2] To borrow a similie from the Maitri Upaniṣad, man, the frog helplessly struggled in a well of *Saṁsāra* which was without water and sought freedom from desire and the dreary cycle of birth and rebirth by attempting to escape the realities and miseries of life. The outlook which was joyous in the Vedas has been replaced by a pessimistic one in the age of the Upaniṣads and the ideal of world renunciation has developed.

Pessimism in Buddhism and Jainism

The pessimism of this age was not typical of Brāhmanism. It is suggested that it also affected Buddhism and Jainism which adopted the attitude of loathing towards the human body and detestation towards the transient *Saṁsāric* world. The Jain Sutras and Pali Pitakas are full of these pessimistic notes.[3]

In Pali texts we come across a number of *Bhikkhus* and *Bhikkhunis* who left the world to escape pain and sorrow.[4] The number of such suffering souls as we hear from the Therigāthā was bigger in the *Saṅgha* of women than that of men. Sorrow was due more to illness, death and pain than poverty. Many of the psalms recapitulate the

[1]*Bṛhad. Up.*, IV.4.22; III. 5-1.

[2]In the famous legend of the Buddha (before he left the princely life), he sees a monk (*śramaṇa*) and ask him the reason for his adopting a homeless life, the śramaṇa replies: *Janmamṛtyubhitaḥ śramaṇaḥ pravajitosmi mokṣahetoḥ* —*Buddhacaritam*, V-17.

[3]*Therigāthā*, p. 4, 15, 17, 16, 74, 15; *DP.*, 147, 148, 150, 197-199, 277-278; Jacobi, *JS.*, I. p. 21; II. p. 18, 348; I. pp. 3 ff, 8, 21, 28.

[4]*Thera*, p. 6, 10, 34, 75, 190.

shallowness and the unsatisfactoriness of the life led in the past by the reputed authors.[1] Dissatisfaction and the uneasiness arising from unfulfilled desires drove many to join the *saṅgha*.[2] Of all the unendurable elements in life, the greatest impetus to join the other came from grief.

The chief guiding impulse which supported several of them in their decision to join the order was the hope of freedom from worldly troubles, cares, responsibilities, temptations, griefs from boredom and from the cloying senses or in the wider sense release from the round of existencies.[3] The largest number of women joined the *saṅgha* due to grief and frustration arising from loss of kith and kin.[4]

However, it will be wrong to suggest that the Buddha's philosophy was pessimistic.[5] He attempted to make the common man to accept life as it was though full of misery and has suggested: 'Get yourselves rid of this vast suffering by becoming possessed of perfect knowledge, by acts of faith, good conduct, exertion, meditation, investigation into the truth and enlightened consciousness.'[6] The Buddha thus preached a positive way to be free from the misery of life. He showed a sure way to lead a happy life: 'Let us be free from hate, ailments and lust, live happily among those who hate, who are ailing and filled with lust, let us dwell free from hatred, ailments and lust.'[7] The certainty that there is a way to end suffering can lead neither to despair nor to pessimism.

The Mahābhārata

Coming to the Epics, in the Śāntiparva of the Mahābhārata, we come across an interesting dialogue between Yudhiṣṭhira and Bhimasena which throws a flood of light on the ascetic institution especially with regard to human motives which force a man to embrace a life of renunciation. After the great war is won, Yudhiṣṭhira's heart is full of pity and sorrow as a result of the cruelties,

[1] *Theri*. xi, xxi, xxxix, xlii, xlix,li, liv, lxiv, lxxi, lxxii.
[2] ibid, lxxii.
[3] Horner, I.B,, *Women Under Primitive Buddhism*, pp. 165 ff.
[4] *Theri*, p. 51, 13, 50, 63, 17, 69, 47.
[5] See article by Keny, *The Buddha and Pessimism* (*Buddha āṇi niraśāvād*; Sadhana), May 24, 1956, pp. 29-32.
[6] *DP*., pp. 197-199.
[7] ibid.

slaughter and consequent misery the war had brought in its wake. Overcome with deep frustration, he wants to renounce the world and become a *saṁnyāsi*. With an agitated heart and burning with grief, he wants to 'abandon the whole of his kingdom and all the worldly objects and go to the forest, escaping from the worldly fetters, freed from grief and without affection for anything.'[1] The life of renunciation, he thought, would dissipate all sorrow, behind which lay aversion and disgust for the world. He is dissuaded by his borthers and wife from renouncing the world. The arguments of Bhima in this connection are of special interest:

'It has been laid down that (a life of) renunciation should be adopted only in times of difficulty (by kings), attacked with decrepitude or defeated by enemies.'

'Wise men, therefore, do not praise renunciation as the duty of a Kṣatriya. On the other hand the clear-sighted think that the adoption of such a life is a transgression of the law.'

'The persons who are shorn of prosperity and wealth and who are unbelievers (*nāstikaihi*), have laid down this precept of the Vedas as the truth. In reality, however, it is a falsehood looking like truth.

'He who can support life by prowess, he who can support himself by his own exertions, does not live, but really deviates from his duty by following the life of renunciation.'

'That man only is capable of leading a solitary life of happiness in the forest who cannot support sons and grandsons and the deities and Ṛṣis and guests and Pitṛs.'

'As the deer and boars and birds cannot attain to heaven even so these Kṣatriyas who are shorn of prowess cannot attain to heaven by leading only a forest life. They should acquire religious merit by other means.'[2]

These passages reflect the total disparagement of renunciation (*saṁnyāsa*). They go to suggest that there was a section of society which regarded *saṁnyāsa* as an *āśrama* simply to avoid responsibility which a person owed to the society and the family. The third passage has been interpreted by Altekar to mean: 'renunciation appeals only to those who are unsuccessful in life.'[3] Frustration is

[1]*Mbh.*, XII.7.41.

[2]*Mbh.*, XII. 10.17-18, 20-23.

[3]Altekar, *The Position of Women in Hindu Civilisation*, p. 425: Śriya vihinairadhanairnāstikaiḥ saṁpravartitaṁ Vedavādasya vijñānaṁ satyābhaśamivanṛinam, XII.10.20.

made here the motive behind renunciation. The next two verses, make meaning quite clear. That man is looked upon as successful in life who can support sons and grandsons, the deities and Ṛṣis, the guests and Pitṛs. These truely give a man religious merit. But a man who cannot support himself by his own labour, as Bhima asks, can he ever think of acquiring religious merit? Thus the argument indeed supports an active life, not a life—denying attitude arising from retirement or inaction. In other words, those who cannot discharge their day-to-day life, attend to the needs of the family and the society and the three debts (*ṛṇas*) only think of renunciation.

What is of special interest is the fact that *saṁnyāsa* is referred to as *nāstikya* and it is said that men of learning do not acknowledge it. Further, it is said that (according to scriptures) a man should enter *saṁnyāsa*, at the time of (the fall of some) calamity or when he is old or is harassed by his enemies.[1] Bhima clearly suggests that it is the man who is dejected and frustrated takes to a life of *saṁnyāsa*.

Summing Up

In the Ṛgvedic Muni, we seem to have the familiar figure of the *shaman* of the primitive society. The descriptions of his abandoning the body, divining the thoughts of others, flying in the air, roaming at will in different regions suggest that he was an ascetic who has acquired magical powers (*siddhis*) very similar to the primitive medicine man. The prescriptions of the Atharvaveda which have a whole collection of magic, indicate that some classes of Āryan society believed in magic practices. The Vedic hymns were used as having a peculiar magic property; it was thought that if correctly used in sacrifices they brought about desired results. Sacrifice was invested with magic. The *ṛta* and *satya* were believed to have sprung in the beginning of creation from *tapas*; similarly the primeval principle described as neither *sat* nor *asat*. Just as this mysterious principle controlling the whole universe could be known through sacrifice, so it came to be believed that the ascetic was able to control nature and gods by the force of his *tapas* and also obtain supernatural powers. Thus originated asceticism or *tapas* from the acquisition of magical powers or *siddhis*. At the same time

[1] *Mbh.*, xii.10.17.

the idea to achieve *ojas* seems to have been dominant with many ascetics as an essential condition for the attainment of celibacy and the highest spirituality.

Climate as a factor leading to pessimism and asceticism is examined. It is found to be an important factors haping the religious temperament of the people of ancient India. It is to the intellectual craving for a higher life, the spiritual urge for self-realisation that the ideal of renunciation is to be traced. However, the idea where it first appears in the Bṛhadāraṇyaka Upaniṣad is made both the cause and effect of self-realisation. But soon after, with the Vedic outlook turning into a pessimistic one, the idea develops. As the Āryan mind reflected on the finite and limited character of human existence, it was overcome by fear. When the fear became conscious of itself due to suffering and *Karma* theory, it turned into anguish. To be free from it demanded destruction of desire as also extinction of the bondage of *Karma* which seemed perpetual. This led to all worldly objects being considered transitory and the human body an abode of evil. Pleasures were short-lived and hence to be rejected. But this was not enough. *Tapas* was insufficient to lead to the knowledge of the self. *Karma* theory operated to create more *Karma* and add to the sense of pessimism. A deep psychological uneasiness and a deep feeling of insecurity as also frustration and suffering, brought in their wake increasing pessimism. It was an unhappy and unsatisfying world to be escaped from at all costs. As the material life believed to be evil and deceptive was a hindrance to a life of the spirit and the release from the eternal cycle of birth and death lay in the total destruction of desire, turning away from the world was the next logical step. It was thus thought necessary to break away from all the ties of this earth which bound man to the world, its desires and temptations. We thus find in the age of the Upaniṣads the ideal of renunciation taking a firm shape.

This ideal of renunciation came to be practised as the result of many forces like: intellectual craving for a higher life and thirst for spiritual wisdom; the fear of present ills and the unending cycle of births and rebirths, the inadequacy of *tapas* for self-realisation, the emergence of anti-hedomistic tendency, the impermanence of the world and a mood of psychological uneasiness and insecurity—all resulting into a pessimistic view of life.

Chapter 4

Asceticism in the Indus Civilisation

In the earliest dawn of prehistory man was primitive. His story is traceable in the tools and implements he had used and in the remains of his habitation, burial or cremation. The nature of tools viz. stone and metals like copper, bronze and iron marks out different epochs of his cultural evolution through various stages viz. Palaeolithic, Neolithic and Chalcolithic. Thus the study of all that which concerns him till the time writing appears belongs to prehistory.

It is obvious that writing and literature appeared much later in human history as products of man's necessary progress in culture and education. In India too the oral traditions were not reduced to writing for a long time. The Vedas were heard as *Śruti* and were transmitted by the teacher to the taught by word of mouth from generation to generation. From the beginning of the Indus Valley Civilisation to the Mauryan period, India had its protohistoric period. Writing was known but was not useful to know history.

Every region, in which civilisation has developed and in which art, literature and science have flourished, has a cultural background extending for thousands of years and dating from Palaeolithic or Neolithic times. India is no exception. This is suggested and proved by the discoveries of some rock paintings and engravings, celts, stone implements and weapons of that age.

The earliest record of rock paintings was that of Archibald Carlleyle who discovered them in the year 1880 in shelters somewhere in the northern cliffs of the Kaimur Range when he was working in Rewah and Mirzapur. The drawings depict animals especially a stag and men engaged in hunting rhinoceros.[1] Of these paintings Carlleyle writes: 'These illustrated in a very stiff and archaic manner scenes in the life of the ancient stone clippers; others represent animals or hunts of animals by men with bows and arrows, spears and hatchets.'[2] It is doubtful whether the cave drawings are as old as Cockburn believes them to be.

[1]Cockburn, 'Cave Drawings in the Kaimur Range' *JRAS* (1889), pp. 89-97.
[2]Gordon, *The Prehistoric Background of Indian Culture*, p. 100.

The Kaimur paintings were followed by another set of such engravings discovered by C. W. Anderson in some caverns at Singhanpur in Raigarh State.[1] The subjects of these paintings were hunting scenes, groups of human figures, picture writing or hieroglyphics and animals, reptiles etc. The hunting scenes depict lifelike portraits of the chase of bison, elephants or mammoths by the hunters with spears or clubs. The human figures appear to be dancing or engaged in some religious ceremony.

These paintings do not have any indication of any form of writing like hieroglyphics. Anderson seems to ignore the fact that writing is an element of proto-historic period and the caves are referred to by him as prehistoric. We can accept the caves as prehistoric without the hieroglyphics which do not exist in the caves.

Still more cave paintings were found by Cockburn[2] in the Kaimur Ranges in the various caves of Ghormangar, Chundri, Lorri and Likhunia rocks. These were similar to those discovered and described by Carlleyle. The drawings were executed on vertical rocks in rock shelters. There were scenes of a rhinoceros hunt, a man spearing a stag which had an arrow stuck in the throat and was also shown as attacked by dogs; a man with a torch encountering a panther. Some of the animals drawn were spotted deer and rhinoceros.

It may be pointed out that the dog is a domesticated animal and the palaeolithic age was ignorant of the domestication of animals which development took place only during the neolithic age.

Cockburn[3] also refers to similar but cruder drawings from the Banda District. Silberrad[4] has found similar rock drawings at Sarhat, Malwa, Kuria-Kund and Karpatia in the same region. These consist of several archers on horseback pursuing sambhar stags, horses caparisoned and led by men apparently armed with some sort of wooden weapon. There are several crude representations of men, an elephant and a bird.

Now horses were not existing in India before the migration of

[1]Anderson, 'Rock Paintings of Singhanpur,' *JBORS*. 1918, pp. 298-306; Mitra, *Prehistoric India*, pp. 254-255; Adam Leonard, *Primitive Art*, pp. 121-122.

[2]Cockburn, loc. cit., & *JASB* (1883), pp. 56-64.

[3]*JASB* (1907), pp. 467 ff.

[4]*Rock Drawings in the Banda District, JASB.*, Vol. III, 1907, pp. 567-568.

the Āryans. They were introduced in India by the Āryans. Therefore, either the paintings do not belong to the palaeolithic times or the animals represented are not horses.

From the Kapgallu in the Bellary District have been found more than 20 groups of figures of birds and beasts of various degrees of artistic execution.[1] There is a hunting scene depicting two men with upraised right arms as if for hurling javelins, having something like shield on their left arms proceeding towards a bull. All the figures are interesting and occur in a neolithic site.

Fawcett[2] discovered a series of such carvings from Edakad cave, Wynaad, situated about 56 miles from Calicut. The carvings represent human beings and objects for human use and symbols, but they so run into each other and are placed so closely together that it needs close study to make anything of them. The symbols might have had some meaning to those who drew them but they convey nothing to us at all.

By far the greater number of the paintings and carvings can be summed up as those depicting events—encounters with wild beasts and wild ritualistic dances. Stone implements, celts, spears, arrows and stone knives found in the various caves have been examined by the museums to which they were sent. Their verdict was that in material, in shape and in manufacture, the polished and chipped celts of the first two classes closely resemble those found in various parts of Europe, America and Australia.[3] This is a definite proof that the paintings belong to the neolithic times. They represent religious beliefs and practices of the prehistoric people. Hunting scenes represent their every day life of hunters, seeking food in the form of the flesh of the animals hunted. The paintings suggest their belief in animism.

The materials and objects of these prehistoric art do not throw any light on any ascetic practices and beliefs prevailing in stone age.

Protohistoric Times

The archaeological excavations at Mohenjodaro, Harappa and Chanhu-daro conducted between 1921 and 1935 pushed back the

[1]Bruce Foot, *New Antiquary*, pp. 88-89.

[2]'Rock Carvings in the Edakad Cave,' *IA.*, 1901, pp. 413-421.

[3]Carnac, 'On Stone Implements from the NWP of India,' *JASB.*, 1883, p. 221.

history of India by nearly 2,000 years with one stroke. The recent discoveries in different centres in India indicate that the civilisation flourished over a vast area from Saurashtra, Cutch and Gujarat to Rupar on the upper Sutlej and upto the Gangetic basin. Particularly Lothal in Saragvala village fifty miles southwest of Ahmedabad, has been identified as a Harappan settlement. Kalibangan between Hanumangarh and Suratgarh in Rajasthan has turned out to be another big Indus Valley city.

The discovery of Mohenjodaro and Harappa was the beginning of a new period in the history of man. It brought to light the relics of a highly advanced pre-Āryan civilisation which flourished in the era which witnessed the glories of the Egyptian, Assyrian and Babylonian civilisations.[1]

Religion

Religion has always played a dominant part in all ancient cultures and more so in India where religion has moulded the lives of countless generations of people from the earliest times to the present day. It is unthinkable that it could have been otherwise in the case of the Indus people. Our main source of information for the religion of the Indus people is the fine collection of seals and amulets, clay sealings and copper tablets, a variety of figurines of terra-cotta, faience and metal, and a few stone images. We have to rely purely on the archaeological evidence. The mysterious Indus script in which the various inscriptions on the seals are found, still remains undeciphered in spite of the attempts of the various scholars so far.[2] The decipherment is expected to unlock the secret of the rise and fall of the Harappan civilisation and at the same time may throw new light on the religious beliefs and practices of the Indus people.

Despite the ignorance of the Indus script, Eliade[3] Wheeler[4] and Piggott[5] hold the view that a dominant religious element was the source of authority of the Indus Valley civilisation. According to them the rulers of Harappa administered their city in a fashion not remote from that of the priest-kings or governors of Sumer and

[1]cf. Hrozny, *Ancient History of Western Asia, India and Crete*, p. 158.

[2]Heras, For summary of these attempts, see *Studies in the Proto-Indo Mediterranean Culture*, pp. 29-129.

[3]Eliade, *Yoga: Immortality and Freedom*, p. 353.

[4]Wheeler, *The Indus Civilisati‿n*, pp. 29-30.

[5]Piggott, *Prehistoric India*, pp. 151-153.

Akkad. In Sumer, the wealth and discipline of the city state were vested in the priesthood or a priest-king. From the archaeological evidence of the Harappa civilisation, the reasonable deduction seems to be that 'it was a state ruled over by priest-kings, weilding autocratic and absolute power from two main seats of Government.'[1] In such a state it is easy to imagine the role of the temple as a centre of religious or administrative life. Piggott observes: 'The civic focus was the exalted temple, centre of an elaborate and carefully ordered secular administration under divine sanction.'[2]

The Mother Goddess

It is believed that a large number of female figurines of terracotta are those of the Earth or Mother Goddess.[3] An oblong sealing from Harappa depicts a nude female figure upside down with legs apart and with a plant issuing from her womb.[4] This suggests the idea of an earth-goddess concerned with vegetation. The numerous clay figurines of women suggest that there was some form of worship of a Mother Goddess in which these figures played their part in household shrines.

The Male God

Side by side with the Mother Goddess, there appears on a square seal, a three-faced deity in a typical *Dhyāna-Yoga* posture. Marshall describes the deity thus:

'The God, who is three faced, is seated on a low Indian throne in a typical attitude of *Yoga*, with legs bent double beneath him, heel to heel and toes turned downards. His arms are outstretched, his hands with thumb to front, resting on his knees. From wrist to shoulder, the arms are covered with bangles, eight smaller and three larger; over his breast is a triangular or perhaps a series of necklaces or torques, like those on the later class of Goddess figurines from Baluchistan and round his waist a double band. The lower limbs are bare and the phallus (*urdhva medhrā*) seemingly exposed. Crowning his head is a pair of horns meeting in a tall head-dress. To either side of the god are four animals, an elephant and tiger on his proper right, a rhinoceros and buffalo on his left. Beneath the

[1]Piggott, ibid, p. 153.
[2]ibid.
[3]John Marshall, *Mohenjodaro and the Indus Civilisation*, Vol. I, p. 49.
[4]ibid, Pl. XII, Opp. p. 52.

throne are two deer standing with heads regardant and horns turned to the centre.'[1]

Marshall recognises this three-faced male god as 'a prototype of the historic *Śiva.*' He also calls him *Paśupati* and *Mahāyogi.*[2] Following Marshall, scholars like Wheeler, Piggott, Gordon and Mackay have accepted the nude figure of the male God as the prototype of the later historical Śiva called Paśupati. We should have no hesitation in accepting this identity.[3]

Besides the worship of the Mother Goddess and three-faced male God, certain trees such as the pipal were also held sacred. The worship of the phallic emblems, the *linga* and the *yoni* was also prevalent.

Among several pieces of stone sculpture from Mohenjodaro, there is a stone-head of a bearded man wearing an embroidered garment. With eye-lids more than half-closed, he appears to be in meditation, with eyes fixed on the tip of the nose.[4] This is believed to be a representation of an ascetic or a Yogi by scholars like Mookerji[5] and Chanda.[6] Marshall believes it to be the statue of a priest, may be of a king-priest.[7] The thick lips, broad-based nose, low forehead, short stunted neck and the fact that the figure is draped in an embroidered garment, probably a shawl, belie any identification with that of an ascetic. But Yogic practices, however, even by those placed in high position, cannot be ruled out. The statue may be that of a priest-king, associated with religion, having the knowledge of the art of meditation.

Summing Up

All the deities reflect the then existing conditions. The representation of the statuette of the Father God with the soles of his feet touching each other, his hands resting on his knees and squatting on the seat like the Yogi, and the bust of the so-called priest-king,

[1]Marshall, op. cit., p. 52, See illustration 'A' opposite.

[2]ibid, p. 53.

[3]Heras identifies him as Ān, the Supreme Lord of the Indus Valley. Art. 'The Plastic Representation of God amongst the Proto-Indians,' *Sardesai Comm.* Vol. (1938), p. 223.

[4]See illustration 'B' opposite.

[5]*Ancient India*, p. 42.

[6]*Chanda*, 'Sind Five Thousand Years Ago,' *Modern Review* (August, 1932), p. 158.

[7]Marshall, op. cit., p. 54.

A. The three-faced deity of Mohenjodaro

B. The Priest King

with the half-closed eyes looking at the tip of the nose, certainly indicate the practice of meditation of those times; and the three-faced nude male deity also suggests a definite proof of the existence of ascetic practices in India as early as 2500 BC.

Chapter 5

Asceticism in the Early Vedic Literature

The Vedas are the earliest available literary record of the Āryans, particularly their philosophical thought and religious practices during the first thousand years or more of their settlement in India. By the Vedic literature we mean not any particular book, but the whole mass of literature produced by them. We generally include in it the four *Saṁhitās*, the *Ṛgveda*, *Sāmveda*, *Yajurveda* and *Atharvaveda*, the Brāhmaṇas on the one hand and the Āraṇyakas and the Upaniṣads on the other which came into existence in different periods of time.[1] Even in each of the *Saṁhitās*, we find evidences of collections of hymns of different periods, grouped together under one common name. Thus Vedic civilisation means various lines of primitive thought and practice of the Āryans which grew and developed over a vast span of time.

The earliest of the *Saṁhitās* is the Ṛgveda wherein we come across the idea of definite gods, as a normal evolution from the striking phenomena of nature. The same Saṁhitā shows that the development of the Āryan religion and philosophy proceeded along two well-marked directions. On the one hand, we find the idea of propitiating the different gods by means of worship, which led to the religious sacraments known as *Yajña* or sacrifice. On the other hand, there developed a more philosophic concept about the nature of these gods which culminated in the idea that all these gods were but the manifestations of a higher spirit: *ekam sad viprā bahudhā vadanti.*[2] The later Vedic literature saw a further development in these directions. The Brāhmaṇas developed the ritualistic

[1]Āpastamba in the *Yajñaparibhāṣāsūtra* has defined the Vedas as the collection of *mantras* and *brāhmaṇas: Mantrabrāhmaṇyorveda nāmadheyam.* Similar definitions have been given by other scholars. Most of the Upaniṣads are included in the Brāhmaṇa portions of the Vedas, though there are a few which are included in the *mantra* portions also.

[2]*ṚV.*, I. 164. 46. cf. *ṚV.*, X. 114. 5: *Ekaṁ santaṁ bahudhā kalpayanti.* Also *ṚV.*, I. 79. 10: Aditirdyorditirantarikṣamaditirmātā sa pitā sa putraḥ Viśve devā aditiḥ pancajanā aditirjātamaditirjanitvaṁ.

side of the sacrifice, while the philosophical ideas were developed in the Upaniṣads.

The ideas that prompted the Ṛgvedic Āryans to perform sacrifice can be gathered from various hymns. The poet, himself in a reminiscent mood notices the variety of ideas,[1] viz. the propitiation of the divinity with a view to secure favour,[2] protection against the enemy,[3] protection from sin,[4] attainment of fame,[5] wealth and strength,[6] material progress,[7] and expiation[8] behind the performance of sacrifice. Thus the Ṛgvedic people performed sacrifices accompanied with prayers to the various gods, viz. Indra, Agni, Varuṇa, Mitra, Aśvins and Uṣas etc. They were conscious of the might of gods who symbolised power, strength, wealth and vigour and whom they evoked for the attainment of worldly comforts with a view to enjoy the blessings of the world. Their worship was sincere but utilitarian. Their ideal of happiness was quite simple and materialistic on the whole. It comprised mainly a desire to live a natural duration of human life which was hundred years,[9] full term of life of hundred autumns,[10] hundred springs,[11] hundred winters[12] and a keener desire for progeny[13] and cattle.[14] The desire for sons was so dominant that they longed to see sons of their sons.[15] The prayers of the Ṛgvedic people thus mainly centered round the desire for prosperity, progeny and safety from misfortunes. Life was thought of as a blessing which they loved in all its fullness and the joys and pleasures of this world deeply interested them.

About the Ṛgvedic life, Radhakrishnan observes: 'We find in the hymns of the Ṛgveda, a keen delight in the beauties of nature, its greatness, its splendour and its pathos. The motive of the sacrifices

[1] *ṚV.*, III. 55. 3.
[2] *ṚV.*, II. 28. 1; I. 114. 3, 108.4, 114.4, 101, 1-7, III. 32-13.
[3] *ṚV.*, I. 103. 8.
[4] *ṚV.*, I. 136.5; II. 26.4, X. 63.6.
[5] *ṚV.*, I. 9. 8, 44.2; VIII. 65. 9, 23. 21.
[6] *ṚV.*, III. 19. 1.
[7] *ṚV.*, VI. 6. 1; VII. 61. 4.
[8] *ṚV.*, I. 185. 8, 114. 4; VII. 51. 5.
[9] *ṚV.*, VII. 66. 16, 101. 6; cf. *AV.*, I. 31. 3; VIII. 2. 8.
[10] *ṚV.*, X. 18, 2-3-4-6; 85. 39; 161. 2-3-4.
[11] *ṚV.*, X. 161. 4; cf. *AV.*, III. 11. 4.
[12] *ṚV.*, X. 161. 4; IX. 74. 8.
[13] *ṚV.*, I. 66, 83. 6, 54. 11; II. 4. 8; III. 3. 7, IV. 2. 11.
[14] *ṚV.*, I. 180. 8; VII. 8. 65; III. 54. 18; V. 41. 17.
[15] *SV.*, II. 11. 9.

is love of the good things of the world. We have yet the deep joy in life and the world untainted by any melancholy gloom.'[1] The estimate of life which finds expression here was inspired by a healthy appreciation of the good things of the world and to seek its pleasures. The life depicted was simple, fresh and full of zest. There was a vigorous pursuit of material life and the desire for prosperity. Though the prevailing spirit of the hymns is optimistic, there is sometimes a note of sadness in them as in those addressed to the goddess of Dawn, the Ushas, which pointedly refer to the way of men.[2]

There is a voice of doubt as to the power, even to the existence of the gods. In one of the hymns, it is said of Indra: 'Of whom they ask, where is he? Of him, indeed, they also say, he is not?'[3] In another hymn, the priests are invited to offer a song of praise to Indra, 'a true one, if in truth he is! for many say: 'There is no Indra, who has ever seen him? To whom are we to direct the song of praise?'[4]

We also find in some verses references to death. The Ṛgvedic people did not try to forget or ignore death. The sober realism of their outlook comes out in the recognition that death was the 'comrade' (*bandhu*), the unseen companion of the race of man.[5] The term 'comrade' suggests a manly, undisturbed attitude towards death, untainted by fantasy or fear. What they prayed for in the beginning, was relief from premature death. 'Let not my thread of life be snapped while I am weaving my song, nor the measure of my work broken up before its time,' prays a Vedic poet to Varuna.[6] When the melody of life was completed, he was perfectly willing to leave the concert hall of life. But the incomplete song seemed sad. He prayed for life for a hundred autumns, life with its full powers, with sight and hearing, the strength of the arms and the keenness of the mind, unimpaired.[7] When his own sons had become fathers in their turn, he was ready to depart.[8] Not only the Ṛgvedic

[1] Radhakrishnan, *IP*, I., p. 111.

[2] *ṚV.*, I. 124. 2: abhinati daivyāni vratāni praminati manuṣyā yugāni iyuṣināmupamā śaṣvatināmāyatinām prathameṣa vyadauta.

[3] *ṚV.*, II. 12. 5-12.

[4] *ṚV.*, VIII. 100. 3 ff.

[5] *ṚV.*, VIII. 18. 22: Ye ciddhi mṛtyubāndhav āditya manavaḥ smasi.

[6] *ṚV.*, II. 28. 5.

[7] *AV.*, XIX. 60; *ṚV.*, X. 158. 4; X. 186. 1.

[8] *ṚV.*, I. 89. 9.

Āryans prayed for long life of prolonged youth and vigour but their outlook on life was also robust and cheerful. The Ṛṣis even called them 'the sons of immortality' (*amṛtasya putrā*) and 'the possessors of celestial natures.'[1]

Despite this robust optimism, we find sometimes the notes of pathos in the Varuṇa hymns when Vasiṣṭha prays to Varuṇa: 'What was the gravest sin, O Varuṇa, committed by me that you want to forsake me, a friend and praiser of yours?'[2] But though references to death and notes of pathos are to be found here and there and disturb their cheerfulness for a while, the Ṛgvedic Āryans were, on the whole, in the rosy dawn of life.

Against this picture of the Vedic society of a happy pastoral people, taking a keen pleasure in worldly things, desiring material prosperity and living a full life of zest and vigour, we come across a small section of society which does not seem to seek the delights of this world and appreciate its comforts. The reference is to the Munis figuring in the tenth *maṇḍala* of Ṛgveda. Basham calls them 'a class of holy men, different from the Brāhmaṇas.'[3] According to Kane, they lived 'a life of poverty, contemplation and mortification.'[4] They look somewhat out of tune with the whole image of the Ṛgvedic society engaged in the performance of sacrifices and the worship of deities. Some scholars argue: 'In the Ṛgveda no evidence of an ascetic *weltanshauung* is found so that the inference seems natural to follow that such an outlook derived from the Dravidians or from aboriginal inhabitants of the land.'[5] This view, which seems to be correct, is partly explained by stating that the hymns to the Muni which are found significantly in the tenth book of the Ṛgveda 'Represents a definitely later stratum of composition.'[6] The reason seems to be that it is a natural development of thought aided by the persistence of magical ideas drawn from lower and more primitive religions.[7] There is no doubt that some of the strange practices and beliefs of the Muni throw light on the ascetic institution which in

[1]*ṚV.*, X. 13. 1; cf. *Sveta. Up.*, II. 5. Sṛnvantu viśve amṛtasya putrā ā ye dhāmāni divyāni tasthuḥ.

[2]*ṚV.*, 86, 2-4.

[3]Basham, *The Wonder that was India*, p. 244.

[4]Kane, *HDS.*, II, Pt. I, pp. 419-42.

[5]Geden, *ERE.*, II, p. 88; Bouquet, *Hinduism*, p. 33.

[6]Macdonell, *HOSL.*, p. 45.

[7]cf. Chapter 4.

course of time came to occupy an engaging attention in the life and thought of the people ancient India.

Firstly we turn to the austerities, ascetic practices (*tapas*) and then to the *Muni*.

Tapas

We find in the following passages the original meaning of *tapas* as 'heat' or 'burning':

The sun burns untroubled sending forth heat: *Sūryastapati tapyatuvṛthā*[1] The sun heats the earth: *tapanti śatrum svarnabhūma*[2] Fire heats milk: *nāśiram duhne na tapanti gharmaṁ*[3] They burn their foes as the sun burns the earth: *tapanti śatrun mahāsenaso amebhireṣāṁ*[4] Chase with thy *tapas* for ally, our foeman: *tapasā yujā vi jāhi śatrun*[5] Burn him: *tapā tapiṣtha tapasā tapasvān.*[6] With heat, O bull, on every side consume them: *tapā vṛsan viśvataḥ sociśā tān.*[7] Agni, burn up the unfriendly who are near us: *tapā canśam araruśaḥ parasya.*[8] Smite ye him down with your most flaming weapon: *tapiṣthena tapasā hanmanā.*[9] The idea of tormenting or distressing is also implied here. Consume with flame most fiercely glowing: *tapiṣthena śociśā ya sūradhiḥ.*[10] With hottest blaze pierce the man who love deception: *tapaṣthena hesasā droghamitran.*[11] Agni is prayed: consume our enemies with thy hottest flames, preserve us from distress: *tapaṣthair ajaro daha.*[12] Make the fiery pit friendly for Atri's sake: *tapaṁ gharmaṁ omyāvantaṁ Atraye.*[13] The frogs who had been burnt and scorched by hot weather: *taptā gharmā aśunavate visargaṁ.*[14] Thus the word *tapas* is used to mean: 'the heating,' 'the burning of sun and fire,' in the psychological sense, 'to give pain,' 'to make to suffer'; and 'to consume by fire and heat, evil or enemies.'

[1]*ṚV.*, II. 24. 9.
[2]*ṚV.*, VII. 34. 19.
[3]*ṚV.*, III. 53. 14.
[4]*ṚV.*, VII. 34. 19.
[5]*ṚV.*, X. 83. 3; cf. *AV.*, 4. 32. 3.
[6]*ṚV.*, VI. 5. 4.
[7]*ṚV.*, VI. 22. 5; cf. *AV.*, 20. 36. 8.
[8]*ṚV.*, III. 18. 2.
[9]*ṚV.*, VII. 59. 8; cf. *AV.*, VII. 77. 2.
[10]*ṚV.*, IV. 5. 4.
[11]*ṚV.*, X. 89. 12.
[12]*ṚV.*, VII. 15. 3.
[13]*ṚV.*, I. 112. 7.
[14]*ṚV.*, VII. 103. 9.

Tapas as heat or fervour is extended to mean heat of mind or zeal in doing things. It is said that gods befriend none except those who have been tried: *Na ṛte śrāntasya sakhyāy devāḥ.*[1] *Tapas* is the unflagging, unsparing effort in the achievement of higher things; the infinite pains one has to take to do something really worthwhile.[2] Tapas is also conceived as a mighty power lying at the beginning of all great things. Truth (*satya*) and order (*ṛta*), for example, were born at the beginning out of *abhiddha tapas.*[3] Gods and sages too performed noble things through austerities, *tapas.* Indra, for example, conquered heaven by *tapas.*[4] Agni was produced by Angirases by *tapas.*[5] Manyu, the personification of Wrath became a mighty warrior through *tapas.* He was praised to chase his enemies with *tapas.*[6]

The practice of austerities (*tapas*), was said to deliver from sins, lead to heaven and to the gods[7] and make one invincible.[8] The fathers (pitṛs), it is said, practised *tapas* when they were on the earth.[9] This suggests that the practice of *tapas* led to the reward of heaven. Some are also said to have become invincible (*anādhṛśya*) through *tapas.*[10] According to Sāyaṇa there is here a reference to *tapas* of various forms such as austerities like *Kṛchacāndrāyaṇa* whereby the ascetic is rendered invincible (*anādhṛsya*), sacrifices whereby he attains heaven, and penances of the highest order (*mahat*), that is *Rājasūya*, *Aśvamedha*, forms of *Upāsana* (Yoga) like Hiranyagarbha.[11] Sāyaṇa seems to have misunderstood the development of post-Ṛgvedic civilisation with the Ṛgvedic one. The ideas of the austerities like *Kṛchacāndrāyaṇa* are to be met with in the Dharmaśāstras. Even the sacrifices like the Rajasūya and Aśvamedha are definitely post-Ṛgvedic developments. Even the Ṛgvedic Hiraṇyagarbha is not associated with any form of Yoga (*Upāsana*) but it is a term used to indicate the Puruṣa or Prajāpati or the one 'as a Golden Germ.' Sāyaṇa has thus implied certain ideas which came

[1] *ṚV.*, VI. 33. 11; cf. *ṚV.*, VIII. 2. 18.
[2] Bose, A.C., *The Call of the Vedas*, p. 56.
[3] *ṚV.*, X. 190. 1.
[4] *ṚV.*, X. 167. 1.
[5] *ṚV.*, X. 169. 2.
[6] *ṚV.*, X. 83. 3.
[7] *ṚV.*, X. 154. 2.
[8] *ṚV.*, X. 167. 1.
[9] *ṚV.*, X. 154. 4.
[10] *ṚV.*, X. 154. 2; cf. *AV.*, 18. 2. 16.
[11] Sayana on X.154.2; cf. Radha Kumud Mookerji, *Ancient Indian Education*, p. 24.

to be associated later with *tapas*. No doubt, what exactly was the nature of *tapas* which brought about these great and mysterious results is nowhere described. *Tapas* was also at the root of the power and inspiration of the Rṣis. The great Seven Ṛṣis of the pristime age are described as absorbed in *tapas*.[1]

The power of *tapas* is further stressed when we are told in the creation hymn (*Nāsadīya Sūkta*) that *Kāma* (desire) was born out of *tapas*.[2] The *sūkta* also depicts the Primal Being as practising *tapas* before the creation of the world.[3] Griffith renders *tapas* here as fervour or penance.[4] Muir translates it as inward fervour.[5] Wilson means the contemplation of things that were to be created: *Jagat-sarjan viśayaṁ paryāloknaṁ*.[6] *Tapas*, it seems, is used here both in the senses of the fervour of austerity and reflection. However, Agrawala gives a different interpretation. *Tapas* elsewhere is known as the primeval heat (*Agraja tapas*), *Devaushṇya*, the divine heat or an incalculable explosion of energy called *Abhiddha tapas*.[7] Agrawala observes: 'The source, nature and effect of this tapas which could have existed and functioned as an infinite ocean of the waves of Prana (*Samañchana—prasāraṇa*) or Light and Heat (*Jyoti* and *Ghraṁsa*) cannot be determined. What actually happens as a result of this activity is the creation of individual centres as whirl-pools of energy which the Ṛṣi here speaks of as Ekam.'[8] This suggests that the Āryans regarded *fervour*, warmth behind the *tapas*, as the principle explaining movement, life and thought.

An interesting cosmic use of the verb *tap* is found where the axle of the world is said to get hot: *tasya nākṣastapyate*.[9] The use of *tapas* in its technical meaning of self-inflicted heat and pain, ascetical practice, giving superhuman power is suggested in: *tanvānāsta-*

[1] *ṚV.*, X. 109. 4: devā etasyāmavadanta purve saptarṣayaḥ tapase ye niṣeduḥ. *ṚV.*, X. 154. 5: ṛṣin tapasvato yama tapojāṁ api gachchatāt.

[2] *ṚV.*, X. 129. 4.

[3] *ṚV.*, X. 129. 3.

[4] Griffith, *Hymns of the Ṛgveda*, II, p. 575.

[5] Muir, *OST.*, V.

[6] cf. Griffith, op. cit., II, p. 575; cf. Sāyaṇa on *AV.*, XIX. 53. 8; cf. Panini: *Tapaḥ ālocane.*

[7] *ṚV.*, X. 190. 1; cf. Agrawala.

[8] Agrawala, '*Nasadiya Sukta*', *Bharati* '62-63, No. 6, pt. II, p. 10. He adds: 'This one also was an unknown factor called *Avyaya Purusa* or *Aja* and *Kimapisavid*, something which is beyond comprehension (*ṚV.*, I. 1. 64. 6).'

[9] *ṚV.*, I. 164. 13.

pasābhyapaśyaṁ.[1] In the tenth *maṇḍala* this seems to be the characteristic meaning of *tapas*.

Tapas is also used in the Ṛgveda to indicate devotion and its results: 'I saw thee meditating in thy spirit, what sprang from *tapas* and thence developed: '*Apaśyaṁ tvā manasā cekitānaṁ tapaso vibhutam.*[2] And in a prayer for truthful life to libation (Indu): 'Flow towards Indra, pressed with words of *ṛta* with *satya* with *śraddhā* and *tapas*: *ṛtavākena satyena śraddhayā tapasā suta Indrāyendo pari stva.*[3]

It seems that *tapas* is indirectly connected with a world-producing sacrifice in the sense of the *Puruṣa sūkta* sacrifice.[4] Sayana too has linked *tapas* more directly with sacrifices, particularly with the *dikṣā*, preparatory to the sacrifice.[5] But wherever the sacrifice (*Yajña*) is thus connected with *dikṣa* or *tapas*, it is no longer the early simple sacrifice, to win the favour of the gods; its conception comes very close and is very similar to that of the later Brāhmaṇic cosmic and magic idea of *Yajña*.

We find in the Ṛgveda the gradual development of the idea of *tapas*. From its original meaning of heat, it becomes physical heat and practise of religious austerities or penance and devotional fervour. The idea that Agni can burn enemies to ashes is close to the idea of the magical power of *tapas* in its technical sense. The psychological meaning of *tap*, 'to give pain' prepares the later meaning of 'voluntarily inflicted heat and pain' hence austerities or ascetical practices. Life, denied of comforts and pleasures, becomes austere, often painful and *tapas* eventually led to austerity or ascetic practices. The *tapas* of the five fires (*pancāgni*) is obviously connected with the physical heat given by Agni. *Tapas* is also connected with cosmic creation.

The Muni

The word Muni occurs five times in the Ṛgveda. In one of the hymns to the Māruts the course of the leader is compared with that

[1] *ṚV.*, VIII. 59. 6: Indrāvaruṇā yadṛṣibhyo maniṣaṁ vāco matiṁ śṛtamadattamagne Yāni sthānānya sṛjanta dhirā yajñaṁ tanvānāstapasābhyapaśyaṁ.

[2] *ṚV.*, X. 183. 1.

[3] *ṚV.*, IX. 113. 2.

[4] cf. *ṚV.*, VIII. 59. 6; *ṚV.*, X. 90.

[5] Sāyaṇa on *ṚV.*, X. 183. 1: Tapaso jātaṁ tapaso vibhutaṁ tapasaḥ dikṣārupādvratāt jātaṁ punṛtpannaṁ tapasaḥ anuṣṭhiyamānādyajño dvetoḥ vibhutaṁ. Also on IX. 113. 2.

of the Muni (*Muniriva*: like one inspired).[1] Here an unusual power of the Muni is celebrated. The mighty god Indra is called the friend of the Munis: *Munināṁ sakhā*.[2] In both the cases, Griffith takes the Munis as 'sages', 'saintly men' or 'ascetics' whereas Sayana takes 'Ṛṣis' for the 'Munis.' *Munināṁ sakhā*, according to him is the Ṛṣis' friend.[3] Extending the same meaning to the wind-girdled Munis, *Vātaśranā munyo* in the *Muni-sūkta* (*ṚV*., X.136.1-7), Sāyaṇa gives us a picture of the Munis as 'the sons of Vātarśana,' 'seers' and thinkers' (*mananāt muniḥ*), who can see things beyond sense-perception (*atīndriyārthadarśino*).

The chief characteristics of the Muni or the *Keśin* as described in the Muni-sūkta are:[4]

(1) He is long-haired (keśin), clad in soiled yellow (*piśangā vasate malā*), gridled with wind (*vātarśanāḥ*) and into whom the gods enter (*deveṣito*). He supports Agni and moisture, heaven and earth; he resembles the sky and the light.

(2) He proclaims: 'In the intoxication of ecstasy we are mounted on the winds. You mortals can see only our body.'

(3) He flies through the air and is a friend of the gods.

(4) He is steed of the wind (*vāta*), the friend of *vāyu*, impelled by the gods (*deveṣito*) he inhabits the two seas, that of the rising and that of the setting sun.

(5) He travels by the path of the Apsarases, the Gandharvas and wild beasts and he knows thoughts or secret desires.

(6) He drinks with Rudra from the cup of poison.

In the verses 1, 6 and 7 the word *Keśin* is used and the *Muni* is used in the verses 2, 3 (*mauneya*), 4 and 5. From the description, the first impression we gather is that the Muni is not an ordinary mortal. The qualities of treading the aerial path and filling the two worlds with golden lustre, helping the rain-god Indra can easily belong to the sun-god. Thus is the verses 1, 4 and 5 where the word *Keśin* is used, Sāyaṇa thinks that the deity glorified is either the Sun or Wind or Fire or all the three together.

Mauna is abstinence from speech. It is regarded as helpful for meditation. *Mauna* itself is a kind of austerity. The Muni

[1] *ṚV*., VII. 56. 8: śubhro vaḥ śuṣmaḥ krudhmī manāmsi dhunir muniriva śardhasya dhuṛṣnoḥ cf. *Unādi-sūtra*, IV. 122 fr. *man* impulse, eagerness. Any one who is moved by inward impulse, an inspired or ecstatic person, enthusiast.

[2] *ṚV*., VIII. 17. 14.

[3] cf. Griffith, op. cit., p. 142, also f.n.

is described as maddened with silence (*unmaditā mauneya*). There is a suggestion here that silence (*mauneya*) and solitude are conducive to ecstasy and concentration (*ekāgratā*). The fact that the Muni is solitary is indicated by Sāyaṇa when he explains the Muni's ecstasy as *laukikasarvavyahar visarjanen unmaditāḥ.*[1] The Muni is in an abnormal state of suspended consciousness or ecstatic trance.[2] In that state he behaves like a madman.[3] This agrees with the fact that Aitaśa Muni of the Aitareya Brāhmaṇa is regarded by his son as deranged and his speech as *Aitaśapralāp.*[4] It is significant that even Sāyaṇa links the *Keśin* walking on the paths of Apsaras and Gāṅdharvas with Ṛṣi Etaśa.[5]

The ecstasy of the silent Muni seems to have heightened owing to his drinking with Rudra, a potent draught from a magic cup which is poison to ordinary mortals. Probably the use of some poison or narcotic drink to produce exhilaration or hypnosis is suggested here. To the hypnotic effect of drinking *Soma* by the gods and men, there are many references in the Ṛgveda. One hymn describes those inabriated with the drink thus: 'We have drunk *Soma*, we have become immortal, we have entered into light, we have known the gods.'[6] Thus possessed they regarded themselves as being into whom the gods had entered. In an ecstatic trance, the Muni is said to be in the state of divine possession or impelled by the gods (*deveṣito*). So inspired, he is believed to possess extraordinary powers of being uplifted, above the world and attaining to communion with the gods. Roth observes: 'The hymns show the conception that by a life of sanctity (*mauneya*) the Muni can attain to the fellowship of the deities of the air, the Vāyus, the Rudras, the Apsarasas and the Gāṅdharvas; and furnished like them with wonderful powers, can travel along with them on their course.'[7] Thus we see in the Muni a case of the effort to obtain religious

[1]Sayana's comment on *ṚV.*, X. 136. 3.

[2]Ecstasy connotes: *pramādaḥ, unmādaḥ, madaḥ, praharṣaḥ, moha, saṁmoha, āṅanda, harṣonmattatā, romaharṣaḥ, atyantāhldaḥ=DSE.* (MW), p. 217.

[3]Sayana's comment: *Unmaditā*=unmattā unmattāvadacarantaḥ yad vā utkṛṣṭaṁ madaṁ harṣaṁ prāptāḥ.

[4]*Ait. Brah.*, VI. 33. 3.

[5]Sāyaṇa on *ṚV.*, X. 136. 5: Yadvā jñatavyāsyasyaṣeretaśasya sakhā svādayitā rasayitā.

[6]*ṚV.*, VIII. 48.

[7]Q. b. Muir, *OST.*, IV, p. 319.

exaltation through ecstatic practices which seem to endow him with certain magical powers.

The Muni is described as having long hair (*Keśin*), wearing the yellow (*piśaṅgā*), dirty (*malā*), garments (*vasate*). Sāyaṇa suggests vestments of bark (*vasate*: *valkalrupāṇi*). The dirt (*malā*) of both person and garments of the Muni suggests his being engaged in some sort of austerities (*tapas*). What exactly was the nature of *tapas* is not described. It was probably some method which produced bodily heat and made the body refulgent. The poetic description that the Muni resembled the sky and the light and filled the two worlds with golden lustre may be interpreted that he was engaged in *tapas*. Sāyaṇa's view that the Munis, by the might of their penance (*tapas*) become gods is significant.[1] This also suggests that they devoted themselves to austerities (*tapas*).

Roth also holds the view that the Muni is engaged in *tapas*. He explains why he is called the Kesin and why he should resemble Surya, Agni or Vayu. He is long-haired (*Kesin*) because, according to him, he does not shave his hair during the time of his austerities and upholds fire, moisture, heaven and earth and thus resembles the world of light.[2] We come across many such ideas in later literature.

The Muni is regarded as traversing the path of the Apsarasas, the Gandharvas and the beasts of the wild forests. He is regarded as dwelling in the eastern and western oceans. This power of the Muni to roam at will in different regions and paths may be the root of the later notion prevalent that the Yogin developes supernormal powers which generate the faculty of untrammelled movement at will. But as already discussed, even *Shamans* or medicine men in primitive cultures possessed such magical powers.[3] The Muni's powers seem to reflect the impact of the pre-Āryan magical practices of the *Shaman* or the medicine man.

About the Ṛgvedic Munis, Schweitzer observes:

'In these hymns (*mūni-sūkta*) we encounter men who know they are uplifted above this world. They are the *Shamanas* and medicine men—later called, Yogins—who get themselves into a state of ecstasy through drinking the intoxicating Soma, through mortifica-

[1]Sāyaṇa on *ṚV*., X. 136. 2: Yadā devāsaḥ devāḥ tapaso mahimnā dipyamānāḥ santaḥ avikṣata devtāsvarupaṁ prāviṣan.

[2]Muir, *OST*., IV. p. 319.

[3]cf. Chapter 3.

tion of the flesh and by self-hypnosis. Thus possessed, they regard themselves as beings into whom the gods have entered, and believe themselves in possession of super-natural powers . . . . They regard this state of being uplifted above the world as something that only came under consideration for themselves because they possessed the capacity of attaining to community with the gods.'[1]

Some scholars like Belvalkar and Ranade also consider the Muni to be the prototype of the Yogi.[2] Sampurṇanand is of the view that the *Mūni-sūkta* refers to 'Yogis in general and not to any one specific group of individuals (the *vātarśaṇās*).' He writes: 'If Sāyaṇa's interpretation that Keśin refers to Sūrya, Agni and Vāyu is accepted, then the Yogis are called Keśins because of their identification with Vāyu through their practice of Prāṇāyama. . . . It is, therefore, quite conceivable that in these *mantras* the Yogis are referred to as Keśins namely Jatādharis.'[3] Eliade sees in the Muni 'an ecstatic who only vaguely resembles the Yogin, the chief similarity being his ability to fly through the air—but this *siddhi* is a magical power that is found everywhere.'[4] He points out that only the rudiments of classic Yoga are to be found in the Vedas. The ascetic disciplines and ecstatic ideologies which these ancient texts refer to, are not always related to Yoga, properly speaking, though they have found a place in the Yogic tradition.[5] *Prāṇāyama* is an important purificatory process in the Yoga system but it is difficult to determine how early in the Vedic culture Yogic technique was known and practised.

We are thus led to conclude that the Muni was an ascetic, though the word *tapas* does not occur in the *sūkta*. He had acquired magical powers (*siddhis*) very similar to the primitive medicine man, the *shaman*. His figure seems to have inspired many *vānaprasthas* and *saṁnyāsis* of later times who practised severe austerities and lived a life of self-mortification and self-abnegation. Even his long hair and soiled yellow garments became typical of ascetics in the full-fledged system of the four *āśramas*. The dirt of his person in later times seems to have developed in a practice of besmearing the body with the ashes. Many an ascetic, like the Keśin, grew matted hair

[1]Schweitzer, *Indian Thought And Its Development*, p. 22.
[2]Belvalkar & Ranade, *HIP*., p. 405.
[3]In his letter of March 24, 1963 to the writer.
[4]Eliade, *Yoga: Immortality and Freedom*, pp. 102-103.
[5]ibid.

and came to be known as *Jatādhāris*. Even Śiva as a Mahāyogi is a *jatādhāri* and Rudra, a Kapardine or Dhurjati. Their *upāsaks* kept long hair (*jatā*) and many sādhus still keep the *jatā*. The yellow robe through the centuries became the commonest symbol of the austere life in India.

The Yajurveda

The Yajurveda represents the sacrificial literature proper as we find in it the exceeding growth of ritualism and an immense development in the various branches of the sacrifice. The main object namely the appeasement of the gods by prayers and minor rites was gradually lost sight of and a more mechanical form of religion based on complicated and elaborate ritualism developed. The sacrifice was no longer an offering to the gods as free personal beings but something that had power in itself. It regulated mechanically the relation of man with them which was controlled and guided by the art of the Brahmin priests, and their wonderful insight into the meaning of all the technical acts. As a result, the priestly class whose monopoly was to perform rites and rituals rose steadily in power and prestige. We find stray references to *tapas* where it means heat, energy, exhaustion and pain.[1]

The Sāmaveda

In this Veda, the hymns taken from the Ṛgveda were set to music for use at the sacrifices. Here too the ritualistic forms assumed importance. Hence the very purpose of its subject-matter like the Yajurveda almost precluded any scope to ascetic practices (*tapas*).

The Atharvaveda

The Atharvaveda is a collection of charms and incantations. It was originally called not the Veda but Atharva-Angiras and was not included in the canon of sacred books till about 300 BC. The Ṛg., Yajur and Sāmaveda were an expression of the buoyant spirit of the Āryans whereas in the Atharvaveda we find a dread of evil spirits and their magical powers. The spells and incantations were designed to accompany magic rites to gain freedom from various diseases and relief from pain and for the attainment of almost every

[1] *TS.*, I. 18, V. 6, XII. 15; XIV. 23, XV. 57; *VS.*, XV. 57, XXX. 6. 12; *KS.*, XXXV, 4.

conceivable and of human life. Ritual, sacrifice and prayer were regarded as themselves powers alongside the gods and spirits. They had ceased to be the means whereby the worshipper was brought into touch with the gods with the result that the gods tended to fall more and more into the background. The Atharvaveda thus reflects the practises of the lower side of religious life and is closer to the common people than the priestly atmosphere of the Ṛgveda. It is the religion of the masses that one meets with throughout.

Tapas

We come across *tapas* used in the original sense of heat or fervour. There is a reference to the heat of the sun: *udgādayatāditryo viṣven tapasā saha.*[1] Sacrifice is said to have been wrought by power of Brahma (*Brāhmaṇo*) and the gods are prayed to assist with fervour (*tapsā*).[2] The people who have originated from thy (the sun's) *tapas* are described as following the calf, the Gāyatri.[3]

Those who practised great austerity (*tapo ye cakrire mahastānśi*) and having become invincible through religious fervour (*tapasā ye anādhṛṣyāḥ*) are said to reach heaven through penances (*tapasā ye svaryayuḥ devāpi gacchatāt*).[4] Ṛṣis austere, practising austerities (*Ṛṣintapasvato*) are said to be born through penance (*tapojāṁ*).[5] Religious austerities are meant here. In the earlier usage, Kill him with Your hottest bolt (*tapiṣṭhena haṅmanā*)[6] is substituted austerity, penance: *tapiṣṭhena tapasā.*[7] The change indicates an increasing magical power of *tapas*.

Tapas is also used in cosmogonic hymns where it may suggest the creative heat or fervour that is symbolised by brooding over eggs.[8] But in religious language, *tapas* means religious or devotional fervour, the inspiration of the ṛṣi and thus related to *brahman*, the holy word: *tadbrahma ca tapasca saptaṛṣaya upjīvanti.*[9] *Tapas* may have had a partly physical connotation. The sacrificial ritual itself,

[1]*AV.*, XVII. 1. 24.

[2]*AV.*, XIX. 72: Kṛtamiṣtam brahmaṇo viryena tena ya devā tapasāvateha.

[3]*AV.*, XIII. 1. 10: Yāste viśastapasaḥ sambabhūvūḥ vatsaṁ Gāyatrimanu tāihāguḥ.

[4]*AV.*, XVIII. 2. 16; cf. *TA.*, VI. 3. 2.

[5]*AV.*, XVIII. 2. 15-18; cf. XI. 1. 26: ṛṣinārṣeyāṁs tapso-adhijātā.

[6]*ṚV.*, VII. 59. 8.

[7]*AV.*, VII. 77. 2; cf. *TS.*, IV. 3. 13. 3.

[8]*AV.*, X. 7. 1; XI. 8. 2 and 6.

[9]*AV.*, VIII. 10. 25.

performed over the sacred fire was 'heating' to the officiants. For these reasons, *tapas* occurs as a cosmic force. Occasionally it is a First Principle itself but more often the creator exercises *tapas* in making the world. In prayers to time (*kāla*) personified as a primordial power, *tapas* is associated: *kāle tapaḥ kāle jyeṣṭham*,[1] and *brahma tapo diśaḥ*.[2]

The Atharvaveda speaks of the earth as upheld by Dharman—'eternal Law.'[3] *Tapas* is described, together with *satya*, *ṛta*, *dikṣā*, *brahma* and *yajña*, as upholding the earth (*pṛthiviṁ dhārayanti*).[4] *Tapas* is also described as the leavings of the sacrifice (*uchhiṣta*) together with *ṛta*, *satya*, *rāśtrā*, *śrama*, *dharma* and *karma*.[5] Those versed in Brahma (*Brahmavido*), it is said, go with *tapas* and *dikṣā*.[6]

The word *tapas* in the Atharvaveda is mentioned in connection with the Brahmacāri. Earlier, he was described as a member of the god's own body (*devānāṁ avaiyekamangaṁ*), through whom Bṛhaspati obtained his consort (*tena jāyāmanvavidaṁ Bṛhaspatiḥ*).[7] Basically, he is one who possesses *Brahma*, the cosmic power, the one from whom Brahmā originates (*tasmad jātāṁ brāhmaṇaṁ brahma jyeṣṭham*).[8] The Brahmacāri moves about stirring both hemispheres: in him the gods become of equal mind, he supports heaven and earth and fills his teacher with *tapas*.[9] Thus the essentially cosmic—magical function of the Brahmacari seems evident: the heat or fervour of his *tapas* is creative of the cosmic power, *Brahma*, by which the gods and world are produced, upheld and protected. The Brahmacārī practices are so necessary that even an *Ācarya* cannot do without them if he wants to find a true Brahmacari disciple.[10]

On the other hand, a teacher is indispensable to the Brahmacāri who at the time of initiation ceremony (*upanayan*) is made to enter

[1]*AV*., XIX. 53. 8.
[2]*AV*., XIX. 54. 1.
[3]*AV*., XII. 1. 17; cf. *Mbh*., VIII. 69. 59: pṛthiviṁ dhārayeti dharmaḥ.
[4]*AV*., XII. 1. 1.
[5]*AV*., XI. 7. 17 *Śrama* is rendered as asceticism by Bloomfield, *Hymns of the Atharvaveda*.
[6]*AV*., XIX. 43. 1.
[7]*ṚV*., X. 109. 5: Brahmacari carati; cf. *AV*., XI. 5 (7) 1.
[8]*AV*., XI. 5. 5; Shende, *The Foundation of the Atharvanic Religion*, p. 110.
[9]*AV*., XI. 5 (7) 1.
[10]ibid.

as it were the womb of the teacher.[1] The Brahmacāri stays with the teacher apparently for a long time (he grows a beard); he dresses in the skin of a black antelope; a girdle (*mekhalā*) described as the daughter of faith (*śraddhāyā duhitā*) and born of spiritual fervour (*tapaso adhijātā*),[2] firewood and toil (*pariśrama*) are the symbols of the means, by which he fills the world with *tapas*. *Mekhalā* could well stand for a symbol of ritual continence as also the Brahmacāri is without wife.[3] We are reminded here of Agastya who practised *tapas* while living a pious life of a householder: *ubhau varṇau pupoṣa*.[4] It is by means of *tapas*—connected with *upanayana* ceremony—that the Brahmacāri wants to master *Brahma*, the cosmic power. For it is due to Brahmacāryaṁ, the *ascetical-magical* power over Brahma, that the world-order is established, that the king protects his kingdom, that a girl obtains a husband, a horse gets fodder, the gods get immortality and Indra becomes the king of the gods.[5] *Brahmacarya* is thus assimilated by *tapas*. *Brahmacāryaṁ* as a stage of life, an *āśrama*, though not yet legally or traditionally imposed, seems to have been already accepted by society.

The words *tapasvin* and *tapasvi* denoting the ascetic are to be found[6] though according to Keith, *tāpasa* (ascetic) is not found in the Vedic literature till the *Bṛhadārāṇyaka Upaniṣad*.[7] All the three words are identical in meaning and denotes one who practised austerities (*tapas*).

Brāhmṇas

The Brāhmaṇas are an inexhaustible mine for the history of sacrifice, religious practices and the institutions of priesthood.[8] The idea that the sacrifice nourished the gods[9] assumed great importance now and almost grotesque proportion. The creative activity of

[1]*AV.*, XI-5 (7) 3.
[2]*AV.*, VI. 133. 4.
[3]cf. *ṚV.*, X-109. 5.
[4]*ṚV.*, I. 179. 6.
[5]*AV.*, XI. 5. 7. 17-19. On *AV.*, XI. 5, Zaehner comments: 'In the Brahmacārin hymn the identification of the microcosm and macrocosm is complete... the identification of microcosmic man not only with the universe but with the creator of the universe had already reached its extreme limit.'—*Hinduism*, p. 63.
[6]*AV.*, XIII. 2. 25.
[7]*Vedic Index*, I, p. 307.
[8]Bloomfield, *Religion of the Vedas*, p. 45.
[9]*ṚV.*, I.181, 1; III.20.1, 35.9; IV.24.6; VIII.18.19.

Prajāpati was represented as exhausting him so much that his power required to be continually renewed partly by his own exertion, austerity (*tapas*) and partly by the food of the sacrifice.[1] Stories are related as to how the gods and the *asuras* competed for world-power and how the gods only won through the correct knowledge of the sacrifice.[2] If anything went wrong not only the sacrifice was useless but it was also believed that misfortune would attend the offerer. Hence the Brāhmiṇ specialist who could do it was in great demand. On his part, he strove to make the rites more and more intricate and indispensable. The over-emphasis on sacrifice reduced religion to an artificial, mechanical and stereotyped form. The sacrifice became greater than the gods and the priests who manipulated the sacrifice greater than all. The Brahmins rose to such an exalted position that they came to be known as veritable 'gods on earth (*bhūmideva*). The Aitareya Brāhmaṇa explains the position of the priest in unmistakable terms.[3] As a result, the Brāhmaṇic religion became unintelligible and uninspiring to the illiterate masses and quite extravagant and meaningless to the literate. The masses found the bloody sacrifices of innocent animals quite shocking. The result was a general unrest and discontent with the Brāhmanic cult.

Tapas

There was not much scope for reference to austerities, *tapas* in Brāhmana literature which is concerned almost entirely with the order and interpretation of the sacrifice, with cosmology and mythology. The practice of *tapas*, however, was recognised and enjoined. Its significance is illustrated firstly by its reference to the divinities. It is said that the gods became divine through the practice of *tapas*.[4] By means of *tapas* the Ribhus obtained the right to a share in the *soma* drink.[5] It is said that the gods conquered the heavenly world through sacrifice (*Yajñena*), austerities, penances, (*śrameṇa*) (*tapasā*) and sacrificial oblations (*āhutibhihiḥ*).[6] The

[1]*Tandya Br.*, IV.10.1.

[2]*KS.*, XXII.9; *TS.*, V.33; *Tandya Br.*, XVIII.1.2.

[3]*AB.*, VIII.24.25; also *SB.*, II.2.2.6, II.4.3.14.

[4]*TB.*, III.12.13.1.

[5]*AB.*, III.30. arbhavaṁ saṁsatybhavo vai deveṣu tapasā somapīthamabhyajayamstebhyaḥ prāptaḥ.

[6]ibid., II.13: Devā vai yajñena śrameṇa tapasāhutibhihiḥ svargaṁ lokamajayam.

divine ṛṣis are said to be born from *tapas*.[1] Prior to each act of creation, Prajāpati was believed to have practised *tapas*. On one occasion, it is said that he practised such *ugraṁ tapas* that the lights, stars came forth from all the pores of his body.[2] He produced the world through *tapas*.[3] Elsewhere, Prajāpati, we are told, created the world by 'heating' himself to an extreme degree through *tapas*[4]—that is he created it by a sort of magical sweating. For Brāhmaṇic speculation, *Prajāpati* was himself the product of *tapas*; in the beginning (*agre*) non-being (*asat*) became mind (*manas*) and heated itself (*atapyata*), giving birth to smoke, light, fire and finally to *Prajāpati*.[5] *Tapas* thus came to be regarded of great value and power; the gods and even Brahma performed it. It is enjoined that 'we must do what the gods did in the beginning.'[6]

The Taittiriya Brāhmaṇa illustrates the great virtue of Brahmacarya in the sense of studying the Veda with due self-control. The decayed and old Bhāradvāja, when asked by Indra, how he would use another life if granted, said he would use it in practising *brahmacarya*.[7] The Gopatha-Brāhmana extols a *Brahmacārin* who goes to a hermitage, where Munis like Vasiṣṭha, Vāmadeva and Jāmadagni practised rigid austerities (*tapas*), like standing in water for a thousand years and observing strict celibacy (*brahmacarya*).[8] Here the word '*āśrama*' occurs in the sense of a hermitage and hence the ṛṣis seem to be hermits or *vānaprasthas*. *Brahmacarya* has acquired a significant place in a life of *tapas*.

In the Aitareya Brāhmaṇa we come across a passage in which sage Nārada tells the childless King Harischandra: 'What is the use of smearing this body with ashes (*mala*)? Why don the deer skin (*Ajina*)? Why grow matted hair (*śamśru*)? Why practise penances (*tapas*)? O, Brāhmaṇas, pray for sons.'[9] Sāyaṇa takes *mala* for

[1] *AB.*, II.27: ṛṣyo daivyāsastanupāvānastanvastapojā upa māṁṛṣyo daivyāso vhayatāṁ.

[2] *SB.*, X.4.4.2.

[3] ibid., XI.5.8.1.

[4] *AB.*, V.32.1: Prajapatirakāmayat prajayeya bhuyan tasyāmiti sa tapo' tapyata sa tapastaptavemāṁ lokanasṛjata.

[5] *TB.*, II.2.9, 1-10; *SB.*, XI.1.6.1; *SB.*, VI.7.4.9: *Devānāṁ vai ridham anu manuṣyāḥ.*

[6] *SB.*, VII.2.1.4, III.2.1; cf. *TB.*, I.5.9.4: *tad vā etad briyate yad deva akurvan.*

[7] *TB.*, III.10.11.3.

[8] *GB.*, I.2.7.

[9] *AB.*, XXXIII.11: *kimu mālaṁ kiṁ ajinaṁ kimu smaśruṇi kiṁ tapaḥ putraṁ brāhmaṇā icchadvaṁ.*

grihasthāśrama ajina for *brahmacarya* and *smaśru* and *tapas* for the last *āśramas*.[1] This does not seem satisfactory. What was the use of denouncing *mala* and wishing for a son? The incongruity would be removed if all the four epithets are applied to the last *āśrama* of *Saṁnyāsa*. *Mala* then will be dirt accumulated on the body of an ascetic like the *Ṛgvedic Muni*,[2] *ajina* the hide of a deer for the ascetic to squat on, his hair and beard grown (*śmaśru*), and practising penance (*tapas*). The age of the *Saṁhitās* and *Brāhmaṇas* held that the sacrifices should be continually performed till death. To give them up in favour of austerities (*tapas*) and renunciation (*saṁnyāsa*) would not have appealed to the society. *Yajña* was the best karma and the ideal was heaven. It was still believed that the gates of heaven were barred against the one who had no son.[3]

Āraṇyakas

As the name Āraṇyaka (*arayṇe avyetavyaṁ āraṇyakaṁ*) suggests the Āraṇyakas were the works to be read in the forest in opposition to the Brāhmaṇas which were to be read in the villages. According to Sāyaṇa, they were intended for persons who had retired from the busy scenes of every day life and adopted the condition of *vānaprastha*: 'From the circumstances of their being read in the forest these works are called Āraṇyakas. It is obtained that they should be read in the forests and none should hear them who is not duly qualified.'[4] As against the external show and formal sacrifices and the elaborate rituals of the Brāhmaṇas, the Āraṇyakas deal with the efficacy of the inner or mental sacrifice and helped the bridge between the Brahmaṇas and the Upaniṣads. The Āraṇyakas thus form a natural transition to the speculation of the Upaniṣads. As a matter of fact some of the oldest Upaniṣads are included in the Āraṇyaka-texts.[5] The Saṁhitās and the Brāhmaṇas are called the *Karma-kāṇda* whereas the Āraṇyakas and the Upaniṣads are called the *Jñāna-Kaṇda*.[6] Some people include the Āraṇya-

[1]Kane holds the same view. *HDS*., II. pt. I, p. 420.
[2]cf. *ṚV*., X.136.2: *munyo vātaraśanāḥ piśaṅgā vasate malā*.
[3]*AB*., IV. 3, 4, 3.
[4]Sayana's commentary on the *Taittiriyaraṇyaka*: araṇyādhyayanādetadāraṇyakamitiryate araṇye taddhiyitetavyaṁ vākyaṁ pracakşyate etadāraṇyakaṁ sarvaṁ nāvrati śrotumarhati.
[5]cf. Radhakrishnan, S. *IP*., I. p. 47.
[6]Sharma, *A Critical Survey of Indian Philosophy*, pp. 13-14.

kas in the *Karma-kāṅda* but really speaking, they represent a transition from *Karma-kāṇḍa* to the *Jñāna-kaṇḍa.*[1]

In the Taittirīya Āraṇyaka, Prajāpati is declared to have practised penance (*tapas*) and performed a kind of self-sacrifice. The sacrifice consisted in shaking his body after the practice of *tapas.* The consequence is described to have been as follows: 'From Prajāpati's flesh arose three kinds of Ṛṣis. They are Aruṇas, Ketus, and Vātaraśanas. From his nails arose Vaikhānasas; and from his hair Vālakhilyas.'[2] Sāyaṇa describes the Vātaraśamas as *Śramaṇas* and *Urdhvamanthis.*[3]

The fact that in the Taittirīya Āraṇyaka, *Vātaraśana* Ṛṣis are said to have existed in former times whom Sāyaṇa calls *Śramaṇas* is significant. The term *śramaṇa* means 'one who was toiling.' It should be noted that even in the Bṛhadāraṇyaka, Upaniṣad which cannot be much later than the Taittirīya Āraṇyaka, the terms '*śramaṇa*' and '*tāpasa*' occur in one passage. The passage describes the nature of the high stage of perfection. It is a stage in which a thief becomes a non-thief (*steno'steno bhavati*), a cāṇḍāla a non-cāṇḍāl, a śramaṇa a non-śramaṇa, a tāpasa a non-tāpasa and so on.[4]

Sāyaṇa explains the term '*śramaṇa*' in the above passage to mean *parivrājaka*, ascetic, *saṁnyāsi*, that is one who is in the last *āśrama.* He takes the term *tāpasa*, that is one who practises austerities (*tapas*) to stand for *vānaprastha*, the third of the four *āśramas.* When the full theory of the four *āśramas* came to be developed, *tapas* came to be prescribed for a person in the third *āśrama*, though he was called a *vānaprastha.* A distinction was made between forcible constraint of passions (*tapas*) and spiritual renunciation (*nyāsa*). *Tapas* was for the *vānaprastha* who was in the lower stage and *nyāsa* for the *saṁnyāsin.*[5] In later Upaniṣads where the *āśrama*

[1]Sharma, *A Critical Survey of Indian Philosophy*, pp. 13-14.

[2]*TA.*, I.23.2.

[3]*TA.*, II.7.1. Accepting the interpretation of Sāyaṇa in *ṚV.*, X.136.2, Ghurye argues that 'in the Ṛgvedic times there were not only ascetics who were known as '*munis*' but also others who went about naked, exhibiting their great Yogic achievements of keeping the penis in tumescent condition without feeling and showing any excitement.' *Indian Sadhus*, pp. 12 ff. The expression *vātaraśana* is rendered by some scholars to mean naked, 'one having only the wind or air for his waist-girdle.' Dutt, *EBM*, p. 9 f.n., Ghurye, op. cit., p. 12. But if the Ṛgvedic Muni was naked, he cannot be called *piśangā vasate malā.*

[4]*Bṛhad. Up.*, IV.3.22.

[5]Radhakrishnan, S., *Philosophy of the Upaniṣads*, p. 91. *Nyāsa* means mentally invoking God, and holy texts to come to occupy certain parts of the body

theory is given, the term *śramaṇa* is conspicuous by its absence. After the Buddha, it came to be monopolised by the Buddhists so that the compound expression *Śramaṇa-Brāhmaṇa* came to denote the two opposing religious systems of the Buddhists and the Brāhmins.[1]

The passage in Taittirīya Āraṇyaka, however, makes it clear that the *vaikhānasas* were *ṛṣis*. In the *vaikhānasa sāman* they are said to be *ṛṣis*, dear to Indra.[2] A certain Rahasyu *Devamalimluc* killed them at a place called 'Muni's death' (*muni-maraṇa*).[3] Thereafter, Indra revived them by a *sāman*, when the gods had asked him about the whereabouts of the *Vaikhānasas*. Indra called Rahasyu and asked him as to who had killed the *Vaikhānasas?* When Rahasyu replied that he did, Indra replied that by doing so he had killed Brahmins.[4] Thus it seems that *vaikhānasas* were *tāpasi ṛṣis* of the established Brāhmanic society who practised austerities with a view to subdue physical senses and joining *tapas* to the offering of sacrifices. Probably they used to live somewhat away from the centres of Brāhmanic community in the forests, where a group of them was killed. Their tradition was, however, revived by the Brāhmaṇic society. Later references to the reputed author of a Vaikhānasa-sūtra,[5] dealing with the rules of forest-dwellers suggest that relatively early, the Brāhmanic society had come to accept the ideal of a way of life of penance and offering of sacrifices in the forest. The *vaikhānasas* may be called the predecessors of the *vānaprastha*.[6]

The *Āruṇaketuka-vrata* is prescribed for the first time. The *Ṛṣis*,

to render it a pure and fit receptacle for worship and contemplation. Kane, *HDS.*, II, Pt. I, p. 319.

[1]cf. *Aśtādhyāyi*, II.4.12.2: śramanbrāhmaṇaḥ yeşāṁ virodhaḥ sāśvatikaḥ.

[2]*Tandya Br.*, XIV.4.6-7.

[3]*Pancavmsa. Br.*, XIV.4.7.

[4]*Jaimini. Br.*, III.190.

[5]cf. *Manu*, VI.21 mentions it.

[6]*Baudh. DS.* (II.6.18) identifies them: *Vaikhānas'opi vānaprastha eva:* Also II. 11.14. Kalidas in the *Śakuntala* speaks of the life led by the charming Śakuntalā in Kaṇva's hermitage as *vaikhānasa-vrata* (I.27) *Bṛhat-Parasara* (Chapter XI. p. 290) speaks of four divisions of *vanaprasthas*: *vaikhānasa, udumbara, vālakhilya* and *vanevāsi*. The *Vaikhānasasmārtasūtra* (VIII.7) says that the *vānaprasthas* are either *sapatnika* or *apatnika* and the first are of four kinds: *Audumbara, Vairiñca, Vālakhilya* and *Phenapa*. The *apatnika* hermits are of innumerable kinds; they have no names but are referred to in accordance with their ascetic practices those who live like pigeons, those who eat only what has been dried by the sun, etc. (VIII.8).

it is laid down, should live on water or every day eat whatever is obtained by begging—should worship Agni; they should not have any possession; they should live in forest; wear the '*Kśauma*' garment, either yellow or white and carry on the pursuit of knowledge.[1] Similarly, a *tapasvi*, says the text, should learn knowledge of the Brahman (*svādhyaya*) in forest, whether he be talking, standing, walking or sleeping.[2] These men seem to be *vānaprasthas*.

According to the Sāṅkhyāyana Āraṇyaka, a man should perform the Brahman sacrifice in his body, which is purified by renunciation and should constantly brood on the Ātman, by means of *tapas*, *brahmacarya* and fasting.[3] The practice of *tapas*, it is said, will enable him to be indifferent to desire and the Brahman sacrifice will drive death away.[4] The Āraṇyaka also explains the allegorical speculations of the ritual and the efficacy of the inner or mental sacrifice.[5] Breathing exercises are more and more emphasised. It is said that he who chants the *Gāyatra-strotra* should not breathe.[6] The idea of *upāsanā* or internal worship to gain *Brahmavidyā* has developed. *Tapas* is now connected with meditative worship.

Thus we see in the Āraṇyakas the order of hermits or anchorites later called the *vānaparsthas* who devoted themselves to sacred practices which had three aspects: *sacrifice*, *tapas* and *meditation.* Sacrifice was no longer an external show but an inward exercise in which the meanings of the mantras were meditated upon. The idea of *tapas* as both physical and mental training to attain *Brahmavidyā* had come to be recognised. Some of the thinkers took to secluded forest-life, reflecting over the ultimate problems of life.

Upaniṣads

The word '*Upaniṣad*' is derived from *upa* (near)+*ni* (down)+ *sad* (to sit) i.e. sitting down near.[7] Groups of people used to sit near the teacher to learn from him the philosophical doctrine. In the sylvan solitude of hermitages the Upaniṣad thinkers pondered on the problems of the deepest concern and imparted their

[1] *TA.*, I.32.
[2] ibid, II.12.
[3] *SA.*, XV.1.
[4] ibid, XIII f.
[5] ibid, V.5-8, X.1-8.
[6] *Jaimm. Br.*, III.3.1; *Kau. Br.*, XXIII.5.
[7] Radhakrishnan, S., *PU*, Introduction p. 19.

knowledge to fit disciples near them. By its very nature, this knowledge was a secret, *rahasyaṁ*, to be communicated only to the tested few. In the words of the Upaniṣads it was *guhya ādeśaḥ*[1] and *paramaṁ guhyaṁ*.[2] Thus 'Upaniṣad' meant the secret doctrine taught by the teacher to his worthy pupils.

Śankarācārya derived the word *Upaniṣad* from the root *sad* (to loosen, to destroy) with *upa* and *ni* as prefixes.[3] He interpreted it to mean 'that which destroyed all ignorance and led one to Brahman.' The word 'Upaniṣad' has since come to be accepted as brahma-knowledge by which ignorance, which is the root-cause of worldly existence, is loosened or destroyed. It was the qualified *ācārya*[4] who imparted to his disciple, sitting devotedly near him or at such private sessions, the secret instruction which dispelled all ignorance of the pupil and helped him in self-realisation. Towards this end, the Vedānta prescribed a long training which was threefold: *śravana*, *manana* and *nididhyāsanā*.[5]

The Upaniṣads are the utterances of spiritually minded people who obtained glimpses of the highest truths by earnest meditation. They belong not to a single thinker but to the seers of a whole age. This is one reason why some scholars think they do not present a coherent or consistent system of philosophy. According to them it is difficult to say definitely what the teachings of the Upaniṣads as a whole are.[6] However, Radhakrishnan points out that different aspects of the Upaniṣadic doctrines are not exclusive of each other and they can give us a single coherent view.[7]

There cannot be disagreement on one point that the Upaniṣads are in the main, concerned with the knowledge of the spirit, the inner being, the spiritual life that leads to eternal peace and immortality. In other words, spiritual knowledge is the subject-matter of the Upaniṣads. By spiritual knowledge, they mean the attainment of salvation through the doctrine of the Brahman-

[1]*Chand. Up.*, III.52.

[2]*Katha. Up.*, I.3.17. cf. *Sveta. Up.*, VI.22: *Vedante paramaṁ guhyaṁ*.

[3]Introduction to the *Katha. Up*. In his commentary on *TU.*, he says: *upanisannaṁ vā asyāṁ paraṁ śreya iti.*

[4]He was to be *Brahmaniṣṭha* according to *Mund. Up.*, I. ii.12.

[5]*Bṛihad. Up.*, II.4.5: ātma vā are draṣṭavyaḥ śrotavyo mantavyo nididhyāsitvyaḥ.

[6]Majumdar, R.C., *The Cultural Heritage of India*, IV, p. 33; Hiriyana, *OIP.*, p. 19; Dasgupta, *Hindu Mysticism*, p. 29; Zaehner, *Hinduism*, p. 97.

[7]Radhakrishnan, S., op. cit., pp. 137ff.

Ātman. The pathway leading to this knowledge has come to be accepted as the *Jñāna-Mārga*.

Emphasis on Jñāna

The word *Jñāna* is used in our religious literature in two different senses—a lower sense and a higher sense. In the lower sense it means only intellectual knowledge of religion and philosophy learnt from books or teachers. In the higher sense, it means the direct realisation of God through one's own personal experience. The Upaniṣads in many places point out the difference between a man of intellectual knowledge and a man of spiritual realisation. Though they regard the knowledge of scriptures necessary, they emphatically declare that the knowledge of scriptures is not the knowledge of God.

The Chāndogya Upaniṣad narrates the story of Narada to illustrate this supreme truth. Nārada approaches Sanatkumara and tells him that he knows all the scriptures and all the sciences and arts of his time, but has no knowledge of the self. The pointed statement put into his mouth is: I know only the *mantras* but not the Self—*mantravideva asmi na ātmavit.*[1] It is not the knowledge of scriptures but the realisation of the Self that brings liberation to the spirit of man. This is the true perspective which the Upaniṣads expect, rather demand from a seeker in his quest for knowledge. The higher knowledge by which Brahman is realised is called *para-vidyā* and the knowledge other than that is called lower, *apara vidyā.*[2] The Upaniṣads are mainly concerned with *para-vidyā* and proclaim salvation by knowledge or realisation rather than by faith or works.[3] Brahman becomes the goal and *jñāna* the means of reaching it. These two concepts come to occupy the foreground of religious life. All other things like *yajña*, *tapas*, *upāsanā*, *yoga* and *karma* become subsidiary.

Attitude to Sacrifice (Yajña)

Like all ceremonies and rituals, the Vedic sacrifices had become mechanical. It was the desire for the fulfilment of some wish that

[1]*Chand. Up.*, VII. 1.3.
[2]*Mund. Up.*, I. 1.4-5.
[3]*Chand. Up.*, II. 23.1: *Brahma-saṁsthomṛtatvaṁ eti Sveta. Up.*, III. 10: tato yaduttarataraṁ tadrūpamanāmayam etadviduramṛtāste bhavanti athetare duḥkhamevāpiyanti.

prompted their sacrificial performances. But some found that this only led to the progressive increase of their desires and not to the diminution thereof and consequently it neither put an end to worldly sorrow and suffering nor did it bring peace of mind. There was thus by this time deep dissatisfaction about the whole of the ritualistic way of life which had failed to satisfy the demands of the intellect and the heart of an entightened section of the community. It was from this small section of society, the Brahmins as well as the Kṣatriyas, that investigations on the deep problems of spirit arose. This dissatisfaction is clearly felt when the Muṇḍaka-Upaniṣad compares sacrifice with unsteady boats (*plavā adṛdhā yajñarupā*) incapable of taking one beyond the sea of existence.[1] It is also said that those who regard sacrifices as the highest good of human life go again and again from old age to death. Full of desire they fall down from their places in the heavens as soon as their merit is exhausted. Thus it is said that the faithful performance of sacrifice takes a man but to the world of fathers (*pitṛloka*) whence he will return to earth in due course.[2] *Yajña* could only take him to heaven from where he had to come down to earth after a brief stay.

This has given rise to many contrary views on the part of many scholars, European as well as Indian regarding the Vedic sacrifices and Brahman, the Absolute in the Upaniṣads.[3] The gist of their views is the main doctrine of the Vedas (excluding the Upaniṣads) is that the Vedic sacrifices should be performed to reach heaven whereas the main doctrines of the Upaniṣads are that Vedic sacrifices are useless and should not be performed, that minor deities do not exist, there being only the Supreme Deity called Brahman and that one should try to attain salvation by acquiring the knowledge of Brahman.

We shall now quote passages from the Upaniṣads in which it is explicitly stated that by performing sacrifices one could go to heaven, that minor gods did exist and that sacrifices should not be given up.

We find in the Īśopaniṣad a prayer to the god of fire (Agni) to lead the soul by a nice path after death.[4] The Śvetāśvatara Upaniṣad

[1] *Mund. Up.*, I. 2.7.

[2] *Bṛhad.*, I. 5.16, VI. 2.16; *Chand.*, V. 10.3; *Prasna.*, I. 9; *Mund.*, I. 2.10.

[3] Muller, Max *RPU.*, p. 21; Macdonell, *HOSL.*, p. 215; Wintermitz. *HIL.*, p. 237; Hume, *TPU.*, p. 53; Radhakrishnan, S., *IP.*, I, pp. 71-72; Dasgupta, *HIP.*, I, p. 28; Hiriyana, *OIP.*, p. 48; Ranade, *CSUP.*, p. 6; Majumdar ed. the *Vedic Age*, p. 493.

[4] *Isa.*, 18.

alludes approvingly to Agni and Soma, the chief sacrificial deities and commends a return to the old ritualistic worship.[1] In the Kenopaniṣad it is stated that the gods Agni, Vāyu and Indra surpass the other gods as they touched Brahman from the nearest place.[2]

In the Kaṭhopaniṣad we find Naciketas addressing Yama thus: 'Oh God of death, you know how god of fire (Agni) is to be worshipped so that one may attain heaven. Please teach it to me. I have full faith in you.'[3] When Naciketas asks about Brahmajñāna, Yama says: 'In the past the gods also wanted to know it.'[4] Again Yama says: 'All the minor gods rest in Him (Brahman).'[5] The same Upaniṣad says: 'Out of fear of Brahman, Agni gives heat, the Surya also gives heat, Indra, Vayu and the fifth god Yama perform their respective functions.'[6] The Praśnopaniṣad says: 'Those who perform sacrifices and excavate tanks go to the heaven which is the moon.'[7]

The Muṇḍakopaniṣad begins by saying that of all the minor gods Brahmā first came into existence.[8] It also asserts the truth of the Vedic sacrifices: 'All this is true, the rituals which are revealed to the sages and which were inherent in the *mantras*.'[9] It also enjoins on the performance of Vedic sacrifice: 'You should constantly try to perform these sacrifices with the desire for attaining the ultimate truth.'[10] It is also stated: 'They (who perform sacrifices) enjoy the fruits thereof in heaven and are born again in this world or even in lower worlds.'[11] To give the minor gods their due importance, it is said: 'The minor gods were created out of the Supreme God (Brahman).[12] The Taittiriya Upaniṣad prescribes the performance of sacrifice: 'You should not neglect to perform the rites in honour of gods and ancestors.'[13] The rites for the gods, it is stated, are the sacri-

[1]*Sveta.*, II. 6-7.
[2]*Kena*, IV. 2.
[3]*Katha*, I. 1.13.
[4]ibid, 2.1.9.
[5]ibid.
[6]ibid, 2.3.3.
[7]*Prasna*, 1.9.
[8]*Mund*. 1.1.
[9]ibid, 1.2.1.
[10]ibid.
[11]ibid, 1.2.10.
[12]ibid, 2.1.7.
[13]*TU* 1.11.2.

fices; the rites for the ancestors are *śraddhā* and *tarpaṇa*. The Upaniṣad affirms: 'Pursue the path of religion.'[1] Śaṅkarācārya comments: 'So long as one does not realise one's identity with Brahman, one should carefully perform the rites laid down in the Vedas and Smṛtis.'[2]

The Chāndogya Upaniṣad says: 'The path of religion can be divided into three parts: Sacrifices, study and gifts constitute the first part.'[3] According to the Bṛhadāraṇyaka Upaniṣad: 'The Brāhmins desire to know the Brahman by the study of the Veda (*vedānuvacana*), by sarifice (*yajña*), by gifts (*dāna*), by penance (*tapas*) and by fasting (*anāśaken*).[4] Commenting on this passage Sānkarācārya observes: 'Those persons whose minds are purified by the performance of Karma can know without hindrance Brahman as revealed by the Upaniṣads.'[5]

It sbould be of special interest that in the Chāndogya and Bṛhadāraṇyaka Upaniṣads those who are engaged in performing sacrifices also discuss philosophical questions.[6] It is pointed out that the rituals which the sages contemplated in the hymns were developed in various ways in the three Vedas and these should be performed always with a sincere desire.'[7]

From the above discussion it appears that some Upaniṣads continue the philosophy of the Brāhmaṇas. Some of them even suggest the importance of a number of minor deities whose worship led to the heaven. Majority of the Upaniṣads, however, discard these beliefs and suggest a new path—*Jñāna-mārga* as the only means of salvation. It is a better path for the liberation of man. All the different views expressed in the Upaniṣads, therefore, need not create confusion. It is quite possible that the Upaniṣads referring to the minor gods and sacrifices continue the Brāhmaṇic phase and hence are nearer the Brāhmaṇas and belonging to the earlier phase of Upaniṣads. However, Sampurṇananda lends a proper perspective. He aptly observes: 'It has become a fashion to study the Upaniṣads by themselves. This method of study often leads to the conclusion

[1]*Dharmam cara: TU.*, 1.11.2.

[2]prāg brahmātmapratibodhānniyamenātuṣṭheyāti śrotasmārtakarmāṇi.

[3]*Chand.*, 2.23.1.

[4]*Bṛhad.*, IV. 4.22.

[5]Karmabhiḥ saṁskṛta hi viśuḍdhātmānaḥ śaknuvanti ātmānaṁ upaniṣad prakāśitaṁ apratihandhen hi veditum.

[6]*Chand.*, I. 11. ff.

[7]*Mund. Up.*, I. 2.1.

that they represent some kind of an intellectual revolt against the ritual and priestcraft of the Vedic hymns. No importance is attached to the fact that Vyāsa and his commentator Śaṁkarācārya, the greatest exponents of the *Jñāna Mārga* support the study of the Vedas and the performance of the rites enjoined by them and speak of them as absolutely necessary.'[1]

It has also to be remembered that the cross-section of the social picture that appears in the Upaniṣads does not represent the whole society of those days. It certainly comprises such sections of society as were busy with spiritual and philosophical problems. The remaining strata of society continued to believe in the efficacy of the sacrifices and the existence of the minor deities. It was the god Agni and the other gods who acted as witnesses at the marriages performed according to the Vedic rites. They were still presiding deities of the *mantras*.

Mysticism

The philosophy of the Upaniṣads centre round the concept of Supreme Truth or Ultimate Reality called Brahman. From the objective point of view, this Reality is called Brahman (the Self) but from the subjective point of view, the same is called Ātman (the Self), for God is present both in the universe and in the heart of man. The two words are generally used synonymously in the Upaniṣads. And the central theme of the Upaniṣads is that Brahman is Ātman and Ātman is Brahman.

The Upaniṣads abound in expounding the nature of Brahman, the Supreme Reality. They employ all kinds of similies and metaphors to describe what it is not. They never tire of telling us again and again that it cannot be comprehended by the study of the scriptures or by the power of intellect or by much learning.[2] Logic, discussion, scholarship and the scriptures do not help. It is also said that not only can it not be perceived by the eye (*cakṣusā*) or described in speech (*vācā*), it cannot be also gained by the other senses (*nānyair devaiḥ*), by ascetic practices (*tapasā*) or by sacrificial performances (*karmaṇā vā*).[3] Thus the realisation of this Reality is beyond speech, beyond thought and beyond all sense-percep-

[1]Sampūrṇananda, *The Evolution of the Hindu Pantheon*, p. 7.

[2]*Katha. Up.*, 2, 23; nāyamātmā pravacena labhyo na medhyā na bahunāśrutena *Mund. Up.*, III. 2.3.

[3]*Mund. Up.*, III. 1.8.

tion. Often a seeker of truth indulges in apparent contradictory terms: 'I do not think that I know it well. Nor do I think that I do not know it. Among us he who knows it—knows it. And he too does not know that he does not know.'[1]

The Maṇdukya Upaniṣad, however, states that there is the *turiyā* state in which one is in the state of a deep dreamless sleep when neither the knower nor the known can be distinctly felt. In that superconscious state one has the experience of the liberated spirit.[2] This is a state which is not within the experience of ordinary men. Here we find an allusion to the great experience which springs from a deep insight transcending all reasoning and which can only be apprehended intuitively. As the same Upaniṣad says: 'The relation of truth is possible only through the most perfect moral purity which results in a natural illumination of intuitive perception when one seeks to attain this Reality through meditation.'[3] Ranade calls this state; 'immediate, intuitive first-hand experience' which is to be attained 'more by way of mysticism than by the way of thought.'[4] According to Dasgupta it is 'ineffable, intuitive experience regarded by the Upaniṣadic sages as absolute and ultimate truth.'[5] Only the mystics can attain and testify to this intuitive experience for Dasgupta points out that they possess 'the higher intuitive knowledge *(pragñāna)* as distinguished from *jñāna* or cognition.'[6] It is, therefore, no surprise that the Upaniṣads do not lay down any definite method for arriving at the perception of this truth.

[1]*Kena, Up.*, II. 2: nahaṁ manye suvedeti no na vedeti veda ca yo nastad veda tad veda no na vedeti veda ca cf. ibid, 1.3: anyadeva tadviditadātho aviditādadhi.

[2]*Mand. Up.*, 12: amātraś caturtho vyavahāryaḥ prapañcopaśamaḥ śivodvaita evaṁ aumkāra ātmaiva, samviśaty atmanātmanaṃ ya evaṁ veda. According to Gaudapada (III. 35) liyate hi susupte tan nigṛhitaṁ na liyate tad eva nirbhayaṁ brahmā jñānalokam samantataḥ.

[3]*Mund. Up.*, III. 1.8: jñāna-prasādena viśuddha-sattvas tatas tu taṁ paśyate niṣkālaṁ dhyāyamānaḥ. cf. Dasgupta, *Hindu Mysticism*, p. 56.

[4]Ranade, *CSUP.*, pp. 286, 324; cf. Dasgupta. *Indian Idealism*, p. 18.

[5]Dasgupta, op. cit., p. 42. The *AV.*, passage (X. 8.44) which contains the earliest occurrence of the word Ātman in its philosophical sense takes pains to make clear the reason for knowing that Ātman: akāmo dhiro amṛtaḥ svayaṁbhu rasen tṛpto na kutaścanonaḥ: tameva vidvān na bibhāya mṛtyo ātmānāṁ dhiramajaraṁ yuvānaṁ. A knower of the Brahman-Ātman is possessed of all these qualities. See *Bṛhad.*, I. 5.20, IV. 3.37, *Chand.*, VI. 25.2, VIII. 12.6.

[6]ibid, pp. 55-56, 41.

Ranade, however, opines that the Upaniṣads afford us certain basic conditions for attainment of the self. These are: 'complete elevation of moral life, including the absolute control of all passions and desires, the abandonment of worldly ambitions and hopes and the attainment of an unruffled peace of mind.'[1] But the *Kaṭhā Upaniṣad* warns us that it is a very difficult path—like the edge of a sharp razor: *kṣurasya dhārā niśitā duratyayā durgaṁ pathaḥ.*[2] No effort, however tremendous is of any avail. The reason is: this Self can only be realised by those to whom it reveals itself.[3] Thus without divine grace, man is without any hope. All his efforts are rendered futile and he continues to float aimlessly in the ocean of *saṁsāra.* The very nature of the Reality and the pathway to attain it are such that only the rare intellectually and morally elevated beings who possess *prajñāna* like the Upaniṣadic ṛṣis or seers could realize it. For the ordinary people there was no hope.

About the Upaniṣadic mysticism Ranade says: 'The Upaniṣadic mysticism was the mysticism of men who lived in cloisters far away from the bustle of humanity, and who, if they permitted any company at all, permitted only the company of their disciples. The Upaniṣadic mystic did not come forward with the deliberate purpose of mixing with them in order to ameliorate their spiritual condition.'[4]

Inspite of the profundity and brilliance of the Upaniṣadic ideas it can be said that they cannot be regarded as sufficient for the moral or religious needs of the masses. The Upaniṣadic thinkers, who were mystics, lived in their splendid ivory tower, more concerned with their own salvation and approachable by only a few of the intelligentia to whom the subtle philosophy of the Brahman-Ātman could make its appeal. Moreover, they followed an intuitive process and conclusions were not based on an intelligible chain of reasoning and argument but held out merely as the experience or realization of great minds. They were, therefore, to be accepted on faith.

[1]*Mund. Up.*, I. 2.13, *Bṛhad Up.*, IV. 4.23, Ranade, op. cit., p. 329; cf. Dasgupta, op. cit., p. 61.

[2]*Kathā*, 3, 14.

[3]*Kathā Up.*, II. 23: Yamevaiṣa vṛṇute, tena labhyastasyaiṣa ātmā vivṛṇute tanūṁ svām. Also *Mund. Up.*, III. 2.3; *Sveta. Up.*, 3.20, 1.6; *Chānd. Up.*, VI. 14.2.

[4]Ranade, *Pathway to God in Marathi Literature*, p. 1.

Tapas

The Upaniṣads, as discussed earlier, emphasise the path of knowledge towards self-realization. Knowledge should lead to experience and finally to direct perception of God: *ātmā vā are dṛṣṭavyaḥ.*[1] That is why *Nididhyāsanā* is insisted on in the last stage of the spiritual journey. Also prescribed are certain exercises in meditation as preliminary steps which are called *Upāsanās* viz. meditations on the five elements, Prāṇa and Aum.[2] As these *Upāsanās* trained the aspirant and prepared him for the higher stages of meditation, they were of considerable value to the development of the concept of *tapas*. It was no longer confined to mere self-mortification. It took on a distinctly ethical colouring. It became a training directed towards exercises of an inward kind. The *Kena Upaniṣad*, for example, says: 'Austerities (*tapas*), self-control (*dama*) and work (*karma*) form the support of the secret teaching relating to Brahman. Vedas are all its organs (*sarvāṅgāni*) and truth (*satya*) is its abode.'[3] This indicates that those who sought spiritual illumination should cultivate qualities of *tapas* and *damaḥ* to acquire sense-control so necessary for meditation. *Tapas* is also recognised together with truth (*satya*), right knowledge (*samyag-jñāna*) and practice of chastity (*brahmacaryam*), as one of the means of attaining the self.[4] According to Śaṅkara, *tapas* here refers to the focussing of the mind and the senses on the eternal self.[5]

In *Bṛhadāraṇyaka* and *Taittirīya Upaniṣads*, there occurs a phrase in the creation of legends: *sa tapo'tapyata.*[6] It literally means: 'He exerted himself, he performed *tapas*.' It is translated by Winternitz: He tortured himself and mortified himself.[7] This meaning does not fit in here. *Tapas* here means austere thinking or reflection. It is to be taken in the sense of knowledge (*jñāna*), thought or reflection (*ālocana*) as it is very clear from the words whose

[1]*Bṛhad*, II. 4.5.

[2]*Aitareya Br.*, V. 32; *TU.*, I. 5.4, I. 6-8 *Aum* is the *praṇava*, which by the time of the Upaniṣads, is charged with the significance of the entire universe. Radhakrishnan, *PU.*, p. 615.

[3]*Kena*, IV. 8.

[4]*Mund.* III. 1.5.

[5]cf. Radhakrishnan. op. cit., p. 688: manasaścendriyānaṁ ca aikāgryaṁ paramaṁ tapaḥ.

[6]*Bṛhad.* I. 2.6; *TU.*, II. 6.1.

[7]Winternitz, *HIL.*, p. 220.

tapas is in essence *jñāna*: *yasya jñānamayaṁ tapaḥ*.[1] Śaṅkara in his commentary observes: *tapas* here means *jñāna*, there being no possibility of other kind of *tapas*, for his desires are already satisfied (*āptakāma*) and so he cannot perform any austerity. Hence the phrase means that he reflected upon the creation of the world He is about to make.[2]

In the *Aitareya Upaniṣad* there is the metaphor of God 'brooding' over the world egg.[3] Radhakrishnan comments: *Tapas*, the enerzing of conscious force, austere thinking, the inward travail of the spirit, is the 'brooding' which is responsible for the creative work. It is the force by which some mighty possibility is actualised.[4] It is thus described in the *Taittirīya Upaniṣad* that Brahman performed *tapas* and thereby created all that we see around us and having created them entered them (*anuprāviśat*).[5] In a number of passages that follow, *tapas* is identified with Brahman: *tapo Brahma*. It is asserted that Brahman underwent *tapas* (*tapo tapyata*).[6] Śaṃkara means by *tapas* knowledge.[7] Brahman willed, he thought and he created. In the same manner elsewhere Prajapati is described to have practised austerity (*tapotaptya*).[8]

In the *Praśna Upaniṣad tapas* is used as sense restraint (*indriya-saṁyama*). *Tapas*, *brahmacarya* and *śraddhā* are considered indispensable conditions of knowledge.[9] Study of the Vedas (*svādhyāya*) and teaching (*pravacana*) have been described as *tapas*.[10] It is said that Brahman can be known by *tapas: tapo brahmeti*.[11] It is also said that Brahman can be realised by knowledge (*vidyayā*), austerity (*tapasā*) and medition (*cintayā*).[12] *Tapas* is a requisite for perception of the Ātman which is said to have its roots in self-knowledge and penance (*ātmavidyā tapomūlaṁ tad brahmā*).[13] It is said that the

[1] *Mund. Up.*, I. 1.

[2] Saṃkara on *Praśna. Up.*, 1.4; cf. Sayana on *TA.*, VII. 2.

[3] *AU.*, I. 4, III. 2; cf. *Parmārthasāra* 10: avyaktādaṇḍa mabhūdaṇḍād brahmā tataḥ prajāsargaḥ.

[4] *East and West in Religion*, p. 76.

[5] *TU.*, 2.6. 1.

[6] ibid, 3.2. f.

[7] *tapa iti jñānaṁ ucyate. tapaḥ paryālocanaṁ.*

[8] *Bṛhad. Up.*, I. 2.7; I. 5.2.

[9] *Praśna. Up.*, I. 2; V. 3.

[10] *TU.*, 1.9.

[11] ibid, III. 2.1; III. 3.1; III, 4.1; III. 5.1.

[12] *Maitri. Up.*, IV. 4.

[13] *Śveta. Up.* I.15.16; *stayenai tapasā yo'nupaśyati.*

Supreme is attainable through proper *tapas*.[1] *Tapas* is also considered necessary for instruction in sacred knowledge.[2] By contemplative power (*tapasā*) Brahma is said to have expanded (*ciyate Brahmā*).[3] *Tapas* here is the energy by which the world is produced.[4] It is austerity or meditation: *tapa saṁtāpa iti, tapa ālocaṇa iti.*[5]

From the above passages it can be seen that *tapas* means energy, self-effort, thought, self-control, study, austerity and meditation. *Tapas* is preliminary to creation and instruction in sacred knowledge. Brahma is built up by *tapas*. Through *tapas* is all creation effected. The Supreme is attainable through *tapas*. *Tapas* is also a a requisite for perception of the Ātman. It is notable that the concept of *tapas* in the Upaniṣads is of a pure nature. It is regarded not as a means to the attainment of mundane or extramundane benefits but as a means to enlightenment or self-knowledge. The ascetic life (*tapas*) has become ancillary to the search for knowledge.

Towards Renunciation

As meditation and knowledge came to be regarded as superior to sacrifice, so *tapas* also was viewed as capable of producing wonderful results. But there came a stage in the Upaniṣadic times when *tapas* came to be depreciated in comparison with *knowledge* as an inferior, secondary way to the highest bliss, to Brahman. A gradual development of this tendency can be clearly seen.

Tapas is more powerful than sacrifice.[6] But it was believed to lead only to the lower bliss of the world of the forefathers (*pitṛlokaṁ*).[7] *Tapas* in itself seems to be powerless without a reshaping of the mind: it came to be associated with faith (*śraddhā*) and *brahmacaryaṁ*.[8] *Brahmacaryaṁ* and *tapas* are spoken of together[9] and later on *brahmacaryaṁ* is itself regarded as *tapas*.[10] *Brahmacaryaṁ* here is used in the sense of a studious life, lived in continence

[1] *Mund. Up.*, 1.2.11, 3.2.4.
[2] *TU.*, 3.1; *Maitri. Up.*, 1.2.
[3] *Mund. Up.*, I. 1.8.
[4] bahusyāṁ iti saṁkalpa rūpena jñānena brahmā sṛṣṭyunmukhaṁ bhavati *Rangaramanuja*, cf. Radhakrishnan, *PU.*, p. 673.
[5] Radhakrishnan, ibid.
[6] *Chānd.* II. 23.1.
[7] *Bṛhad.* VI. 2.16.
[8] *Chānd. Up.*, V. 10: *Ye ca ime araṇye śraddhā tapa eti upāsate.*
[9] *Praśna Up.*, I. 9.10.
[10] ibid, I-15.

and implying a mental discipline. *Śraddhā* is the attitude of mind which accepts a reality beyond the reach of the senses and is determined to give up worldly things to obtain it. The *Chāndogya Upaniṣad* distinguishes only two ways of life: the *Gṛhastha* and the *Brahmacārī*, the latter category apparently including Vedic students and Upaniṣadic hermits in the woods. Here not noly the need for *brahmacarya* advocated but also the equivalence of certain sacrifices to *brahmacarya* is stressed on.[1] The waning influence of *tapas* could be seen in the words of *Yājñavalkya* to Gargi that a thousand years of *tapas* without the knowledge of Brahman is of no avail.[2] The utter futility of *tapas* is demonstrated in the case of king Brihadratha, who having performed the highest penance—that too acquiring *vairāgya*, has failed to attain self-knowledge.[3] *Tapas* thus occupies a secondary, subordinate precondition to bring about a change of mind, leading up to the *Brahma-state*, difined as *jñāna*. Once it is fully realised that the Brahma-experience stands out of all proportion to sacrifice and *tapas*, *tapas* is dropped and *brahmacarya* and *jñāna* are pointed out as leading up to Brahma realisation.

In complete harmony with the spirit of these texts, the Upaniṣads, now speak of the one who stands firm in Brahman (*brahma-saṁstha*) and who attains life eternal.[4] In comparison with this state of *brahma-saṁstha* sacrifices, study and charity; and austerity (*tapas*), *naiṣṭhika brahmacārī* in pursuit of sacred wisdom, staying with the teacher all his life are said to attain only to the worlds of the virtuous (*puṇya-loka*).[5] Śaṁkara suggests that *brahma-saṁstha* refers to the *parivrāt* or the monk who alone obtains eternal life, while others who practise active virtues obtain the worlds of the virtuous. According to him, the true *brahma-saṁstha* is the *saṁnyāsin* who gives up all actions.[6] The three branches of *Dharma* mentioned

[1]*Chānd. Up.*, VIII. 5.1-3.

[2]*Bṛhad. Up.*, III. 8.10: Yo vā etadakṣaraṁ gārgyaviditvā asmin loke juhoti yajate tapastapyate bahuni varṣa sahasrāṇi antadevāsya tadbhavati.

[3]*Maitri. Up.*, 1.2.

[4]*Chānd. Up.*, II. 23.1: *brahmasaṁsthomṛtatvameti.*

[5]ibid, Trayo dharmaskandhāḥ; yajño dhyānaṁ dānamiti; prathamaḥ tapa eva, dvitiyo brahmacaryācārakulavāsi, tṛtiyo'tyantaṁ ātmānaṁ ācaryakule vasādayam: sarva ete puṇya. loka bhavanti. Sankara on *Vedantasutra* (III. 4.20) speaks of the third *āśrama* as *vaikhānasa* as indicated by the word *tapas* here.

[6]*Karma-nivṛtti-lakṣanaṁ parivrājyam brahma-saṁsthatvaṁ*; cf. Radhakrishnan, *PU.*, p. 375.

by the *Chāndogya Upaniṣad* seem to be alternative paths for religious and spiritual development leading to *puṇyaloka*. Immortality is possible only for the one who knows the Brahman (*Brahma-saṁstha*). He stands apart from the three paths of *gārhasthya*, *tapas* and *naiṣṭhika-brahmacarya*. Thus the *Brahma-saṁstha* seems to be identical with the *Atyāśramin* who knows the Ātman and is beyond *āśrama*.[1] Here no chronological idea is suggested that the one who knows Ātman is in a period of life. A transcendency is expressed as in the *Brahma-saṁstha*. Both the states point to renunciation of the world.

We have already seen that the *vānaprastha* stage has been accepted by the Brāhmanic society in the Āraṇyakas. *Tapas* is distinctly associated in the Upaniṣads with the life of the anchorite in the forest, the *vānaprastha* for whom the practice of *tapas* is especially obligatory but it is said, he must add faith (*śraddhā*) to it.[2] Those who practise *tapas* and *śraddhā* in the forest are said to be free from passion (*virajāḥ*), tranquil and wise (*śānta vidvāṁso*) and leading the life of a mendicant (*bhaikṣācaryaṁ carantaḥ*).[3] Who are they? They are the ascetics (*yatayaḥ*) with their imperfections done away and who behold this self within the body, of the nature of light and pure.[4] Thus those who live in the forest purified by austerities (*tapas*) and those who know and are learned become almsmen, religious mendicants (*bhikṣus*). A new mode of life of a wandering beggar, a religious mendicant (*parivrāta*, *bhikṣu*) to attain the highest bliss, the Brahman has come to be recognised for the first time.[5]

The *Bṛhadāraṇyaka Upaniṣad* refers to such class of men who are world-forsakers and almsmen when Yājñavalkya tells king Janaka: 'Him Brahmins seek to know by the study of the Veda, by sacrifices, by gifts, by penance (*tapasā*), by fasting. On knowing Him, in truth, one becomes an ascetic (*Muni*). Desiring him only as their worlds, mendicants (*pravrājino*) wander forth (*pravrajanti*). Because they know this, the ancient (sages) did not wish for offspring. What shall we do with offspring (they said), we who have attained this Self, this worlds. They, having risen above the desire for sons, the

[1] *Śvetā. Up.*, VI. 2.1.

[2] *Chānd. Up.*, V. 10: *Ye ca ime araṇye śraddhā tapa eti upāsate.*

[3] *Mund. Up.*, I. 2.11.

[4] ibid, III. 1.5: antah-śarire jyotir-mayohi śubhro yam paśyanti yatayaḥ kṣiṇadoṣāḥ.

[5] Dutt holds the view that almsmanship was customary; *Buddhist Monks and Monasteries of India*, p. 45.

desire for wealth, the desire for the worlds, led the life of a mendicant (*bhikṣācaryaṁ caranti*).'[1] The *Ātma*-Knowledge is then the final, culminating point, leading up to which, other paths of life are but stages of development. Behind their spiritual urge to attain this supreme wisdom, the Upaniṣadic thinkers have realised that worldly goods did not give lasting happiness. The true and everlasting happiness was to be found in the bliss of *Ātman*.

The same Upaniṣad sets forth this ideal of renunciation elsewhere thus: 'The Brāhmins, having known that Self, having overcome the desire for progeny, the desire for wealth, the desire for worlds, live the life of mendicants (*bhikṣācaryaṁ caranti*).'[2] Here the life of mendicancy is suggested as the outcome of knowing the Ātman whereas in the first passage (IV. 4. 22) it is a means to the self-knowledge (*etam eva pravrājino lokaṁ icchantaḥ pravrajanti*), as the *saṁnyāsa* in the last stage of life (*āśrama*) came to be understood. In the second passage (III.5.1) the mendicants, having realised the self which is the only desire (*ātma-kāma*) have realised all their desires (*āpta-kāma*), the state which the ascetic or *saṁnyāsi* aspires to reach. (IV.4.22). It is significant that in III.5.1, 'a Brahmin, after he has done with learning,' is advised 'to desire to live as a child.' It is said that 'when he has done (both) with the state of childhood and with learning, then he becomes silent mediator.'[3] The Ṛgvedic Muni was silent; maunam, *mauneya* was his chief trait. The Upaniṣadic Muni takes to *pāṇḍityaṁ*, *manan*, thought, meditation. After *manan*, *maunaṁ* is again recommended to him. The true knower of Brahman has to devote himself exclusively to the contemplation of the self and shun all other thoughts as distractions. In the silence of his own soul (*ātman*) he has to find (*Brahman*).

We thus find that the thirst for spiritual knowledge to attain self-realisation inspired the ideal of religious mendicancy and renunciation of the world. The greatest of the Brahmavādins of the Upaniṣadic age Yājñavalkya renounces the worldly life and takes to the life of a *pravarājyā* after he has divided his property between

[1]*Bṛhad. Up.*, IV. 4. 22.

[2]ibid, III. 5.1: *etam vai tam ātmānāṁ viditvā, brāhmaṇāḥ putraisaṇāyāś* ca *vittaiṣānāyāś ca lokaisaṇāyās* ca *vyutthāya, atha bhikṣācaryaṁ caranti.*

[3]Tasmād brāhmanaḥ pāṇḍityaṁ nirvidya bālyena tiṣṭhāset; balyam ca pāṇdityaṁ ca nirvidya, atha muniḥ; amaunaṁ ca maunaṁ ca nirvidya, atha brāhmaṇaḥ.

his two wives, Maitreyī and Kātyāyanī. The conversation between him and Maitreyi aims at showing that the giving up of all worldly possessions and retiring to the world of the forest completely dedicated to a life of *tapas* was indispensable for the knowledge of Brahman and the attainment of salvation.[1] With the emergence of the doctrine of Brahman-Ātman, the miseries and sufferings of human life came to be attributed to the absence of self-knowledge. The eternal Ātman was bliss and everything else painful and transistory: *ato anyad ārtam.* The world was believed to be deceptive and life evil. To this phase of pessimism were added other forces, as described in the third chapter. According to the doctrine of transmigration and law of Karma, *saṁsāra* was full of misery and ruled by Karma resulted in a perpetual bondage of birth and death. The fear of present miseries and future sufferings of rebirths made the world a miserable place to escape at all costs. The Upaniṣadic thinkers preached that the seeker after saving knowledge must get rid of all desires for worldly things. This naturally meant detachment from normal human life; not because it was painful, transitory and negligible but because it was also distracting. It impeded the attainment of the highest goal by involving man in mundane interests. Thus developed in the Upaniṣadic times the ideal norm of the wandering mendicant (*saṁnyāsin*, *bhikṣu*, *samaṇa*, *muni*), the homeless ascetic, living on alms, cut off from family ties, possessions and all worldly life. He stood outside of everything, even of caste. He died to the world only to live in the world of Brahman-Ātman.

Summing Up

In the Vedic literature we find that the Āryans still lived a full life though in the Upaniṣads, there is an emphasis on the life of the spirit and self-realisation, due to the development of the doctrine of Brahman-Ātman. The institution of *tapas* has developed from its basic meaning of heat or warmth or fervour to ascetic practices and devotional fervour. In the Upaniṣads it has come to be accepted as a means of elightenment or self knowledge. Sacrifice through discredited as leaking boats and incapable for attaining salvation had still an important place in the life of the common man. Though the Upaniṣadic thinkers held out that self-realisation was necessary to obtain salvation and which could only be had through the intuitive

[1]*Bṛhad. Up.*, IV. 5.2.

knowledge of Brahman, the path was confined to a few who could understand the subtle-philosophy of Brahman-Ātman and who could completely elevate life on intellectual and moral planes. The few regarded the Brahman-experince not only as ineffable and intuitive but also as absolute and ultimate truth. The masses, however, continued to rely upon sacrifices and minor gods to reach heaven. Spiritual knowledge was not the monopoly of only Brāhmins. Even the Kṣatriyas, some of whom were kings, were in possession of it and instructed even the Brāhmins in the secret doctrine. It was believed that salvation was obtainable by living a righteous life of *Artha*, *Kāma* and *Dharma* according to Vedic prescriptions. Even kings like Janaka were said to have obtained salvation while still ruling and there was no need to give up worldly life and its interests. However, a minority of thinkers and mystics endeavoured to attain salvation and immortality through self-realisation and as a result of realising Brahman, and wandered as mendicants. For the very purpose, others took to a life of *Saṁnyāsa*. Due to pessimism arising from Brahman-Ātman philosophy as also other factors like *samsāra* and *karma*, the *saṁnyāsa* ideal came to be developed in the Upaniṣadic times.

Chapter 6

Asceticism in Buddhist Literature

The times which saw the rise of the religious systems of Gautama, the Buddha and Mahāvira, the Jaina, were one of an intensive speculative activity, spiritual unrest and intellectual ferment. The country was seething with a multitude of more or less opposing theories on all sorts of questions, ethical, philosophical and religious. In the sixth century, thus we find, an upheaval of new ideas leading to the rise of new philosophical tenets and religious sects, often of a revolutionary character such as ancient India has never seen before or since. Many of these philosophical dogmas or religious sects had a merely temporary vogue and gradually faded away. A few however, came to stay and left a permanent impress on Indian religious thought. Of these, four played an important part in subsequent history. These are Jainism, Buddhism, Vaiṣṇavism and Śaivism. The first two are more important because they broke themselves away from the orthodox Vedic tradition and were offshoots of a heterodox movement. We deal here with Buddhism.

On the importance of Buddhism as a religion, observes Havell: 'It was much more a social than religious revolution.'[1] The question arises: What were the main features of the broader human situation that Buddha confronted? In general, it appears, that 'the situation was one of radical social readjustment and deepening religious need.[2] In order to understand this historical situation which Buddha found himself challenged to meet, we have to consider the environment of his times which is naturally influenced by its background in the earlier religious thought of India. It is essential, therefore, to view the life and times of the Buddha and the social, religious and cultural background against which he is to be understood, with regard to the role he played and the message he preached on the vast stage of Indian thought.

[1]Havell, *The Āryan Rule in India*, p. 50.
[2]Burtt, *The Teachings of the Compassionate Buddha*, Introduction p. 19.

The Conditions of the Time

The philosophy of the Upaniṣads was meant only for the initiated few. The Upaniṣadic teachers were not concerned with common people or earthly matters. The cult of the sacrifice which developed out of the prayers in the Vedic Saṃhitās had still a powerful hold on the people. Religion had become mechanical. To the mass of men it consisted in regular ceremonials, purifications and prohibitions applicable to almost all relations of human life. The slaughtering of animals for sacrifice became exceedingly common. Emphasis was placed on the correct performance of rite and ceremony. Goodness was judged on the one hand by the standard of ritualistic correctness, and on the other by asceticism, torture and penance, in the search for the ultimate truth.

The Brāhmāns had became powerful through their knowledge of the sacrificial arts, which the hereditary priests especially made it to a high degree esoteric and exclusive. The Vedas were frequently taught by them as a collection of authoritative texts rather than as living truths to be tested and re-interpreted, if need be, at that time. The *Dīgha Nikāya*, having referred to the names of the ten rishis or hymn composers of the Vedic tradition,[1] points out that the Brāhmins of the Buddha's times were merely repeaters of the hymns composed by the ancient sages.[2] The goal of these sacrificing priests was mainly the union of Brahma by merit through sacrifices or austere practices.[3] The Brāhmāns sought to perpetuate their own social ascendency by inculcating the doctrines of their own superiority as custodians of a divine revelation and as expounders of sacred laws. Besides, by virtue of their birth they enjoyed the high social esteem of the masses irrespective of their character. This was, however, challenged by the non-orthodox teachers like the Buddha. In *Sonadaṇḍa Sutta* for example, the Buddha vigorously contests the exclusive claims of the Brāhmāns to social superiority birth.[4] According to him, character and deeds, virtue and wisdom were the characteristics of the true Brāhmān.[5] He also points out that the

[1]*Dīgha. Nik.*, I. 104. Also *Maj. Nik.*, II. 200. The rishis named are: Atthaka, Vāmaka, Vāmdeva, Vessāmitta, Yamataggi, Angirasa, Bhāradvāja, Vāsettha, Kassapa and Bhagu.

[2]Tevijja Sutta *Dīgha. Nik.*, I, 13.

[3]*Maj. Nik.*, II. 197 ff.

[4]*DOB.*, I, pp. 144 ff.

[5]*SBE*, Sūtta Nipāta, p. 115, Sonadaṇḍa Sutta, p. 154.

real union with Brahma lay not in sacrifices and ascetic practices but in the cultivation of virtues like love, pity, compassion and poise which truly freed the heart from wrath and malevolence, sensuality and sluggishness.[1]

Religious thinkers, in attempt to satisfy their metaphysical curiosity, were championing varied cosmological systems, each heaping argumentative scorn on the theories of his opponents. Moral life suffered, since metaphysical subtleties and theological discussions absorbed the energies of the elite. Dogma and pristhood, sacrifice and sacrament reigned supreme. Religion was straying through these and other vices away from the insistent, poignant and practical needs of common men and women. It was not leading them towards true fulfilment and more dependable happiness; it was being entangled in obstructive tradition, repetitious rite and dead dogma. 'The age' as Radhakrishnan observes, 'was one of spiritual dryness, where truth hardened into tradition and morality stiffened into routine. Life became a series of observances. The mind of man moved within the iron circle of prescribed formulas and duties. The atmosphere was choked with ceremonialism.'[2] It was left to the thinkers like Gautama, the Buddha and Mahavira, the Jaina to break through or sweep away these obstructive tangles, to find an enduring solution to the real problems of men and to bring to India and the world a saving message of light and love.

Before the time of Buddha, there was not one vast Indian empire, but only princes of particular tribes and clans who were trying to form small states. According to Buddhist texts sixteen great states (*Solasamahājanapada*) flourished, shortly before the time of Gautama, the Buddha.[3] In northern India, wars were frequent between the petty princes and rival clans. Society was moving more and more in the direction of a rigid caste system.

Religious and Ascetic Sects

The Pali texts give us an exceedingly concrete picture of the movements of the religious world of the times in which a number of reli-

[1] *Maj. Nik.*, II, 203-208.

[2] Radhakrishnan, *POU.*, 142.

[3] They are Aṅga, Magadha, Kāśi, Kośala, Vriji (Vajji) Malla, Chedi, Vatsa (Vaṁsa), Kuru, Pāncala, Matsya, Sūrasena, Aśvaka or Aśmaka (Assaka) Avanti, Gāndhara and Kamboja; *The Age of Imperial Unity*, p. 1; *Ang. Nik.*, I, 213; IV, 252, 256, 960; *Mahavastu*, I, 34, II, 3; *Vinaya*, II, 146 fn; *Niddesa*, II, 37.

gious and philosophical sects, ascetic orders, groups of hermits and wanderers played their part. A picture of the variety of religious beliefs current at the time is obtained from some Buddhist texts, like *Aṅguttara Nikāya*, *Mahāniddesa* and *Chullaniddesa*.

According to the *Aṅguttara Nikāya*, the ten main religious sects of the times were:

(1) Ājīvika	(2) Nigantha
(3) Muṇḍa-Sāvaka	(4) Jatilakā
(5) Parivrājaka	(6) Māgandika
(7) Tridaṇḍika	(8) Aviruddhaka
(9) Gautamaka and	(10) Devadhammika

Ājīvikas

The Ājīvikas formed a third heretical sect beside those of Buddhism and Jainism. Its founder was Makkhali Gosāla. The religion of the Ājīvikas, called Ājīvikism, which 'played a part of some importance if not of glory'[1] and which is aptly termed as 'a vanished Indian religion' by Basham[2] has its own history and doctrines. We purposely indicate its early beginnings here, as when the Buddha came on the scene, the term 'Ājivikas' did not connote a regularly 'organized' religious sect with distinct doctrines of its own. At this time Gosāla had not yet commenced his ministry.

The word 'Makkhali' before the proper name Gosāla suggests that it was a title. Makkhali or Maskarin was a fairly common appellation of a staff-bearing ascetic. The word is explained by Pāṇini as a mendicant who bears a *maskara* or bamboo rod.[3] The etymology of the word has been established by Hoernle. 'It describes Gosāla,' he writes, 'as having originally belonged to the Makkhali or Maskarin class of religious mendicants.'[4] Ājīvika Upaka is also referred to as bearing a staff.[5] That such staff-bearing ascetics existed is clear from various references to *maskarins* and *ekadaṇḍins*.[6] Though Pāṇini's etymology seems only to imply that the word *maskarin* means a mendicant bearing a staff, of whatever class or order, staves probably became a regular mark of the Ājīvika order.

[1]Barnett, '*The Ajīvikas*,' Introduction p. xi.

[2]Basham, ibid, p. 288.

[3]*Aṣṭādhyāyi*, vi, 1, 154: Maskara Maskariṇi veṇu parivrājakayoḥ cf. Agrawala, Art. (Word Notes on the Divyāvadāna, *Bharati*, No. 6, Pt. II, p. 68.

[4]*ERE.*, *I*, p. 260.

[5]Latthi-Hattho, *Theri*. 291.

[6]*Tittira Jat*. iii. p. 542; *ERE.*, i. pp. 266-7.

The Ājīvika ascetics in the Pali texts appear usually to have lived in a state of nakedness. Pūraṇa Kassapa is described as a Nirgantha clothed in the garment of righteousness (*dharma-śātapraticchanna*), the phrase is obviously an euphemism for a state of total nudity.[1] Both Gosāla and Pūraṇa are described as completely naked.[2] The Ājīvikas performed penance of the most rigorous nature. A typical account is given in the *Kassapasihanāda Sutta*[3] Their asceticism often terminated like that of the Jainns in death by starvation.[4] The typical Ājīvika of the early period was usually completely naked, no doubt covered with dust and dirt, perhaps bent and crippled and armed with a bamboo staff.[5]

A detailed account of the Ājīvikas is given elsewhere.[6]

Niganthas

The leader of the Niganthas (Nirganthas) was Nigantha Nātaputa or Mahāvir Vardhamān, now acknowledged as the last Tirthankar of the Jaina tradition. But in the early period the terms '*Niganthas*' and '*Ājīvikas*' seem to have been used synonymously. *Nigantha Saccaka* or Aggivessana names the six heretics as the leaders of his order.[7] These six teachers are usually portrayed in the Pali texts as a group though occasionally brief references to an individual teacher may be found. The *Sandaka Sutta* refers to all of them, including the great leader of the Niganthas, Nigantha Nātaputa, in the general category.[8] It seems probable that in the days of the Buddha both the terms *Ājīvika* and *Nirgantha* originally had a wider connotation and were applicable to almost any non-Brāhmanical naked ascetic.[9] In some later texts Ājīvikas are clearly distinguished from Niganthas.[10] The Niganthas practised asceticism of a severe type which often amounted to death by starvation.[11] The Jainas are

[1] *Divya*, p. 165.
[2] Buddhaghosa, *Sum. Vil.*, i. pp. 143-4.
[3] *Dīgha Nik.*, I, 161-177.
[4] Basham, op. cit., pp. 127-131.
[5] Basham, ibid, p. 109.
[6] Vide Chapter 7, Jainism.
[7] *Maj. Nik.*, I. 238.
[8] ibid, I, pp. 513 ff.
[9] Basham, op. cit., p. 102.
[10] *Sūtta Nipāta*, 381 *Ye ke c'ime tithiyā vādaśila, Ājīvika vā yadi va Niganthā.*
[11] Vide Chapter 7 Jainism.

known to be the successors of this school of the Niganthas.

Muṇḍa-sāvaka (*Muṇḍa-Śrāvaka*)

According to Buddhagosa they were the same as Niganthas.[1]

Jatilakās

The *Jatilakās* were those who wore their hair in braids. To do so was the rule for the orthodox hermits (the *Vānaprasthas* or *tāpasas*).[2] They were fire-worshippers as the Pali expression '*aggikā Jatilakā*' suggests.[3] There is a reference to their wearing matted hair which they are said to have shorn off on receiving *Upasampadā*.[4] They lived outside society, did penance (for which their leader Kassapa Uruvela was specially renowned),[5] performed sacrifices and kept up the sacred fire.[6] From this description it becomes certain that they were in the *Vānaprastha* or *Tapas* stage of life.[7]

Paribbajakas (Parivrājakas)

The term *Paribbajaka* was applied to the homeless community of men who lived outside the organisation of the society. They were called by various names—*Parivrājaka*, *Bhikkhu* (*Bhikṣu*), Śramaṇa (*Samaṇa*), *Yati* and *Saṁnyāsi*. The last name, however, was seldom used in Buddhist and Jaina literature. However, the denomination *Parivrājaka* is common to all. They have one more essential characteristic in common viz. that they are all professed *religieux*, homeless and nomadic. The common phrase in the Pali scriptures for one who embraces this mode of life is, *Agārasma anagāriyaṁ pabajjati* (passes from the household to the household state). The character of the community is so varied and miscellaneous that it is extremely difficult to generalize upon it. They lived by begging, had no settled dwelling, moved about from place to place and were either ascetics practising austerities or celibates.[8]

[1]cf. Rhys Davids, *DOBI.*, p. 221.
[2]*Gaut. D.S.*, III, 34.
[3]*Mahāvagga*, i. 38. 11, cf. Kern, *Manual af Buddhism*, p. 78.
[4]ibid, i. 20.19.
[5]ibid, 22,4.
[6]ibid, 15, 2; 19, 1; 20, 19.
[7]Rhys Davids and Oldenberg regard the Jatilakās as Brāhmanical Vānaprasthas—*Vinaya*, *SBE.*, pt. I, p. 118 fn. 1.
[8]Dutt feels that the Parivrajaka stage is not exactly the culmination of

Out of the *Parivrājakas* were formed from time to time groups who expressed their allegiance to a certain teacher or subscribed to some common tenets, marks or styles of dress. Of these we may refer to *Māgandikas*,[1] *Vekhanass*,[2] *Pārāśariyas*,[3] *Jatilals*,[4] *Tedaṇḍikas*,[5] *Aviruddhakas*,[6] *Devadhammikas*[7] and *Gautamaka*.[8]

According to Buddhaghosa all these groups were the followers of non-Buddhist teachers (*Titthiyas*).

Tridaṇḍika (*Tedaṇḍikas*)

As opposed to *Ekadaṇḍins*, they were the bearers of the triple staff. The technical term is not to be found earlier than the latest part of Manu.[9] Probably they were Brāhmaṇ *bhikṣus* who carried three staves bound up as one, as a sign, of their self-restraint in thought, word and deed. The idea of the three-fold division of conduct recurs in the *Dharmasūtras* and in Manu.[10]

The *Mahāniddesa* and *Cullaniddesa* mention the *Ājivikas*, *Niganthas*, *Jatilas*, *Parivrājakas* and *Aviruddhakas* along with the worshippers of the elephant, horse, cow, dog, crow, fire, serpent, goblin, Vāsudeva, Baladeva, Purṇabhadra, Maṇibhadra, Agni, the Nāgas, the Yakṣas, the Asuras, the Gāṅdharvas, the Mahārājas, Chandra, Sūrya, Indra, Brahman, Deva and Dik. In the account given of the various superstitious beliefs current among the ancient people for the attainment of purity, a few ascetic practices are mentioned e.g. strict observance of *śilas* (moral precepts), living the life of animals

the 'stages' but something apart, not exactly comprehended by the *āśrama* theory, but a condition of life represented by men who may not have gone at different stages of life through the disciplines of graded duties and responsibilities imposed by Vedic culture and its requirements: *Buddhist Monks and Monasteries of India*, p. 39.

1 *Maj. Nik.*, I, 501-13.

2 ibid, ii.21.

3 ibid, ii.324 f.

4 ibid, II, pp. 40-44.

5 Vinaya, II, p. 132, 196; Lalitavistāra, p. 238.

6 *Sūtta Nipāta*, Verse, 365, 704, 854.

7 *Cullanidessa*, p. 173.

8 *DOB.*, p. 221.

9 '*Saptangasyea rajyasya vistabdhasya tridandavat*' (Manu xii. 10).

10 *Gaut. DS.*, III, 17; *Baudh. DS.*, xi, 6, 11, 23; *Manu*, V.165; IX, 29. According to the *Mbh.* (XIV.105.8-9), a *Saṁnyāsin* should be revered irrespective of his having one or three staves, being shaved or otherwise and even when he has only reddish-brown cloth.

e.g. elephant, horse, cow and so forth, rubbing the body by earth and cow-dung.[1] The account furnishes us with two lists of *religieux* (*Samanabrāhman*) who seek emancipation through the performance of *Vatas*, *Vratas*, (vowed observance) and *Mutas*. The Vata-suddhikas are Hatthivatika, Assavatika, Govatika, Kukkuravatika, Kākavatika, Vasudevatika, Baladevavatika, Punnabhaddavatika, Manibhaddavatika. The Mutasuddhikas are those who in proper time rub their body by earth, harita and gomaya.[2]

These two lists which are quite exhaustive, are interesting and instructive. They demonstrate the existence, side by side with well-known religious sects, of a bewildering variety of primitive faiths and popular cults—a characteristic feature of Indian religious life throughout the ages.

The lure of renunciation or other-worldliness was very much in the air at the time. The ascetic was the most prominent figure in religious life as opposed to the Brāhman priest who fllled the religious and literary stage of the earlier period. The system of *āśramas* or the four stages of life was evolved and the last two, those of the *vānaprastha* and *saṁnyāsa* gave opportunities for speculation on the problems of ultimate reality and absolute happiness. In Brāhmiṇ circles asceticism had become popular and numerous Brāhmiṇs were found to be living in forest hermitages (*āśramas*) or wandering ascetics (*parivrājakas*) or *yatis* and *saṁnyāsis*. They emphasised the ideal of renunciation of the world—but only from the point of view of the *Āśrama* theory according to which the Āryan had first to pass the stage of the student of the Veda (*Brahmacāri*) and of the householder (*gṛhastha*) who founded a family, offered sacrifices and honoured the Brāhmiṇs, before he is allowed to retire from this world as an hermit (*vānaprastha*) or an ascetic (*saṁnyāsi*). They debarred other castes from entering the ascetic life. Excessive formalism had developed in this scheme. The monopoly on the part of the Brāhmins meant treating those debarred from entering the ascetic life as in every way inferior. This created in the latter a sense of denial to have opportunities to rise to the full heights of their powers. This fact was naturally most keenly felt by the clever and critical *Kṣatriyas*. It is from the ranks of these that the Jaina as well as the Buddhist reformers sprang.

[1]cf. 'Browsers' These were solitaries of Mesopotamia and were so called because they lived on grass like cattle. *ERE.*, VIII, p. 783.

[2]*Mahaniddesa*, I, p. 89.

Buddha and Mahāvīra preached against the sanctity of the Vedic lore, rejecting the sacrificial prescriptions of the ritualists and repudiating claims of spiritual superiority asserted by the Brāhmins.

Asceticism was now the only door open for non-Brāhmins who sought spiritual, mental and intellectual fulfilment and realisation and hence the life of the wandering mendicant was considered superior to that of the Brāhmin priests. It was equally the opportunity for magicians, necromancers and sorcerers as for those who used it as a technique for the acquisition of superhuman powers and knowledge, whereby they would have a privileged place in society, even if they, like Makhali Gosāla, one of the Ājīvika teachers, belonged to an inferior caste.

The ascetics of different orders were described by the general term *Samaṇa-Brāhmaṇa*, leaders in religious life. This indicates that there were two different representatives of religious life—the *Samaṇas* (recluses) and Brāhmanas. Samaṇas were non-Brāhmana ascetics including the Jainas and Buddhists. The Buddhist Samaṇas were also called *Pabbajjakas* or *Bhikkus* (*Bhikṣus*). The *Brāhmaṇa* ascetic orders depended on birth and were recruited exclusively from one caste, those of *Samaṇas* were thrown open to all high born or low born, who would adopt, ascetic life. The practice of adopting a wandering religious life had become a characteristic feature of the society.

There are frequent references[1] in Buddhist literature to six *senior contemporaries* of the Buddha who were the prominent leaders of the non-Buddhist ascetic sects (*titthas*):

(1) Pūraṇa Kassapa	(4) Pakudha Kaccāyana
(2) Makkhali Gosāla	(5) Nigantha Nātaputa
(3) Ajita Kesakāmbali	(6) Sanjaya Belatthiputta

Each is described in the same stock terms. Each is referred to as the leader of an order (*gaṇācariyo*), well-known, famous, the founder of a sect (*titthakaro*), respected as a saint (*sādhu-sammato*), revered by many people, a homeless wanderer of long standing (*cirapabbajito*) and advanced in years.

Each of them had his pet theory of holy living, philosophical doctrine[2] and a band of followers. Throughout the *Nikāyas*, the Buddha's polemic is focussed, outside wanderers and Brāhmaṇism, on these six leaders of heretic sects.

[1]*Digha Nik.*, I, 47-59; *Maj. Nik.*, I, 198, 250; *Sutta Nipāta*, III, 6; ibid, II 2.
[2]See Basham, op. cit., pp. 13-17.

Of these six leaders, Nigantha Nātaputa is no other than Mahāvīra, and according to the Jaina tradition the last prophet or the *Tirthaṅkara*. He preached ethical doctrines which had been held long back by an incomparably senior ascetic, Pārśva. The latter is now acknowledged to be Mahāvīra's predecessor and the founder of Jainism. In the *Sāmmañaphala Sutta* Nigantha Nātaputta is mentioned as having held the doctrine of four-fold restraint: restraint from the use of cold water as it contains life and from sinful activities such as killing and sexual intercourse.[1] 'Nigantha' or 'Nirgantha' suggests that he was free from all bonds and had purified himself. In the *Uduambarika Sīhanāda Sutta* the restraints ascribed to him are identical with the four vows of Pārśva with minor differences.[2]

The next important contemporary of the Buddha was Makkhali Gosāla. He belonged to the sect of the *Acelakas* or 'Naked Ones'[3] and as the first part of his name indicates carried a staff of bamboo (*maskarin*). It is said that he was for some time a disciple of Mahāvīra but later broke away from him. Afterwards, he founded an independent school known as the Ājīvikas. Later writers mention two predecessors, Nanda Vaccha and Kisa Sankicca[4] thus giving this school three teachers. This sect is now extinct, but seems to have enjoyed popularity and even royal patronage.[5] The remaining four teachers did not leave their mark on posterity as did Mahāvīra and to a lesser degree, Gosāla.

An analysis of the doctrinal or philosophical tenets of the non-Vedic sects shows that the number of such teachers or religious leaders and their schools was very large. The Jain Sutras[6] mention as many as 363, while according to the Buddhist *suttas* the number is 62 or 63.[7] The Jainas group their 363 schools broadly into four,

1 *DOB.*, I. p. 74. Also cf Siyodagam va taha biyakāyam ahā yakammam taha itthiyāo eyaṁ jānam paddisevamāna agārino assamanā bhavanti. *Suyagada*, 2, 6, 8.

2 *Digha Nik.*, III, 48.

3 The word *acelaka* connoted any naked ascetic; *DP.*, I, p. 309. When Buddha asks the *Nigantha* Saccaka Aggivesana how the Ājīvikas maintain themselves, he replies referring to Nanda Vaccha, Kisa Sankicca and Makkhali Gosāla as the *acelakas*: *Maj. Nik.*, p. 238.

4 *Maj. Nik.*, I, 238, 524.

5 Asoka's P.E , VII; Also Dasaratha's inscriptions of the Hill Caves. cf. Basham, op. cit., p. 151-152.

6 *Stkr.*, ii, 2.79.

7 Brahmajala Sutta, *DOB.*, I, p. 52-53.

namely the *Kriyāvāda*, the *Akriyāvāda*, the *Ajñānavāda* and the *Vinayavāda*,[1] Mahāvīra being shown as the champion of the Kriyāvada.[2] Mahāvīra had declared complete renunciation as the right and only norm of conduct. In Jainism the ascetic life as the only path of salvation has remained a cardinal point.

The generic term for the wanderers, whom Havell calls 'a fraternity of mendicant sophists'[3] was Paribbajakas or Parivrājakas of both the sexes. Much information about them is to be found in *Samana Mandika* and *Cūlasakuludāyi Sutta*.[4] The *Anguttara*[5] *Nikāya* mentions two classes of *Parivrajakas*: *Brahmana* and *Annatitthiya* i.e., other non-Buddhist ascetics. The Brāhmaṇa Parivrājakas are characterised as *Vādaśila* (*disputations*)[6] *Vitaṇḍās* and *Lokāyatas* (*sophists*, *casuists* and *materialists*);[7] *Tevijjas* (versed in the three Vēdas);[8] *Padakas* (versed in metre); *Veyyākaraṇas* (versed in grammar) and proficient in *Jappa*, recitation or *Jalpa*; *Niganthu* (vocabulary); *Ketubha* (etymology, Itihas etc.)[9] The Parivrājakas also included a number of wandering teachers and scholars (*carakas*) who also had their disciples. The *carakas* were celibates but not necessarily ascetics who resembled, in scholasticism and discussion, the Greek Sophists, who fulfilled the intellectual requirements of the people.[10] Some of them were described as 'Eel-wrigglers'[11] or 'Hair-splitters' and the Eternalists (*Sassatva-vāda*).[12] These *Parivrājakas*, except during the rainy season, spent the remaining seven or eight months wandering in different regions expounding their doct-

[1] *Suyagada*, 1, 12, 1-2.
[2] ibid, 1, 12; 11-20-21. Also for Māhavīr's Kriyāvad: Chapter 7 *Jainism*.
[3] Havell, op. cit., p. 50.
[4] *Maj. Nik.*, II, 23-38.
[5] *Ang. Nik.*, IV, 35.
[6] Sutta Nipāta, 382.
[7] *Cullavagga*, V.3.2.
[8] Sutta Nipāta, 594.
[9] ibid, 1020.
[10] 'The religious atmosphere of the time is perhaps comparable to that which prevailed in the Roman Empire, when many people had lost their implicit faith in traditional verities, and were ready to support any new cult which offered a more plausible and attractive system of belief. In Rome the changing spiritual requirements were met in large measure by mystery cults imported from the East. In India, in the 6th and 5th centuries BC., the wandering ascetics filled the need.' Basham, *The Ājīvikas*. p. 96.
[11] *DOB.*, I, p. 52.
[12] *DOB.*, I. p. 224; cf. Rhys Davids, *Early Buddhism*, p. 4; *Jat.*, iii, pp. 346ff.

rines, meeting new teachers and learning from them and disputing with them, thus winning the allegiance of rulers and peoples. Their philosophical discussions often resulted in conversions and borrowings as between their different sects and schools. The importance of these wandering scholars both Brāhmaṇa and non-Brāhmaṇa to the history of Indian thought is that they were responsible for a wide-spread movement to encourage speculation for its own sake and to repudiate sacerdotalism, authority and tradition, if they were not compatible with their rationalism.

An interesting picture of the conditions which must have prevailed at the time is given in *Neru Jātaka* where we find a certain Buddhist bhikkhu preaching in an unnamed frontier village, and winning considerable support from the villagers. On his departure his place is taken by an eternalist (*sassatavādi*), then by an annihilationist (*ucchedavādi*), and finally by a naked ascetic (*acelaka*), who in turn gain the temporary loyalty of the villagers.

Ascetic Practices

At the time of the rise of Buddhism, the belief in the efficacy of self-mortification, self-torture and holiness of austerity (*tapas*) would appear to have reached its zenith. Asceticism was regarded as identical with religiousness. Piety was synonymous with self-torture. In both Brāhmanism and Jainism which were flourishing, great stress was laid on the ascetic way of life which had become the symbol of sanctity. Even Gautama was taught by his two teachers Ālara Kālāma and Rudrak Rāmputra who were Brāhmana ascetics to follow the ascetic practices of the day. By the sacred life was meant a matter of raiment, dressing in a rough garment or going naked or shaving the head or wearing matted hair or abstaining from fish or flesh or fasting and starving to death or assuming ascetic postures such as lying on the bare earth or besmearing the body with dust or covering oneself with dirt or living under a tree or in the open or never sitting down or merely tending the sacrificial fire and chanting the *mantras*.[1]

The Niganthas and Ājīvikas took a sort of pride in outdoing their Brāhmanic rivals as regards rigorous conduct, mistaking nastiness and filthiness for the highest pitch of ascetic virtue. This is illustrated by a story of a number of naked ascetics who were

[1] *Maj. Nik.*, I, 282; Sutta Nipata, *SBE.*, X, p. 40; *DP.*, 106-7, 141.

assembled in the house of the daughter of Anātha Pindika. Calling her daughter-in-law, Sumāngadhā, she told her to go and see those 'highly respectable persons.' Sumāngadhā ran overjoyed but was horrified to see the ascetics with their hair like pigeon wings, covered by nothing but dirt, offensive and looking like demons.[1] Even the Jaina scriptures admit that pious householders were disgusted by the ascetics who asked for a lodging in their houses—'naked, unwashed men, foul to smell and loathsome to behold.'[2] This was the sort of life which the Buddha called *anāriyam*, ignoble or barbaric. With such degradation of humanity, he would have nothing to do. He forbade nakedness as well as garments of hair and another uncomfortable dress.[3] Jainism teaches that twelve years of asceticism of the severest type were necessary for salvation. The ideal life for a Jaina monk is described in the *Ācāranga Sutra* which involved self-torture and self-mortification leading logically to suicide.[4] These austerities practised by the Jaina monks form but a poor illustration of the extent to which asceticism had been pushed in Buddha's time—in excess, fanaticism and morbidity. They are to be read to be believed.

The *Udumbarika Sīhanāda Sutta* gives us a detailed picture of the extent to which the austerity of self-mortification was carried out by the ascetics:

"The ascetic (*tapassi*) goes naked, is of certain loose habits, licks his hands, respects no approach nor stop; accepts nothing expressly brought, nor expressly prepared, nor any invitations. He accepts nothing taken from the mouth of cooking pot nor placed within the threshold, nor within a mortar, nor among sticks, nor within a quern, nor anything from two eating together, nor from a pregnant woman in intercourse with a man, nor food collected in drought, nor from where a dog is, nor from where flies are swarming, nor will he accept fish or meat, not drink or intoxicants or gruel. He is either a one-houser, or one-mouthful man; or a two-houser, a two-mouthful man; or a seven-houser, a seven-mouthful man. He maintains himself on one alms, on two or on seven. He takes food once a day, or once every two days, or once every seven days. Thus he dwells addicted to the practice of taking food according to

[1] *SBE.*, X, p. 39.
[2] Acara, 11.2.2.
[3] Vinaya, I.30.4.
[4] *SBE.*, XXII, p. 84-87.

rule, at regular intervals, up to even half a month. He feels either on potherbs, or on the powder of rice rusks, on rice-scum, on flour of oil seeds, on grasses, on cowdung, on fruits and roots, from the woods or on windfalls. He wears coarse hempen cloths, discarded corpse cloths, discarded rags, or antelope-hide, or bark garments. He is a hair and beard plucker, a stander-up or a croucher on heels. He uses iron spikes or thorns on his couch. He uses a plank-bed or sleeps on the ground. He sleeps only on one side. He is a dust-and-dirt wearer, an open-air man, a where-you-will sitter and a filth-eater."[1] The catalogue of these austerities is identical with the list in the *Kassapasīhanāda Sutta* where the various practices are also explained.[2]

In the Nikāyas, we repeatedly meet with enumeration of similar kinds of ascetic practices which were popular in ancient India. The catalogue of the Buddha's four-fold austerities in the *Mahā-Sihanāda Sutta*, vividly presents the ideals of mortification of the flesh (*tapas*). The Buddha says that he has lived the four-fold higher life: "He has been an ascetic of ascetics, foremost in loathliness, foremost in scrupulosity and foremost in solitude.'[3] To such a pitch of asceticism he has gone that he says: 'Naked was I, flouting life's decencies, licking my hands after meals, never heeding when folk called to me to come or to stop, never accepting food brought to me before my rounds or cooked expressly for me, never accepting an invitation. I have had but one meal a day, or one every two days or every seven days or only once a fortnight, on a rigid scale of rationing. I have lived on wild roots and fruits or on windfalls only. My raiment has been of hemp, of rags from the dust-heap, of bark of the black antelop's belt, of grass, of strips of bark or wood, of hair of men or animals woven into a blanket. In fulfilment of his vows, I have plucked out the hair of my head and the hair of my beard, have never quitted the upright for sitting posture, have squatted and never risen up, have couched on thorns, have gone down to the water punctually thrice before night-fall to wash (away the evil within). After this wise, in diverse fashions, have I lived to torment and to torture his body.'[4]

In the *Culadukkhakkhandha Sutta* there are references to the

[1] *Digha Nik.*, III, pp. 37-56.
[2] *Digha Nik.*, III, pp. 161-177. Also *Maj. Nik.*, I, 238ff, 342 ff, II, 161f.
[3] *Maj. Nik.*, I.78-79.
[4] ibid.

Jain practices, to a number of Niganthas who always stood and would never sit down and were undergoing paroxysms of acute pain and agony. They subjected themselves to all these pains because Nātaputa, their teacher, had taught them to extirpate evil done in the past by these severe austerities.[1]

In the *Apaṇṇaka Sutta* there are references to recluses and Brāhmaṇas 'who hold and affirm that there is no such thing as alms or sacrifice or oblations; no such thing as the fruit and harvest of actions good or bad; no such thing as this world or the next; no such thing as either parents or spontaneous generation; no such thing in this world as recluses and Brāhmaṇas who have achieved success and walk aright, who have, of and by themselves, apprehended and realized this world and the next and make it all known to others.'[2]

As a contrast to this view, we meet with the freak practices of some naked ascetics who lived like 'dog-ascetics' and 'ox-ascetics,' whose asceticism consisted in feeding and living exactly after the manner of dogs and oxen. The *Kukkuravatika Sutta* refers to Puṇṇa Koliyaputta who was a Bovine. To support his bovine character, he wore horns and a tail and affected to browse on grass.[3] The story is also told of a naked ascetic (*acela*) called Seniya, who was a canine, and squatted like a dog. He had fully and completely developed the dog's habits, the dog's principles of conduct, the dog's mind and the dog's behaviour. He had punctually discharged the vows of his canine vocation and thought that it was the highest life.[4]

An identical picture is given by Aśvaghoṣa in his *Buddhacarita*. The Buddha is told by an ascetic in the forest how different ascetics lived like birds, by picking up grains left in the fields; others ate grass like animals; some lived with snakes; some sat still like ant-hills, with nests of birds in the tangles of their long hair and snakes playing on their bodies; some lived in water, with tortoises eating

[1] *Maj. Nik.*, I.93.

[2] *Maj. Nik.*, I.401-402.

[3] ibid, I.387f; *Dhammsangani*, p. 261.

[4] ibid, I.388-389. Gibbon refers to certain Christian anchorites who were called 'bovines', who 'derived their name from their humble practice of grazing in the fields of Mesopotamia with the common herd.' In the words of Gibbon, they 'aspired to reduce themselves to the rude and miserable state in which the human brute is scarcely distinguished above his kindered animals.' q.b. Chalmers, *DOB.*, I, Introduction, p. xvi.

parts of their bodies, thinking that misery itself is virtue and that the highest happiness in Heaven can be achieved by undergoing sufferings of all kinds.

We thus see that long before Gautama's day the ascetic life was the accepted mode of religious culture. Asceticism was considered the outward and visible sign of holiness. All canons of hygiene and decencies were discarded and austerities were reduced to self-torture of the most ugly types—in excess and fanaticism. Mortification of the flesh was considered the way to salvation. These practices were the salient features of all the schools – from the orthodox Jatila to the Jaina—which sought to surpass one another in the extremes. No new doctrine or speculation could hope to win acceptance or indeed a respectful hearing without the credentials of asceticism. The way from the human to the superhuman was to be found in asceticism alone: such was the abnormal current of thought at that time.

Having presented an exhaustive picture of the environment of his day, let us briefly reconstruct the Budha's life-story in order that we may understand his attitude towards ascetic thought better, as also to know the correlation between his teachings, his actions and experiences.

Buddha's Life

It is difficult to penetrate the mixture of legend and history that partially discloses, and partially shrouds, the life of Gautama, the Buddha, who was one of the giant intellects of human history. In Buddhist tradition it is a moving version idealised by pious imagination and devotion. Though the Pāli texts do not narrate the biography, in a connected form, they do give us details about the principal events in the Master's life which are well-known.

He was born a prince of the Sākya Clan at Kapilavastu. His family name was Gautama and his first name was Siddhārtha. At the age of sixteen, he was married to his cousin, Yaśodharā and they had a son named Rāhula. His early days till he reached manhood were spent in splendour, ease and luxury. He lived a life where the world's miseries were unknown. For almost twenty five years, he saw only the beautiful, knew only the pleasant. The Buddha himself presents to us a vivid picture of the world in which he moved and lived—amid scenes of luxury in palaces and surrounded by all the paraphernalia of sensuous enjoyment. Says he:

"I was delicate, O Monks, extermely delicate, excessively delicate. In my father's dwelling lotus pools had been made, in one blue lotuses, in another red, and in another white ones bloomed, all for my sake. I used no sandalwood that was not of Banaras, my dress was of Banaras cloth, my tunic, my under-robe and cloak. Night and day a white parasol was held over me so that I should not be touched by cold or heat, by dust or weeds or dew. I was lapped in the pleasures of the five senses and revelled in sights, sounds, odours, tastes and touch—which are desirable, agreeable, pleasant and attractive, bound up with pleasures of sense and exciting. Three palaces were mine, one for the rainy season, another for the winter and another for the summer. In the palace of the rainy season, I lived during the four months of the rains, entertained by female musicians, never coming down from the palace. While in the dwelling of others, food from the husks of rice was given to the slaves and workmen together with some gruel, in my father's dwelling rice and meat was given instead to the slaves and workmen."[1]

The Buddhist tradition tells us that on the four occasions when he went out of his palace, he happended to see four persons in four different stages. He saw an old man and felt that he was subject to the frailties of old age, saw a sick man and felt that he was also subject to sickness, saw a corpse and felt that he was also subject to death and met a monk with a peaceful countenance who had, leaving all desires, left the world and adoped the traditional way of the seekers of religious truth.

Siddhārtha thus became acquainted with the sad facts of old age, of disease and of death; for the first time he new the major miseries to which human nature is inevitably subject in a world of decay and dissolution. This experience moved him to anxious and puzzled reflection on the problems of life. He thought he must learn the meaning of life in such a strange world: he must discover the truth—the essential and saving truth—about life and death, about sorrow and hapiness. He resolved to gain freedom from old age, sickness and death. He rembered the words of the mendicant who told him:

Nara—pungava janma mṛtyu bhītaḥ
Śramaṇaḥ pravrajito'smi mokṣā-hetoḥ

(I am a śramaṇa, an ascetic, who in fear of birth and death have left home life to gain liberation.)[2]

[1] *Maj. Nik.*, I. 505; *Ang. Nik.*, I. 145.
[2] Asvaghoṣa, op. cit., V. 17.

The sight of the holy man, healthy in body, cheerful in mind and serene in spirit without any comforts of life impressed him strongly for he says:

Sadhū subhāṣitamidaṁ mama rocte ca
Pravajya nāma vidubhihi satataṁ praśastā
Hitamātmanasca parasatvahitaṁ ca yatra
Sukhajivitaṁ sumadhuraṁ amṛtaṁ phalaṁ ca

(Yes I like this. The learned men always praise such a homeless life. There is happy living and it bears sweet immortal fruit.)[1]

He felt convinced that such a life would help him to find the origin of suffering and sorrow and the means of extirprating them. He decided to renounce the world and as was the fashion of his day, left his home and family and retired to forests to seek after truth.

There are different versions of the reason for this momentous step of renunciation by Gautama. The mere sight of an old man, diseased stranger or even of a dead body, would be insufficient by itself to work so powerful an effect on the mind of one so as to induce him to abandon the world. But we find in this ancient tradition, an expression of what in the main we must ourselves believe to be the possible explanation of the cause of his renunciation. It is also suggested that a feeling of revulsion came upon him when he saw in the night in his palace, the dancing girls in their sleep in ugly postures which aroused in him a disgust for worldly pleasures.[2] He could sense the reality behind the shadows, the sham substance behind the splendour. He decided to be free from the life of lust and luxury and fled into the forest. In the earlier texts like the *Sutta Nipāta* or the *Arīyaprīyesana Sutta*, their is no reference to the above mentioned causes for Buddha's renunciation. It is simply stated: 'A hole-and-corner life is all a home can give.'[3] And 'full of hindrance is household life, a path defiled by passion; free as the air is the life of him who has renounced all wordly things. How difficult is it for the man who dwells at home to live the higher life in all its fulness, in all its purity, in all its bright perfection.'[4]

[1] *Lalita Vistara*, 14.15.

[2] Samavekṣya tataḥ ca tāḥ śayanāvikṛtasya yuvtīradhīrceṣṭāḥ Gunavat apuṣo'pi balagubhāso nṛpasūnuḥ sa vigarhyāḥ cakāra Asvagosa, op. cit., v. 63. Also Yuvatistāḥ śayita vigarhamāṇaḥ: ibid., V. 67.

[3] *Maj. Nik.*, I. 241, I. 179.

[4] ibid.

Gautam placed himself under the guidance of the wisest hermits of his day—Ālāra Kālāma and Rudraka Rāmputra. He studied all their teachings and endeavoured to follow their example. Kālāma taught him Sāṁkhya school of philosophy[1] while Rāmputra who had reached the stage of highest meditation taught him Yoga. But Gautama was dissatisfied. He left both of them and began to practise rigorous ascetic practices, which were in vogue then, along with five other Brāhmaṇa ascetics, who afterwards deserted him. He tried to purify himself by ceremonies and sacrifices, by starvation and austerities, by nakedness and self-torture. He has himself described how for six years in the jungle of Uruvela he patiently tortured himself and suppressed all the wants of nature. He led the most rigorous ascetic life. Says he: 'I have been an ascetic of ascetics; loathly have I been, foremost in loathliness; scrupulous have I been, foremost in scrupulosity; solitary have I been, foremost in solitude.'[2] His body became emaciated and shrunken, so much so that his arms and legs looked like withered reeds, his buttocks resembled the hump of a camel and his ribs projected like the rafters of a house.[3]

Gautama pushed his fast even to such an extent that at last he fell into a swoon from sheer starvation and exhaustion. When he returned to conciousness again, he found no revelation had come to him in his senselessness. He felt convinced that this was not the right way—such radical punishment of the body brought no spiritual illumination and peace but exhaustion, torpor and impotence of mind. He decided to give up ascetic practices and resume normal intake of food and drink so that he recovered his strength.

He pondered over the fruits of his self-mortification and felt convinced that this was not the path to the wisdom he sought. He found that 'with all these severe austerities, he failed to transcend ordinary human limits and to rise to the heights of noblest understanding and vision.'[4] Just as he realised in his palace that the way from human suffering did not lie in the indulgence of worldly pleasures, so did he now realize that fasts and penances did not advance him in his search for deliverance from misery. He tried it all and found it wanting.

[1] Asvaghosa, op. cit., XII. 17-65.
[2] *Maj. Nik.*, I. 78.
[3] ibid, I. 80.
[4] ibid, I. 246.

After he gained bodily health and mental vigour he spent seven weeks under the shade of the tree now called a Bodhi, sitting in a state of deepest and most profound meditation. One night towards the dawn he finally realized the Truth. He thus became Buddha (the Enlightened One). He attained both insight and knowledge and knew for certain that he had achieved full emancipation. He says: 'The Deathless—*amṛta*, enternal life has been found by me.'[1] This was the understanding and liberation he had sought. After the enlightenment, the Buddha refers to himself in the third person as the Tathāgatā—'he who is gone away like (the other Buddhas).'[2] Tathāgatā also means: bringing the truth (*tathā*)[3]; he who has arrived at the truth. The great 'Samaṇa'[5] and the 'Jaina' are[6] also one of the titles of the Buddha.

In the joy of his assured enlightenment Buddha arose and after a brief stay wandered slowly towards the sacred city of Vārāṇasi. His problem was: how could he make his *Saṁbodhi*—sublime knowledge full comprehension, complete enlightenment—intelligible and persuasive to others, so that it might guide them also toward true happiness and peace? Apparently there was a strong temptation to keep his illumination to himself, but it became clear that he must make the attempt to share it with the world: *bhaujana-sukhāya, bahujana-hitāya*.[7] But it meant formulating the basic truth about

[1]*Mahavagga*, I. 6.14; *SBE.*, XIII, p. 93.

[2]Budhaghosha gives eight reasons, which are explained in detail, for calling the Buddha, the Tathāgatā:

(i) He has come in the same way; (ii) He has gone in the same way; (iii) He is endowed with the sign of Tathā (truth); (iv) He is supremely enlightened in Tathādhamma (truth); (v) He has seen Tathā (truth); (vi) He preaches Tathā (truth); (vii) He does Tathā (truthfully); and (viii) He overcomes all. *Sum. Vil.*, I. pp. 59-68.

[3]cf. Chalmers, *Suttam Nipaha*, Introduction, p. xx.

[4]cf. Radhakrishnan, *2500 Years of Buddhism*, Foreword, p. VI.

[5]*Sutta Nipāta*, p. 95.

[6]*Mahavagga*, I, 60,10, *SBE.*, XIII, p. 91.

[7]Isolation from society was no object of the Buddhist Sangha. It was towards the *Bahujana* that its eyes were turned. It set out on its historic career with this goal. The Buddha preached: 'Go forth, O Bhikkhus, on your wanderints for the good of the many, in compassion for the world (*bahujanahitāya bahujanasukhāya lokānukaṁpāya*)—for the happiness of gods and men. Let not two of you go the same way. O Bhikkhus, proclaim that *Dhamma* which is gracious at the beginning, at the middle and at the end.' *Mahavagga*, I.2.1.

life in the halting, inadequate medium of human speech; and then it meant speaking the truth in love, so that others capable of responding to it would sense the answer to their living need too, and would not rest until they had mastered its promise and its power. At Sāranāth, he preached his first Sermon and won his first converts. Then for forty years he continued to proclaim his message, expanding it in its bearing on the problems that sincere inquiries raised and adapting it to the special needs of all who found hope and cheer in his presence. He travelled from place to place, touched the lives of hundreds, high and low, princes and peasants. They all came under the spell of his unique personality. At the age of eighty he passed in the arms of Ānanda, his beloved disciple, with the words: 'Decay is inherent in all compound things. Work out your salvation with diligence.'[1]

Rationalism of Doctrine

The Buddha was a thinker of unexcelled philosophic power. He started on his enquiries in order to solve the problems of life, not to search for the existence of God. His quest ended with a solution of that problem. He broke away completely from that religious tradition of India which believed in 'innumerable gods, ghosts and miracles.'[2] He sought and found the consummation of his quest without the intermediation of the concept of God. The principle on which he based his speculative enquiries was itself philosophic. For him the goal of human endeavours was to find a solution of the problem of life without recourse to any divine agency. Thus he exhibited a keenness of analytic understanding, a rational approach to human problems, discarding all claims to special revelation. He expounded the truth as he had discovered it. He found his standard of truth and his way of discriminating it from error, in the common reason and experience of men as they can be brought to bear on the universal problem of life. In this sense he was the Buddha: 'One who has attained Bodhi.'[3] By Bodhi is meant 'an ideal state of intellectual perfection which can be attained by man by purely human means.'[4] It is on the basis of human means that he expounds

[1]Vayadhammā saṁkhāra, appamādena sampādethāti: *DOB.*, III, Mahaparinibban Sutta, p. 156.

[2]*Mahanidessa*, I, p. 89.

[3]Narasu, *The Essence of Buddhism*, p. 1.

[4]ibid.

the Four Noble Truths (*catvāri ārya satyāni*) which are the results of his personal experience. His goal is to lead man into *Nirvāṇa*, an ideal state produced by the destruction of craving (*tanhā*). The way to the attainment of this goal is through the eight-fold moral path. Nirvāṇa is the state, 'marked on the positive side by a sense of liberation, inward peace and strength, insight into truth, the joy of complete oneness with reality, and love towards all creatures in the universe.'[1]

Not only the Buddha approached human problems with a peculiarly positive way of reasoning, he even discarded all appeals to authority or tradition. He believed in man's capacity to believe, his capacity to see, to feel and to understand. He repeatedly asked his disciples not to accept anything merely on the authority of others or to give unqualified assent to propositions, the truth of which was not clear and distinct. The Buddha exhorts in *Kālāma Sūtta:*

'Believe nothing on mere heresay; do not believe traditions because they are supposed to have been received by some ancient sage; do not believe anything, either because people talk much about it, or because presumption is in its favour, or because the custom of many years bids thee to regard it as true. Indeed, believe nothing on mere authority of the teachers or priests; but whatever according to thy own experience and after thorough investigations agrees with thy reason and is conducive to thy own weal and that of all other living beings, that accept as truth and live accordingly.'[2]

In Buddhism nothing is affected by authority or compulsion, not even by pursuasion. The Buddha does not impose his ideas on others. He tells his disciples to accept his words after examining them and not merely out of regard for him.[3] He also tells them to 'speak only of that on which you yourselves have meditated which you yourselves have known, which you yourselves have understood.'[4] He says: 'I will not force you as a potter his raw clay.'[5] It is for this reason that he does not claim anything exoteric and esoteric with regard to his doctrine. He tells Ānanda: 'I have preached the truth without making any distinction between exoteric and

[1]Burtt, op. cit., p. 29.

[2]*Ang. Nik.*, iii. 653.

[3]Parikṣya bhikṣavo grāhyam mad vaco na tu gauravāt.

[4]*Maj. Nik.*, I. 259; cf. Radhakrishnan, *Occasional Speeches and Writings*, II, p. 233.

[5]ibid, cxx, 11 cf. Radhakrishnan, ibid, II, p. 234.

esoteric doctrine; for in respect of Dharma, Ānanda, the Tathāgathā has no such thing as the closed fist (*baddhamuṣṭi*) of a teacher who holds something back.'[1]

Even while the Buddha lived, he was so far from exercising authority over his own disciples that when requested by weeping Ānanda to leave instructions as touching the Order, he said just before he passed away: 'The Tathāgatā does not think that it is he who must lead the brotherhood or that the *Saṅgha* is dependent upon him. Why then should he leave instructions in any matter concerning the Order?'[2] His faith in the inherent capacity of every man to work out here, in this life, his own salvation is aptly brought out when in his last moments he exhorts Ānanda: 'Rely on yourselves and do not rely on external help. Be ye lamps into yourselves. Hold fast to the truth as a lamp. Seek salvation alone in the truth. Look not for assistance to any one besides yourselves.'[3] The Budddha resisted every form of tyranny over the mind of man.

The Buddha's main concern was to reduce human suffering by explaining its causes; he wanted to expose the evil tendencies in man and show how they could be cured. He was confident that a rational analysis of the basic lessons taught by experience can locate the root of evil as it lies in the inner nature of each human being. That evil was *tanhā* which leads man ever from birth to birth. Its destruction demanded an inward transformation of the human being by a correct life and a correct thinking. The Buddha's keen intellect could probe through the virtue and the deceptions of the thought of his day. He set out, therefore, to preach the knowledge he gained, the truth of his discovery, attained through self-experience. And he started with a view to purify ascetic life first in which he found himself.

Against Asceticism

The Buddha was well conversant with the contemporary ideals of asceticism. Having himself gone further with austerity than the most fanatical of ascetics, he had found penances and selfmortification quite unsatisfactory. He declared himself as an enemy of asceticism and pronounced bodily austerities and self-torture to be not only futile but positively harmful. The self-mortification was an

[1]*Mahaparinibbana-Sutta, SBE.*, XI, p. 36.
[2]ibid.
[3]ibid, p. 38.

actual hindrance. It turned men's minds away from more essential matters. The Buddha, therefore, condemned asceticism, morbid ascetic practices, fanatical excesses and its exaggerations into most ugly types. In lieu of asceticism he preached the simple life of studied and purposeful temperance in all bodily matters, with the body as the mind's obedient servant. He rejected both the extremes of self-indulgence and self-mortification and preached the Middle Path by which the wayfarer avoids the two extremes. The path consists of the *Four Noble Truths* and the *Eight-fold Steps*, and leads one to vision, knowledge, tranquillity and *nirvāṇa*. Each step in the process is an inevitable advance on the path leading to the ideal.

The Buddha gave his message against the background of religious practices which he sought to condemn. He preached a moral path which avoided the two extremes of the pursuit of sensual pleasures on the one hand and severe ascetic discipline culminating in the annihilation of the body on the other. He announces the discovery of this new path in the following words in his First Sermon, which is the basis of all his subsequent teaching:

'There are two extremes, Oh Bhikkhus, which he who has given up the world ought to avoid. What are these two extremes? A life given to pleasure, devoted to pleasures and lusts; this is degrading, sensual, vulgar, ignoble and profitless. And a life given to mortifications; this is painful, ignoble and profitless. By avoiding these two extremes, Oh Bhikkhus, the Tathāgatā has gained the knowledge of the Middle Path which leads to insight, which leads to wisdom which conduces to calm, to knowledge, to *Sambodhi* (enlightenment), to *Nirvāṇa*.'[1]

The Buddha then expounds the Middle Path comprising of the *Four Noble Truths* and the *Eightfold Path* which helped him attain the Bodhi or enlightenment. All that he taught later was either a clarification, amplification or explanation of these fundamental tenets. Thus he set into motion as the legends assert, the wheel of the Dhamma (*Dhamma-cakka-ppavattana*). It is to this Dhamma that the Buddhist Bhikkhu dedicates himself along with the Buddha and the Saṅgha—the 'Three Jewels' when he takes the three vows: 'I take my refuge in the Buddha, I take my refuge in the Dhamma, I take my refuge in the Saṅgha.'

[1]*Mahavagga*, I. 6-17.

The essence of the Path can be stated as follows:

i. Existence is unhappiness (*dukha*)
ii. Unhappiness is caused by selfish craving (*tanhā*)
iii. Selfish craving can be destroyed
iv. By following the eight-fold path whose steps are:
   1. Right views (*Samyag dṛṣti*)
   2. Right intention (*Samyag saṁkalpa*)
   3. Right Speech (*Samyag vāk*)
   4. Right Action (*Samyag karma*)
   5. Right Livelihood (*Samyag ājīva*)
   6. Right Effort (*Samyag vyāyāma*)
   7. Right Mindfulness (*Samyag smṛti*)
   8. Right Concentration (*Samyag samādhi*)

The three steps of Right Speech, Right Action and Right Livelihood lead to physical control (*śila*), Right Effort, Right mindfulness and Right Concentration to mental control (*chitta*) and the first two Right Views and Right Intention to intellectual development (*prajñā*). Nothing short of complete destruction of (*tanhā*) will bring true and dependable well-being to oneself and to others.

In his sermon to the five Bhikṣus in the Deer Park at Vārāṇasi the Tathāgatā explained the Middle Path, the true means of salvation thus:

'Let me teach you, Bhikkhus, the Middle Path, which keeps aloof from both extremes. By suffering the emaciated devotee produces confusion and sickly thoughts in his mind. Mortification is not conducive even to worldly knowledge: how much less to a triumph over the senses! "Mortifications are painful, vain, profitless. And how can any one be free from self by leading a wretched life, if he does not succeed in quenching the fires of lust? "All mortification is vain so long as selfishness leads to lust after pleasures in this world or in another world. But he, in whom egotism has become extinct, is free from lust; he will desire neither worldly nor heavenly pleasures, and the satisfaction of his natural wants will not defile him. He may eat and drink to satisfy the needs of life.'

'On the other hand, sensuality of every kind is enervating. The sensual man is a slave of his passions and pleasure-seeking is vulgar and degrading.' But to satisfy the necessities of life is not evil. To shelter the body from the weather, to cover it decently and comfortably, to protect it against the numerous external causes of pain, to save it as far as possible from fatigue, to eliminate sensations that are disagreeable, in short *to keep the body in good health, is a duty, for otherwise we shall not be able to trim the lamp of wisdom and keep our minds strong and clear.*

'This is the Middle Path, O Bhikkhus, that keeps aloof from both extremes.'[1]

Thus Buddha rejecting both asceticism and sensuality preaches self-control and self-culture by the destruction of ego and leading the simple life of studied and purposeful temperance in all mere physical matters. The body's functions should be respected so far as health required. The Buddha knew that bodily torture was injurious to strength of mind, so necessary for the understanding of philosophical truths. What was of the utmost importance to him was the good life and all else was secondary.

Asceticism in Buddhist Literature

Elaborating his earlier theme on asceticism as to why it is painful, ignoble and useless, the Buddha now discusses with the wanderer Nigrodha in the *Udumbarika Sīhanāda Sutta*, the different ramifications of his attitude towards the self-mortifications. He asks Nigrodha: in what does the fulfilment or non-fulfilment of these self-mortifiations consist? Except saying that they hold self-mortifying austerities, Nigrodha has no other reply. The Buddha, then dwells at length upon how austerity by self-mortification involves blemish *(upakkileso)* in several ways whereas one who does not practice self-mortification keeps away from these blemishes, and to that extent keeps himself pure.

Enumerating various blemishes in the austerities of self-mortifiation the Buddha says:

'When an ascetic undertakes a course of austerity, he becomes self-complacement. He starts thinking that now his aim is satisfied, who is equal to him in this practice? This thought makes him exalted and he despises others. He becomes inebriated and infatuated and careless. He procures gifts, attention and fame which make him more complacent. He makes a distinction between foods, saying: This suits me, this doesn't suit me, deliberately rejecting the latter and waxing greeedy and infatuated over the former, cleaving to them and enjoying them without seeing the danger in them or discerning that they are unsafe; he does not think out of his

[1] *Mahavagga*, I. 6-17. *Buddhacarita*, XV. 26-8.

longings, for gifts, attentions and fame. Rajas, his nobles, Brāhmaṇas, householders and founders of schools—all pay him attentions. And then he grumbles at some recluse or Brahmana who, though lives on all sorts of things like tubers, and is still being revered and honoured by the citizens as a holy man. Thinking that though he lives an austere life he is neglected, he is full of envy and grudge at the citizens. He sits in the public[1] and when on his round for alms among the people says: 'This is part of my austerity.' He works miracles and when asked if he approves of this or not, he deliberately tells untruths. And then if the *Tathāgatā* or a disciple of his, teaches the Norm, uses a method worthy of appreciation, the ascetic does not appreciate it. He, on the contrary, loses his temper and bears enmity. He is liable to be hypocritical and deceitful, as well as envious and grudging; cunning and crafty, hard-hearted and vain; entertains evil wishes and becomes captive to them. He entertains false opinions, becomes possessed of metempirical dogma (*attānam adassayamāno*), misinterpretes his experience, is avaricious and adverse from renunciation. All these things are blemished resulting from asceticism and self-mortification.

'In the opposite case of one who does not practise asceticism, he is free from the above blemishes. He takes the path of self-restraint: not to inflict injury on living thing, not to help in any way in the injury being inflicted nor approves them. He does not take what is not given, does not utter lies, does not crave for the pleasures of senses; neither causing these to be committed nor approving them. As a result he advances upwards and turns not back to lower things. He spends a life of meditation, does not hanker after the world and thus purifies his mind of coveteousness and enmity. He becomes compassionate towards every living thing. Gradually his heart becomes full with equanimity, abounding, sublime and free from hatred and ill-will. Thus living a higher life he attains understanding and realizes insight.'[2]

This is the pattern of holy life that the Buddha suggests which according to him will prevent 'corrupting, entailing birth renewal, bringing suffering, resulting in ill, making for birth, decay and

[1]Buddhaghosa explains: He sits in some meeting (lit. seeing) place and where they can see him, he executes the bat-rite of hanging head downwards like a sleeping bat, the five-fold austerities or stands on one leg, or worships the sun. *Sum. Vil.*, cf. *Jat*, III. 235, IV. 299. I. 493.

[2]*Digha Nik*, III., 37-56.

death in future.'[1] He emphasises that it is for the putting away of these that he teaches the Norm, the Dharma. Thus according to him the ascetic is not one who punishes the body but he who roots out egoism and purifies the soul. The Buddha demands self-sacrifice rejecting asceticism; he inculcates purity discarding austerities. He urges a healthy simplification in living, discerning that the higher life must be rooted in hygiene and not in hysteria. He, therefore, regards the mortification of all desire, the stultification of the will, as mere madness.

Having rejected asceticism which was regarded identical with religiousness and holy living, the Buddha directs his attack against the ascetic's regimen. Says he in the *Cūla-Assapura Sutta*: 'It is not the robe which makes the recluse, nor nakedness, nor dust and dirt, nor bathing thrice a day, nor living under a tree, nor living in the open, nor never sitting down, nor *punctilio in regimen*, nor intoning texts, nor a shock head of matted hair. If the mere wearing of the robe could banish, greed, malice and wrong outlook, then as soon as a child was born, his friends and kinsfolk would make him wear the robe and the greedy will put from them their greed, the malicious their malice, and those of wrong outlook will put from them their wrong in their outlook.'[2] Similarly, he exhorts: 'It is not the shaving of the head, nor the moving of the chin, nor the donning of the yellow robe (*samjnā bhikṣu*) nor the taking of the vows (*pratijnā bhikṣu*), nor the begging of food (*bhikṣaṇā śilo bhikṣu*), nor even the strict observance of the rules of the Vinaya (*jñāpti-caturtha karmadyupasaṁpasanno bhikṣu*) that constitutes *bhikṣutā*, but it is *bhinna kleśatā*, the weeding of the heart from passion and pride, from lust and greed.'[3] Not the external state or habit but the inward purity is that what matters most.

Very rightly, the Buddha maintains in the *Kassapasīhanāda Sutta* that the insight, self-control and self-mastery of the path or of the system of intellectual and moral self-training laid down for the bhikkhu are really harder than the merely physical practices so much more evident to the eye of the vulgar.[4]

Then to the questions: Who is a *Śramaṇa*? Who is a true *Bhikṣu*? he replies in his characteristic vein. The *Śramaṇa* is not he who is

[1] *Digha Nik.*, III. 57.
[2] *Maj. Nik.*, I. 283.
[3] cf. Narasu, op. cit., p. 151.
[4] *Digha Nik*, I, pp. 161-177.

shaven perforce, who speaks untruth, and covets possession, or he, who is a slave of desire like the rest of men; but he who is able to put an end to every wicked desire, to silence every personal preference, to quiet his mind and put an end to selfish thought.[1] And again, the *bhikṣu* is not he who at stated times begs his food, not he who, walking uprighteously desires to be taken as a disciple, with a view to pass for a man of character: but he who has given up every source of sin, who by vision is able to crush every evil inclination, and who lives continently and purely.[2] Restraint in life, habit and thought, seems to be his special virtue. Says the Dhammapada: 'Restrained of hand, restrained of foot, restrained in speech, the best of the self-controlled, reflective, calm, content, alone—it is he that is a true *bhikṣu*.'[3]

The Fruits of Recluse's Life

A question raised by many who became acquainted with the life of the Buddhist monks was also raised in India in the early days of Buddhism: What values, significant for this life and verifiable to others, were attained by those who renounced the world and took to monastic life? The Buddha's answer to this question is charmingly presented in the *Sāmmañaphala Sutta*. King Ajātasattu of Magadha, after pointing out the advantages derived from their occupations by the ordinary people in the world, enquired of the Buddha whether the members of his order derived any such benefits? In reply the Buddha narrated the advantages of the recluse life:

1. The honour and respect shown to a member of a religious order
2. The training in all those lower kinds of morality set out in the *Śilas*, the details of which can be summarised as follows:
   (i) Mercy and kindness to all living beings
   (ii) Honesty, chastity, truthfulness; peacefulness, courtesy and good sense in speech
   (iii) Abstinence from luxury of twelve different kinds and freedom from trickery and violence
   (iv) Not injuring plants
   (v) Not laying up treasure of seven kinds

[1]cf. Narsu, op. cit., p. 151.
[2]Ibid.
[3]*DP.*, V. 362: hathasaṁyato pādasaṁyato vācāsaṁyato saṁyuttamo ajjhattarato samāhito eko santusito tamāhu bhikkhu.

(vi) Not frequenting shows, playing games, using luxurious rugs and toilet luxuries and not taking vain things
(vii) Not using sophisticated and rude phrases when talking of higher things
(viii) Not acting as go-between
(ix) Not practising trickery and mystery under the guise of religion
(x) Not gaining a living by low arts (as described)

3. The confidence of heart, absence of fear, resulting from the consciousness of right action
4. The habit of keeping guarded the door of his senses,
5. The constant self-possession he thus gains and the power of being content with little, with simplicity of life
6. The freedom of heart from the five hindrances to self-mastery and perplexity resulting in the joy and peace which fill his whole being
7. The practice of the four Ghānas
8. The insight arising from knowledge (*nana dassana*)
9. The power of projecting mental images
10. The five modes of mystic insight (abhiñña): the practice of *Iddhi*, hearing heavenly sounds, knowledge of others' thoughts, memory of his own previous births
11. The realisation of the Four Truths, the destruction of the Āsavas and attainment of Arhatship.[1]

When the Buddha concluded his sermon the king confessed that he would treat a person who has joined the Order as one worthy of honour and respect.

Summing Up

Among the world's religious teachers Gautama, the Buddha, alone has rightly judged the intrinsic greatness of man's capacity to work out his own salvation without any extraneous aid. He professed no more than to teach men the way by which they could liberate themselves as he had done himself. He made reason the foundation of his philosophical doctrine and strove for man's freedom in all forms, in order to set free his spirit.

Apart from his being a rationalist, he was the first founder of a disciplined and organised monastic order. He laid emphasis on

[1] *DOB.*, I 47-85.

good conduct instead of rituals and formalities of religion. He rejected asceticism as a means to salvation and demanded self-sacrifice, discarded austerities as painful, ignoble and profitless and created saintliness devoid of morbidity. He found that though renunciation was necessary for transcending suffering, severe mortifying practices which crippled the normal faculties and functioning of man, were detrimental to his pursuit of the highest spiritual goal. He also condemned self-indulgence which was vain, unworthy and fit for the worldly-minded. He, therefore, advocated a more practical and rational Middle Path, which kept aloof from the extremes and preached a life of self-control and self-culture.

Chapter 7

Asceticism in Jaina Literature

Jainism is a monastic religion, which like Buddhism, denies the authority of the Vēdas and is, therefore, regarded by Brāhmanism as heretical. The Jain Church consists of the monastic order and the lay community. It is divided into two rival sections, the Śvetāmbaras and the Digaṁbaras. They are so called because the monks of the Śvetāmbaras wear white clothes and those of the Digaṁbaras originally went about stark naked.[1] The dogmatic differences between the two sections, which were of slow growth, are rather trivial and are based more on conduct and practice rather than creed and philosophy.

Modern historical research has established beyond doubt that Vardhamān Mahāvīra, well-known as the last Tirthaṅkar is not a mythical figure like so many of his predecessors in the tradition of the Tirthaṅkaras 'or ford-makers across the stream of existence.'[2] Pārśva, who too has been proved to be a historical person[3], was the immediate predecessor of Mahāvīra and is believed to have lived 250 years before him. Mahāvīra has been identified with Nigantha Nātaputta, one of the six heretical teachers who are represented in

[1]At the time of Alexander the Great's invasion of India (327-326 BC.) the Digaṁbaras were still numerous enough to attract the attention of the Greeks, who called them 'Gymnosophists' or 'naked philosophers.' They continued to flourish side by side with the Svetāmbaras until after 100 AD., when through Moslem rule they were forced to put on clothes.

[2]*Bṛihat—Svayambhu—Stotra*: Yena pranitaṁ pṛthu dharmatirthaṁ jyeṣṭham janāh prāpya jayanti dukhaṁ.

[3]Jacobi makes out a strong case regarding his historicity. *JS.*, II, *SBE.*, XLV, p. XX-XXII; Kosambi has brought together a mass of material, particularly from the Pāli Books, to show how Buddha himself came into contact with the followers of Parśvanāth even before as well as after his enlightment and how the tenets of that earlier system influenced him in the formulation of his own teachings: *Parśvanāth's Caturyama Dharma.* (Marathi). Pt. Sukhlaji has further supported the thesis and has also tried to show what exactly was the practice of the followers of Parśvanātha. Art. Bhagwān Parśvanātha ki Virāsat (*Darśana aur Cintana*, pt. II).

the Buddhist canon as the Buddha's contemporaries, and especially Mahāvīra, who is depicted therein as the Buddha's opponent and rival.[1] The Jaina tradition, however, ascribes the origin of Jainism to Ṛṣabha, who is believed to have lived many centuries back.[2]

There is no other evidence than literary to prove the authenticity of the Jaina traditions regarding Mahāvīra and Pārśva. The Jaina epigraphical evidence is so far remote from the age in which they had flourished that nothing can be definitely built upon it. But as early as the third century BC, we have a reference to the Niganthas as a distinct class of Indian recluses, in the Seventh Pillar Edict of Aśoka. The Niganthas mentioned in this famous epigraph along with Brāhmaṇa, Śramaṇa and Ājīvika, were no other than the followers of Mahāvīra. This very class of recluses has been honoured in the the Hāthigumpa inscription of Kharavela as the *Arhat Śramaṇas*—Śramanas who were believers in the faith of the Arhatas (*Arhaṁtapasādānam samaṇanam*).[3]

Buddhist Evidence

The Buddhist canon supplies us with very useful information about the Niganthas, who were the followers of Nigantha Nāttaputta, the name by which Mahāvīra was and has been known to the Buddhists, as well as to his own followers and contemporaries. The term Niganthas (*Nirganthas*) means 'the unfettered ones.' The name Nigantha Nātaputta is composed of two separate epithets, Nigantha and Nātaputta. He was Nigantha (*nirgantha*) in a literal as well as in a figurative sense: 'Outwardly unclothed and inwardly unfettered,'[4] free from all wordly bonds and ties. He was called Nātaputta because he was a scion of the *Nāya*, *Nāta* or *Jñātṛ* clan of Kṣatriyas, just as the Buddha was called Sākyaputta, a scion of the Sākya clan. His followers were accordingly called Nirganthaputta (Nirganthaputras) or simply Niganthas. And his lay followers

[1]*The Ājīvikas*, p. 55: According to Basham, 'Rather than Mahāvīra, it is Makkhali Gosāla, who emerges as the Buddha's chief opponent and most dangerous rival.

[2]*Kalpa*, *SBE.*, XXII, pp. 281-285; Riṣabha's life story is narrated in the Kalpa.

[3]*Epi. Ind.*, XIII. As a matter of fact, all the cave-dwellings (lenas) on the Udayagiri and Khandagiri hills were made by Kharavela for the residence of Jaina recluses.

[4]cf. Law, *Mahāvīra*, p. 5.

became known as *Nigantha-Sāvaka.*[1] Later on the lay-followers were simply called the *Sāvakas*, which term is still in usage.

We come across many references with regard to the Niganthas in the Pāli literature. Some of the Suttas introduce to us some of the immediate disciples and contemporary lay followers of the Jaina Tirthaṅkara.[2] The *Cūladukkhankhandha Sutta* faithfully presents the fundamental doctrine of the Nirganthas with a criticism from the Buddhist point of view.[3] The *Sāmaññaphala Sutta* attributes to Nigantha Nātaputta certain religious discipline which was in a way the cult of the earlier Niganthas, the followers of Pārśva.[4] One Sutta yields a faithful description of the *uposatha* as practised by the Niganthas.[5] The *Upāli Sutta* correctly hints at the fact that the lay supporters of the Nigantha Nātaputta were called *Sāvakas* or *Śrāvakas* instead of *Upāsakas.*[6] The *Sāmagāma Sutta*[7] clearly states the name of the place, Pāvā, where Mahāvīra died, which is in agreement with Jaina tradition.[8] The same *sutta* also describes how immediately after his demise, his followers became divided into two camps. There are several references in which Nigantha Nātaputta is associated with five other teachers who passed as notable personalities and leaders of thought.[9] The *Mahāvagga* tells us that the Nigantha Nātaputta taught *Kriyāvāda* while the Buddha taught Akriyāvād.[10] Even some light is thrown on the Nigantha doctrine of *Kriyāvad.*[11] The *Kassapa-Sīhanāda Sutta*[12] furnishes a catalogue of the punctilious ways of certain naked ascetics of the time which might be shown to be precisely the practices observed by the Jinakalpas among the Niganthas, and which remarkably coincide with those depicted in the Jaina texts.[13]

The same set of texts introduce to us the kings and clans and classes

[1] *Culla-Nidessa*, p. 173.
[2] *Vinaya, SBE.*, XVII, pp. 108 ff.
[3] *Maj. Nik.*, I pp. 91 f.
[4] *Digha Nik.*, I. pp. 47 ff. cf. Jacobi, *SBE.*, XLV, p. xxi-xxii.
[5] *Ang. Nik.*, I, pp. 205 f.
[6] *Maj. Nik.*, I, pp. 371 f.
[7] ibid, II, pp. 243 f.
[8] *Kalpa, SBE.*, XXII, p. 269.
[9] *Digha Nik.*, I. pp. 47 ff.
[10] VI. 31, *SBE.*, XVII, p. 108 ff.
[11] *Ang. Nik.*, III. 74.
[12] *Digha Nik.*, I, pp. 161 f.
[13] Jain, *IHQ*, II, pp. 698 ff: 'The Jain references in the Buddhist Literature' cf. Law, op. cit., pp. 10-12.

of people who directly and indirectly supported the Nirgantha movement in Northern India in Mahāvīra's life time. The Jaina canon also mentions as contemporaries of Mahāvīra the same kings as reigned during the Buddha's career and one of the latter's rivals. Mahāvīra is also represented in the *Abhayarājakumar Sutta* as personally interested in the welfare of Devadutta who fomented a schism within the Buddhist order of the time.[1] We also come across accounts of the conversion by the Buddha of the lay disciples of Mahāvīra.[2] At the same time we are told that two recluses, Dirghatapasvi[3] and Satyaka of *Agniveśyāyana gotra*[4] and one wanderer (*parivrājaka*) who were much influenced by the teaching and personality of Mahāvīra. There is also a mention of a great many (*saṁbahula*) Nigantha recluses, who following the instructions and example of the Tirthaṅkar, practised a rigorous form of penance on a ridge of Mount Ṛṣigiri near Rājagṛha.[5]

Such are the main outlines of the early activities of the Niganthas and their leader Nātaputta which may be drawn with the aid of Buddhist literature. Together with the Jaina texts, these sources enable us to breathe the very atmosphere of thought and life in which Mahāvīra moved with his Nigantha followers.

The Conditions of Mahāvīra's Time

Being the contemporary of the Buddha, Mahāvīra lived, moved and preached at a time when the social, political, economic and religious conditions of the time were identical with those of the time of the Buddha.[6]

Alongwith Mahāvīra, the other five religious contemporaries of the Buddha and their doctrines are described in the *Sāmmañaphala Sutta*.[7] The names of the six were:

1. Pūraṇa Kassapa
2. Makkhali Gosāla
3. Ajita Kesakāmblin
4. Pakudha Kaccāyana

[1]*Maj. Nik.*, I, pp. 392-393.
[2]*Mahavagga*, VI. 31 ; *Maj. Nik.*, I. 56.
[3]*Maj. Nik.*, I, p. 371.
[4]ibid, I, p. 237.
[5]ibid, I, p. 92
[6]vide Chapter 6.
[7]*Digha Nik.*, I, pp. 47 ff.

5. Sanjaya Belatthiputta and
6. Nigantha Nātaputta (Mahāvīra)

Each is described in the same stock terms, a formula applied to the six heretics in the Pāli canon.[1] The phrases have a certain importance since they at least indicate the celebrity and influence which the early Buddhist tradition attributed to the six teachers. Each is referred to as the leader of an order (*gaṇācariyo*) well-known, famous, the founder of a sect (*titthakāro*), respected as a saint (*sādhu—sammato*), revered by many people, a homeless wanderer of long standing (*cira-pabbajito*) and advanced in years.[2] All the six teachers, including Mahāvīra, died before the Buddha.[3]

The mental life of India was at this time in ferment, and was permeated by a mass of mutually contradictory theories about the universe and man's place therein. Many theories independent of the Vēdic tradition are referred to in the *Suyagaḍaṅga* which describes the four heretical creeds of the time: *Kriyāvāda*, *Akriyāvāda*, *Ajñānavāda*, and *Vinayavāda*.[4]

It is clear that several teachers like the six named above, gathered group of followers together and founded *saṅghas*, perhaps in some cases loosely linked one with another. From some of these developed *Ājīvikism*, a third heretical sect, beside those of Buddhism and Jainism, which survived the death of its founder, Makkhali Gosāla 'for nearly two thousand years and was at least, locally a significant factor in ancient Indian religious life.'[5] It is believed that Ājīvikism had some influence on Mahāvīra's religious doctrine. This is based on the fact that Makkhali Gosāla stayed with Mahāvīra as his disciple for six years but parted company due to some differences. We shall deal with the Ājīvikas later.

It was an age of the wandering philosophers many of them were mendicants generally grouped as the *Parivrājakas*. They represented the intellectual and spiritual life of the time along with *Śramaṇas* as opposed to the *Brāhmaṇas*. In the Pāli works, the *Parivrājakas* are described as wanderers whose chief object was to meet distinguished religious teachers and philosophers, listen to their discourses and enter into discussions with them 'on matters of ethics and

[1] *Jat*, I, 509; *Digha Nik*, II, 150.
[2] *Digha Nik*., I, p. 49.
[3] *Maj*. *Nik*., II, 243.
[4] *Suyagad*, I. 12.1.
[5] Basham, op. cit., p. 3.

philosophy, nature lore and mysticism.'[1] We get a typical description of them in the Buddhist *Nikayās*[2] and the *Jātakas*[3] which afford an interesting picture of the conditions prevalent at the time. The Jaina text *Bhagvati Sutra*[4] also mentions the regions of Kosala, Magadha, Kāśi and Videha and Campā as the homes of peripatetic philosophers of the Ājīvika type. These seasoned wanderers maintained a wide range of doctrines and varied rules of conduct. They were known by various titles, which usually denoted loosely knit classes of ascetics rather than regularly organized orders, as the Buddhist *bhikkus* and the Jaina *Śramaṇas* later became.

Besides the terms '*bhikkhu*' and '*śramaṇa*' we also find others such as '*acelaka*', '*nigantha*' and '*ājīvika*', which are used quite loosely and obviously do not imply membership of any organized religious body. The world '*acelaka*' was used at the time in a general sense in the same way as the word '*śramaṇa*' because we find the *Naganthas* also mentioned as *Acelakas.*[5] Similarly the term Ājīvika like Nirgantha was probably used to denote almost any non-Brahmanic naked ascetic.[6] The *Sandaka Sutta* seems to embrace all the six heretical teachers, including Nigantha Nātaputta, in the general category of Ājīvikas.[7] As if to clear the confusion of all these terms, the *Dhammapada* commentary, describes the ascetic with unsettled mind (*anavaṭṭhita-citto*), who may start as an *acelaka*, then becomes an *ājīvika*, then a *nigantha* and finally a *tāpasa.*[8] The same work refers to a group of ascetics as *nagga-samana, acelaka* and *ajīvika.*[9] But by the time Nigantha Nātaputta becomes the Jina and Mahāvīra after his omniscience (*kevalship*), we find a gradual, fixation of these terms: 'acelakas' are used to designate the followers of Pārśva, *niganthas*, those of Mahāvīra and Ājīvikas as those of Makkhali Gosāla.[10]

The Buddhist texts offer a typical description of the punctilious ways of all Indian ascetics of the time, and we have already

[1]Rhys Davids, *Buddhist India*, p. 141.
[2]Udumbarika-Sihanad Sutta, *Digha Nik.*, III, pp. 36 ff.
[3]*Neru. Jat.*, III, pp. 264 ff.
[4]*Bhag.*, XV, Su., 550 f, 674.
[5]Patika Sutta *Digha Nik.*, also *Divya*, p. 427.
[6]Basham, op. cit., p. 102.
[7]*Maj. Nik.*, I, pp. 513 ff.
[8]Buddhaghosh, I, p. 309.
[9]ibid.
[10]Basham, op. cit., pp. 96-101.

attempted to offer a detailed picture of the ascetic beliefs and practices then prevalent.[1] The ascetics practised self-mortification and self-suppression with unwavering faith as a means of gaining superhuman powers and insight. The belief in the efficacy of asceticism would appear to have reached its acme. It was regarded as identical with religiousness and was popular with almost all religious sects. In both Brāhmanism and Jainism great stress was laid on asceticism but as regards religious conduct the latter even surpassed the former.

With a view to assess how asceticism in its most extreme form came to be accepted in Mahāvīra's philosophy and his religious system, let us briefly touch upon certain aspects of his life to consider what role asceticism played in his final attainment of omniscience as a *Kevalin* or a *Tirthaṅkar*.

Life of Mahāvīra

He was born in a suburb of Vaiśāli, and belonged to the Naya clan known as Nāta, or *Ñata* (P) and *Jñatṛi* (Sk). His parents were Siddhārtha, a wealthy nobleman and Triśalā, sister of Chetaka, an eminent Licchhavi prince of Vaiśāli.[2] His original name was Vardhamān. At the age of thirteen, he married Yaśodā and had a daughter called Anojja or Priyadarśana.[3] Anojja was married to Jamāli, a Kṣatriya, who after becoming one of Mahāvīra's followers and fellow workers, subsequently disagreed with him.

Not to grieve his parents, Vardhamān renounced the world only after their death and with the permission of his relatives. Thirteen months later, he gave up his clothing and began to wander about as a naked monk. This was probably the first important step in the reformation of the teaching of Pārśva which allowed clothing. The *Ācārañga Sutra*[4] gives us a vivid picture of the way in which he performed his meditation and spent his days in austerities and also

[1]vide chapter 6.

[2]Tradition emphasises the importance of Mahāvīra's noble birth and tells of the transference of his embryo from the womb of the Brahmana lady Devananda, wife of Ṛṣabha, to that of Trisala: *Kalpa,* p. 255; *Smv,* p. 89a; *Than.*, p. 523b; and *Acar.* II, 15, 4-5. According to Jacobi, the idea seems to have been borrowed from the Purānic story of the transfer of the embryo of Krishna from the womb of Devaki to that of Rohini. *JSI.*, Introduction p. xxxi.

[3]According to the Digambaras, he was unmarried. *Age of Imperial Unity*, p. 411.

[4]*SBE.*, XXII, pp. 84-87.

of the treatment he received from the unfriendly people of the neighbouring regions.

For the next twelve years he underwent a course of rigorous bodily mortification at the end of which he attained omniscience. He was given the titles of *Jina* (spiritual conqueror), *Mahāvīra* (great hero) and *Tirthaṅkar* (omniscient). Then for the next thirty years he led the life of a wandering missionary, teaching his religious system and organising his order of ascetics. At the age of 72, he obtained *Nirvāṇa* at a place called Pāvā.[1]

One important event in this period of Mahāvīra's life was his meeting with Gośāla Maṅkhaliputta, the founder of the Ājīvika sect, also known as Makkhali Gosāla.[2] He became a pupil of Mahāvīra in the second year of his monkhood and remained with him for six years. Then came a breach between the two due to some differences and Gosāla went his own way. It is quite probable that the rules about diet current among the Niganthas may have come from the code of the Ājīvikas and some significance must be attached to the coincidence of Mahāvīra giving up his clothing in the year of his meeting with Gosāla.

Mahāvīra, a Reformer

The Jaina tradition represents Mahāvīra as a reformer of an existing religion, most probably that of Pārśva rather than the founder of a new faith. This is corroborated by the Pāli canon which views him merely as a leader of a religious sect of the Niganthas already existing at that time.

Pārśva, the predecessor of Mahāvīra seems to have collected a good number of adherents to his faith. The *Kalpasūtra* says that he had 16,000 monks under Āryadatta, 38,000 nuns under Puṣpacūlra, 1,64,000 laymen headed by Suvrata and 3,27,000 laywomen, the chief among was Sunandā. Besides these he had a number of monks as his disciples who were well-versed in the *Pūrvās* and endowed with various supernatural powers, as also those who were destined to liberation in that very birth.[3]

Apart from the Jaina references to the followers of Pārśva, the Buddhist texts also refer to them. It may be noted that with the aid of these references Jacobi finally proved the pre-Mahāvīra antiquity

[1] *SBE.*, pp. 189-202; *Kalpa*, pp. 217-69.
[2] *Bhagavti*, XV, su., 541, fol. 660-3.
[3] *SBE*. XXII, p. 274; also *Smv.*, pp. 316, 65a, 101 to 103a, 104b.

of Jainism.[1] These texts besides giving the details about his religion called as '*cāujjāma dhamma*,' as we shall see later on, refer to his disciples like Upali,[2] Abhaya,[3] Siha,[4] Asibandhakaputta,[5] Sacea and Patācara.[6]

The religion of Pārśva was called 'Cāujjāma Dhamma'[7] or the fourfold religion consisting of abstinence from hiṁsā (*pāṇaīvāya*), untruth (*musāvāya*), stealing (*adiṇṇādāna*) and possession (*bahiddhādāṇa*).

Other aspects of his religion are revealed by the practice of repenting for the transgressions done, as resorted to by the parents of Mahāvīra. They also practised fasting upto death by lying upon a bed of Kuśa-grass.[8] The practice of giving up all clothing in order to practise the life as a Jinakalpaka monk towards the end of one's career is also referred to in the case of Municandra who was the follower of Pārśva.[9]

It seems certain that the Buddhists were also aware of a similar fourfold religion (*Cātuyāma-saṁvara*) which they attributed to Nigantha Nātaputta:[10]

> 'A Nigantha is restrained with a fourfold self-restraint. He lives restrained as regards all water; restrained as regards all evil; all evil he has washed away; and he lives filled with the sense of evil avoided.'

From this description, it can be gathered that Nigantha Nātaputta held the doctrine of fourfold restraint: restraint from the use of cold water as it contains life[11] and sinful activities,[12] as a result of which

[1] *SBE.*, XLV, pp. XIV-XXI; *IA.*, IX, pp. 158-63; Also see Charpentier, *CHI.*, I, p. 153; Dasgupta, *HIP.*, I., p. 173.

[2] *Maj. Nik.*, *I*, Uppali Sutta.

[3] ibid, I, Abhayarajkumar Sutta.

[4] *Mahavagga*; VI. 31.

[5] *Sam. Nik.*, IV. 317 ff.

[6] *Jat.* III. 1; *Naya*, 139, 218; *Tha.*, p. 457b; *Bhag.*, p. 455a, *Uttara.*, 23, 12; *Rayap.*, 147.

[7] The asceticism of Pārśvanātha has been called 'Cāujjāma' (Sk. Cāturyāma) and the name has been given even to the system of Mahāvira in the Pāli Books. Cāujjāma is also called Sāmājiya Sanjama (SK. Sāmāyika Samayama). Jain, 'The Practice of the Earlier Tirthaṅkaras', *AIOC.*, II, pp. 75-81.

[8] *Acar*, II, 15-16.

[9] *Avasyaka-Comm.*, pp. 285, 291.

[10] *Digha Nik.*, i, p. 74.

[11] *Sum. Vil.*, p. 168: 'So kira sitodake sattasanni hoti.'

[12] cf. *Suyagada*, 2. 6, 8: As killing and sexual intercourse are implied.

he was free from all sins or bonds—Nirgantha and had purified himself. According to Jacobi these fourfold restraints are intended to represent the four vows of Pārśva.[1] However, as we have seen above, these vows were quite different.

But elsewhere in the *Udumbarika-Sīhanāda Sutta*[2] the Buddha in his conversation with the wanderer Nigrodha refers to the fourfold restraints which seem to be ascribed to Nigantha Nātaputta[3] viz. (i) not to inflict injury on any living being, (ii) not to take what is not given, (iii) not to utter lies and (iv) not to crave for the pleasures of sense. Out of these, three are identical with the three vows of Pārśva. Pārśva's fourth rule of *aparigraha*, not to have any worldly possessions (including a wife), was split up into two by Mahāvīra to make up his code of five, viz. to lead a celibate life and not to have worldly possessions. The main difference in the practical or external aspects of Pārśva's and Mahāvīra's code of conduct thus seems to have been that the code of Pārśva allowed monks to wear an under and upper garment, that of Mahāvīra forbade clothes.[4] These two schools, we are told, some 250 years after the death of Pārśva, became one when the disciples of Parśva and Mahāvira met at Śrāvasti and brought about the union of the old branch of the Jaina Church and the new one.[5]

We have thus the evolution of the five great vows (*pañca mahāv-vyas*) that were binding upon every Jaina monk. The five great vows are:

(1) *Ahiṁsā*—not to cause or tend to cause pain or destruction to any living being by thought, speech or conduct.
(2) *Satya*—truth in speech, thought and deed.
(3) *Asteya*—to take nothing, unless and except it is given.
(4) *Brahmacarya*—chastity.
(5) *Aparigraha*—not to have worldly possessions, renunciation of all earthly concerns.

These form the basis of every field of Jaina monastic conduct.

[1] *Uttar.*, *SBE.*, XLV, pp. XX-XXI, *IA.*, IX, p. 160.
[2] *Digha Nik.*, III, 48, para 16.
[3] cf. Vaidya, *2500 Years of Buddhism*, p. 16. Mahāvīra's five Great Vows are mentioned in *Acar*, II, 15, i, 4; 15, V, 5, *SBE.*, XXII, pp. 202-210. Māhavīra was himself observing the all comprehensive and omnibus *Sāmāyika Saṁyama* and it was only after his enlightenment that he preached the Five Vows i.e. Chedovatthāniyama—Jain, loc. cit., p. 78.
[4] *Uttar*, XXIII., 13, p. 121.
[5] ibid, Su., 23.

Even the sixth vow as given in the *Dasaveyāliya* and consisting of the abstinence from taking food at night is apparently the corollary of the first vow. The observance of these basic vows which comprised the whole fabric of Jaina monachism led to the development of numerous rules and conventions which have survived to this day.

Against this background we may say that the religion advocated by Mahāvīra was not a creation of his own. The only thing he did was the organization of moral and disciplinary aspects of the then existing Jaina Church. That he stood for a stricter code of discipline of the body and of the mind is evident from his inclusion of the fifth vow of celibacy (*brahmacarya*) to the aggregate of four vows of Pārśva.

Mahāvira's Kriyāvād

The theory of Karma is the key stone of the Jaina system and the ethical and ascetic practices of the Jains are to be regarded as the logical consequences of this theory.[1] The statement emphasises the importance of the Karma doctrine in the teachings of Mahāvīra, and its application to moral and disciplinary aspects of asceticism, monasticism and the life of the laity.

Mahāvīra is represented as an exponent of Kriyāvād as opposed to the Buddha who taught Akriyāvād.[2] *Kriyā* denotes the existence of soul (*jiva*) and those who admit the existence of soul are called *Kriyāvādins*. It is stated that one who knows the torture of beings below in hell, one who knows the influx of sin and its stoppage, one who knows the misery and its annihilation is entitled to expound the *kriyāvād*. The principle tenets of the *kriyāvād* school are that misery is the result of one's own acts and is not caused by anything else; that release from *saṁsāra* can be secured by knowledge of the highest truth and by good conduct. The doctrine admits the existence of soul or self, this world and the next, believes in reward and action and holds that there are causes of misery which can be controlled.[3] The doctrine invests man with moral responsibility for all his deeds. On its logical or dialectical side it came to be described as a doctrine of *nayas*,[4] and on its pragmatic or practical side as *Kriyāvāda*.[5] The

[1]*ERE*., pp. 469-470.
[2]*Mahavagga*, VI. 31; *SBE*., XVII, p. 108 ff, *Ang. Nik*., IV, pp. 180-181.
[3]*Suyagad*, I. 12, 11-20-21.
[4]*Uttar*., XXVIII, 24.
[5]*Stkr*., I, 12, 21.

three spheres of the self to which it was required to be represented by these three terms: *jñāna* or sphere of knowledge and intuition, *darśana* or sphere of faith and devotion and *caritra* or sphere of conduct and behaviour.[1]

We are introduced to the doctrine of *kriyāvad* which forms the basis of Mahāvīra's teaching by Abhaya, a learned prince of the Licchhavi of Vaiśāli in these words: 'The Nigantha Nātaputta knows and sees all things, claims perfect knowledge and faith; teaches the annihilation by austerities of the old Karma and prevention by inactivity[2] of new Karma. When Karma ceases, misery ceases.' Karma presupposes belief in *saṁsāra* and soul. An elaboration of the same teaching is presented elsewhere by way of clarification thus: 'Whatsoever a person experiences, whether it is pleasant or painful or neither pleasant nor painful, is due to his *Karma* (totality of deeds in the past. Hence by extenuating through penance (*tapasā*) the effect of all past deeds and by not accumulating the effect of fresh deeds, the future gliding in rebirth stopped, the past is wiped out; with the past wiped out, ill is no more; with ill no more, painful feelings are no more; with painful feelings no more, all ill is outworn (exhausted) or negated.'[3] Here penance (*tapa*) means the practice of austerities (*dukkaracariyā*).

The Jaina counterpart to these tenets can be easily cited. It is said of the Nirgantha that 'By austerities, he cuts off Karman;'[4] by renouncing activity he obtains inactivity, by ceasing to act he acquires no new Karman and destroys the Karman he had acquired.'[5] We are told that 'Karman is the root of birth and death and birth and death, they call misery.'[6] Thus the practice of asceticism is necessary to put an end to misery. The goal of treading such a path is made quite clear: 'A man who is indifferent to the object of the senses and to the feelings of the mind is free from sorrows; though still in the *saṁsāra*, he is not afflicted by that long succession of pains, just as the leaf of the lotus is not moistened by water.'[7] The purpose of the austerities (*tapas*) is to prevent the

[1]*Stkr.*, I, 6, 14.
[2]*Uttar*, XXVIII, 24.
[3]*Ang. Nik.*, I, pp. 220-221; *Maj. Nik.*, II, p. 214.
[4]*Uttar.*, XXIX, V. 27.
[5]ibid, XXIX, V. 37.
[6]ibid, XXX, V. 7.
[7]ibid, XXXII, verses 34, 47, 60, 73, 86, 99 condensed.

formation of new Karma as well as to put an end to the old Karma with a view to be free from the cycle of birth and death. The goal is *Nirvāṇa* or final liberation

We are thus led to the sphere of Jaina ethics which has for its end the realization of *nirvāṇa* or *mokṣa.* The necessary condition for reaching this end is the possession of right faith (*samyag darśana*), right knowledge (*samyag jñāna*), and right conduct (*samyag carita*) metaphorically called the 'three jewels' (*triratna*).[1] Right faith consists in believing the true ideal (*āpta*), scriptures (*āgma*), and teacher (*guru*).[2] Right knowledge consists of the nature of the soul and non-soul, devoid of doubt or error.[3] Right conduct means living a life in accordance with the light gained by the first two jewels, right conviction and right knowledge. It must be such as to keep the body down and elevate the soul. The barrier is the *karmic* matter which obscures the true nature of the soul.

The consideration of the problem of how the obstacle of Karma (*karmic* matter) 'which binds the soul in *saṁsāra*'[4] be removed, brings out the necessity of having a code of conduct, both for laymen and ascetics, which must directly or indirectly be conducive to this central aim. Naturally the rules for ascetics are stricter than those for laymen and provide a shorter *albeit* harder, route to *nirvāṇa*, which is the goal for the layman also, but one which he reaches by a longer and a slower process. Of the first importance, are the five vows (*mahāvrata*) referred to earlier, the first four of which are also acknowledged by Brāhmanism and Buddhism. These vows are to be strictly observed by monks who take them on taking initiation (*dikṣā*).[5] Jainism thus lays down that for attainment or *nirvāṇa*, the highest goal is to get rid of Karma (*nirjarā*)[6] and meanwhile to acquire no new Karma. The path of asceticism (*tapas*) can help to speedily annihilate the old Karma than would happen in the common course of things. Therefore the whole apparatus of monastic conduct in Jainism seeks to prevent the formation of new

[1] *Tattva.*, i, 1: Samyag darśanjñānacaritrāṇi moksamārgaḥ.

[2] *Ratnakaranda—Sravakacārya*, 4.

[3] *Dravya Saṁgraha*, 42.

[4] *Panchāstikāya-gatha*, V. 27: Jivo tti Kammasaṁjutto.

[5] Lay people, however, should observe them so far as their conditions admit, hence they are called the small vows (anuvrata). The duties of a *Śrāvaka* intent on following the path of salvation are laid down in the *Sagar-Dharmāmṛta.* Summarised by Jaini, *Outlines of Jainism*, p. 68.

[6] *Tattva.*, IX. 3: Tapasā nirjarā ca.

Karma. By living an austere life of purity and virtue one can escape the ills of life which are due to the endless cycle of birth and death. Jainism, however, considers the life of renunciation as the best life and hence the shortest way to *Nirvāṇa.* Asceticism thus acquires a conspicuous status in Mahāvīra's doctrine.

Asceticism in Jaina System

The Nirgantha argument of the practice of penance or austerity is clearly set forth in the *Majjhima Nikāya*: 'Beatitude cannot be reached through mundane happiness. It is attainable through the mortification of the flesh. Had it been possible to reach beautitude through mundane happiness, King Śrenika Bimbisāra of Magadha would certainly have attained it.'[1]

Mahāvīra, by his own life, furnishes a pattern of an extraordinarily rigorous application of ascetic practices to be followed by the monks in their religious life. This has been accepted as the ideal life for a Jaina monk which is described vividly in the *Ācārańga Sūtra* as follows:

'Giving up his robe, the Venerable One was a naked, world relinquishing, houseless sage. When spoken to or saluted, he gave no answer. For more than a couple of years he led a religious life, without using cold water; he realized singleness, guarded his body, had got intuition and was calm. For 13 years he meditated day and night and was undisturbed in spirit. Practising the sinless abstinence from killing, he did no injurious acts; he consumed nothing that had been prepared for him; he consumed clean food. Always on his guard, he bore the pains caused by grass, cold, fire, flies, gnats, undisturbed. Whether wounded or unwounded, he desired not medical treatment. Medicines, anointing of the body and bathing cleansing of the teeth, did not behove him after he had learned the path of deliverance. Sometimes the Venerable one did not drink for half a month or a month. Sometimes he only ate the sixth meal, or the eighth or the twelfth. Without ceasing in his reflections he wandered about and killing no creatures, begged his food. Whether he did or did not get such food—moist or dry or cold, he was rich in self-control.'

[1]*Maj. Nik.*, I. 93=Na sukhena sukhaṁ adhigantabbaṁ dukhena kho sukhaṁ adhigantabbaṁ sukhena ca sukham adhigantabbaṁ abhavissa, rājā Magadho Seṇiyo Bimbisāro sukhaṁ adhigacheyya.

The privations Mahāvīra suffered at the hands of the hostile populace are also described:

'He wandered naked and homeless. People struck him and mocked at him—unconcerned, he continued in his meditations. In Ladha the inhabitants persecuted him and set the dogs on him. They beat him with sticks and with their fists and threw fruits, clods of earth and potsherds at him. They disturbed him in his meditations by all sorts of torments. But Mahāvīra withstood it all.'[1] In short, he had cut off all earthly ties and was not stained by any worldliness. Like a lotus-leaf he remained unsoiled.

It is no exaggeration to say that even while the Master was alive, the Nirgantha recluses sought to imitate his life. In both Brāhmanism and Jainism which were in a flourishing condition in the time of the Buddha, the Niganthas took a sort of pride in outdoing their Brāhmanic rivals, as regards rigorous conduct. The Jaina religion teaches that twelve years of asceticism of the severest type are necessary to gain salvation. From the various penances recommended for a monk, it seems that practices of bodily mortification were held in high esteem. These, no doubt, reveal a high standard of asceticism and self-control.

Tapas as an Institution

One of the most important institutions of Jainism is asceticism, austerities or *Tapas*.[2] The truth of this statement becomes evident if we examine the practice of asceticism as (i) important for the right conduct of those who strive to attain *Nirvāṇa* and (ii) its observance as a rigorous mode of monastic life.

Tapas is divided into (a) external and (b) internal *tapas*; the former comprises the austerities practised by the Jainas, the latter their spiritual exercises, concerning self-discipline, the cleansing and purifying of the mind, especially by the Jaina monks.

Both the internal and external were further divided, each into six sub-divisions, which were as follows:[3]

External Tapas

Among austerities, fasting is the most conspicuous. The Jainas

[1] *Acar*, *SBE.*, XXII, pp. 84-87.
[2] *ERE.*, VII, p. 469.
[3] *Than.*, p. 364b; *Smv.*, 11b. *Uttar.*, 28, 34; 30, 8; *Bhag.*, 29a, 921a.

have developed it to a kind of art and reach a remarkable proficiency in it. These six types are:

(1) *Aṇasaṇa* (*Anaśana*)—fasting.

(2) *Ūṇoyariyā* (*Anavāpta*)—eating less than what one desires.

(3) *Bhikkhāyariā* (*Bhikṣācarya*)—begging food (in a peculiar way). It consisted of imposing certain restrictions upon oneself regarding the mode of begging or the nature of the donor or the quality of food or the way in which food was offered.

(4) *Rasapariccāya* (*Rasa-parityāga*)—Renunciation and suppression of taste and of dainty food.

(5) *Kāyakilesa* (*kāyā-kleṣa*)—mortification of the body. It consisted of the practice of various bodily postures.[1]

(6) *Samlinayā* (*saṁlinatā*)—Living with perfect self-control in a pure and lonely residence which is in all likelihood devoid of any temptations.[2]

One of the form of fasting is starving oneself to death (*māraṇantiki saṁlekhanā*), also called religious suicide.

Internal Tapas

(1) *Pāyacchitta* (*Prāyaśchitta*)—Penance in expiation of any fault, committed consciously or unconsciously.

(2) *Vinaya*—modesty—It consisted of perfect self-control and purifying the mind by means of right knowledge, faith and conduct.

(3) *Veāvacca* (*Vaiyapritya*)—service to others. It consists of sincere and actual attendance on old, infirm and sick sadhus.

(4) *Sajjnāya* (*svādhyāya*)—reading the scripture, study.

(5) *Jhāna* (*Dhyāna*)—meditation.

(6) *Viūsagga* (*Vyutsarga*)—non-attachment to the body. It consisted either of giving up food, or the care of the body or the four passions.

The application of the internal and external *tapas* in the life of

[1]Summarised by Deo, *HJM.*, p. 188.

[2]According to Digaṁbar texts, *bhiksācaryā* and *samlinatā* are replaced by *vrttiparisankhya* and *viviktasayanasana*. *Mul*, 5, 148-49; *Tattva*, 9, 19.

A very useful summary on the subject is given by Deo, who groups some representative transgressions covering the various fields of monastic life and the punishments prescribed for these. Deo, *Jaina Monastic Jurisprudence*, pp. 61-80.

the monk amounts to denying him every form of comfort and merely keeping him alive. Especially internal *tapas* embraces all that belongs to spiritual discipline, including contemplation e.g. confessing and repenting of sins.

We shall now take certain facets of monastic life with a view to show its rigorous code which is but an extension of the belief and practice of asceticism in its most extreme form.

Clothing and Nudity

The Digambaras maintain that as the Tirthaṅkaras in their highest stage never wore clothes, in the same way the monk should be naked too, in order to symbolise the ideas connected with *nirganthatva* (boundlessness) and *aparigrahatva* (non-possession).

Early texts like the *Ācāraṅga*[1] state that it was Mahāvīra who started the practice of nudity after a period of thirteen months after his renunciation. The *Sthānāṅga*[2] also refers to the fact that Mahāvīra himself told his disciples that 'I have laid down the practice of nudity (*mae acelate dhamme paṇṇatte*). The same view is expressed by the *Daśavaikālika*[3] which disallows all efforts of bodily decoration to the monk as he is *nagiṇa* (naked) and *muṇḍa* (tonsured) The *Uttarādhyāyana*[4] also lays down nakedness as the sixth *parīsaha*.[5] The *Thānāṅga*[6] gives five advantages of nudity. It may be noted that celibacy and nudity are closely related from the point of view of controlling the senses and non-attachment to bodily pleasures and external needs. Thus 'freedom from bonds' was the main idea behind the practice of nudity.[7]

Though nakedness was considered a necessity for salvation as practised by Mahāvīra himself who was habitually naked, it seems

[1] *Acar.*, I, 8. 1. 3.

[2] *Than.*, p. 460b.

[3] *Dasa.*, 6. 65; 4. 2. 1.

[4] *SBE.*, XLV, p. 9.

[5] *Uttar.*, Chapter 2, *Smv.* p. 40b. There are twenty-two troubles (*parīsahas*) to which a monk was often subjected to. There were: hunger, thirst, cold, heat, mosquitoes and flies, nakedness, dissatisfaction with the objects of control, women, wandering life, places of study, lodging, abuse, death, asking for something, not to get what is wanted, illness, pricking of grass, bodily dirt, kind and honourable treatment, knowledge and reason, ignorance and equanimity.

[6] *Than.*, p. 342b, 343a. Comm. attributes it to the Tinakalpas.

[7] On this point of Jaina practice (of nakedness), Benarasi Dass makes some interesting remarks with an illustration of the well-known story of the expulsion of Adam and Eve from heaven: *Lecture on Jainism*, p. 69.

he made slight concessions to public opinion and human frailty. He permitted his followers to wear a minimum of covering to avoid embarrassment and the accusation of indecency. Thus inspite of such constant references to nakedness, the rules about clothing did not seem to make it a compulsory item.[1] On the other hand the Ājīvikas in the times of Mahāvīra practised complete nudity.[2] And yet the vow of non-possession in its severest form emerged in the vindication of nudity so peculiar to the Digambar Jainas.[3]

Celibacy

In all the three principal systems—Brāhmanism, Buddhism and Jainism, celibacy or *Brahmacarya* forms the common basis of the ethical foundation along with the principal vows of *ahiṁsā*, *satya*, *asteya* and *aparigṛaha*.

A well-controlled mind led to the practice of ideal celibacy. All that which tempted and disturbed the mind was prohibitive to the monk. He was asked not to look at females or walk along with them; was not allowed to be alone with a woman or to use beds slept over by them, or tell stories regarding them or to remember former enjoyments or to eat spicy food or eat too much or gaze at wall-paintings of women. He was asked to remain aloof from a woman even if she was disfigured and hundred years old for 'they are to monks what a cat is to a chicken.'[4] The monk, thus, was not allowed to take bath, or clean his teeth, or use flowers and scents or fan his body.[5] All his life he was to carry the dirt on his body and no attempts of external purity were encouraged.[6] Use of purgatives[7] or of enema, applying collyrium, playing dice[8] and going to all sorts of recreation like dramas etc.,[9] were the forbidden items of monk life.

[1] *Acar.*, I, 6, 2, 3; I, 7, 7, 1; *Stkr*, 2, 1, 56; *Uttar.*, 23, 32-33, 2, 12-13.

[2] Hoernle, *ERE.*, I, p. 262; *Divya*, p. 165; cf. Basham, op. cit., p. 109.

[3] In Brahmanism, the Paramahaṁsa and the Turiyātita remained naked: *Nāradaparivrājaka*, *UP.*, *MU.*, pp. 174-175, which classifies *Samnyasis* in six kinds: *Kuticaka*, *Bahūdaka*, *Haṁsa*, *Paramahaṁsa*, *Turiyatita* and *Avadhuta*.

[4] *Stkr.*, 1, 4, 1, 5; *Uttar*, 16, 1-10; *Than.*, 444a; *Smv.*, 151; *Dsv.*, 2, 4, 7-11, 8, 54-58.

[5] *Dsv.*, 3, 2-3; 61-64; *Sam.*, 35b; *Than.*, 460b; *Stkr.*, 1, 9, 13.

[6] *Uttar.*, 2, 37; *Acar.*, II, 13, 1-23.

[7] *Dasa.*, 3, 9.

[8] ibid, 3, 4; *SBE.*, XLV, p. 303.

[9] *Acar.*, II, 11, 1, 18; *SBE.*, XLV, p. 305.

Loya

It was a custom with many *Saṁnyāsis* and *Bhikkhus* to cut or shave off their hair but a peculiar and most painful custom of the Jaina is that all monks, as a proof of their power of endurance, must practice *loya* or uprooting of the hair on the head and beard.[1] It is the extremest form of the idea of the non-decoration of the body and of self-control. 'Only those can do it who have no love with their flesh and bones.' It is looked upon as a sign that the monk or nun will have no thought for the body.

Ahiṁsā

It is the Jainas who far more than any other religion emphasize Ahiṁsa. In thought and practice they aim at an extraordinarily rigorous application of the doctrine which finds the foremost place in the *mahāvratas* of the Jaina monk. The underlying idea is an extreme reverence for life and of a dogmatic belief that not only men, animals and plants but the smallest particles of earth, fire, water and wind are endowed with living souls. Consequently a very large part of the Jaina monk's attention was directed to using the extremest care not to injure any living being, or thing, by speech, thought or conduct.

If we examine the whole set of rules regarding food of the monk, we find that it is reduced to three categories. According to these, a monk was to accept such food as was free from the acts of killing beings, free from the doubt of its purity and free from the faults of preparation, acceptance and begging.[2]

The element of *ahiṁsā* was foremost in these rules which made a monk forego not only raw, powdered and vegetable food but even that which was given with a wet hand or with a ladle besmeared with other impure articles. Not accepting cold unboiled water, not traversing over mud or bridge or rain-water or ash etc. implied the effort in the strict practice of *ahiṁsā*. The rule of not taking food at night was also as a result of such considerations. For the same reason, the monk cleaned his requisites,[3] scanned the places of easing

[1]The typical phrases used in this connection are 'munde bhavitta agārāo anagariyaṁ pavvaio', *Smv.*, 37a. *Than.*, 46a, 176b, 307a, 400b or 'pañcamutthiyaṁ loyaṁ karei' (in five handfuls) *Naya.*, p. 218; *Bhag.*, 430b, 620a.

[2]*Bhag.*, 293a; *Comm.*, p. 294a; *Than.*, p. 452a.

[3]*Dsv.*, 8, 17.

nature,[1] did not do any fire activity[2] and covered his face or the place where his sneezing or yawning or vomitting was likely to spread.[3] Not only that, he had to be careful in not hurting the feelings of others by his speech or behaviour.[4] The reason behind that was that 'all living being desire to live and not to die. Therefore, the Nigganthas give up killing of living beings.'[5] The very fact that he had to avoid forty-six faults in the course of his begging round prove the utmost sanctity attached to the doctrine of *Ahiṁsā.* In fact, he was more particular about minor living beings than himself. That is why Charpentier remarks that Mahāvīra 'seems in reality often to care much more for the security of animals and plants than for that of human beings.'[6] If non-injury to life was so much respected, why not the same attitude be applied to human life as well?

Voluntary Death

The monk always yearned to escape from the cycle of births and rebirths and the sooner he reached the end of worldly existence the more happy he was. So eager was he to part with the world that in his uttermost anxiety he parted even with a scrap of clothing or a blade of grass. The whole outlook of life being that of non-attachment, he practised the most severe self-mortification sustaining his body so far as it served his purpose of a religious life. Logically, self-mortification should lead to suicide. And in Jainism, while all other kinds of killing are strictly forbidden, suicide or voluntary death is highly praised. The proper method for such a death is to retire, after practising mendicancy and the approved austerities for twelve years necessary for salvation, to a secluded spot and having cleared it of all living creatures, starve one's self to death. 'This method,' says the *Ācārańga Sūtra*, 'has been adopted by many who were free from delusion. It is good, wholesome, proper, beautifying and meritorious.'[7] This is called *'maraṇantiki saṁlekhana'* fasting unto death. Actually a planned scheme of mortification

[1] *Dsv.*, 8, 18; *Than.*, 380a; *Uttar.*, 24, 17-18; *Acar.*, II, 10, 1-22.
[2] ibid, Chapter 4.
[3] *Acar.*, II, 2, 3, 28.
[4] *Dasa.*, Chapter 7.
[5] ibid, 6, 11.
[6] *CHI.*, I, p. 162.
[7] *JS.*, *SBE*, XII, p. 307.

spread over a period of twelve years as a prelude to fast unto death is prescribed.[1]

A monk took recourse to voluntary death with the permission of his teachers when he found that he could no more sustain his body. It was better to commit suicide than to fail to practice austerities. Various forms of death are described in the *Aṅgas*, with the sole aim of gradually preparing oneself for the last journey. In all these cases, the monk goes without any food and drink till death overtakes him. Some of the forms are; (1) *Bhaktapratyākhyāna*[2] (awaiting death after total abstinence from food and drink), (2) *Ingitamaraṇa*[3] (awaiting death lying on a bare piece of ground free from living beings), (3) *Pāovagamaṇa*[4] (awaiting death standing motionless like a tree) and (4) *Saṁlehaṇa*[5] (*pandita-maraṇa*). All these were known as '*sakāma*' or wise man's death as it was met with one's will for it. As a contrast as many as twelve kinds of death[6] are condemned by Mahāvīra and hence unfit for ideal monks.

The method of voluntary death considered to be the best mode is included as one of the internal austerities (*tapas*). It is known as *Utsarga* which consists in showing and feeling absolute indifference to the body and its needs. Its furthest development leading to death is termed as *Pādopagamana Santharo*, which is, as a rule, practised by the monk.[7] In this connection, Mrs. Stevenson rightly observes: 'It is strange that a religious system which begins with the most minute regulations against the taking of the lowest insect life should end by encouraging human suicide.'[8] For a while, she forgets that the Jaina tradition has put a stamp of religious sanctity on this method, turning it into an institution down the ages.[9]

From our examination of the Internal and External *tapas*, together with certain aspects of monastic life viz. Clothing and Nudity,

[1] *Uttar*., 36, 249-54; *Than*., *Comm*., pp. 95ab, 96a; *Naya*., pp. 46, 157, 200.
[2] *Acar*., I, 7, 8, 7-10.
[3] ibid, I, 7, 8, 11-18.
[4] ibid, I, 7, 8, 19-23.
[5] *Uttara*., 5, 2-3: *Than*., 93b. 175a.
[6] *Than*., 93b, 94ab, *Acar*., II, 10, 13: For details see *Deo*, *HJM*., p. 202.
[7] Stevenson, *The Heart of Jainism*, p. 168.
[8] ibid.
[9] In the law-books also the hermits and *Saṁnyāsis*, who have attained the highest stage of asceticism, are recommended starvation. Āpastamba says: 'Next he shall live on water then on air, then on ether.' See *Ap*. *Ds*. 22, 4; 23, 2, *SBE*., II, pp. 154, 156, *Manu*., VI, 31; *Yaj*. III, 55; cf. Bühler, *Indian Sect of the Jainas*, p. 16, fn. 5.

Celibacy, Loya, Ahiṁsa, Voluntary Death by Starvation, etc. the emphasis on the extreme form of self-suppression and self-torture can easily be seen.

Ājīvikas

Out of the philosophic ferment of the sixth century BC at least three unorthodox sects developed in the same region, all seeking more satisfying explanation of the cosmic mystery than those of sacrificial Brāhmanism and the Upaniṣadic gnosis. These sects, named heretical by the Brāhmanas, were built round the doctrines of the Buddha, Mahāvīra and Gosāla, and the creeds came to be known as Buddhism, Jainism and Ājīvikism. As the legend goes, Gośāla, the founder of the Ājīvikism, as we have referred to him earlier,[1] was closely associated with Mahāvira, the Jaina Tirthaṁkara, but later on their partnership was broken.

While concluding the study of the Ājīvikas, 'their long but by no means glorious existence,' Basham gives an outline of their history thus:[2]

'Closely allied to Gosāla were Pūraṇa Kassapa, the antinomian, and probably Pakudha Kaccāyana, the atomist, whose doctrines were adopted by the later Ājīvikas, Gosāla's fatalism inspired the new sect, which developed around groups of naked wanderers, devoted to asceticism, but accused by their opponents of secret licentiousness.[3] A vigorous lay community supported the Ājīvika sect, which held its own until the Mauryan period, when it appears to have reached its zenith and to have received the patronage of Aśoka and of his successor Daśaratha. After this, however, the Ājīvika community in Northern India dwindled rapidly and soon became insignificant.'

[1]According to Basham, the account of the circumstances of the meeting seems by no means reliable and was probably introduced to stress the inferiority of Ājīvikism to Jainism and of Gosāla to Mahāvīra. *The Ājīvikas*, p. 40.

[2]ibid, pp. 278-288.

[3]The Buddhist accused the Ājīvika ascetic of secret indulgence in rich foods behind a cloak of false austerity, while by the Jaina he was often condemned for his unchastity.

Vide: *Mahasaccaka Sutta*, *Maj. Nik.*, I, p. 238; *Vinaya*, IV, pp. 223 ff *Stkr.*, II, 6, 8 fol. 390.

Mrs. Stevenson, with the aid of certain Jaina sources, paints Gosala as living a life 'of sin and shame.' She calls him characteristically—Mahāvīra's 'Unruly disciple': op. cit., pp. 58-60.

However, in South India where Ājīvikism reached in the Mauryan period, it survived there longer than in the North at least until the fourteenth century.

Various views regarding the interpretation of the term 'Ājīvikas' are examined by Basham,[1] which also throw some light on their belief and practice. We can do no better than summarise them:

(*i*) According to Hoernle, the term '*Ājīvika*' is derived from '*Ājīva*' (livelihood) and means 'the mode of life or profession of any particular class of people, whether they live as householders or as religious mendicants.' It may also mean 'one who observes the mode of living appropriate to his class.'[2]

(*ii*) The term 'Ājīvika' like 'Nirgantha' originally had a wider connotation than the organised followers of Makkhali Gosāla and might be applied to any non-Brāhmanical naked ascetic.[3]

(*iii*) The proposition ā in the term 'Ājīvika' has more often the force of 'until' than 'as loag as,' but 'it may denote the limit 'to,' 'until,' 'as far as,' 'from,' either including the object named or excluding it.'[4] This possibility becomes clear from the *Dīgha Nikāya*, where a certain 'acela' ascetic Kandara-Masuka is referred to as maintaining seven life-long vows. The first of these was: 'As long as I live, I will be naked and will not put on a garment.'[5]

His other vows viz. perpetual chastity and demiliting the area in the four directions beyond which he undertakes not to travel are vows of a Jaina type.

(*iv*) It denoted in its narrowest sense the disciples and followers of Makkhali or Mankhaliputta Gosāla.[6] This included free-lance ascetics of a similar type or followers of other leaders who later merged with the Ājīvika order.

Ājīvika practices, doctrines and their influences on Jainism

The Pāli texts refer to all six, heretical teachers together in such a manner as to suggest that their relations were by no means always mutually antagonistic. Numerous points of similarity in Jaina and

[1] op. cit., pp. 101-104.
[2] *ERE.*, I. p, 25a, cf. ibid, p. 102, Basham, however qualifies (i) by (ii).
[3] Basham, ibid, p. 102.
[4] *SED.*, (MW), *SV.*, a.
[5] *Digha. Nik.*, III, p. 9: Yāvaj-jivam acelako assaṁ, na vattham paridaheyam.
[6] Barua, *ABORI.*, VIII, p. 183; q.b. Basham, op. cit., p. 97.

Ājīvika doctrine and practice suggest the early interaction of the two teachings.

The cardinal point of the doctrines of the Ājīvika founder, Gosāla, was a belief in predestination, 'in the all-embracing rule of the principle of order, *Niyati*, which ultimately controlled every action and all phenomena, and left no room for human volition, which was completely ineffectual.'[1] He did not believe in human effort, and held that all creatures were helpless against destiny. His followers, the Ājīvikas, were utter fatalists who claimed that no amount of virtue and asceticism could hasten or shorten the natural biological process of rebirth, that goodness did not help toward the final release. An atomic theory, which was perhaps the earliest in India, if not in the world, was later on developed on the basis of strict determinism, which was the foundation of the Niyati doctrine.[2] The Ājīvikas classified humanity according to its spiritual colour (*abijāti Sk*) which classification has much in common with the Jaina *leśyās.* Whereas the former classification is based on creed or occupation, the latter on man's psychic development and virtue.[3]

The Ājīvikas practised asceticism of a severe type which often terminated like that of the Jainas, in death by starvation. They practised total nudity, which inspired Mahāvīra in introducing the custom in the Jaina order. The motive was the same as Mahāvīra's the acquisition of complete indifference to all physical sensation.[4] The typical Ājīvika was usually complete naked, covered with dust and dirt, bent and crippled and armed with a bamboo staff.[5]

The Jaina *Aupapātika Sūtra* contains a significant list of the types of the Ājīvika mendicant.[6] These include :

(1) *Dugharantariyā*: who were in the habit of begging food at every third house only.
(2) *Tigharantariyā*: who begged at every fourth house.
(3) *Sattagharantariyā*: who begged at every eighth house.

[1]Basham, op. cit., p. 3.

[2]ibid, pp. 3-4.

[3]ibid, pp.244-245. According to this classification, the Ājivika regarded the Jaina as second to himself in sanctity, the Buddhist bhikkhu was a poor third and the Brāhman, the lowest.

[4]*Acar.*, I. 7, 7, 1.

[5]Basham, op. cit., p. 109.

[6]*Aup. Su.*, 41, 101. 196; Also *Ovavaiya Su.*, 41, p. 196.

(4) *Uppala-bentiyā*: who under a special vow employed lotus stalk in begging and who perhaps used lotus leaves as begging receptacles
(5) *Gharasamudāniyā*: those who begged at every house
(6) *Vijjuantariyā*: who were ascetics and who entered large earthen ports in order to do penance.

The *Sthānaṅga Sūtra*[1] gives a further list of Ājīvika ascetic practices, which are said to be severe penances, terrible penances, the abstention from liquids (*rasa*)[2] and indifference to the pleasures of the sense of taste.

The Ājīvikas' reputation for asceticism apparently reached the Far East. Chinese and Japanese Buddhist literature classes the *Ashibikas* (i.e. Ājīvikas) and the *Nikendabtras* or Nirgranthas as practising severe penance. 'They both hold that the penalty for a sinful life must sooner or later be paid and since it is impossible to escape from it, it is better that it be paid as soon as possible so that the life to come may be free from enjoyment. Thus their practices were ascetic—fasting, silence, immovability and the burying of themselves upto the neck were their expressions of penance.'[3]

The most detailed description of the begging customs of naked mendicants is contained is the *Mahāsaccaka Sutta* of the *Majjhima Nikāya.* The passage therein seems to give a convincing picture of the begging habits of Makkhalī Gośāla and his two shadowy predecessors, who are named in the text (Nanda Vaccha and Kisa Sankicca).[4] It might be inferred that it also applies to the community which he established. But its reliability, as applying to the Ājīvika order is questionable. For in another passage of the *Majjhima* the same words are put into the mouth of the Buddha himself, when he describes his own ascetic conduct before his enlightenment.[5] This indicates that the description of ascetic begging practice applies to the wide class of *acelakas* or naked ascetics, which class seems to have included not only organized Ājīvikas, but freelance Ājīvikas and Nirganthas or Jainas, as well as independent

[1]*Than.* IV. 309, cf. *Nanguttha*; *Jat.* I, p. 144, 493.

[2]Comm. Abhayadeva interprets it as ghee etc.—*ghṛtādi rasa partityāgah.*

[3]Sugiura, *Hindu Logic as Preserved in China and Japan*, p. 16 quoting Hyaku-ron So i, 22. The passage has been noticed by Hoernle (*ERE.*, I. p. 269), who adhering to his own theory, identifies the Ashibikas with the Digambara Jainas.

[4]*Maj. Nik.*, I, p. 238.

[5]ibid, I, p. 77.

ascetics and members of the smaller mushroom communities of the time.[1] Some of the practices referred to may have been followed by Makkhālī Gośāla's Ājīvikas, but there is no reason to believe that they followed all of them. However, one interesting but minor rule of their begging practice was that they did not beg for their female relations, because Gośāla himself was once disappointed at not receiving alms, presumably from his own kin.[2] In general, the begging and dietary habits of the Ājīvikas were somewhat less lax than those of the Buddhists and less strict than those of the Jainas.[3] The Ājīvikas were like the Buddhists and Jainas believers in Ahiṁsa and usually vegetarian[4] though a passage in the *Bhagavatī Sūtra* describes them eating animal food.[5]

Some of the Ājīvikas used to practice *Suddhapāṇaé*[6] penance, a sort of 'religious suicide,' awaiting voluntary death like the Jainas but the former differed in the sense that it involved death not from starvation but from thirst. The ascetic finding his physical powers waning would enter on the six months course of austerities. At some stage in his penance, he would refrain from all drinks but the four *pāṇagāim*, 'kinds of liquid suitable to an ascetic.'[7] At the final stage he would only allow himself the four *apānagāim* (the four substitutes for drink).[8] This shows that the Ājīvika ascetic of greatest sanctity like the Jaina cheerfully died a lingering death for the sake of his spiritual welfare, by pursuing the traditional religious path of pain and fast.

The Saṁnyāsi as the Model for the Jaina Ascetic

It was Max Müller, who first observed that the Brāhmin ascetic (the *Samnyāsin*) was the model from whom the monastic orders of the Jainas and Buddhists borrowed many important practices and institutions of ascetic life.[9]

[1]Basham, op. cit., p. 119.

[2]*Vihimaggapava* of Jinapaha Suri. q.b. Basham, ibid, p. 54.

[3]Basham, ibid, p. 50.

[4]Basham, ibid, p. 123.

[5]*Bhag.*, VIII, su. 329 fo. 369.

[6]It consisted of eight finalities (*carimāim*), the four drinks (*panāgāim*) and the four substitutes for drink (*apānagāim*). *Bhag.*, XV, su. 544, fol. 679 *Comm.* fol. 684.

[7]Abhayadeva's Comm. *Bhag. Su.*, 554 fol. 680.

[8]Barua believes that Gośāla himself practised the penance. *JDL.*, II, pp. 36-37.

[9]*Hibbert Lectures*, p. 351.

Likewise, Bühler[1] and Kern[2] held a similar view. Working on this premise, Jacobi compared the rules of the Brahmin ascetics from the quotations[3] and Baudhāyan's law books with those of the Jaina and Buddhist monks, and has conclusively proved that the originals of the monastic orders of the Jainas and Buddhists are to be found in the Hindu ascetic.[4] In his investigation, he considered: the five great vows of the Jainas and the five cardinal sins and virtues of the Buddhists versus the five vows of the *Saṁnyāsins*, chastity, rules regarding residence during the rainy season, begging, restraining of the mind, speech and body; nudity, ahiṁsa; the outfit of the ascetic and his ways of eating, drinking etc. From the historical point of view, even, many of the Jaina ethical principles can be shown to have been inherited from older religious classes of Indian society.

Why Extremist Asceticism in Jaina System?

In the discussion Jacobi does not fail to point out that regarding the dress, the Jaina ascetics are forbidden to wash or dye their clothes and that they must wear them in the same condition in which they are given.[5] He observes that the Jainas have carried into the extreme the original intention of the Brāhmanic rule viz. that the dress of ascetics should be as simple and mean as possible. For the Jainas seem to take a sort of pride in outdoing their Brāhmanic rivals as regards rigorous conduct: the former never bathe; are covered with uncleanliness; they smell badly, they are disagreeable, they are loathsome.'[6] They, thus, considered nastiness and filthiness for the highest pitch of ascetic virtue. As a contrast the Buddhists observed principles of hygiene and conducted themselves in accordance with the dictates of humanity. Secondly, he emphasises how the Brāhmanic rule 'to be indifferent towards (all)

[1]*Baudh. DS., SBE.*, IV, 191-192.

[2]*History of Buddhism in India.*

[3]The law giver Gautama who, teaches the complete system of Brāhmanic asceticism, was older than the rise of Buddhism—Bühler, *SBE.*, II, p. XIIX. introduction.

[4]Jacobi, *JS.*, *SBE.*, XXII,—introduction, pp. XXII-XXIX cf. Ghoshal, 'Rules for Ascetics in Jainism, Buddhism and Hinduism,' *JA.*, 1, No. IV, 1936, pp. 67-81.

[5]*Acar.*, II, 5, 2, 1; I, 7, 7, 1.

[6]ibid, II. 2, 2, 1.

creatures, whether they do him any injury or kindness'[1] was strictly carried out by Mahāvīra who 'with equanimity bore, underwent and suffered all pleasant or unpleasant occurences, arising from divine powers, men or animals.'[2] He quotes that the Jaina ascetic in the last stage of his spiritual career 'does desire neither life nor death.'[3] As we have seen earlier he is on the path of religious suicide, longing and lingering for death to overtake him. This is considered as 'wholesome, proper, beautifying and meritorious." The conclusion is obvious and inevitable that the Jaina system recognises and preaches the extremest asceticism. The practice of the *loya* and the rigid adherence to *ahiṁsā*, in thought, word and deed, and the system of internal and external *tapas* for the monk, all these strengthen the conclusion. The question arises: Why did Mahāvīra make his moral code so extremely ascetic? As Jacobi does not provide an answer, we have to seek it ourselves.

It is a fact that Mahāvīra adopted Pārśva's ethical code of four rules and enlarged it into five great vows (*Mahāvṛatas*). The fourth rule of Pārśva, that of *aparigraha*, not to have any worldly possessions was split up into two by Mahāvīra viz. not to take a wife or to lead a celibate life and renunciation of all worldly concerns (*parigraha—tyāga*). He symbolised these two in his own life by practising ideal purity by thought, word and deed and complete nudity. Thus he found the necessity of preaching these two to his followers by his own example and their strict enforcement became a part and parcel of his ethical code. Basham hints at the reason behind the necessity when he points out that 'Mahāvīra founded his order upon a looser group of ascetics, wearing clothing and by no means in their chastity.'[4] The Jaina accusation of the Ājīvika of sexual laxity points to the state of impurity existing in the Ājīvika order. According to the *Sūtrakṛtāṅga*, Gośāla is made to declare that according his *dhamma*, the ascetic incurs no sin from women.[5] The same source also speaks of indifferent ascetics, the slaves of women, who maintain that there is no more sin in intercourse with women than in squeezing a boil.[6] 'A wise man,' states the *Sūtra-*

[1] *SBE.*, II, p. 192; *Gau. DS.*, III, 24.
[2] *Kalpa*, p. 260.
[3] ibid, p. 307.
[4] ibid, p. 108.
[5] *Stkr.*, II, 6, 8, fol. 390.
[6] ibid, I. 3, 4, 10, fol. 97.

kṛtāṅga, 'should consider that these (heretics) do not live a life of chastity.'[1] The nature of the relations of Gośāla with his patron Hālāhala, the potter woman, are nowhere explicitly stated but it seems to be implied that they were not honest.[2]

There is a reference to the Ājīvika sexual laxity in the Vinaya.[3] We hear the distant echoes of their bad reputation even in later literature.[4] The conclusion becomes certain that there existed a lack of purity amongst the ascetics of Mahāvīra's times especially the Ājīvikas.

When the long Jaina tradition maintains that the Ājīvikas were not celibate, the Jainas themselves could not be regarded blameless in this regard. Mahāvīra found that many ascetics belonging to other sects including the proto-Jainas (*achelas*) who followed Parśva, took no vows of chastity.[5] The legendary *ṛṣis* shared their austerities with their wives and must have had later counterparts. Their own religious literature shows that the Jaina monks themselves were not always strict in the maintenance of chasity.[5] Their occasional lapses of misconduct are also referred to.[7] Mahāvīra must have been dissatisfied with the state of existing physical laxity amongst the ascetics around him and with a view to enforce strict observance of chastity from his followers, introduced a distinct vow of chastity (*brahmacarya*).

Not only that Mahāvīra was dissatisfied with the lack of chastity amongst the ascetic order including his own, but the accusation of laxity in discipline in the religious order of the Buddhists and the Ājīvikas, it seems was a source of embarassment and even disturbance to him. The Buddhist accused the Ājīvika ascetic of worldliness who wore a cloak of false austerity.[8] The Ājīvika accused the Buddhist of laxity in discipline. Even the Buddha is called a 'shaven householder' (*muṇḍa-gahapatika*).[9] Amongst their rivals

[1] *Stkr.*, I, 1, 3, 13, fol. 45.

[2] Gośāla in his 24th year, starts his career as an ascetic, making his headquarters at Savatthi in the workshop of the potter-woman Hālāhala and was surrounded by many disciples: *Bhag. Su.*, XV. su. 539, fol. 658.

[3] *Vinaya*, IV, pp. 223 ff., *Samantapasadika*, IV, p. 906.

[4] *Rajtarangini Epi Car.* II (edn.) No. 234, p. 209.

[5] *Uttar.*, XXIII, 11-12, *SBE.*, XLV, p. 121 f.n. 2.

[6] *Stkr.*, IV. 2.

[7] Jaina, *Life in Ancient India According to the Jaina Canon*, pp. 199-202.

[8] *Maj. Nik.*, I, p. 238, 438.

[9] *Vinaya*, IV, p. 91.

the Buddhists enjoyed the reputation of being 'preachers of ease' (*sāta-vādin*) who favoured the 'way of comfort' (*puṣṭimārga*).[1] In the *Vinaya* there are many references where the Buddhists monks are accused of having the ways and pleasures of worldly men. All these accusations and counter-accusations created a doubt in many of the simpler lay folk of the time who were naturally inclined to estimate the sanctity of a religious order by the severity of its discipline, and to bestow their alms accordingly. With each sect attempting to win members from the others, the sanctity of a religious order was an important aspect not to be ignored. Logically it follows that the stricter the discipline, the more sacred a religious order, and more chances of winning the followers. In the circumstances it would appear that Mahāvīra, to distinguish his order from the others, found the necessity of making his ethical codes more rigid, more ascetic and hence more respectable in the eyes of his contemporaries especially his lay adherents. There is no reference to his giving freedom to a monk to leave his monastic order, as was the practice with the Buddhist order to allow the monk to give up monastic life, if his mind still hankered after worldly life or if he found the monastic discipline too severe. The Jaina list excluding the persons from joining their order as compared with that of the Buddhist also reflects its rigid internal organisation and the anxiety to preserve its purity.

With regard to Mahāvīra's religious doctrine in which asceticism finds a prominent place, we have to consider the conditions of the time which gave rise to it. The general atmosphere was of intellectual confusion. When countless doctrines and theories, some philosophical and other non-philosophical, were expounded by many religious teachers and leaders of the time.[2] For instance, out of his own group of six heretical teachers, Ajita Kesakāmbalin was the utter materialist, Puraṇa Kassapa, the amoral cynic, Pakudha Kaccāyana, the hedonist and Sanjaya, the sceptic who rejected all possibility of the knowledge of self. Apart from the problem of the universe and man's place therein, most of the doctrines were

[1]*JS.*, II, p. 269, I, 3, 4, 6; cf. Narasu, *The Essence of Buddhism*, p. 142.

[2]For example, Kriyāvād alone comprised one hundred and eighty schools and Akriyāvād, eighty four schools. (*Suya. Ti.*, 1.12, p. 208a, 209). In *Brahma Jala Sutta*, are set out 62 varieties of existing hypotheses and after each of them has been rejected, the doctrine of Arhatship is put forward as the right solution. For details of 62 heresies, see Rhys Davids, *Buddhism*, pp. 31-33.

concerned with the aims or values of human life which centered round man's happiness and sorrow. It would be thus clear that both Mahāvīra and the Buddha had to face thinkers who held extreme views on the subject.

Gośāla thought that the characteristics of all things were predetermined and that there was no cause or condition which predetermined them. The *Cārvāka* belief was that the aims or values of human life were realised by the enjoyment of worldly pleasures. Mahāvīra's views was that happiness and sorrow were due to one's own deeds or that they were due to some other cause; he answered the problem in terms of his *Anekāntavda* or *Syādvāda.* The aims of human life according to the ascetic school, which was a powerful force, lay in self-mortification. While Mahāvīra clung to the doctrine of self-mortification, as against Kaccāyana, Ajita, Gośāla and Sanjaya, the Buddha preached the *Majjihimapatipadā* or the Middle Path. He rejected the path of asceticism as of no value.

The various reasons or motives which prompted persons to join the monastic orders of the Buddha and Mahāvīra, it becomes apparent that the lure of renunciation was to be seen at its height and people generally sought freedom from *Karma* and *Saṁsāra* in the ascetic life of renunciation. This was a barometer of the people's dissatisfaction with the conditions in the society. The extraordinary hold which the ideas of *Karma* and *Saṁsāra* had on the Indian mind, can be demonstrated by the fact that the Buddha discarded much which belonged to the current religion but retained these traditional ideas. While the Buddha has no place in his thought for soul, Mahāvīra made it the basis of his *Kriyāvāda,* according to which soul exists (in *saṁsāra*) in combination with Karma (karmic matter).[1] *Nirjarā* consists in the wearing out of accumulated effects of Karma on the soul by the practice of asceticism. *Mokṣa* logically follows from *nirjarā* which signifies the final deliverance of the soul from the bondage of Karma, the bondage of sin. Asceticism has to burn out sin in its fire to attain freedom from *Karma.*

The path to salvation as taught by the Buddha appeared to Mahāvīra too comfortable a mode of life, which meant: *Mokṣa,* a pleasant thing was to be arrived at through a comfortable life, another pleasant thing.[2]

[1]Panchāstikāya-Gāthā: jivo tti kammasamjutto.
[2]*JS.*, II, p. 269, f.n. 3-4; *Stkr.*, V. 27, i, 3.4.6.

Mahāvīra declared that

Na sukhena sukhaṁ adhigantabbam,
dukkhena sukhaṁ adhigantabbam.[1]

The disciples of the Jaina were called to seek *sukha* or infinite bliss or Nirvāna by *dukkha* or painful and difficult path of rigorous practice of asceticism. *Samvara* or practice of self-restraint with regard to the body, speech and mind was just the other aspect of *tapas*. The practise of austerities or penances was to be resorted to as a means of wearing out and ultimately destroying the effects of sinful deed of former existence and that of the three-fold self-restraint as a means of not giving effect to a new *Karma*.

According to this teaching, mental and bodily penances should be practised. He who possesses virtuous conduct and life, who has practised the best self-control, who keeps from sinful influences and who has destroyed *Karma* (through asceticism) will obtain *mukti*.[2] Thus asceticism in its extremest form came to be accepted in Mahāvīra's philosophy and his religious system.

Summing Up

The era of the two great reformers, the Buddha and Mahāvīra was lit up by their personalities. Both were Kṣātriyas; both organised religious orders, both ignored God and denied the Vedās; both led a revolt against the superiority of the Brāhmins over the Kṣātriyas and derided the four stages of life (*āśramas*) stressing only the life of a *bhikṣu*. They broke away from outworn grooves of thought, intensified inward outlook of man, turned religion into a pure spiritual discipline and encouraged and popularised monastic life, which was open to all, irrespective of caste, creed or sex. For both self-realisation was possible only through renunciation, hence the best life was the life of renunciation. It was thus the shortest way to salvation.

Both the monachisms emphasized that there was no God or creator and man's emancipation from suffering did not depend upon the mercy of any such being. Man was the architect of his own density. By living an austere life of purity and virtue he could escape the ills of life.

[1]*Maj. Nik.*, I Culadukkhakkhandha Sutta, pp. 93-94.

[2]According to Silanka, Kriyāvādins hold that action (kriyā) alone leads to liberation even though it be unaccompanied by right knowledge and right faith: *Suya Tika.*, p. 218a.

However, the Buddha after having practised the most severe type of asceticism for six years, found it defective for attainment of knowledge. He, therefore, condemned extreme asceticism as ignoble and useless and taught the middle way between self-mortification and allurements of senses. The only asceticism he permits is bodily self-control as aid to mental self-control. In contrast, greater austerity and self-mortification cannot be found in any religion other than in Jainism. Mahāvīra greatly emphasised the practice of penances even to the point of death. In his doctrine asceticism finds a prominent place as a pathway to *nirvāṇa*.

There is no doubt that the time of the Buddha and the Jaina was known for the traditional practice of asceticism. It is but natural, therefore, that these Teachers started with the usual ascetic practies which were current as means of salvation in those days. The Buddha, however, revolted against the traditional asceticism as he realised by personal experience that it was not at all useful for the salvation of man. Mortification was not the goal of man, whereas people of these times saw salvation only in it. It was forgotten that mortifications were, if anything, only the means. The Buddha realised that the goal was forgotten in vain gloriousness of austerity. But he also warned those who may swing to the other extreme path of sensuality and pleasure which he considered as degrading and vulgar. He advocated the middle path. Mahāvīra, on the other hand, not only continued to respect the traditional belief and practices of asceticism but carried them to their most severe form. Death by starvation was the best path of salvation to him. It is thus clear that various teachers in the sixth century BC viewed asceticism in different ways. In other words the institution of asceticism had not yet developed in its rigidest form as it later became in the hands of Mahāvīra.

Chapter 8

Asceticism in the Epics

(*i*) *Mahābhārata*

The *Mahābhārata* and the *Rāmāyaṇa* form two great Sanskrit epics of ancient India. Both have been a national inheritance for 2,000 years or more and have exercised a continuous and pervasive influence on the mass mind. Both embody the spirit and culture of ancient India. Emphasizing their importance in the life of the Indian people as a living force, forming the basis of their thoughts and of their moral and ethical ideas: Havell observes with particular regard to *Mahābhārata* how in the Gupta age, "The *Sādhu* and *Saṁnyāsin* carried it throughout the length and breadth of India, as the bhikkhus of the Saṁgha had formerly spread the message of the Buddha. Both in the original Sanskrit text and in vernacular translations it played the same part in moulding Indian character and forming the synthesis of thought called 'Hinduism.' "[1] The homage is equally applicable to the Rāmāyaṇa. For it is said: "If the *Mahābhārata* teaches the lessons of life, the *Rāmāyaṇa* preaches the highest ideal of it."[2] That ideal is the conjugal devotion and fidelity as represented by the inherent purity of Rāma and Sīta.

Varṇa System in the Mahābhārata

In the *Mahābhārata*, the startification of the society of the times was less complex than that of the modern one. "In the final recast of the epic, the varṇa system is found to be almost rigid with a regularly established social hierarchy formed on the basis of birth."[3] The truth of this statement will become evident when we will examine the institution of asceticism in the epic. The epic describes the occupations of the four varṇas—the *Varṇāśramadharma*.[4] No doubt the epic reflects here and there the injustice involved in such

[1]Havell, *Āryan Rule in India*, p. 157.
[2]Vaidya, *Riddle of the Rāmāyaṇa*, p. 53.
[3]Vora, *Evolution of Morals in the Epics*, p. 124.
[4]xiii, 141, 47, 54, 55, 57, 67.

a system but it soon tries to justify it on other considerations. Thus we come across a rigid *varṇa* system in the *Mahābhārata.*

Of the many voices of injustice inherent in the system, the first one we hear is of the sage Parāśara who puts forwards *tapas* to be the basis of the *varṇa* distinction. He narrates a long list of sages achieving higher status in society by their austerities. Thus he tells king Janaka: 'O King! those great souled ones who have made themselves pure by austerities even though born of low parentage can not be considered low, only because of their low birth. O King! in ancient times, the sages had produced sons in lowest wombs and yet they had transformed themselves into sages due to the power of their austerities.'[1] Here Parāśara indicates asceticism as bestowing certain qualities, possibly a high ethical standard which could turn a person of low birth into one of higher birth. But this story of Parāśara seems to be the only example suggesting the mobility of the caste system. Almost all other evidences suggest its rigidity.

The story of Mātaṅga, for example, narrated in the *Anuśāsana parva*[2] shows, how impossible it was for a non-brāhmin to achieve brāhminhood in spite of a highly developed moral character. Mātaṅga was supposed to be the son of a Brāhmin. In fact, he was an illegitimate son, a *cāṇḍāla* born out of a Brāhmin woman and a śūdra father—a fact which he did not know. By a curious turn of circumstances, he comes to know of this fact and he performs severe penances (*tapas*) in the forest to achieve Brāhminhood. Indra becomes pleased with him. Mātaṅga requests him to grant him his heart's desire. Said Indra: 'O Mātaṅga, it is very difficult to attain Brāhminhood. You will destroy yourself because of this unreasonable desire of yours. Simple austerities can never achieve for you—a cāṇḍāla—that which is unobtainable even to gods, *asuras* and men.'

These words suggest that the society did not approve of a low born to aspire for a higher status in society through the efficacy of asceticism. Mātaṅga, not convinced by Indra's reply, persisted in more severe penances till he fainted. Indra returned to him trying to explain the impossibility of the task he was bent upon achieving. 'O Indra,' he said, 'I can obtain your grace by austerities but cannot obtain Brāhminhood. I am a person who has concentrated on becoming a Brāhmin, who has obtained release from happiness

[1]xii. 285, 12-16.
[2]xiii. 27.

and misery, who has no family. I am always non-violent and controlled in respect of the senses. Even then, how is it that I am not fit to attain Brāhminhood? What bad luck for me, O Purandara, that even though I am a knower of Dharma, I have attained this position due to the fault of my mother. I am sure that a man may strive and strive but fate is all powerful!' Neither *tyāga* of worldly possessions nor austerities nor *dharma* but fate seems to be all powerful. Thus birth imposed certain religious and social disabilities on the low born. It is not left to him to develop and to grow, independently of birth.

There is another story[1] which describes how a śūdra is rewarded with the position of a *Kṣatriya* King *in the next life* as a result of his performing the *pitṛ-kārya* with the help of a Brāhmin ascetic and by leading an ascetic life though his *varṇādharma* was to serve the three higher castes. The Brāhmin ascetic who helped him got degraded in the next birth and was born as the priest of the king who was śūdra in his former life. The moral is that a Brāhmin should never preach a person of low birth; he incurs no sin if he preaches, only the three twice born. Another noteworthy factor is that the śūdra's leading the ascetic life worthy of a Brāhmin does not entitle him to a high social status in the present birth. What is the use of a high status in the next life when an ascetic life does not improve his lot in the present life?

If *tāpas* in general could obtain superhuman qualities for the *tapasvī*, how could Mātaṅga not obtain them? Is it because he was a *cāṇḍāla*? Does it mean that *tapas* was associated with castes and the quality of the *tapas* depended upon the caste of *tapasvin?* It appears that Brāhminhood was suggested to be a difficult goal for a *cāṇḍāla* despite to whatever limits he possessed the power of asceticism. It seems that though asceticism could make a man as powerful as gods, he could not reach the higher status in society.

Practice of Austerities

Besides the examples of a cāṇḍāla like Mātaṅga and a śūdra practicing austerities (*tapas*) the epic abounds in illustrations of men and women engaged in *tapas*. Not only the ṛṣis, the hermits but even the kings and *asuras* practise austerities to propitiate the gods, to gain power or some material end.

The famous episode of Viśvāmitra describes him as the king of

[1]xiii. 10 ff.

Kānyakubja who tries to seize ṛṣi Vaśiṣṭha's cow, Kāmadhenu. Having failed in the attempt he feels disgusted with Kṣātriya prowess as inferior to that of a Brāhmin, turns an ascetic and attains Brāhminhood by the power of austerities.[1] Viśvāmitra and Vaśiṣṭha challenged each other in respect of the superiority of their penances.[2] Due to their rivalry in asceticism, a great enmity arose between them. Ṛṣi Śaradvat studied *dhanurvēda* in preference to the Vēda and by his austerities came to master all weapons.[3] Ṛṣi Kapila practised severe penances for a hundred years and obtained hundred sons.[4] *Muni* Bāladhi, in grief for death of a child practises austerities in order to have an immortal son and he gets one.[5] Yavakrita, whose father was slighted by the Brāhmins, performs austerities to obtain the knowledge of the Vēdas and to become learned.[6] King Aświapati who was childless undertakes austerities and is blessed with a daughter who came to be known as Sāvitri.[7] The king of Vidharbha is engaged in austerities for obtaining an offspring.[8] King Kauśika is said to have practised austere penances with a desire of getting Indra for a son;[9] Arjuna, to obtain celestial weapons from Mahādēva.[10] Seeing that the sun had no power to rise in the usual time if he was asleep, *muni* Jaratkāru, began to practise austerities.[11] *Asura* Dhundu undergoes fierce austerity with the object of destroying the triple world.[12] The *asura* brothers Sunda and Upasunda by means of severest penances obtained from Brahma, a boon, by means of which they became incapable of being killed by any one except one by the other.[13] In the ancient flood-story, the venerable Manu stands on one leg (*ekapādasthitas*) and hangs upside down (*ūrdhvabāhuḥ*) for ten thousand years.[14]

[1]I.175, 1.48.
[2]IX. 42, 1-41.
[3]I. 63. 104-127.
[4]xiii. 18-1-83.
[5]III. 135. 45-55.
[6]III. 135-136.
[7]III. 291.
[8]III. 96 f.
[9]xiii. 49-4.
[10]iii. 38 ff.
[11]I. 47. 1-43.
[12]iii. 85 ff.
[13]I. 209.211.
[14]iii. 187. 4 ff.

Devoted to severe austerities, Pāṇḍu stands on one foot all day with the most extreme concentration (*samādhi*) with a view to propitiate Indra.[1] He is credited with the possession of *tapoyogabala*.[2] Śrutavati, the daughter of ṛṣi Bhārdvāja practised austerities with a desire to obtain Indra for her husband,[3] Bhadrā, for getting Utathya[4] and Umā for obtaining Śiva,[5] as husbands. Ambā practised penance to take vengeance on Bhiṣma.[6] Arundhati devotes herself to ascetic penances during a draught of twelve-years when her husband ṛṣi Vaśiṣṭha had gone away with other ṛṣis in the forest of Himavat.[7]

There are references to female ascetics who devoted themselves to life long austerities and remained unmarried. They seem to have taken to life-long celibacy (*Naiṣṭhika Brahmacarya*). They include king Yayāti's daughter Mādhavi, the daughters of ṛṣi Kuṇigarga and Śāndilya, Sulabhā and Prabhāvatī.

Sulabhā[8] was a Kṣatriya girl born in the family of a royal sage and had become a mendicant because she could not find a suitable husband. She was a woman who possessed deep philosophical insight and understanding. She won a victory over King Janaka when both entered into a discussion about the relative merits of *saṁnyāsa* and *gṛhastha dharma*. The daughter of Śāndilya was so much advanced in austerities that she acquired supernatural powers to curse semi-divine creatures like Garuda, and a Brāhmin like Gālava.[9] The daughter of sage Kuṇigarga preferred to remain unmarried and performed severe austerities following the footsteps of her father. She had attained proficiency in Yoga which enabled her to assume any form she liked.[10] Hanuman and other vānaras in the command of Sugrīva who set out in search of Sītā[11] came across Prabhāvati engaged in austerities. Mādhavi, King Yayāti's daughter, remained unmarried throughout her life and practised

[1] i. 123.26 āṅrādhyayiṣur devam.
[2] i. 121. 37.
[3] ix. 48.
[4] xiii. 154. 10. 31.
[5] xiii. 19 ff.
[6] V. 173-187.
[7] IX. 48.
[8] xii. 308. 7. 308 ff. 320. 60.
[9] V. 3. 1-16.
[10] IX. 52-54.
[11] iii. 282.

austerities.[1] It appears, therefore, that generally women were also supposed to be proper upholders of asceticism like men.

We come across in the epic typically detailed descriptions of the ascetics (*tapasvins*) engaged in austerity or *tapas*, immune to their surroundings and indifferent to bodily needs.

The Brāhmin Jajali is described as standing as a wooden post, rapt in *Yoga*, so much engrossed in *tapas* that a pair of Kuliṅga birds built their nest in the matted hair of his, mated and the female one laid eggs and the young ones came out. Only when they did not return even after a month, he left the spot.[2] Angiras performed a wonderful *tapas* in his hermitage, excelled even the fire-god, the carrier of oblations in splendour and in that state he illumined the whole universe.[3] Ṛṣi Cyavana assumed the posture called *virāsana*, quiet and still like an inanimate post and for a long period remained at the same spot. Covered all over with creepers, he was turned into an ant-hill. After the lapse of a long period, crowds of ants enveloped him. Covered all over with ants, he looked exactly like a heap of earth. He continued practising *tapas* enveloped on all sides with that ant-hill.[4] Arjuna is described as clad in rags, made of grass and furnished with a black deer-skin and a stick. He commenced to eat withered leaves fallen upon the ground. He ate in the first months only fruits at the interval of three nights, then at the interval of six nights, then fortnight and finally began to subsist on air alone. With arms upraised and leaning upon nothing and standing on the tips of his toes (*pādāṅgushṭāgradhisṭhitaḥ*), he continued his austerities. He wished not for heaven, not for prosperity, not for long life, but to obtain celestial weapons.[5] Different *tirthas* where various ascetics performed their sacrifices and austerities are also described.[6]

In the epic descriptions of the hermit (*vānaprastha*) and of the parivrajaka (*Saṁnyāsin*) are found.[7] It will be noticed that it confines

[1]V. 115.23.
[2]xii. 262.
[3]iii. 217, 1-21.
[4]iii. 122 ff.
[5]iii. 38 ff.
[6]iii. 88 ff.
[7]xii. 191 f; xii. 243 ff. These descriptions agree almost verbally with those of Manu,

the rights and privileges of an ascetic life only to the twice-born.[1] Here only a summary of the descriptions is given.

The Vānaprastha Stage

"It is the mode of life followed by those who live in forests as hermits and who living with their wives pain themselves by way of austerities. At what stage of life a householder should become a hermit is stated. When he sees his body wrinkled and hair white on his head and children of his children, he should then retire into the forest and pass the life of *vānaprastha*.

'Hermits (*Vānaprasthas*) in order to acquire virtue sojourn to sacred waters, rivers and springs and practice penances in solitary and secluded forests. They forsake all sorts of raiments, food and enjoyments which people in society like. They live abstemiously upon wild herbs, fruits, roots and leaves of various kinds. The naked earth is their seat and bed. They are clad in grass, animal skins and barks of trees. They never shave their heads and beards or pare their nails. They perform ablutions at regular times. They pour unfailingly libations on the ground and on the sacred fire at the proper time. They bear without any concern cold, heat, rain and wind and become emaciated in performing various kinds of rites, vows and acts. Gifted with great patience and calmness, they live always practising the quality of goodness.'

The ṛṣis, munis and sages the epic speaks of are mostly forest-dwelling hermits. The *Umā-Maheshwara Saṁvāda* also throws some light on their mode of life. To Umā's question: 'What is the religion of the Vānaprastha?' Śiva replies: '*Virāsana*, *māṇḍūka-yoga*, *purṇamāsya*, *cāturmāsya*.' The reply sums up the daily routline of the hermit life consisting of postures, Yogic penances, rituals and vows. To another question: What is the religion of the Munis in their doctrine of perfection?, the reply given is: 'They live unrestrained in the forest together with their wives. Their characteristics are: the shaving of the head, yellow robes, passing the night at home, ablutions three times a day, *hōtra*, *samādhi* and adherence to the path of the good.'[2]

The Saṁnyāsa Stage

The description of the fourth mode of life—of the *saṁnyāsin* as

[1]xii. 192. 6, xii. 244. 28.
[2]xiii, 141. 1-115.

given by the epic is summarised as under:

Practising austerities while living like a forest hermit (*Vānaprastha*) one should shave off his hair and bristles and pare off his nails and having purified by acts pass into the last holy mode of life in *Saṁnyāsa*. He should leave off Vedic study and the sacred thread which marks his birth and having given to righteousness and under complete control, seek the knowledge of the self.

He should not regard death with joy. Nor should be regard life with joy. He should only wait for his hour like a servant waiting for his master's command. He should purify his heart and mind of all short-comings, purge himself of all sins. He should abstain from injury, regard all creatures impartially and should devote himself to truth. He is gifted with fortitude, has his senses under restraint and extends protection to all beings. He is free from attachments of every kind, has nothing which he can call his own, leads a lonely life.

'Such a man does not eat more than five or six mouthfuls sanctioned for the *Vānaprastha*. He performs sacrifice in his own self, makes a libation of his senses and mind. He wanders on the earth like one not attached to anything. He is shorn off anger and error; regards equally a clod of earth and a lump of gold; does not care for praise or blame and the agreeable and the disagreeable. He possesses equanimity of soul.'[1]

The sage Hārīta also describes the mode of life of the *Saṁnyāsin* which is identical with the above description.[2]

The epic mentions Agastya and the seven Ṛṣis: Madhuchhandas, Aghamarshana, Sāukriti, Sudivātaṇḍi, Ahoviryya, Kavya, Taṇḍya and adds the names of Medhātithi, Karmanirvaka and Shunyapāla to the list of those who were the authors of the mode of the life of *Saṁnyāsa*. These *ṛṣis*, the epic states, themselves practising the course of duties pertaining to *Saṁnyāsa* had all gone to heaven.[3] Many who observed the vows of *Saṁnyāsa* are referred to as living in a sacred asylum on the Himavat.[4]

Power of Asceticism

The epic eulogises asceticism, its efficacy and its power. There is

[1]xii. 244 ff. 245 ff.
[2]xii. 278.
[3]xii. 244. 16-18.
[4]xiii. 10. 10.

nothing superior to asceticism and it is by its might that a person achieves great results. It is mentioned that an ascetic engaged in severe *tapas* acquires supernatural powers; such a Yogin can assume many forms, have many experiences and take them all back to himself.[1] Austerities bring to the credit of the *Tapasvin* a store of religious merit won by asceticism, in addition to boons granted by gods. The epic is replete with instances where such ascetics endued with the power of *tapas* and *yoga* shakes the very throne of the lord of celestials, Indra, who gets alarmed by the penances of these great sages and he sends down the Apsarases equipped with all the armoury of womanly charms to destroy their tapas. The classical instance is the episode of ṛṣi Viśvāmitra and Menakā.[2]

It is said that a muni lives in the forest after withdrawing himself from all worldly objects. But though he never seeks to possess things, he may yet get them by his ascetic powers.[3] Many a great ṛṣi have attained exalted psychic powers through *tapas* and are able to move freely through space between heaven and earth and to appear and disappear at will.[4] Outstanding names are: Nārada, Mārkaṇḍeya, Vaśiṣṭha, Viśvāmitra, Agastya, Bhṛgu, Bṛhaspati, Sanatsujāta and Vyāsa. Ṛṣi Viśvāmitra attains Brāhminhood by the power of his asceticism.[5] Arjuna acquires the fierce weapon *Brahmasira* which arose from *Amṛta* and which Rudra had obtained by means of ascetic practices, together with the *mantras* for hurling and withdrawing it and the rites of expiation and revival. He also acquires *vajras* and *daṇḍas* and other celestial weapons from Yama and Kubera, Varuṇa and Indra by performing penances.[6] It is said that due to Arjuna's austerities, heated with asceticism, the earth is smoking all round and all the great *ṛṣis* are moved.[7] Endowed with miraculous powers by asceticism, Agastya drinks the waters of the ocean to expose the wicked Kālakeyas who were hiding in it and stops the growing of the Vindhyā mountains.[8] He is able by his *tapas* to get all the wealth in the world.[9] A Brāhmin Kaśyapa, who

[1]VII. 202-203; XII. 285-286; XIII. 13-14-18.
[2]I. 69-74.
[3]I. 91. 5.
[4]I. 126; II. 80; XIII. 26; XIV. 14.
[5]xiii. 4.
[6]xiii. 91 ff.
[7]iii, 38 f.
[8]iii. 100-105.
[9]iii. 97. 21-22.

had become conversant with all the authorities on religion etc. crowned with ascetic success (*siddham*) was able to move everywhere at will (*kramamāṇam*) knew the science of disappearing at will, roving with invisible *siddhas* and celestial musicians.[1] It is said that Ailavila practising austerities at Kuber-tirtha obtained the lordship of all treasures (*dhanādhipatyam*) and all kinds of wealth came to him of their own accord.[2] Vipula protected his preceptor Ṛṣi Devaśarman's wife, Ruci, from the amorous advances of Indra by supernatural powers acquired through austerities and entering into her body.[3] Indra conferred a boon on Mātaṅga so that he could move at will in the sky by the power of his austerities.[4] Śiva bestowed the eightfold supernatural power upon ṛṣi Jaigiśavya who was practising *tapas*.[5] Sage Jamadagni's wife Reṇuka once went for a bath where she saw king Sahastrārjuna dallying in the water with his numerous wives and a desire arose in her mind at this sight and she stood there dreaming that she was in the position of the queen. Jamadagni was omniscent and could know her thoughts and what she had seen though he was in his hermitage. He was so enraged that as soon as Reṇuka came back he ordered his eldest son to cut off her head. The episode emphasises the Yogic power of the sage which enabled him to visualise even a slight mental, lapse on his wife's part.[6]

The female mendicant Sulabhā who practised Yoga and wandered over the earth, had heared from many *tridaṇḍins* about king Janaka who had a control over his senses and was a student of *Mokṣa Dharma*, the emancipatory knowledge. By her Yogic power, she assumed a beautiful form and went to Mithilā. On the pretence of begging alms, she presented herself before the king, who was surrounded by his ministers and learned scholars. It is depicted that she entered the king's consciousness by her own consciousness (*sattvam sattvena*). Then they conversed upon *Mokṣa Dharma.*[7] Ambā with a view to take revenge on Bhiṣma performed a severe *tapas* and having reborn as Śikhaṇḍī killed Bhiṣma in the great

[1]xiv. 16. 1-46.
[2]IX. 47. 1. 33.
[3]xiii. 40. 14 ff
[4]xiii. 27 ff.
[5]xiii. 18. 1-83.
[6]III. 116.
[7]xii. 321. 1-190.

war.[1] The daughter of the sage Kuṇigarga had acquired such supernatural power by performing life-long austerities that she could assume any form she liked. When she learnt from sage Nārada that without marriage she will be unable to attain heaven, an ascetic called Śṛṅgavān married her on the condition that he would stay with her only for one night. The old lady by her *Yogic* power transformed herself into a young maiden of incomparable beauty, properly adorned with ornaments, fine cloths and perfume. The sage was rather happy to stay with her not only for one but more than one night, but the ascetic woman left her body on the very next day, as it was settled and attained heaven.[2] The daughter of Śāṇdilya was so much advanced in her austerities that she acquired supernatural powers to cure semi-divine creatures like Garuda and a Brāhmin like Gālava.[3]

Thus *tapas* seems to be an extraordinary power by which one could perform superhuman feats.

Limitations of Asceticism

We have already referred to austerity or *tapas* being performed with various motives but broadly speaking either to attain power or some material end. *Tapas* also can be directed toward attainment of *mokṣa* or emancipation.[4] The epic, however, emphasises that austerities must be accompanied by ethical behaviour. A *Yogin* or a *Saṁnyāsin* who was an aspirant of the knowledge of Brāhman, is advised to develop ethical qualities as detailed below. Lack of ethical behaviour is considered a breach of *dharma*. Even some of the *rākṣasas* have to their credit a store of religious merit won by their austerities in addition to boons granted by gods, but their unethical behaviour which upsets the peace and tranquility of society leads them to destruction. *Tapas* thus seems to be a moral force.

In one of the tales it is formally taught that the exercise of mastery (*aiśvarya*) which could be attained through *tapas* diminishes the store of *tapas*. Thus Lopamudrā wants luxuries and tells her ascetic husband that he 'is able by his *tapas*, (*iṣah tapasā*), to get all the wealth in the world' but Agastya replies: 'That is as you

[1]V. 173-187,
[2]IX. 52.
[3]V. 3, 1. 16
[4]xiii. 141. 80-87.

say, but it would cause a diminution of the *tapas*.'[1] The true *tapas* rises above the riches of the world.

The true and the false *tapas* are distinguished from one another: 'Fasting though for a fortnight, which ordinarily men count for *tapas*, is merely a castigation of the body, and is not regarded as tapas by the good; renunciation (*tyāgaḥ*) and humility are the noblest *tapas*; he who practises these virtues fasts unceasingly and his virtue is never found wanting.'[2] And again: 'Study of the Vēda and avoiding injury to any living being, men call bodily asceticism; the true spiritual asceticism is control of speech and thought.'[3] Here the emphasis on certain ethical qualities is quite evident. The *Gītā* also brings out the concept of *tapas* which is essentially ethical; it defines three types of tapas—physical, verbal and mental (*mana-vācā-karmaṇā*).[4]

With the ethical basis of *tapas* in view, the epic advises a *Saṁnyāsin* to concentrate upon the avoidance of the fundamental vices like desire, anger, vanity, lust, pride, violence etc. which would come in his way of self-conquest.[5] He is also advised to avoid the various social crimes: murder, insult (*niṣkṛti*), theft, censure, jealousy, violence, cruelty, deceit (*anṛtam*); for one who practises these does not gather any *tapas*, while one who avoids these advances in *tapas* [6] The epic, however, goes further to extend the practical aspect of the teaching to be applicable to all the stages of life. While describing the *āśramadharma* of the individual, it emphasises the following qualities in a *gṛhastha*: 'Compassion towards all creatures, sweet speech loving to the ears, abandonment of cruelty, ignorance, pride, hypocrisy and non-violence, truth and peaceful nature, these are the real *tapas* in all stages of life.'[7] This passage enumerates the active as well as passive virtues and proclaims them to be a sort of *tapas* for an individual in all the stages of life.

That asceticism without ethical virtues or *dharma* is not of much value is stressed through the instances of Brāhmins like Kauśika and Jājali who are proud of their asceticism and who seek the

[1]iii. 97. 21-22: *evam etad yatha 'ttha tvaṁ tapovyayakaraṁ tu tat.*

[2]xii. 217.

[3]xii. 221.

[4]*BG.*, xvii. 14-17.

[5]xii. 185. 3.

[6]xii. 185, 17-18.

[7]xii. 184, 14-15 cf. xii. 154, 14-19.

advice of a Śūdra like Dharmavyādha and a Vaiṣya like Tulādhāra to understand the true *dharma*. In the *Tulādhāra-Jājali Saṁvāda*[1] Tulādhāra tells Jājali that *dharma* lies in having least malice or not having it towards anybody. It does not matter what profession one follows or in whatever station of life one is. If he is a friend of everybody in mind, speech and action, then he has understood true *dharma*. Without this knowledge, Tulādhāra points out to Jājali, the futility of his austerities and the pride that he took thereof. The Śūdra Dharmavyādha tells Kauśika that he himself was the son of a Brāhmin in his previous birth, possessed a good character and was learned in the Vēdas, but he fell down from his position in the next birth, because he accidentally hurt a Brāhmin. He had in his present birth of a Śūdra, had developed an ethical personality befitting a Brāhmin, but he expected to attain Brāhminhood not by the power of these virtues but by serving his parents and performing his *svadharma*.[2] By *svadharma* he means adherence to the duties that belonged to him by birth, to speak the truth always, never envy others, never to speak ill of anything small or great and to live upon what remained after serving the gods, guests and those that depended on him.[3] He suggests that Kauśika's austerities are futile because he has still to control anger and malice. Dharmavyādha rates virtuous conduct much higher than asceticism as he shows Kauśika, the perfect way of the virtuous which lies in freedom from malice, forbearance, peace of mind, contentment, pleasant speech, renunciation of desires and anger and actions regulated according to the ordinances of holy writ.[4] Here beside the virtuous conduct, the *Varṇāshramadharma* is upheld. The cāṇḍāla Mātaṅga's failure to obtain Brāhminhood in spite of his severe asceticism,[5] is another instance in the same direction. These are the well-known instances from the epic.

The *Śāntiparva* declares that pride and anger are two great enemies of human beings.[6] The conquest of anger is considered one

[1]xii. 216-62.
[2]iii. 205, 21-29; III. 206, 4-5; III. 200, 38.
[3]ibid.
[4]ibid, III. 206. 21-22. vidhācā vihitaṁ purvaṁ karma svamanupālayan prayatnācca guru vṛdhau suṣṛs'chaṁ dvijottam satyaṁvade nābhyāsūye yathā-śakti dadāmi ca devatā'tithimṛtyānāmavaśiṣtena vartaye na kutsyāmyahaṁ kincchin garhe balavattraṁ *Mbh.*, III. 206, 21-22.
[5]xiii. 27.
[6]xii. 248, 13-20; also cf. xii. 360; III, 29.

of the requisite qualities of a hermit as well as *Saṁnyāsin*. Viśvāmitra, who by a severe penance tried to attain Brāhminhood, lamented his short temper when due to anger he cursed the *apsarā* Raṁbhā sent by Indra to guile him and determines to conquer henceforward all his senses to be a Brāhmin.[1] The epic presents the ideal of Vasiṣṭha describing him thus, "That Vasiṣṭha, had conquered lust and anger by asceticism and had controlled his senses."[2] Many of the *ṛṣis* that we meet in the epic are short-tempered, who curse on finding the slightest breach in conduct or cause annoyance. Thus anger and cursing were considered vices which reduced the efficacy of the ascetic's religious merit or the power of his *tapas*.

It is surprising that the sages are often described as seducers and desirous of charming girls and are still respected and worshipped as powerful ascetics. Ṛṣis like Viśvāmitra, Dadica and Śaradvata who are reputed to be ascetics of strict vows, happen to see the apsarases sent down by Indra to frustrate their *tapas*, immediately lose control over their mind and stop to desire. The products of their temporary union as a result of their momentary madness are too well known. The sages Vibhāṇḍaka, Vyāsa, Viśvāmitra, Bhārdvāja caused the birth of Ṛṣyaśraṅga, Śuka, Śakuntalā and Śrutavatī. In very rare cases we meet *ṛṣis* firm in their *tapas* who have cursed the Apsarases sent by Indra to disturb their *tapas*.[3]

How much heir to human flesh these powerful ascetics are can be judged by two more examples of Vyāsa and Cyavana. Vyāsa, the illustrious *ṛṣi*, sees the beautiful apsaras Ghṛtachi and becomes suddenly possessed by desire.[4] Engaged in severe penances for a long time and reduced to an ant-hill, having been covered all over with creepers, ṛṣi Cyavana, emaciated in body, but still powerful in vision, seeks Sukanyā, the daughter of king Saryāti, who was lovely and in the prime of her youth, and that 'ascetic of exceeding effulgence' is inspired with desire and addresses her, and ultimately marries her.[5] The ṛṣi who had shown amazing indifference to his body and its needs for a long time suddenly becomes alive to the charms of a lovely maiden! This shows that even in the innermost sanctuary of the sage's heart there lurks a woman who steps out in

1 *Ram.*, i, 64, 17; cf. V. 55. 3-6.
2 I. 173 ff.
3 III. 216-217.
4 xii. 324.
5 iii. 122.

the form of desire which is irresistible and under its powerful sway, he pays homage to the eternal flame that is woman, the best handiwork of God, the supreme artist. And for a few moments of bliss even the ascetic returns to his true nature as a man of this earth, with his longings. And so far he longs he is away from the path of *Saṁnyāsa.*

Kinds of Ascetics as described in the Mahābhārata

We come across in the epic ascetics of various kinds, and observant of various restraints and vows. Their names suggest some peculiar manners of their conduct and certain characteristics which distinguish them from one another.

There are four classes of *bhikṣus*: *kuṭīcaka*, *bahūdaka*, *haṁsa* and *paramhaṁsa*, each in turn being superior to the preceding one.[1] The Kuṭīcaka and Bahūdaka are Tridaṇḍins, the former living alone in a hut and the latter visiting *tirthas*; the Haṁsa and Paramahaṁsa are Ekadaṇḍins, the former living in a hermitage, the latter being 'freed from the three gunas.'[2]

Other kinds of ascetics enumerated are:

Phenapas: who always gather the froth from the *amṛta* that Brahmā drank at the great sacrifice[3]

Vālakhilyas: who adopting the practice of the birds, live by picking up grains, clad in deer skins or bark of trees. They are only as big as the joint of the thumb (*anguṣthaparvamātrāḥ*): they have burnt all their sins by severe penances[4]

Vaikhānasa: *Saikatas*: They are forest hermits. Vālakhilyas, Vaikhānas and Saikatas are described as reaching heaven following the Vānaprastha mode of life—*Vaikhānasadharma*[5]

Yayavaras: those who had the power to see immediately the fruits of their ascetic merit[6]

[1]xiii. 141. 89.

[2]Nilkantha's comm. on xiii. 141. 89. The *Vaikhānasa-smārtasūtra* (viii. 7 f) also divides *apatnika* hermits into four classes: *Kuticakas*, *Bahūdakas*, *Haṁsas* and *Paramahaṁsas*. A paramhaṁsa is shorn of sorrow and happiness; auspicious and freed from decrepitude and death and without any change. The *Nāradparivrājaka Up*. classifies Saṁnyāsins into six kinds: Kuṭīcaka, Bhaūdaka, Haṁsa, Paramahaṁsa, Turiyātita and Avadhuta. *MU.*, pp. 174-175.

[3]xiii. 141. 97-99.

[4]xiii. 141. 100-103; IX. 38; cf. i. 31. 8.

[5]xii. 244-19-21.

[6]ibid.

Dantolukhlikāḥ: those who use only their teeth for cleaning grains[1]
Ashmakuttas: those who use only stones for cleaning grains[2]
Adhomukhas: those who hang themselves from a tree[3]
Cakracaras: those who are described as living in the moon devoted to compassion[4]
Prasaṅkhyānas: those who never used beds but lived only on the earth[5]
Abbhakshāḥ (*Abhravakacaḥ*): those who lived upon water or air alone[6]
Saṁprakshālas: those who lived upon the rays of Soma with passions under complete restraint, they celebrated the well-known sacrifices and worshipped the departed manes under proper forms[7]
Tridaṇḍins: those who carried three staves[8]
Vāyubhakṣāḥ: those who subsisted on air[9]

Many of these ascetics are described as following the forest mode of life, some amongst them using only their teeth for cleaning grains; and some only stones. Some amongst them drank only during the light-fortnight (*śukla-pakṣa*) and ate only lightly boiled gruel of wheat. Others drank similar gruel only during the dark-fortnight (*kṛṣṇa-pakṣa*). Some ate what only came of itself (*vāyathāgatam*). Some practised rigid vows, living upon only roots or on fruits, or upon flowers, following the method of the *Vaikhānasa*.[10]

The Roving Mendicants

There was another group of mendicants (*munirmuṇḍaḥ*) who did not believe in a fixed abode, subsisted only on alms and were constantly on move from one place to another.[11] The epic refers to a large number of such *munirmuṇḍaḥ*, who may be called roving

[1]xiii. 141. 105; xii. 17. 11; IX. 38.
[2]ibid.
[3]i. 30. 2.
[4]xiii. 141. 104-105.
[5]IX. 38.
[6]xiii. 17. 11.
[7]xiii. 141. 106-197.
[8]xii. 321. 8-19.
[9]ii. 4. 19.
[10]xii. 244. 28.
[11]xii. 9. 12-13: Caran bhaikṣyaṁ munirmuṇḍaḥ kṣapayiṣye kalevaraṁ vṛikṣa-mūlaniketo vā tyaktasarvapriyāpriyaḥ.

ambassadors of asceticism as they used to visit kings and other people in trouble and afford succour to them through consolation or better still by proper advice.

In Vanaparva, many eminent sages came to Yudhiṣṭhira all the way to console him, to give him cheer by pointing out that he and his brothers are not the only ones who have suffered in the past and a few of these sages suggested different ways of conduct. Lomāsa accompanied Pāṇḍavas in exile acting as their friend, philosopher and guide. Śaunaka, a sage equally versed in *Sāṅkhya* and *Yoga*, comforts the king and asks him to have mental peace. Mention may be made of Mārkaṇḍeya, the great sage of antiquity who spent a great deal of time with Yudhiṣṭhira. He brought home to him that man reaps the fruit of his actions alone, his action pursues him like a shadow and therefore acquisition of true knowledge alone is the way to final good. Sanatkumāra, the sage of the Upaniṣadic fame, figures in Vanaparva. He is introduced to extol the warrior caste.[1] This view is shared by Mārkaṇḍeya who says in clear terms that 'He who worships a king, the protector and a Brāhmin, the ascetic (*tapasvin*) is relieved instantaneously of his sins.'[2] Bṛhaspati also explains king Vasumana how there would be instability and chaos in the world if there is no king to protect.[3]

Ajagara, a wandering mendicant (*caran Brāhmaṇaḥ*), instructs king Prahlāda in wisdom, learning and behaviour.[4]

Muni Kālakavṛkṣīya who, while consoling a certain king over the loss of his kingdom, points out the futility of earthly possessions and their transitory nature.[5] Elsewhere king Senājit is told by a Brāhman that a loss of a son is not a matter of great grief. After all relations in this world are in the nature of accidental meetings of woods in the stream. We meet by chance and separate by chance. Pleasure and pain spring mutually from one another but the true happiness springs from self alone.[6] At the court of Janaka where many ascetics possessing different disciplines and engaged in discussion regarding rites after death, Panchaśikha advocates the highest release according to the *Sāṅkhya* system and laid a stress on

[1]iii. 185. 25-31.
[2]iii. 200. 193.
[3]xii. 68.
[4]xiii. 179. 25f.
[5]xii. 104. 13: Yatkincinmanyass'stiti sarvam nāstīti viddhi tat.
[6]xii. 174.

the disinterestedness not only in actions but in everything.[1] Nārada quotes Sanatkumāra's teaching that there is nothing higher than knowledge, as miserable as attachment and as good as charity. Truth is the highest god.[2]

Since these wandering mendicants (*caran bhaikṣyaṁ munirmuṇḍah*) have an active interest in the safety and welfare of the world, though they themselves have renounced it, they give advice to kings in the sphere of politics also. In fact there is hardly a subject which they touch and do not adorn. An instance of this is provided by Kalakavṛkṣīya muni who on his own went to the king of the Kośala country and warned him against his evil advisers and ministers. Not content with this he stayed with him for some time and continued to guide the destitutes of his kingdom.[3] Sages like Nārada,[4] Utathya,[5] Vāmadeva,[6] Kāmaṇḍaka, Ṛṣabha and others[7] tender advice on similar lines to various kings, in the matters of kingship and politics. The wandering female ascetic Sulabhā discusses the relative merits of *Saṁnyāsa* and *Gṛhasthāsharma*, with king Janaka, who admits that as soon as the futility of the world is realised, one should renounce the world.[8]

Taking a general review of the teachings of the various mendicants referred to above, it appears that these mendicants had no special philosophy of their own. Whatever philosophy they advocated was akin to the *Sāṅkhya* and *Yoga*. But they were more interested in *Ācāra* and hence even abstract philosophical problems they tackled from this angle. Another noteworthy feature of these sages is that they never arrogated to themselves the sole monopoly of knowledge and greatness. Nārada himself gives to Vāsudava a list of people whom he salutes. The list indicates those who do their duties conscientiously and willingly, who are truly generous and self-sacrificing and who deserve honour even at the hands of the great sages.[9] Above all, these ascetics or mendicants, having themselves accepted the life of renunciation, have never undermined

[1]xii. 219.
[2]xii. 329. 5
[3]xii. 82.
[4]xiii. 81. 13-21.
[5]xii. 90, 91.
[6]xii. 92, 93, 94; cf. 90. 4.
[7]xii. 123, 128.
[8]xiii. 308ff.
[9]xiii. 31.

the theory of āśramas. There were a variety of ascetics some of whom contributed a great deal to improve the lot of the people. The miserable received soothing words from these wandering ascetics in their times of distress and calamity. They gave a helping hand to the needy. This indicates that the ascetics did care for the improvement of worldly life of the people.

Śiva, the Mahāyogi

In one of the passages in the *Mahābhārata*, the Great God Śiva is described in detail.[1] The word '*śiva*' means 'mild' or 'auspicious.' But a prominent side of his character is his fierce asceticism. He loves to haunt the cremation-ground, clad in elephant-hide or tiger-skin, his neck encircled with a necklace of skulls, with serpents in in his hair. He wears the matted locks of an ascetic and the austerities he performs are terrific. Once the god of love had the impudence to disturb his yogic contemplation with the vulgar lures of sex. With a glance of his third eye he reduced the godlet to ashes and would only consent to take his consort Pārvati to be his wedded wife after she too had performed the fiercest *tapas*.

Among all the gods, Lord Śiva excels in *tapas*, living in the icy solitude of the Himālayās. Here is a graphic picture of the inherent asceticism of India, incarnate in the Lord Śiva, the *Mahāyogī* who sits absorbed in meditation, passionless and immovable.

"All the manifold satisfactions of the flesh become a burden. Home and kindred and intercourse with the world become a bondage. Food and sleep and the necessities of the physical life seem indifferent or intolerable. And so it comes that the Great God of the Hindu imagination is a beggar, covered with the ashes of His sacrificial fire, so that He is white like snow, His hair growing untended in large masses, oblivious of cold and heat, silent, remote from men. He sits absorbed in eternal meditation."[2] Here we are in the grip not only of a constructed theory of life but of actual experience which has guided the spiritual quest of the *Saṁnyāsin* through the ages.

Lord Śiva is the typical ascetic and self-mortifier, who has attained the highest perfection in abstract meditation and austerity, of the virtue which could be won thereby, hence called *Mahātapaḥ*, *Mahāyogī*. His exemplary life of a mendicant is described thus:

[1]xvii. 202. 203; also xii. 285. 6; xiii. 13-14-18.
[2]Sister Nivedita, q. b. Rufus Jones, *New Studies in Mystical Religion*, p. 68.

'He, Himself is called the Great God Mahesha. The Himālayās, Nageśa is His father-in-law. Dhanesh, the treasurer of the gods, who is Kuber, is his friend. He has a son like Gaṇesha. (Inspite of these very rich and aristocratic contacts), what is He? Only a mendicant! Great indeed is the wish of Hari'[1]

Such is the model Śiva, the *Mahātapaḥ*, provides for his devotees. And the *Saṁnyāsin* is nothing if he does not reach the perfect state of total abandonment of all worldly desires. Here, once more is the picture of the Saṁnyāsin Bhartṛhari gives:

'He who has the earth for his bed, his creeper-like arm for a pillow, the sky for a canopy, the autumn moon for the lamp, experiences pleasures with his mate called renunciation[2] and fanned on all sides with chowries by the winds, rests like a king.'[3]

Even the king who is the ruler of the earth (*bhūpati*) is no match for him. By giving up everything and desires nothing he has everything: the earth, the sky and the winds serve him—the *Saṁnyāsin*. His enduring peace and a sense of perfect freedom are born of his deep realisation, 'Why should I pursue the transient beauties of the world, when my soul has a beauty which age cannot wither, poverty cannot mar, sickness cannot dim, death itself cannot destroy?' He has found eternal bliss in the Ātman which is *Sat-Chit-ānaṅda*.

Two Trends of Thought

The epic discusses two parallel trends of thought relevant to our enquiry; one favouring the path of renunciation embodied in the *Saṁnyāsa* and the other favouring the path of action embodied in the *Gṛhastha* and clearly shows its preference for the latter.

There were some circles especially those of philosophers following the Upaniṣadic line of thought, who advocated renunciation, showing the ascetic way of life as a necessity to achieve concentration on the highest reality. The *Śāṅtiparva* has many such discussions expounding such a view either by itself or in comparison with

[1]svayaṁ maheśaḥ svasūro nageśaḥ sakhā dhaneśastanayo Gaṇeşaḥ tathāpi bhikşātanameva śambho baliyasi kevalamiśvarecchā.

[2]cf. *Ś'raddha* is called the ascetic's wife: *Vairāgya janakaṁ śraddhākalatraṁ Maitri. Up.*, II. 3. 14.

[3]bhūḥ paryanko nijabhujalatā kandukaṁ khaṁ vitānaṁ dipascāndro virativanitā labdhasaṅgapramodaḥ dikkāntabhih pavanacamarairvi jyamānaḥ samantā bhikşuḥ śete nṛpa iva bhuvi tyaktasarvaspṛho'pi *Vairāgyaśatak* Bhartṛhari depicts an ideal life of a saṁnyāsi in this verse.

the opposite view advocating action.[1] Specially noteworthy in this respect is the dialogue between a father and a son where the father advises the son to follow the *āśramas* in their consecutive order. The son, however, prefers the path of renunciation as against the path of action that was to be followed by a *gṛhastha*.[2] In the *Kapila Gītā*[3] also the sage Kapila, admitting the importance of *gṛhasthāśrama*, nonetheless emphasizes in very clear terms that from the individual point of view, *saṁnyāsa* is the only way to achieve erernal bliss. Thus a view prevailed that *saṁnyāsa* was the stage of life by following which the attainment of *mokṣa* was made easy.

As a reaction to the sentiments expressed in favour of *Saṁnyāsa*, the epic first comes out attaching an equal importance to the *gṛhastha* stage. It defends the four *āśramas* of life which are likened to a ladder or proper training ground for the further development of an individual's character. Then it goes further to declare that the *gṛhastha* stage in itself was self-sufficient for the achievement of *mokṣa*, and not only that but it was impossible for a person who ignored it to achieve *mokṣa*.

The main argument put forward in favour of the *gṛhastha* stage of life is that it is the root of all the other modes of life.[4] The householder who lives like a *gṛhastha*, celebrates sacrifices and practises penances. Whatever is done by anybody for acquiring happiness has for its root the *gṛhastha* mode of life.[5] It is thus implied that the persons in the *gṛhasthāśrama* are the main supporters of society. It is due to their unceasing activities and industry that the persons in the other three *āśramas* were supported. Thus it is said: "Indeed as all the rivers, big and small go in the end to the ocean so men belonging to all the other orders have the householder for their refuge."[6] While thus praising the *gṛhasthāśrama*, the Śānti parva goes to say that it surpasses the other *āśramas*: "All persons acquainted with Vēdas have declared the life of a householder to be superior to all the (other) modes of life."[7] The four different modes of life were at one time weighed in balance. The wise have said

[1]xii. 280 ff. 187-284. 295. 60-61.
[2]xii. 277, 5 ff.
[3]xii. 260 ff.
[4]xii. 234.
[5]xii. 269. 7.
[6]xii. 295. 39.
[7]xii. 12. 6.

that when the life of a householder was placed on one scale, it required the three others to balance it.[1] Not only this but the *gṛhastha* stage of life is considered sacred, for the same Parva says: 'The duties of the orders as also of Brāhmans and of those that have retired from the world are included within those of that sacred mode of life viz. that of *gṛhastha*.'[2] Even the fruits of kingship are equated with the object of *gṛhastha* stage of life. It is said that the king who silently recites his *mantras* every day and who adores the gods according to the ordinances, attains to the object of *gārhasthya* mode of life.[3] It is towards this mode of life that the king's deeds are directed, even his attainments flow to fulfil the object of *gārhasthya*: 'That king who is possessed of knowledge, who makes gifts to worthy persons on proper occasions, who knows how to favour and punish, who follows the injunctions of the scriptures in all his dealings, who has tranquillity of soul, attains the object of *gārhasthya* mode of life.'[4] The king's domestic duties are akin to his best penances.[5] Thus *gṛhasthāśram* is superior to all the three *āśramas*.

A person who ignores such a superior *gṛhastha* stage of life, misses an important link in the training ground for the further development of his personality. Sage Syūmarāśmi, while defending the relative position of *gṛhasthāśrama*, puts forward the same argument. He says, 'To achieve a proper equilibrium of mind in misery as well as happiness, is a necessary step towards achieving *mokṣa*. It should also be noted that without taking resort to the *gṛhastha* stage of life, one does not achieve this state of mind. Just as all the creatures are dependent on their mother for their life, so are all the other *āśramas* dependent upon the *gṛhastha* stage of life.'[6] For the achievement of *mokṣa*, therefore, a person ought to have lived as a *gṛhastha*. And having lived as a *gṛhastha*, he need not renounce worldly life to cultivate detachment as the epic declares: 'Even that householder who satisfies the duties of his life by following (even) the practice of picking up fallen grains of corn from the lines of fields and who gives up sensual pleasure and attachment to action,

[1]xii. 12. 12.
[2]xii. 64. 6.
[3]xii. 66. 23.
[4]xii. 66. 6.
[5]xii. 66. 23.
[6]xii. 261. 5ff.

does not find it difficult to acquire heaven.'[1] Thus *gṛhasthāśrama* in itself was self-sufflcient for the achievement of mokṣa.

Another reason for advocating the *gṛhasthāśrama* was for progeny. We come across many cases of the sages who are refused merit because in spite of great austerities to their credit they have not satisfied their ancestors.[2] Especially the story of Jaratkāru and Mandapāla vividly bring out the futility of austerities, sacrifices and asceticism—for they are all subordinate. "None of these things are equal to progeny. A child is the greatest of religious merits."[3] In spite of the greatest of austerities, he who does not produce children goes to hell—for there is no one to perform *śraddhā* for him. Hence the importance of the *gṛhastha* stage in the times of the *Mahābhārata*. The *Gītā* adds lustre to the *gṛhasthāśrama* by favouring the *pravṛtti mārga* and its philosophy of *niṣkāmakarmayoga*. It does not favour the *nivṛtti mārga* and the ascetic life. It makes the ideal of renunciation a part of the active life *gṛhasthāśrama*.

Besides the importance of *pravṛtti mārga* the *Gītā* itself puts forward the concept of *lokasaṁgraha*. A stagnant society always dies. Only that society which understands the value of cooperation and guides its activity along those lines survives in strife. It is not necessary for a detached person who has already realized oneness with the Supreme Brahman to perform any actions but this they must do, to set an example to the society. Lord Kṛṣna himself being the supreme reality does so for the welfare of the society.[4] Thus the fact that social welfare is the ultimate aim of an individual as *gṛhastha* is stressed in clear terms.

If considered in this light it becomes evident that the importance of *gṛhasthāśrama*, not only as the best but the only *āśrama* supporting the other three, is not exaggerated and the epic spares no words to flatter this position of *gṛhasthāśrama*. It repeats off and on that *gṛhasthāśrama* is the best *āśrama*. Not only that but a *gṛhastha* who executes all his responsibility as shown above need not worry about other *āśramas* but attains heaven by the virtue of the merit earned in it.[5]

[1]xii. 191. 18.

[2]xii. I. 13, 18-20; I. 120. 28.29; I. 229; III. 96. 14-15.

[3]xiii. 58. 34.

[4]*BG.*, III. 20-22: Karmaṇaiva hi saṁsiddhimāsthitā janakādayaḥ lokasaṁgrahamevāpi saṁpaṣyan kartumaharsi na me parthāsti kartavyaṁ triṣu lokeṣu kincan nānāvāptaṁvaptavyaṁ varta eva ca karmaṇi *Gītā*, III. 20-22.

[5]xii. 12. 12.

Let us now look at the other side of the picture. Detachment from the world and practice of austerities have been regarded from *Upaniṣadic* times as means of salvation. As remarked earlier, the epic also recommends these means for *mokṣa*.[1] However, at a couple of places there is a discussion on the value or otherwise of renunciation and it appears as if this mode is derided. It is said: 'The wearing of brown clothes, shaving off the head, bearing of the triple stick and the *kamaṇḍalu* (the begging bowl)—these are the outward signs of one's mode of life. These have no value in aiding one to the attainment of emancipation.'[2] Not only that, but it is maintained that people try to avoid the *gṛhastha* stage of life because of their laziness to shoulder the great responsibility. Thus it is said, 'Those lazy and ignorant who have no faith and wisdom and who have no foresight and social reputation, renounce the world only because they get tired of their worldly duties.'[3]

Bhima echoes the same opinion when he rebukes Yudhiṣṭhira, who, after the great battle is won, is disgusted with the world as a result of the cruelties, slaughter and consequent misery, the war brought in its wake and wants to become a *Saṁnyāsi*. Bhima dissuades him by pouring scorn on the *Saṁnyāsāśrama*. He says, 'Men of learning do not acknowledge renunciation. Those who have acute vision consider it a transgression of law. O King, if man could obtain perfection by renunciation then even the mountains and the trees should very soon attain salvation. They are seen always in renunciation, have no troubles, no possessions and are perpetual celibates.'[4] These words clearly show the futility of the life of renunciation in the forest. Stressing the argument further he declares, 'It is true that a person staying in the forest can stay peacefully because he is not supposed to maintain his family, *ṛṣis* guests or the ancestors, but their life is like that of animals.'[5] Here we have for a while an impression that Bhima while advancing the arguments against *Saṁnyāsāśrama* was prejudiced and was actuated by an earnest desire to dissuade his elder brother from taking to a life of *Saṁnyāsa*.

But we have more evidence to show that this was not so. The

[1] xii. 329. 19. 29. 32; xii. 277, 5ff; xii. 161, 43-48; 176, 4 ff; 177, 178 and 179.
[2] xii. 321. 46. 52.
[3] xii. 161. 10.
[4] xii. 10. 18. 24. 25.
[5] xii. 10. 22.

epic clearly declares: 'He who has merely withdrawn from possessions, cannot be regarded as to have renounced the world. He, however, who remains in contact with the world, but sees its faults may be said to have truly renounced the world.'[1] The world, imperfect as it is, throws a challenge to face the realities of life, not to escape them. For it is said that renunciation appeals only to those who are unsuccessful in life.[2] Thus it might have been possible that many who wanted to avoid the responsibility of maintaining a family and supporting the society might have taken recourse to *Saṁnyāsa* as an escape from the realities of life, disappointed as they might have been also in their expectations in life.

The queen of Janaka-Videhi also gets angry when her husband tries to go to forest, shirking all the responsibility of the kingdom and his household, and angrily she declares: 'O King, all creatures in this world are bound by the fetters in form of the fruits of actions committed in their previous life. So it is doubtful as to when one may get liberated. You, who are desirous of living alone, leaving behind your dutiful, religious minded queens, are absolutely a sinner and there would be no place for you in this life as well as the other.'[3] Here grave doubts are cast upon *Saṁnyāsāśrama* to grant one freedom from the chain of Karma. The queen shows her husband the path of duty when he was bewildered and was thinking of accepting the life of renunciation.

It seems clear that there was a section of society which looked down upon *Saṁnyāsa*. According to it, it was simply avoiding the responsibility which a person owed to the society in which he liveed, and towards the family in which he was born and bred. No doubt *Saṁnyāsa* preached high thinking and as an ideal was the best but the most difficult to be cultivated even while living the *gṛhasthāśrama*. To seek these one need not run away from life. In concentrating upon the individual in the *Saṁnyāsa* ideal, which afforded an easy escape from the realities of life, the society as such was neglected. This was meant for those who could not face the life's battle and fight.

The epic thus does not advocate *Saṁnyāsa*. It does not approve of *tapas*. It brings out their utter futility in these words: 'Asceticism is not mere abstinence from the pleasures of the world. He

[1] iii. 2. 30.
[2] xii. 10. 20.
[3] xii. 18. 13-15.

that is always pure and decked with virtue, he that practises kindness all his life, is a Muni *even though he may lead a domestic life.* Such a man is purged of all his sins, however much they may weaken and dry up the body that is made of flesh and blood. The man whose heart is without holiness, suffers torture only by undergoing penances in ignorance of their meaning. He is never freed from sins of such acts. The fire he worships does not consume his sins. It is in consequence of holiness and virtue alone that men attain to regions of blessedness and fasts and vows of silence, living upon air, the shaving off the head, abandonment of a fixed home, the wearing of matted locks on the head, lying under the canopy of heaven, daily fasts, the worship of fire, immersion in water and lying on the bare ground—these cannot produce such a result.'[1] Adopting a sceptic attitude towards the ascetic practices of all kinds and *Saṁnyāsāśrama*, the epic thus scoffs at them. Praising those who live in *gṛhasthāśrama* it declares: 'They only that are possessed of holiness succeed by knowledge and deeds, to conquer disease, decreptitude and death, acquire a high status.'[2] What is of utmost importance is the virtuous conduct of *maitri* and *karuṇā* of a *Gṛhastha* that can win him even infirmity, disease and death.[3]

The epic further seeks to resolve the conflict between the path of action (*pravṛtti*) and the path of renunciation (*nivṛtti*) which has always faced Hinduism by presenting the system of *āśramas* for the purpose of the highest spiritual and ethical development of the individual. These four stages of life are said to be the four steps of a ladder and by climbing them one by one, a person can reach the summit viz. emancipation.

The scheme of the four *āśramas* provides a proper balancing of the four aims of life, viz. *artha*, *kāma*, *dharma* and *mokṣa*. Adopting the three motives, viz. *artha*, *kāma* and *dharma*, as the incentives for all the worldly activities, the epic emphasizes that these motives should be so guided that they may lead to the ultimate realisation of the inner spirituality—the aim of human life.[4] It is thus an integrated view of human life that the epic unfolds. Any departure from this is considered very grave. This is illustrated by a story related by Arjuna in which Indra condemned, in the days of yore,

[1]III. 199 f.
[2]ibid.
[3]XII. 261-264.
[4]xii. 12. 12.

some Bṛāhmins who had taken to the stage of renunciation straight from *brahmacaryāśrama*. He made them return to the *gṛhasthāśrama*.[1] The story clearly indicates that all the four stages of life ought to be preserved, particularly the stage of a *gṛhastha*, which is said to be the prop of the three stages. This means that *Saṁnyāsa* was disfavoured if it ignored the other stages of life.[2] The epic declares:

'He who disregards the *gṛhasthāśrama*, the source of much happiness and adopts the life of renunciation, is possessed by the quality of darkness.' (xii. 12.9).

A reference should be made here to the Ajagara-Prahlāda *Saṁvāda*[3] which gives us an insight in the integrated view of life. Ajagara, a wandering mendicant, appeared to King Prahlāda as one who is healthy of mind and body, disinterested, child-like but a genius and not following any particular path of duty. The king therefore asked him, 'What is wisdom, learning and behaviour, O Sage?' Ajagara then explains that the origination of beings, their growth and destruction is without any casual efforts, and therefore one should neither rejoice nor grieve. One should sleep happily, wise and contented, seeing that the entire world is under destruction and death. One need not turn one's back to the good things which life has to offer nor hanker after them. Ajagara thus describes his way of life, pure and firm, never swerving from Dharma, free of greed, stupefaction and other afflictions.[4] This Ajagara philosophy is advocated by poets and philosophers alike and Bhisma winds up the whole discussion by saying that it will bring happiness to all. It should be noted that this philosophy explains the experience of a wise man who has seen life whole and fully with an emphasis on tranquility of mind, discipline and complete disinterestedness rather than the negative aspect of *Saṁnyāsa*. But to see life wholly and fully one has to pass through the four *āśramas*, balancing the four aims of life. It implies the gradual ethical evolution of personality through stages, higher and higher till one attains the ideal of *mokṣa*. Thus the epic 'does not advocate a completely ascetic view of morality. It gives due importance to happiness and wealth. It enjoins pursuit of them in due subordination to *dharma*.'[5]

[1]xii. 11. 20. 21.

[2]xii. 12-9.

[3]xii. 179 ff.

[4]xii. 179. 25.

[5]Sinha, *History of Indian Philosophy*, I, p. 68.

The question arises: how should a man pursue happiness and wealth, *artha* and *kāma* and blend them in harmony to serve *dharma?*

The epic, in more places than one, raises this important question, to which Vyāsa emphatically declares: 'Happiness and wealth flow from *Dharma*.'[1] And what precisely is *Dharma?* The epic represents *Dharma* as eight-fold viz. sacrifice, learning the Vedas, gifts and penance on the one hand and truth, restraint of passions, forgiveness and freedom from greed on the other. The first four form the *Pitṛyāna*, leading to the moon; while, the latter, the *Devayāna*, to the union with the Supreme Reality.[2] But in addition to this descriptive aspect, *Dharma* has a directive function. It has an import of obligation, when it means duty.[3] In other words we may render Dharma to mean our whole duty to God and man. The epic equates this duty with *ācāra: ācāra paramo dharmaḥ.*[4] It is also called the main supporter of Dharma.[5] Thus *ācāra* stands for *sadācāra* righteous living or virtuous conduct.

We find *ācāra* eulogised in the epic. Its efficacy is so great that it elevates the *śūdra* to the status of a Brāhmin, if he is endowed with self-restraint, truthfulness and righteousness.[6] If these virtues are to be found in a *śūdra* and if they are not found in Brāhmin, then such a *śūdra* is not a *śūdra* and such a Brāhmin is not a Brāhmin. 'A man becomes a Brāhmin by his *ācāra*.'[7] The observance of *ācāra*, in all circumstances, is the duty which the epic tries constantly to inculcate. It is considered superior to even life and death. 'Do not give up righteousness for greed or fear or for desire or even for the sake of dear life. Virtue is eternal; pain and pleasure are fleeting. Life also is fleeting but not the soul.'[8] The soul like virtue is eternal (*nitya*). Under no temptation, under no calamity should a man, therefore, abandon the path of *ācāra*, righteousness. Moreover, the *ṛṣis* have declared *ācāra* as the root

[1]Dharmadarthascakāmasca sa dharmaḥ.

[2]III. 75-76.

[3]cf. Saṁkaranarayana, *Values in History*, p. 37.

[4]I. 108.

[5]xii. 251. 3.

[6]III. 206.12.

[7]xii. 182-8.

[8]na jātu kāmānna bhayānna lobhāt dharmaṁ tyajejjīvitasyāpi hetoḥ nityo dharmaḥ sukhduḥkhe tvanitye jivo nityo heturasya tvanityaḥ.

of all *tapas*. It is through *ācāra* that the Dharma is to be realised.[1] For a man treading the path of *ācāra*, it is not absolutely necessary to retire to the forest, giving up all his connections with worldly activities. He may stick to the world living a virtuous life. Such a life accompanied by the temperate enjoyment of the world's gifts, blended with *artha* and *kāma*, serves Dharma and enables him to attain *mokṣa*. The virtuous life thus becomes as effective as *Saṁnyāsa* to achieve the final aim of life.

However, the path of virtue is not easier as we are tempted to think than the other paths leading to *mokṣa;* nay it is as difficult and severe. Our frail minds are tempted from the path of virtue even by the prospect of the smallest unjust gain which we can secure without difficulty. What need then to speak of privations and calamities? Hence men who have lived a virtuous and perfect life are few and far between in every age. Even Maharṣi Vyāsa who proclaims this supreme path of virtue cries out loudly: 'With arms uplifted I declare that pleasure and wealth *artha* and *kāma* stem from duty (*dharma*). So why not revere or serve the path of *Dharma?* But no one listens to me.'[2] Not only we sense a feeling of despair behind these words but also an awareness that the path of virtue is not easy to follow. The question arises: What are the qualities essential to lead a life of *ācāra* or righteousness?

The foremost is the courage of one's convictions. It is the most difficult to acquire and to possess. The trials and storms in life which often overtake a virtuous man sometimes shake his convictions. For he sees often in this world that even a vicious man prospers. Even if, therefore, virtue may seem to suffer, it must not allow his conviction in its efficacy to slacken. The path of virtue must be followed for its own sake. One must continue to have intrinsic faith that its reward is sure to come, though now invisible. Yudhiṣṭhira observes to his queen in their exile to the forest: 'I Follow Dharma not because I see any immediate profit from it but from the conviction that virtue is to be followed for its own sake.'[3] It requires the conviction of a Dharmarāja to stick to the path of virtue.

Secondly, what is necessary is the self-denial to resist the

[1]sarvasya tapaso mūlamācāraṁ jagṛhuḥ param.

[2]urdhvabāhuvirobhyeṣa na ca kascitśṛnotimāṁ dharmādarthas ca kāmasca sa dharmaḥ kiṁ na sevyate.

[3]dharmam carāmi śuṣroṇi na dharmaphalakāraṇāt dharma vānijyako hino jaghanyo dharmavādinām.

temptation of worldly gain through improper means. This temptation is as great as the self-abnegation which is required for *Saṁnyāsa*. A virtuous mind fortified by this self-denial is sure to raise the soul higher and higher till the man attains *mokṣa*. This self-denial presupposes 'equableness, harmony, balance, *samatva*.'[1] Here it becomes the basic philosophy to guide a virtuous man in his difficult path. He should possess equanimity of mind, harmony or balance of personality, born out of living a life of *ācāra*, to face life as it comes and accept what it has to offer, for better or for worse. Sukthankar opines that '*samatva* is the keynote of the philosophy of the *Mahābhārata* which is identical with that of the *Gītā*.' He further observes: 'The man who is *sama* clearly does not try to fly from the world. Worldly life brings a multitude of marvellous experiences, most precious, not to be missed at any cost but not to be utterly absorbed in. One who has attained *samatva*, walks *evenly* among the beauties and the perils of the world.'[2] The man who has acquired *samatva* can through self-abnegation stick to the path of virtue. It is only *Gṛhasthāśrama* which trains a man to attain *samatva* and prepares him to live a righteous life.

This can be supported by quoting sage Syūmarāśmi who says: 'To achieve a proper equilibrium of mind in misery as well as happiness is a necessary step towards achieving *mokṣa*. It should also be noted that without taking resort to the *Gṛhastha* stage of life, one does not achieve this state of mind.'[3]

Accordingly, Vyāsa declares that *Gṛhasthāśrama* wherein a virtuous life is possible, is the brightest of all the *āśramas*. It is sacred and worthy of worship.[4] He also considers *Lokasaṁgraha*, the welfare of the world and *lokadharma*, the obligation towards the world, as great values to be cherished and perused. Ajagar *muni* is called *lokadharma vidhānavit*,[5] one who knows, supports and propagates the ideal of *lokasaṁgṛaha*. 'One who is such a protagonist of *lokapakṣa* has to be necessarily an admirer of *Gṛhasthadharma*.'[6] For it is only in the *Gṛhsthāśrama* that the ideal of *Lokasaṁgraha* could be pursued and realised, transcending one's own welfare:

[1]Sukthankar, *On the Meaning of the Mahābhārata*, p. 122.
[2]ibid, pp. 122-123.
[3]xii. 261. 5 f.
[4]xii. 66. 37.
[5]xii. 179. 9.
[6]Agrawala, *Kalā Aur Saṁskriti*, p. 77.

ātmahitāya jagadhitāya ca. It is here that one can learn to live life fully and as a whole, balancing the four aims of life. It is solely here that 'this glowing and rhythmic synthesis of life, a profound and universal philosophy,'[1] can be worked out and lived.

But this is not all. The epic, in no uncertain terms, characterises 'an age of youth,' depicts 'Indian heroic society.'[2] It is not a mere epic. It is a romance, telling the tale of heroic men and women. 'The whole epic is the assertion of the heroic activism of the warrior against the world-denial of the ascetic.'[3] We hear many echoes of the conflict between the *Brāhmin* and the *Kṣatriya* ascetics and warriors. The rivalry between Vaśiṣṭha, the Brāhmin and Viśvāmitra, the king, who becomes an ascetic for the achievement of superior powers, and the legend of Nahuṣa who levied taxes on the ascetics and compelled them to do manual labour are such echoes. The Kṣatriya disdained to die a natural death at home. As the epic points out: 'The death of a Kṣatriya on his bed at home is highly sinful. The man who meets with death in the forest or in battle acquires great glory.'[4] Only after he had lived a life of action in youth and maturity, when the business of life was over, and life, having lost all attachments, was thought to be a burden, that he thought of a life in the forest. He then took the final course like the Pāṇḍavas, who crowning Parikṣita, went out on a pilgrimage, visiting holy places and finally took the great journey—*Mahāprasthāna.*

It was the desire to live a heroic life on the battlefield and to court even death which distinguished the life of a Kṣatriya. If asceticism claimed that withdrawal from the world was the only way to salvation, the warrior-class made the counter-claim that death on battlefield also led to heaven. Karṇa claims: 'I shall win great renown in this world and I shall have access to the highest heaven.' Even Duryodhana is convinced that he shall go to heaven. Says he: 'There is no sorrow for me that my head was kicked by Bhima with his foot. In a moment, crows and vultures are going to place their feet on my head. I die the death which is dear to true Kṣatriyas who follow their own Dharma. Who can have a more

[1]Sukthankar, op. cit., p. 124.
[2]Siddhanta, *The Heroic Age of India*, pp. 114, 188 ff.
[3]Chaitanya, *A New History of Sanskrit Literature*, p. 215.
[4]IX. 5.30 ff.

glorious end than myself?'[1] When the Pāṇḍavas were in deep distress and despair, their mother Kunti recalls the story of queen Vidula, who turned angrily on her son Sanjaya for trying to withdraw from a hopeless battle. 'Flare up like a torch of Tinduka wood, though it be put for a moment, but smoulder not like a fire of chaff just to prolong life. That man whose deeds do not form the subject of tales of wonder, serves but to increase the great heap, he is neither man or woman. It behoves thee not to adopt the idle, wretched, infamous and miserable profession of mendicacy that is worthy only of a coward.'[2] The moral is obvious. It is this heroic side of this illustration which emerges eloquently out of the great epic: to encourage and inspire man to face the battle of life like a warrior, however, hopeless it may be, to fight it out and not run away like an ascetic. It teaches him to go through it all—the joys and sorrows, the beauties as well as the perils of the world—with a smile and behind which to have a vision of the Transcendent Reality.

II. Asceticism in the Bhagavad Gītā

The Bhagavad Gītā, 'Song of the Blessed One,' forms part of the Bhiṣmaparva of the great epic, the *Mahābhārata*. Accepted as a classic and a scripture which has moulded the lives of the millions down the ages, it has acquired along with the *Upaniṣads* and the *Brahmasūtras*, the collective name of *Prasthāntraya*, the principal three-fold canon upon which the spiritual tradition of India is based.

Different opinions have existed amongst the scholars, from time to time, as to whether the *Gītā* teaches the path of knowledge (*jñāna*), devotion (*bhakti*) or action (*karma*). Śaṅkarācārya has with a good deal of analytical and logical skill attempted to prove that the *Gītā* predominantly preaches the way of knowledge. 'The knowledge of its teachings,' he said, 'leads to the realisation of all human aspirations.'[3] The great *ācāryas* like Rāmānuja, Vallabha, Mādhava, Nimbārka and others have laid stress on the path of devotion.[4] In recent times Lokamānya Tilak and others have interpreted the *Gītā's* view as pre-eminently that of action (*karma*).

[1]IX-16; cf. Rajagopalachari, *Mahābhārata*, p. 289.
[2]V. 133, 14-25.
[3]cf. Munshi, *Bhagavad Gītā and Modern Life*, p. 17.
[4]cf. Radhakrishnan, *The Bhagavadgītā*, pp. 17-19, introduction.

It would, therefore, seem that it all depends from which angle one approaches the *Gītā.* In it the materialist finds a code of daily life and conduct, for the philosopher, there is a guide to the knowledge of the Self; to the man of affairs, the path of action is laid bare; while to the devotionally inclined is clear the path of adoration till he merges himself into the Supreme. The author of the Gītā not only recognises many of these ways, already traditional in his own time, but shows familarity with disputes among those who claim superiority for each of them. Instead of taking sides with any of the leading schools of thought, however, he sagaciously explains and evaluates the ways in which each is correct and how each may play its own peculiar role in the total picture of how men quest for the goal of life.

Thus in the Gītā, as Kosami observes: 'We have a brilliant review—synthesis of many schools of thought which were in many respects mutually incompatible. The incompatibility is never brought; all views are simply facets of the one divine mind.'[1] The *Gītā* blends the Ṛgvedic *Veda-mārga*, the Brāhmanic *Karma-mārga*, the Upaniṣadic *Jñāna-mārga* and to this fusion adds the rich stream of *Bhakti*, personal devotion, 'which was the justification, the one way of deriving all views from a single divine source.'[2] Thus in reflecting clearly ideas from every point of view and attempting to harmonise them, it gains the universality of appeal. Though a reflection of the age in which it was written, its message has a timeless value for all, regardless of caste, colour and creed.[3]

The Conditions of the Times

Almost the same circumstances which gave birth to Buddhism, surrounded the rise of Kṛṣṇa, who preached the gospel of the *Gītā*. The Vedic law had fallen into much disuse and also into a lot of misuse. Vedic ritualism and the other-worldly attitude of the Upaniṣads had become exceedingly dogmatic. The Vedic sacrifices were a common feature in the religious life of the people and were popular especially among the orthodox. The priestly and other classes of people practised religious observances only for the sake

[1]Kosambi, *Social and Economic Aspects of Bhagavad Gītā*, pp. 203-204.
[2]ibid, p. 218.
[3]It is called *sarvaśāstramayi Gītā* (*Mhb.*, vi. 44. 4). Having mastered the Gītā, one is in possession of the essential knowledge of all the scriptures. Vyāsa says: Gītā sugita kartavyā kiṁ anyaiḥ śāstravistaraiḥ.

of obtaining happiness and heavenly enjoyment. Their minds remained ignorant of religious knowledge. The ritualistic practice of religion had thus become mechanical. This indicates the low level to which people had fallen after the spirit lying behind the Vedic sacrifices had disappeared and religion had become too formal.

On the one hand were the Vedic *Karmakāṇḍins* who believed in *yagna* with its intricate and elaborate ceremonies and on the other several Upaniṣads enjoined men to give up worldly pursuits and resort to *Saṁnyāsa* for getting salvation. *Saṁnyāsa*, it was believed, lay in running away from the battle-field of life to a safer and quieter valley of the Himālayas. It had become a matter of complete suppression of desires or giving up all actions. It was held that the emancipatory knowledge of the Ātman placed man beyond the reach of all desire; a man of perfect philosophical knowledge, a Jñāni, need not do any actions as they do not affect him as the effect of *Karma* is burnt by the fire of the knowledge. Asceticism consisted of mere physical austerity or *tapas* and was identified with all kinds of self-torture and physical mortification.

The concept of *Ahiṁsā* or non-injury was rapidly coming into favour. There was a growing sentiment that all souls including those of animals were sacred and that it was a sin to kill the animals for obtaining a supposed entry into heaven. More stress was now laid on the necessity of austerities of life and suppression of animal instincts rather than on animal sacrifices. This opposition was first laid by Mahāvīra and then Gautama, the Buddha, who were the great religious reformers of the time. The Buddha revolted against the priestcraft of the Vedic religion and against the demoralisation of the people which had crept into society. By his own example he showed a way of stern ethical code of life to substitute formal religion. There were also new cults of religious philosophy which stressed the ethical aspect of religion and which had no prominence, in the formal Vedic sacrifices. The common man was puzzled as to what his duties were and which way lay his emancipation. There was no proper place for a psychological approach towards religion through devotion (*Bhakti*) to the cosmic manifestations of the Absolute in any of the prevailing cults of religion. People were becoming either too worldly or were drawn away from the world. They had sunk into a sad condition of desperate ignorance. 'In Arjuna,' says Chinmayananda, 'we find a typical representative of the confused and the confounded members of the then society, over-fed with unintelligent knowledge, vaguely repeated, least understood and rarely appreciated.'[1]

There was thus a much felt need to divert men's minds from the barren and downward path of dogmatic formalities of religion to the progressive path of inner life. They now needed a way of life in which knowledge, devotion and obligatory duties should have their proper proportion to guide them in their daily lives. A new lead had to be given to them and a fresh orientation had to be made of the doctrines of life which the Āryans evolved through centuries of thought and meditation. The *Gītā* came to the rescue to evolve such a philosophy which could satisfy the minds of ordinary men, meet their individual needs and situations, without removing the basic beliefs of the Vedic religion. By weaving the web of religion into the texture of worldly life and its challenges, the *Gītā* showed the way that religion must rule even our worldly pursuits. Its message was addressed to the common man, not to the adept only. Its lessons were originally meant for the soldier on the battlefield, but by implication they apply to all who are engaged in the battle of life. Gandhiji looked upon the *Gītā* as a scripture which could guide him through the dark paths of life. According to him, the *Gītā's* teachings had an application to the problems of daily life. About its religious importance he observes: 'What cannot be followed out in day-to-day practice cannot be called religion.'[2] It is for this reason that it is called layman's *Upaniṣad*.

Implications of the term 'Yoga'

To understand the *Gītā's* contribution to asceticism properly, it is important to comprehend the implications of the term 'Yoga' which is the keynote of the whole work, which is also called '*Yoga-śāstra*.' The term is used singly and in combination with other terms viz. *bhakti-yoga*, *karma-yoga*, *saṁkhya-yoga* etc. Every chapter is described at its end as containing a dissertation of a particular kind of *Yoga*.

The *Gītā* employs 'Yoga' in various senses. The Sanskrit word

[1]Chinmayananda, *Bhagavad Gītā*, I, p. 39.

[2]Mahadeva Desai, *The Gītā According to Gandhi*, p. 132. Gandhiji says: 'When doubt haunts me, when disappointments stare at me in the face and I see not one ray of hope on the horizon, I turn to the *Bhagavad Gītā* and find verse to comfort me and I immediately begin to smile in the midst of overwhelming sorrow.'

'Yoga' is derived from the verb 'Yuj' which means 'to join,' 'to attach,' 'to yoke.' Primarily it means joining or union, and is akin to the English word 'Yoke.' Secondarily, it has various shades of meaning such as equilibrium, balance, synthesis or integration and regulation and control of bodily and mental faculties. In the *Gītā* '*Yoga is called Samatvam.*'[1] It means balance or equilibrium, secured by mental discipline. It is also used in the sense of art, device or skill as in 'Yoga is proficiency in doing *karma.*'[2] This skill becomes perfect as we achieve perfect equanimity or serenity of mind under all conditions and circumstances. In some other places its meaning is restricted to performance of actions as compared with *Sāṁkhya* i.e. Knowledge.[3] The word 'Yoga' is also combined with *Buddhi* and *Jñāna*, *Karma* as well as *Bhakti*.[4] At first sight, this may appear where it is stated[5] that the Yogi is superior to a *Tapasvi* i.e. an ascetic, to a *Jñāni* i.e. a man who has mere knowledge of sacred books and also a *Karmin* i.e. a person who merely performs ceremonial rites. But looking to the general tenor of the whole work, it will be reasonable to ascribe the meaning of 'Yoga' as the union of all the three—*Jñāna*, *Bhakti* and *Karma*—with a subjective emphasis on one of them according to the mental development of each individual. In this way each man may search for that particular kind of *Yoga* which is best suited to him. Thus for example different types of Yoga for a man of confused intellect and for a man who is engaged in religious observances are described.[6] Everywhere, there is emphasis on the organic unity of mind and its faculties which should not be disrupted but strengthened by the three-sided progress of *Jñāna*, *Bhakti* and *Karma*. Yoga is thus the art of creating synthesis, integration or harmonious adjustment between various springs of action, which constitute our mental life. They are the various aspects of a single reality namely spiritual life, Kṛṣṇa's exhortation to Arjuna: 'Do then become a Yogi, *Yogi bhava*, *Yogi bhava*'[7] is the central teaching of the *Gītā*. This means that one

[1] *BG.*, II. 48: *Samatvaṁ yoga ucyate.*

[2] *BG.*, II. 50: *Yogaḥ karmasukauśalaṁ.*

[3] *BG.*, III. 3, V. 5.

[4] *BG.*, XVIII. 57, III. 3. 7, chapter XII etc.

[5] *BG.*, VI. 46: tapasvibhyo'dhiko yogi jñānibhyo'pi mato'dhikaḥ karmibhyascādhiko yogi tasmādyogi bhavārjuna.

[6] *BG.*, II. 53; VI. 44.

[7] *BG.*, VI. 46.

should realize the ideal of a perfect man who has 'yoked himself to the way of Yoga (*Yogayukto*) whose mind is purified, whose self has triumphed and whose senses have been subdued, and whose self has, indeed become the self of all beings.'[1] He is verily the Yogin whose understanding is secure from all attachment to objects of senses, is free from fear and wrath and resentment, free alike from likes and dislikes, pleasure and pain. Having stopped all brooding on the objects of the senses, he broods on the Highest and rises towards Him ultimately resting in Him—*Brāhmisthithi*.[2] The *Gītā* calls such a perfect Yogin, a *Sthitaprajña*.

It should be borne in mind that the 'Yoga' that is taught by the *Gītā* is not the technical Yoga of Patañjali. It does not consist of a series of exercises in-thought-control,[3] which is only its restricted meaning. Examining all the contexts in which 'Yoga' is used, Tilak is of the opinion that it has been used in the *Gītā* ın the sense of *ONLY* the Path of Energism (*pravṛtti-mārga*) i.e. the Karma-Yoga. According to him, 'Karma is the only *sādhanā* to salvation.'[4] In other words Karma-Yoga is the essence of the *Gītā*. Even *Jñāna* and *Bhakti* point to Karma as the ultimate goal of life. The great activist that Tilak is, his interpretation is examined by Ranade who points out that even Tilak regarded realisation as being higher than service.[5] Ranade opines that 'God-realisation constitutes the *apurvatā*, the novelty or the supreme contribution of the *Gītā*.' He observes: 'The *Gītā* is one of the greatest works on mysticism that the world has even seen and when God-realisation has been duly stressed, everything else will follow in its wake.'[6] This is amply borne out by the eighteenth chapter of the *Gītā*. Explaining the distinction between *tyāga* and *saṁnyāsa* and preaching *selfless action in this world*, *for the benefit of this world*, Lord Kṛṣṇa assures Arjuna: 'Dedicate thy thought, thy worship, thy sacrifice, thy homage to Me and I solemnly promise that thou shalt come to Me. Disturb not thyself by conflicting duties. Seek refuge in Me. I will deliver thee from sin. Sorrow not.'[7]

[1] *BG*., V. 7.
[2] *BG*., II. 55-72.
[3] *YS*., I. 1.
[4] *Gītā-Rahasya*, I, pp. 76-87.
[5] Rande, *Bhagavad Gītā as a Philosophy of God-realisation*, pp. 111-123.
[6] ibid, p. 123.
[7] *BG*., XVIII. 63-66.

Karma Yoga

'The *Gītā*,' according to Munshi, 'is not a scripture of the next world, nor of asceticism nor of inaction. It is an intensely human document; a guide for every human situation.'[1] This statement focuses the central teaching of the *Gītā* that it is predominantly a gospel of action. Lord Kṛṣṇa is not concerned with running away from life through asceticism or contemplation or ecstatic devotion. He does not want us to flee from a worldly career or the haunts of men to the solitude of the forest. He does not bid us hide in a cave like a hermit or to seek peace on the loneliness of the mountain-top like a *tapasvi*; nor does he urge us to accept cowardly renouncement. When Arjuna wants to escape and says: 'I shall not fight.'[2] Kṛṣṇa chides him and asks: 'Whence has come to thee this dejection of spirit in the hour of crisis? It is unknown to men of noble mind (not cherished by the Āryans); it does not lead one to heaven; (on earth) it causes disgrace.'[3] In his attempt to release Arjuna from his doubts, Kṛṣṇa refers to the doctrine of the undestructibility of the Self, appeals to his sense of honour and martial traditions, reveals to him God's purpose and points out how action is to be undertaken in the world. Says he: 'Yield not to this unmanliness (*klaibyaṁ*) O Pārtha, for it does not become thee. Cast off this petty faint-heartedness and arise.'[4] These inspiring words rouse Arjuna to action, to fight as a warrior.

This urge to action is the dominant note of the gospel, as it is the inalienable feature of human existence. 'No one,' says Kṛṣṇa, 'can remain actionless even for a moment.'[5] He then elaborates this point and gives in support the instance of a *Jñāni* 'who revels in Ātman, who is content in Ātman and who is satisfied only with Ātman. There is nothing he needs to do. That which is done or left undone, does not concern him. He has no ambition to serve.'[6] Such a perfect man also must perform action without attachment, to attain the Supreme. He must work ceaselessly for the welfare of the world (*lokasaṁgraha*). It is pointed out that it was through such work that Janak and others attained to perfection. 'For

[1]Munshi, op. cit., p. 18.
[2]*BG*., II. 9.
[3]*BG*., II. 2-3.
[4]ibid.
[5]*BG*., III. 5.
[6]*BG*., III. 17-19.

whatever a great man does, the same is done by others as well. Whatever standard he sets, the world follows.'[1] Thus the great men are the path makers who blaze the trail that other men follow. The light generally comes through individuals who are in advance of society.

The Lord then cites His own example. 'For me, there is nothing to do in the three worlds, nothing worth gaining that I have not gained; yet I am ever in action. If I withdraw from action and cease to work, My example would be followed by men. This world will fall to pieces. I would be the creator of chaos and creation would then perish.'[2] Not only this, He adds, he Himself takes incarnation from time to time for universal benefit, 'to save the righteous, to destroy the wicked and to re-establish *Dharma*.'[3] Thus even those who reach self-realisation, everyone, including even God, must express themselves through action.

The performance of action which the *Gītā* advocates is disinterested work (*niṣkām-karma*). It says: 'To action alone hast thou a right and never at all to its fruits; let not the fruits of action be thy motive; neither let there be in thee any attachment to inaction.'[4] It is *Karma-phala-tyāga*, the giving up of expectation of the fruit of action, that detached frame of mind which is most important. The *Gītā* declares that before God, the work of man will be judged by the spirit in which it is done, not by the nature of the work. 'Whosoever acts in a spirit of dedication, fits himself for salvation.'[5] The action of such a man does not bind him. 'For he who has renounced attachment to the fruit of action, who is ever content and free from all dependence—he, though immersed in action, yet

[1] *BG.*, III. 20-21.

[2] *BG.*, III. 23-24 Following in the footstepts of the *Gītā*, Tagore says that 'God is a worker, and that, if we love Him, we must work with Him.'

'Our master is a worker and we work with him Boisterous is his mirth and we laugh with his laughter. He beats his drum and we march. He Sings and we dance in its tune. (*Poems*: No. 43)

God is not only a worker, but also a dweller among the lowest of the low who work. Tagore says: 'He is there where the tiller is tilling his hard ground and where the pathmaker is breaking stones. He is with them in sun and in shower, and his garment is covered with dust. Put off thy holy mantle and even like him come down on the dusty soil.' (*Gītāñjali*, XI)

[3] *BG.*, IV. 8.

[4] *BG.*, II. 47.

[5] *BG.*, III. 35.

acts not.'[1] The Gītā thus preaches *niṣkāma karmayoga* which leads one to salvation. And such work becomes holy when dedicated to the lord.

The Institution of Asceticism

The doctrine that release cannot be attained unless one goes out of this painful and insipid worldly life, was first brought into the Vedic religion by the writers of the Upaniṣads and Sāṁkhya philosophers.[2] Several Upaniṣads enjoined men to give up worldly pursuits and resort to *Saṁnyāsa* to gain salvation.[3] Both Jainism and Buddhism were in favour of monachism and had given a great stimulus to the popularity of this ideal. The monastic movement was wide-spread. Some of the best men had given up the world and had embraced the life of renunciation. The author of the *Gītā* was face to face with this serious situation. He realized that if this other-worldly ideal spread any further there would be great harm. There was a danger of men, who, instead of being at the helm of the affairs in the family and the state, leaving for the jungle or the cave and devoting themselves entirely to a life away from society and its concerns. It would spell disaster, and result in the disintegration of society. To check this anti-social movement gathering momentum, some radical remedy was needed. Lord Kṛṣṇa preached the doctrine of *Niṣkāmakarmayoga* through the *Gītā.* He taught that men should perform the various duties belonging to their different stations in life, but in a spirit of dedication and surrender to the Divine. Through the gospel of selfless action He promised salvation from the bondage of repeated births.

In elevating all disinterested work performed in a spirit of dedication to God, the *Gītā* elevates such work to the state of holiness. It declares that *renunciation* (*saṁnyāsa*) and performance of action (*Karmayoga*) both lead to salvation; but of the two, *Karmayoga*, the latter is better than renunciation, the former.[4] Thus renunciation is not cessation from work. It is to be practised not towards work but to the fruits of work. It refers not to the act itself but to the frame of mind behind the act. It means the abandonment (*tyāga*)

[1] *BG.*, IV. 20.

[2] cf. Tilak, op. cit., II, p. 692.

[3] *Bṛhad. Up.*, IV. 4.26; III. 5. 1; also Brahmā, Saṁnyāsa, Aruṇeya, Kanthaśruti, Paramhaṁsa, Jābāla, Āśrama.

[4] *BG.*, V. 2.

of the fruits of all action. A *Saṁnyāsi*, according to the *Gītā* is one who performs actions but without the least faint of expectation of fruits or results. He is not the one who has renounced worldly life. The goal placed before the Saṁnyāsi is *Sarva Saṁkalpa Saṁnyāsa*,[1] which means surrendering his will, desire and action at the feet of the Lord. It is not to evade the social responsibilities. All work is for the welfare of the world, for the sake of the Supreme—*jagad hitāya Kṛṣṇāya*. Says the Lord: 'Whatever thou doest, whatever thou eatest, whatever thou offerest, whatsoever thou givest, whatsoever thou doest of austerity (*tapasyasi yat*), do thou that as an offering unto Me.'[2]

Thus *Saṁnyāsa* is the restatement of the central teaching—*Yogi Bhava*.[3] As *Saṁnyāsa* is well nigh impossible without Yoga,[4] the *Gītā* wants the *Saṁnyāsi* to be a *Karmayogi*. Thus a man who remains in the world and works in a spirit of renunciation or desireless action is as much a *Saṁnyāsin* as he who has retired from the world and renounced all possessions. The *Gītā* does not favour the life of a recluse who escapes from life meditating in a cloistered seclusion, scorning all action. Not the inactive *Saṁnyāsi* but the dispassionate and disinterested householder, a *Niṣkāma-Karmayogi*, is upheld as the ideal. And the householder who performs all actions desirelessly and with the idea of dedicating them to God is called an eternal ascetic (*nitya saṁnyāsin*).[5] This was a revolutionary change the *Gītā* brought about. In all earlier systems, release was possible only for those who gave up worldly life and took to *Saṁnyāsa*. In the *Gītā* release was made available for the layman and his wife while they maintained the household and took part in the business of the world.

While the *Gītā* condemns the ascetic way of life in no uncertain terms and interprets *Saṁnyāsa* as Karma-Yoga, it also takes a clear stand against the ascetic practices prevalent in that age. This it does with an emphasis on the inward process of purifying the mind or self-control and *Vairāgya*. It aims at the necessity of acquiring the discipline to attain the equanimity of the mind, 'a poise of the soul' which enables one to look evenly at life in all its aspects.

[1] *BG*., VI. 4.
[2] *BG*., IX. 27.
[3] *BG*., VI. 46.
[4] *BG*., V. 6.
[5] *BG*., V. 3.

Ascetic practices or *tapas* were taken in those days as going into the forest and mortifying the body (*karṣayantah, ghoraṁ tapyante ye tapo janāḥ*).[1] Various methods of self-torture were practised by some for purposes of display (*daṁbhāhaṁ-kārasaṁyuktā*)[2] hair-shirts or piercing the body and putting it to torture by various devices. Similarly, it was believed that *Saṁnyāsa* consisted in shaving off the hair and throwing away the sacred thread or taking a staff in the hand and going about begging or giving up all action and living in the forest in self-denial and conscious self-persecution.[3] The Gītā condemns these methods of self-torture as demoniac (*āsuri*).[4] It points out that the practice of mortification and meaningless austerities (*tapas*) must be distinguished from self-control which is a matter of discipline.

The *Gītā* asserts that the true discipline of the body, mind and speech constitute the real austerity or penance (*tapas*). This three-fold discipline is described and classified by the *Gītā* as austerity (*tapas*) of the body, speech and mind. Homage to the gods, to Brāhmaṇas, to Gurus and to wise men; cleanliness, uprightness, *brahmacarya* and *ahiṁsā*—these constitute *tapas* of the body. Words that cause no hurt, that are true, loving and helpful, and the practice of the study of the scriptures constitute *tapas* of speech, serenity, gentleness, silence, self-restraint and purity of the spirit—these constitute *tapas* of the mind.[5] This three-fold *tapas*, practised in perfect faith by men, who are not desirous of the fruit, and are disciplined, is said to be pure (*sāttvika*).[6] Not content with this, the Gītā adds: 'Austerity or *tapas* which is practised with an eye to gain praise, honour and homage and for show is said to be *rājas*; it is fleeting and unstable.'[7] Furthermore, 'austerity which is practised from any foolish obsession, either to torture oneself or with the object of destroying another is called *tāmasa*.'[8] Thus austerity which is for the sake of reputation, honour and reverence, is false and impure. That austerity is still worse when it is practised as self-

[1] *BG*., XVII. 5-6.

[2] *BG*., XVII. 5.

[3] *BG*., XVIII. 3: tyājaṁ doṣavadityike karma. *BG*., XVIII. 6: karṣayantaḥ śarīrasthaṁ.

[4] *BG*., XVII. 6.

[5] *BG*., XVII. 14-17.

[6] *BG*., XVII. 17.

[7] *BG*., XVII. 18.

[8] *BG*., XVII. 19.

torture, aiming at hurting another. Real *tapas* is the three-fold control of the body, mind and speech. It is self-discipline. It must be a matter of inner life. It should be an aid to self-control to bring about an equilibrium of all our mental faculties which the *Gītā* Calls Yoga: *samatvaṁ yoga uchyate*.[1] Thus the *Gītā* makes *tapas* a matter of self-discipline, an inward attitude of a purifying process of the mind. This demands the training of the mind. For mind is the man. As the mind so is the individual. The *Gītā* also shows how to train the mind.

Arjuna pointedly asks Kṛṣṇa how to curb and control the mind which is restless, turbulent and as uncontrollable as wind. To this Kṛṣṇa replies that it is really very difficult, but it can be done gradually by constant practice (*abhyāsa*) and disposition (*vairāgya*).[2] *Vairāgya* means without *Rāga* or attachments—detachment from all affections, all aversions (*rāgadveṣaviyukta*) seeking nothing and rejecting nothing. The exercise consists in rising above the pairs of opposites (*nirdvanda*), on the planes of body, mind and feelings—above cold and heat, pleasure and pain (*śitoṣṇasukhduḥkha*) honour and ignominy (*mānāpamāna*).[3] Thus *vairāgya* according to the *Gītā* is not running away from the world, or callousness towards men and matters or going through the routine of life disliking it. It is not indifference or heedlessness in the living of our life. It is the capacity to face the realities of existence and evaluate men, things and events at their true worth, without letting ourselves be affected by any of them. Thus it is the discipline of restraining the mind at all levels and in all circumstances. This is possible only when one has achieved mastery over the mind. Towards this end, Kṛṣṇa does not recommend a negative discipline of self-suppression or denial of the joys of life.

It is an erroneous belief that Indian philosophy regards senses as the seat of nothing but evil and should therefore be suppressed. What is evil is not the senses but the uncontrolled use of them. Sense experience is natural and therefore desirable. The world is to be experienced and enjoyed through the senses. But the enjoyment

[1] *BG.*, II. 48.

[2] *BG.*, VI. 34. 35.

[3] *BG.*, II. 56; II. 38; cf. Manu. (VI. *TS.*, 81) mentions freedom from *Matrāsangha* (mātrāsparśa) (*BG.*, II. 14) and *Iudriya-saṅiga* i.e. *saṅga-tyāga* and freedom from all *dvaṅdas.*; *BG.*, II. 64; II. 14; VI. 7; *BG.*, XII. 17-18; XVIII. 51; *BG.* II. 48, II. 15.

should not only be moderate but controlled without the mind being made a slave of them by attachment. Austerity does not mean annihilation of desires but their restricted use by subordinating them to rational thought. The *Gītā*, therefore, does not support an ascetic life. It repeatedly says that the food and pleasures should be balanced; the body should not be put to torture and that *Prasanna-cetas*, joyful attitude towards life is essential to reach Him.[1]

Thus the *Gītā* takes a synthetic view and teaches that an attempt to crush all desires would only increase the mental conflict. 'All beings follow their nature. What is the use of absolute restraint?'[2] What is required is not suppression but regulation of the senses. It says, 'He who, restraining the organs of action, sits resolving in the mind thoughts regarding objects of senses, he, of deluded understanding, is called a hypocrite. But he excels, who controlling the senses by the mind, unattached, directs his organs of action to the path of work.'[3] Human nature, being what it is, cannot be wiped out by trying to do the impossible. Our lower self is to be lifted up and purified by the higher self and not annihilated. What keeps us low in the scale of life is excessive attachment to sensuos objects and frustration in not obtaining the fruits of action and the fulfilment of our desires. For that purpose it is absolutely necessary to acquire, firstly, a sense of non-attachment (*Anāsakti*) to sensuous objects even while experiencing them; secondly, renunciation of the desires to enjoy the fruits of actions while doing them (*Karma-phala-tyāga*) and thirdly, an equilibrium of all our faculties of the body and the mind (*Yoga*). The *Gītā* teaches us how to acquire these qualities.

Though the *Gītā* stresses self-control through constant practice (*abhyāsa*) and dispassion (*vairāgya*), the teaching never degenerates into mere asceticism. On the other hand, excessive mortification of the flesh is condemned and moderation recommended. It says: 'Yoga is not for him who eats too much, nor for him who eats too little. It is not for him who sleeps too much, nor for him who keeps vigil too long. But to him who is temperate in his food and recreation, who is restrained in all his actions and who has regulated his

[1] *BG*., VI. 16-17; II. 65.
[2] *BG*., III. 33.
[3] *BG*., III. 6-7.

sleep and vigils. Yoga puts an end to all sorrow.'[1] Even the food we daily take has its effect on our psychology and character. The *Gītā* makes distinction between the foods and groups them as of three kinds as also sacrifice, austerity and almsgiving: *Sāttvik*, *Rājasik* and *Tāmasik*. It may be *Sāttvik*, good and strengthening to the spirit; or destructive of serenity, passion-producing, *Rājasik*; or wholly bad, causing deterioration of mind and intellect and increasing inertia, *Tāmasik*.

Lord Kṛṣṇa also asserts that excessive bodily mortification is prohibited even by the *Śāstras* and calls those engaged in it as foolish and fiendish. Says He: 'Vain and conceited men, impelled by the force of their desires and passions, subject themselves to terrible mortifications not ordained by scriptures. And being foolish, they torture their bodily organs and one also who dwell within. Know that such men are fiendish (*āsuri*) in their resolves.'[2] So the natural man in us is neither to be suppressed nor indulged. He is to be wisely controlled and properly directed. In other words, we should learn to move amidst the sense objects with an easy self-mastery, neither attracted nor repelled by them. 'The disciplined soul,' according to the *Gītā*, 'moving among sense-objects with the senses weaned from likes and dislikes and brought under the control of Ātman, attains peace of mind.'[3]

The ideal Yogin of the *Gītā* is, therefore, one who lives in God but works in the world, whose head is in solitude, but whose hands are in society. He is the one who has attained a detached frame of mind. He is not the *Saṁnyāsin*, retired from the world renouncing everything, but is a disinterested householder, a *Niṣkāma-Karmayogi*.

Lokasaṁgraha

The *Gītā* in the concept of *Lokasaṁgraha* shows a practical path not only for the *sādhus* and *saṁnyāsis* but even for the worldly men, how to lead their life of action. It is the *Gītā* concept of active social service for the welfare of humanity.

[1]*BG.*, VI. 16-17. According to Chinmayanand, the world 'Eat' should be understood in a comprehensive sense. 'It is not only the process of consuming things through the month, it includes the enjoyments gained through all the avenues of sense perceptions and inward experiences.' op. cit., II, p. 584.

[2]*BG.*, XVII. 7-10.

[3]*BG.*, II. 64.

The word '*Lokasaṁgrha*' occurs only twice in the *Gītā*.[1] The similar import is meant by the term *sarvabhūtahiteratāḥ*—'engrossed in the welfare of all beings.'[2] 'Saṁgraha' means 'retaining,' 'keeping,' 'regulating,' 'restraining,' 'controlling' and 'protecting.'[3]

In support of the doctrine of Karma Yoga, Kṛṣṇa explains why and for what purpose these actions at all come into existence. His advice to Arjuna is: 'Even having regard to the welfare of the world (*lokasaṁgraha*) You must perform all actions.'[4] Radhakrishnan translates '*lokasaṁgraha*' as 'world maintenance which stands for the unity of the world, the interconnectedness of society.'[5] The Manu-Smṛti uses the words 'welfare of a nation' in the same sense.[6] *Śankarabhāsya* defines '*Lokasaṁgraha*' as 'weaning men from the tendency to take the path of wrong.'[7] Tilak interpretes this to mean 'making use, those persons who behave recklessly as a result of ignorance and keeping them together in a happy state and putting them on the path of self-amelioration.'[8] Taking all the above meanings according to the context of the *Gītā* he means by '*Lokasaṁgraha*,' 'binding men together and protecting, maintaining and regulating them in such a way that they might acquire that strength which results from mutual cooperation, thereby putting them on the path of acquiring merit while maintaining their good condition.'[9] However, Tilak makes it clear that the word '*loka*' in '*lokasaṁgraha*' does not indicate only mankind. It is also interpreted to mean 'the maintenance of various worlds: Lokanam saṁgrahah.' Thus he says, it has been used in the *Gītā* to mean 'the maintenance, not only of human beings, but that the human and all the other spheres, such as the gods etc. should be maintained and that they should become mutually beneficial.'[10] Thus

[1] *BG.*, III. 20; III. 25: Karmaiṇaiva hi saṅsiddhimāsṭhitā janakādayaḥ Lokasaṁgrahamevāpi sampaśyankartumarhasi Saktāḥ karmanyavidvaṅso yathā kurvanti Bhārat Kuryāt vidvānstathā 'saktaś cikirşur lokasaṁgraham.

[2] Labhante brahmanirvāṇam ṛṣayaḥ kṣiṇakalmaṣāh Chinnadvaidhā yatātmanaḥ sarvabhūtahite ratāḥ. *BG.*, V, 25 Samniyanuye' ndriyagrāmaṁ sarvatra samabhddhyayḥ Te prāpnuvanti mām eva sarvabhutahite ratāḥ. *BG.*, XIII. 4.

[3] *SED.*, p. 328.

[4] *BG.*, III. 20.

[5] Radhakrishnan, *The Bhagavad Gītā*, p. 139.

[6] 7. 144.

[7] Tilak, *Gita Rahasya*, I, p. 457.

[8] ibid, p. 457.

[9] ibid.

[10] ibid.

the term *lokasaṁgraha* has a comprehensive meaning and includes 'the putting not only mankind but the entire world, on a proper path and making *saṁgraha* of it i.e. maintaining, feeding, protecting and defending it in a proper way, without allowing it to be destroyed.'[1] It stands for universal welfare. The Gītā emphasises that the welfare of the society is the primary concern of the spiritual man, who identifies self with the self of all beings and who delights in the welfare of all beings.[2]

The implications of the concept of *Lokasaṁgraha* are far and wide. It demands that men should engage themselves in such activities which will prevent the disruption of the self-maintaining and self-uplifting capacity of society. Towards this end, whatever is defective in the prevalent social institutions must be weeded out, having regard to the changing circumstances. One must serve the society and his fellow men according to one's capacity as a matter of duty, imbued with a social vision, social need and social awareness. It is not proper for one to say that if one does not do it, somebody else will; because in that case, not only does one person fall short in the performance of the total work of society and thereby society loses its aggregate power. Society is a living organism; all the organs (individuals) are inter-connected and mutually dependent. If each limb does not contribute its own share of life-force to the others, not only do the others starve and die but the limb itself ultimately shares the same fate. That is the relation between individual and society.

It is true that the followers of the *Saṁnyāsa* school sometimes say that when one's own Ātman has obtained release, one should be satisfied with it; and he should not mind even if the world goes to dogs. 'One should neither perform *lokasaṁgraha* nor cause it to be performed.'[3] This doctrine is one-sided and cannot be true at all times. The *Gītā* says that such an ideal man, if he exists, may live a life of pure seclusion or retire into a forest but even then as an integral limb of society, he should not give up actions but should devote himself to work for the benefit of his fellow beings. If even men who have imbibed perfect knowledge should not completely renounce the world, there is no justification for lesser men to escape from their worldly duties by becoming

[1]Tilak, *Gita Rahasya*, I, p. 457.
[2]*BG.*, V. 25, XII. 4.
[3]*Mbh*, XIV. 46: 39: lokasaṁgrahadharmaṁ ca naiva kūryān na kāryet.

sādhūs and *saṁnyāsis*. A true *Jñāni* is also a *Karma-Yogi*. It must be said, therefore, that the only path which is excellent and is consistent with the *śāstras* is to continue working for the benefit of the society. One should live so long as life lasts, even after he has acquired realisation and with due regard to one's own qualifications. He should follow the glorious example of Lord Kṛṣṇa who takes incarnation from age to age for the universal welfare.[1] Thus a man must lead a balanced life with a disciplined mind for the good of the society in which he lives. That is the only way to get happiness which is another name for peace of mind. Nevertheless, this *loka-saṁgraha* must not be performed entertaining the hope for some fruitful result but being free from attachment. The automatic test of the purity and nobility of even that detachment is the dedication for an ideal viz. service of God as embodied in the good of humanity. The *Yogin* that the *Gītā* regards as the ideal man is he 'whose sins are wiped out, whose doubts are resolved, who has mastered himself and who is engrossed in the welfare of all beings.'[2]

In the context of the Gītā, the word '*Yajna*' is to be understood in a comprehensive sense. The life itself becomes an *Yajña*. '*Yajña*' literally means sacrifice; hence 'worship'; hence 'any sacrificial act or any act of service.' In the words of Gandhiji '*Yajña* means an act directed to the welfare of others, done without receiving or deriving a return for it, whether of a temporal or a spiritual nature. Act must be taken in its widest sense and includes thought and words and *others* embrace not only humanity but all life.'[3] As Radhakrishnan puts it: 'It is sacrificial action in general by which man dedicates his wealth and deeds to the service of the One Life in all.'[4] Thus *Yajña* as an act directed towards the welfare of entire mankind and everything that lives becomes an integral part of the *Gītā's* concept of *Lokasaṁgraha*.

In the concept of *Lokasaṁgraha*, the *Gītā* thus shows us the path of integration of the individual with the social life in which he lives. Just as each limb of the organisation has to do its duty in its own sphere, in the same manner the individual realises himself by discharging the obligations attached to his station in life. Divatia observes: 'Self-realisation means the realisation of one's self in the

[1]*BG.*, IV. 7.
[2]*BG.*, V. 25: kṣiṇakalmaṣāḥ chinnadvaidhā yatātmānaḥ sarvabhūtahiteratāḥ.
[3]Mahadeva Desai, op. cit., p. 177.
[4]Radhakrishnan, op. cit., p. 346.

wider life of our fellow men. The *Gītā* teaches us that there cannot be self-realisation without the integration of the individual self with the larger social self.'[1] We cannot do better than recall Swami Vivekanand's words: 'The poor, the ignorant, the illiterate, the afflicted, let these be your God; know that service to these is the highest religion.'[2] The *Gītā* turns humanity into a temple of worship to which a man should dedicate himself and serve.

Summing Up

The institution of asceticism before the time of the *Gītā* was in its decadent phase, it being considerably influenced by the teachings of renunciation by Buddhism and Jainism. It had become anti-social and parasitical and misunderstood as running away from life and to be engaged in all kinds of excessive and meaningless bodily torture. The *Gītā* corrects the view with emphasis on the inner religion and declares that *Saṁnyāsa* is to be the garb of the mind and not the cloth of the body. It supplanted the *Niṣkāmakarmayogi* householder as the ideal type for the ascetic and promised him salvation through the rich stream of *Bhakti*. Though emphasising *Vairāgya* as a discipline to acquire mastery over the mind, it does not support an ascetic life but recommends a life of moderation in all matters. Neither mere suppression of passions and desires, nor a life of rigorous asceticism, nor mere knowledge of nature, nor mere emotional effusion of mind, nor adherence to rigorous rites and ceremonies, nor running away from his duties, will enable a man to fulfil the mission of his life. The only sure way for the fulfilment of that mission is service to humanity and the integration of the individual self with the larger social self. The *Gītā* blends the three concepts of *Sthitaprajña*, *Niṣkāmakarma* and *Lokasaṁgraha* together in the activist teaching of *Karmayoga*—selfless action in this world for the benefit of this world. Not renunciation but active participation in the activities of the world thus becomes a gospel of supreme importance in the *Gītā*.

[1]Divatia, *The Art of Life in the Bhagavad Gītā*, p. 173.

[2]Akhandananda, *History of the Ramkrishna Math and Mission*, p. 110. Tagore puts the whole teaching of the *Gītā* in a nut-shell, when he says in the last chapter of Sadhana: Where can I meet thee, unless in this my home made thine? Where can I join thee, unless in this my work transformed into thy work? If I leave my home, I shall not reach thy home; if I cease my work, I can never join thee in thy work. For thou dwellest in me and I in thee. Thou without me or I without thee are nothing.

III Asceticism in the Rāmāyaṇa

The two personalities who have fascinated the Indian mind through the ages are undoubtedly Rāma and Kṛṣṇa. In Rāma, sage Vālmiki has depicted not mere nationai hero but divinity, an incarnation of the supreme deity Nārāyaṇa. Kṛṣṇa, as the great friend of the Pāṇḍavas is a well-known figure in the *Mahābhārata* as also the author of the *Gītā*. The nobility and magnanimity of Rāma's character and the conjugal love and fidelity of his wife Sītā, have for a great many centuries exercised a far-reaching moral effect as ideal specimens for emulation among Indians. Sītā, as the ideal wife and the woman of culture, has been looked upon as a pattern of feminine virtue and self-sacrifice by almost all Hindu women. It can be truly said that no work of literature secular in its origin has ever weilded so profound an influence on the life and culture of the Indian people as the *Rāmāyaṇa*, and particularly the masses most of whom look upon it as a source of *dharma* to guide their daily life.

Varṇa System

The three main types of people dealt with by Vālmiki and living in India during the period were the *Āryans*, the *Vānaras* and the *Rakṣasas*.

The epic expressly mentions the existence of the four *varṇas* (cāturvarṇya) viz., Brāhmana, Kṣatriya, Vaiśya and Śūdra.[1] The city of Ayodhyā is described as inhabited by these *varṇas* devoted to their respective duties.[2] The first three *varṇas* are spoken as *dvijas* or the twice born, the 'second' birth being conferred upon them by the Upanayan ceremony, which gave them the status they enjoyed, particularly over the *śūdras*. In all auspicious rites, the ceremonial functions were entrusted to eminent *dvijas*.[3] The study of the Vedas, observance of religions, vows, offering sacrifices and giving gifts are said to be the common duties absolutely enjoined on the *dvijas*.[4] The four *varṇas* in Ayodhyā, with the Brāhmins at their head, always worshipped the gods and the guests and are depicted as grateful and generous.[5] Their privileges related mainly to their principal means of livelihood.

[1]IV. 4. 6; I. 13. 20; VII. 75. 18; VI. 128, 120.
[2]II. 100, 41; I. 6. 17.
[3]I. 15. 4.
[4]I. 6. 12, 15.
[5]I. 6. 17.

The study and teaching of the Vedas (*svādhyāya*) and the practice of penance or austerities were the principal occupations of the Brāhmin.[1] He, however, could not impart instruction in the Vedas to *non-dvijas*.[2] He enjoyed a high social status and as a priest, particularly weilded a strong influence. It is said that at the conclusion of a horse-sacrifice for the birth of a son, King Daśaratha conferred the earth upon the Brāhmins,[3] though the latter, knowing their resources and interests better chose to have something instead, as a price thereof.[4]

The main function of the King and the Kṣatriya warriors under him was the protection of the population from aggression,[5] the cow and the Brāhmin.[6] The kṣatriya was to offer protection to anyone who sought his refuge.[7]

The pursuit of wealth was the special *dharma* of the Vaiśyas. They bore the brunt of the taxation[8] and their wealth provided the economic support to the whole society. They reared cattle and pursued agriculture (*kṛṣi-go-rakṣya-jivināḥ*)[9] and carried on trade. They were entitled to attend and perform sacrifices.[10] Being far more numerous than the other two classes and being also wealthy, they formed the most influential part among the citizens of Ayodhyā. They also had several corporations like Ganas and Naigamas.[11]

The duty of the Śūdras was to serve the three higher castes. They were at times allowed the privilege of attending sacrificial ceremonies.[12] They attended Rāma's assembly in thousands to witness oath-taking ceremony along with the Kṣatriyas and Vaiśyas.[13] But they suffered many disabilities. They were outside the pale of the *dvija* castes. They were not allowed to study the Veda.[14] A Brāhmin could not impart Vedic instruction to them. They were forbidden to

[1] I. 14. 48.
[2] V. 28. 5.
[3] I. 14-15.
[4] I. 14-18.
[5] II. 100. 42.
[6] I. 26. 4-5
[7] VI. 18-27.
[8] I. 7. 13.
[9] II. 100-47.
[10] I. 13-20.
[11] I. 6. 12.
[12] II. 18. 12; II. 83. 11.
[13] I. 13. 20.
[14] VII. 96, 7-8.

practise religious austerities or penance which was a privilege of the higher varṇas.[1] The Cāṇḍālas were the untouchables and were looked upon as the lowest in the social scale. Vālmiki refers to them as the most degraded beings: *Yonināṁ adhamā vayam.*[2] They were deprived of the most elementary rights of citizenship. They could not enter temples, places, houses of Brāhmins and places of worship.[3]

Such is the picture of society during the *Rāmarājya*, a term which in our times has come to be synonymous with a state of piety and righteousness.

The castes were no longer fluid as in the Ṛgvedic times but had become differentiated from one another and their privileges, duties and liabilities had become more or less fixed in the days of the *Rāmāyaṇa.*

Hermitage or Āśrama Life

The forest from ancient times has been accepted as the religious home of India, whose spiritual genius has manifested itself in the solitary retreats of the woodland. It was here that the Āryan retiring from the turmoil of the world, in the peaceful environment, sought to work out within himself the truth of the spirit in a broad freedom from the strict social bonds. The location of such hermitages (*āśramas*) was in an *aranya* or forest with its sylvan surroundings and quiet vicinity and was found to be the ideal place by those who wanted to live away from the disturbance of human habitation,[4] seeking solitude. The forests, mountains, rivers, birds and beasts serve as the backdrop against which Rāma, Lakṣmaṇa and Sitā live their life of *vanavāsa.* The epic affords a many coloured picture of human emotions and feelings in which nature participates. The hills at Citrakūta, the woodlands and the lake at Pampa, the onset of of the night in Atri's *āśrama*, the pageant of the seasons, the rains, the spring and the splendour of the *śarat*, the descriptions of these are intimate, rich and moving, such as is possible only for a poet who has lived in the lap of nature and knows all its moods and delights. Nature was there in all its inexhaustible beauty and glory.

[1] V. 28. 5.
[2] VII. 76. 1-4.
[3] VII. 59a. 21.
[4] VII. 59, 20-21.
[5] cf. pranastajanasambādham ksetrārāmavivarjitaṁ (vanam), II, 52, 98.

And Rāma captivated by the charm of Citrakūta, the famous hermit-centre of the period, exclaims that it was even more delightful than life in the metropolis.[1]

It was first at Citrakūta that Rāma built his cottage which had every recommendation: *Sarvaguṇāvitam.*[2] Nature in all its grandeur of *fauna* and *flaura* had invested it with lyrical background which made it an ideal place, for locating a hermitage. A hermit colony comprised of several huts was known as *āśrama-maṇḍala*[3] or a *tapovana.*[4] The asylums of the anchorites forming the colony were called *tāpasālayas.*[5] Rāma's cottage was situated amidst many hermit-huts (*āśrama-maṇḍala*).

Of the different quarters in a hermitage, the most important was the *agniśaraṇa* or the *agniśālā.*[6] It was indeed the hearth and home of the hermits. It was a spacious chamber housing the sacrificial fire. Room was set apart for the lodging of guests.[7] When Rāma visited the *āśrama* of *Bhārādvāja*, the sage duly welcomed him and assigned for him suitable quarters.[8] Separate places were set apart for the worship of gods, the *Caityas* for offering oblations.[9]

The patriarch ascetic, who acted as the head of such hermits colonies was known as the *Kulapati.*[10] The famous *Kulapatis* of the times were Vālmiki, Agastya, Vasiṣṭha, Bhāradvāja etc. Under their spiritual guidance resided a host of disciples, who included the children of the hermits and men and women who had retired to these religious resorts after a lifetime of strenuous activity and who devoted themselves to religious duties. In the congenial atmosphere of a quiet *āśrama*, they spent their days in worship and pious studies, sacrifices and holy recitations. Those who were equipped for it imparted to others the spiritual knowledge. The epic abounds in the descriptions of the third stage of life in the woodland, *vānaprasthrāśrama*. The renowned hermitages of the age were those of

[1]II. 95. 12.
[2]III. 15. 8.
[3]III. 1. 1.
[4]VII. 47. 15.
[5]II. 99. 4.
[6]III. 1, 4; III. 12. 15 and II. 91. 1.
[7]III. 1. 15.
[8]II. 54. 18.
[9]II. 56. 33.
[10]II. 116. 4.

the sages Agastya,[1] Vasiṣṭha,[2] Atri,[3] Sārabhanga,[4] Vālmiki,[5] Bhāradvāja,[6] Gautama,[7] Sutikṣṇa,[8] Śabari,[9] Tṛṇabindu,[10] Siddhāśrama of Viṣṇu[11] and the Kāmāśrama of Śiva.[12] The greater number of hermits lived in the company of their wives. And sage Kaśyapa is said to have eight wives![13] Obviously, they have not renounced worldly life as yet.

The hermitages are described as encircled with the energy derived from Brahma lore.[14] Proper decorum and gravity of behaviour was to be maintained and frivolous or sportive attitude was discouraged.[15] What was inculcated was piety and right conduct. It is said that the pious atmosphere of the *āśramas* naturally prompted one to desist from untruth and other sins of the body and mind.[16] The spiritual potency of Agastya rendered his *āśrama* inhospitable to persons given to falsehood, cruelty, craftiness, wickedness or unrighteousness of any kind.[17] No wonder such centres of piety and holiness became the centres of learning in ancient India.[18]

Contrary to Ghurye's view that the ascetics were not living in

[1]III. 11.
[2]I. 51. 23-28.
[3]II. 117. 5.
[4]III. 5. 3.
[5]VII. 49.
[6]II. 90.
[7]I. 48.
[8]III. 7. 22.
[9]III. 74.
[10]VII, 2. 7.
[11]I. 29.
[12]I. 23. 15, 22.
[13]III. 14. 11.
[14]III. 11. 21: brāhmyā lakṣmyā samāvṛttaṁ (āśramamaṇḍalam).
[15]III. 1. 9-10.
[16]III. 17. 14.
[17]III. 11. 90.
[18]The hermitages of Kaṇva, Vasiṣṭha and Viśvāmitra were great centres of learning where the students congregated (*Mbh.*, IX. 42; I. 70). Rajagopalachari writes: 'Beside the urban and rural life, there was a very highly cultural life in seclusion of forest recesses, centered round ascetic teachers. These *āśramas* kept alive the bright fires of learning and spiritual thought. Young men of noble birth eagerly sought education at these *āśramās*. World-weary age went there for peace. These centres of culture were cherished by the rulers of the land and not the proudest of them would dare to treat the members of the hermitages otherwise than with respect and consideration.' *Mbh.*, preface, p. 9.

groups at an earlier time,[1] we find a specific mention of different types of ascetics organized into a great *vānaprastha-gaṇa* a community or guild of hermits.[2]

The daily life of the inmates of the hermitage was largely occupied by the recitation of the Vedas and performance of various rites and rigorous vows. They had to observe the rules of an austere life,[3] by adoring the deities and manes, performing the rites of hospitality and offering presents of flowers collected by themselves on the altars.[4] They performed *agnihotra* and the different kinds of sacrifices as prescribed by the scriptures. After finishing their *agnihotra* and *svādhyāya*, the sages sat surrounded by their disciples[5] and carried on discussions on matters concerning religion, philosophy and mythology.[6] On the occasion of a *parva*, some of them remained absorbed in meditation.[7]

In harmony with their abstemious lives, the dress of the hermits was of the simplest and barest quality, made of raw materials which could be had in the woods. They used to be clad in the fibres of *Kuśa* grass (*Kuśa-cira*),[8] black deer-skin (*Kṛṣṇājina dhara*)[9] and bark garments (*valkalāmbara-dhāraṇam*).[10] The valkala served the purpose of the upper garment (*valkalottaravāsas*)[11] the deer-skin being evidently used as a lower garment. The colour of the garment was orange (*Kāṣāya-paridhāna*).[12] On the head *jaṭās* or matted locks were worn.[13]

The hermits had to practise moderation in food (*niyatāhāra*),[14] remaining content with whatever things were obtainable in the forest.[15] They subsisted mainly on tuberous fruits and roots, avoiding meat

[1]*Indian Sadhus*, p. 6.
[2]III. 6. 15; munisaṅgāh, III. 6. 1.
[3]II. 28. 15: Caratām niyamenaiva tasmāt duḥkhtaraṁ vanam.
[4]II, 28. 14; II. 28. 16.
[5]II. 54. 11-12.
[6]II. 54. 34.
[7]III. 38. 4.
[8]II. 50. 45.
[9]II. 99. 26.
[10]II. 28. 13.
[11]II.95. 6.
[12]II. 12. 98.
[13]II. 28. 13.
[14]VII. 9. 39.
[15]II. 28. 17; II. 37. 2.

as a rule.[1] They were required to fast to the best of their capacity.[2] The forest fare they lived on was known as *vanyamāhāraṁ*.[3] It is truely said that *vanavāsa* was beset with innumerable difficulties.[4] Rāma paints for Sītā's benefit a vivid picture of the miserable and taxing life in the wilderness.[5]

Austerities (Tapas)

We find in the epic not only the Āryans, men and women ascetics (*tāpasas*) practising austerities, or penance but also the Rākṣasas and Yakṣas resorting to it for various ends. Even kings and gods are also depicted as practising austerities.

It was common to perform austerities with a view to having a son. The king, Daśaratha is shown as engaged in austerities as he had no son to perpetuate his line.[6] Yakṣa Suketu practises rigid austerities to have an issue.[7] Diti, the wife of sage Kaśyapa also practises austerities with the same view.[8]

Attainment of a divine boon in order to rise above the mortals was also a motive for performing tapas or penance. Rāvaṇa performed a long course of *tapas* to propitiate Prajāpati who confers a boon on him that save man, he could not be killed by gods or demons.[9] It was by virtue of this boon that he could conquer the gods, committed ravages upon the three worlds and carried away the fair sex. He was ultimately killed by Rāma, a man. Having gratified Brahma, Rākṣasa *Virādha* by his penance, received a boon that none in the world would be able to slay him mangling his body with weapons.[10] Mārica is described as practising penance, clad in deer-skin, bearing matted-locks and subsisting on restricted fare.[11] But these Rākṣasas used the powers gained through austerities for evil purposes.[12]

[1]II. 20. 29.
[2]II. 28. 13.
[3]II. 12. 97.
[4]II. 28. 5: Bhaudośam hi kāntāraṁ vanamityabhidhiyate.
[5]II. 28. 4-25.
[6]I. 8. 1-3. Mahatejāh dharmaratovaṣi.
[7]I. 25. 5: tepe mahattapaḥ.
[8]I. 46. 2: dirghataporjitaṁ.
[9]I. 16. 4-5.
[10]III. 3-6.
[11]III. 35-38.
[12]VII. 5. 16: Surasuran prabādhante varadansunirbhayāḥ

The performance of *tapas* was the sole objective that led the anchorites to seek the calm solitude of the forest.[1] The different kinds of self-torture practised by these ascetics, *tapasas*, included keeping legs upward and head downward,[2] standing in water,[3] remaining in the midst of five fires in summer, drenching oneself in the wet season, residing in water in winter, eating[4] once a month (*māsāhāraḥ*),[5] abstaining from food and subsisting on air,[6] standing on one leg, with the arms raised up,[7] the offering of one's own limbs in fire,[8] and similar kinds of excruciating vows (*saṁsita-vratāḥ*). *Tapas*, is, therefore, often called *urgam*,[9] *ghoraṁ*,[10] and *durādharṣaṁ*.[11] The aim was to train the body and mind to bear the pairs of opposite viz. heat and cold, the desire to eat and drink, the desire to remain seated or standing, the absence of words (*kaṣthamauna*) and the absence of gestures that could reveal one's feelings or thoughts (*ākāramauna*).[12]

During the period of austerities, the ascetics were required to be studiously intent on piety, study of the Vedas, restrain their fare, keep their senses under control, tread the path of righteousness, remain firm in honesty, absorbed in meditation and observe purity of conduct.[13] The aspirants bent on different types of penances were to regulate themselves by the codes of morality (*dharma-vidhi*),[14] proper for each. The *Vīrāsana* was a generally adopted posture during meditation.[15] *Maunitva* or silence in penance was an effective aid in combating the evils of anger and lust.[16] Success in penance was associated with particular sacred spots. Citrakūta was eminently suited for penance, since innumerable *ṛṣis* there were reported to

[1]II. 28. 24: Kartavya tapase matiḥ.
[2]VII. 75. 14.
[3]VII. 88. 10.
[4]VII. 10. 3. 4; I. 63. 24.
[5]I. 42. 13.
[6]I. 63. 24; I. 51. 25-27.
[7]VII. 10. 6. 8; I. 63. 24.
[8]VII. 10. 10.
[9]I. 63. 18.
[10]I. 63. 15. 24.
[11]I. 65. 17; I. 61. 4; III. 5. 28; III. 7. 13.
[12]cf. Eliade, *Yoga: Immortality and Freedom*, p. 51.
[13]VII. 9. 39; VII. 10. 3; III. 10. 5. 6.
[14]VII. 10. 2.
[15]10. 4.
[16]I. 30. 4; I. 64. 17.

have attained heaven through austerities.[1] Viṣṇu's Siddhāśrama was so named because his asceticism had attained fruition there.[2]

Penance was considered the live vehicle of the practice of *Dharma.* Vaiśravaṇa, the son of Pulastya, took to rigid austerities, it is said, when his mind became inclined towards the practice of Dharma.[3] The efficacy of the *tapas* is so great that even venerable gods like Viṣṇu are described as resorting to *tapas* to gain an accession of soul-force before embarking on momentous undertaking.[4] Men also could achieve great things through *tapas.* It is said that penance consisted in following Dharma by afflicting one's person.[5] Austerities were also resorted to with some worldly object (*kāmaṁ*) in view.[6] There is a reference to the attainment of Brahmaloka[7] and bodily repairment to the heaven by means of fierce austerities.[8]

Sugriva describes the Kiśkiṅdhā forest where dwelt seven *munis,* having control over their senses, dwelling on the mountains, passing days and nights in water with their heads down and after seven nights living upon air. In this manner, it is said, passing seven hundred years they went bodily to heaven. By virtue of their asceticism, the asylum was walled by trees and made incapable of being conquered even by Indra.[9] Ṛṣyaśṛanga who was brought up in woods was so much engrossed in the study of the Vedas and austerities that he was ignorant of the pleasure that sprang from contact with women.[10]

The great powers which could be acquired through *tapas* are illustrated in the story of King Viśvāmitra, who desires to have from Vasiṣṭha a cow called Śabala, the yielder of all that was desired. Foiled in his efforts to secure the cow, the spirit of emulation was aroused in Viśvāmitra and he gets prepared for abstinence, mortification and self-restraint. He retires to the lonely forests and performs the most severe penances, but meets with formidable

[1]II. 54. 31.
[2]I. 29. 4.
[3]VII. 3. 10-11.
[4]I.29. 3.
[5]Śariklešasambhutaṁ sa dharmaṁ parimārgate, II. 99. 34.
[6]VII. 9.47.
[7]brahmalokaṁ jitamugreṇa tapasā: II. 5. 28.
[8]divaṁ yātā saklevarāḥ: IV. 13. 19.
[9]IV. 13. 18-20.
[10]ṛṣyaśṛngo vanacaratapaḥ svādhyāya tatparaḥ anabhijñaḥ sa nāriṇāṁ-viṣayāṇāṁ sukhasya ca: I. 10. 3. 4.

obstacles on his path of progress which put his mettle to the test. The impediments appear in the form of Triśanku, Śunaḥśepa, Menakā and Raṁbhā. He becomes *Rājarṣi* through severe *tapas* but vanquished again by Vasiṣṭha, takes again to much harder penances to reach perfection. Only *tapas* was not enough. What was needed was the mortification of one's pride, vanity, anger, lust, jealousy, and desire, the lower side of a man's nature which alone was a match for the spiritual fervour of a Brāhmin (*brāhma-teja*). Through most severe *tapas* he conquers these shackles which hindered his onward march. He got gradual recognition from being a Mahārāja, first as a *Rājarṣi*, then as a *Maharṣi*, and lastly as a *Brahmarṣi*. He was not satisfied until Vasiṣṭha claimed him as equal to himself. But not before till Viśvāmitra emerges through long and constant *tapas* of a thousand years, a perfect *personality*.[1]

The merit of Viśvāmitra lies in the fact that he is a wonderful example of one who worked his way to the highest state by dint of his own personal efforts, in spite of natural predisposition to passion of every kind. His example also proves that *tapas* could be utilised as a means of purification to purge the heart of all sinister propensities. It elevates man from all that is base in him, and turns out a perfect product. *Tapas* is thus a spiritual force, a power that leads him to his highest possible state of perfection.

The *tapasvis* or *tāpasas* are described as *tapodhanam*,[2] whose wealth is *tapas*; *mahatejāḥ*,[3] *mahātapāḥ*,[4] highly effulgent by virtue of tapas; *saṁśitvratāḥ*,[5] having control over their senses; *paramtapāḥ*,[6] of great *tapas*; *dharmācar*,[7] righteous; *mahabhāgaḥ*,[8] *satyavādi*,[9] truthful. These attributes also indicate the virtuous effect of *tapas* on human conduct. The ascetic cult engaged in *Brāhmya tapas* is described as highly effulgent, with his vital fluild under control (*ūrdhva-retāḥ*) conferring upon Gandarbhi an excellent mind-begotten son (*mānasaṁ sutaṁ*).[10] When Rāma and Lakṣmaṇa enter the

[1] I. 53, 55, 57, 58, 59, 60, 64, 65.
[2] I. 29. 12; III. 12. 5.
[3] I. 51. 27.
[4] I. 32. 1; I. 51. 27.
[5] IV. 13. 18-19.
[6] III. 12. 24.
[7] IV. 52. 13-18.
[8] IV. 48. 12; II. 117. 8.
[9] IV. 48. 12.
[10] I. 1. 33. 11, 18.

asylum of Ahalyā she is described as magnificent, flaming in ascetic energy.[1] The sage Vāman is described as *tapomayaṁ taporāśiṁ tapomūrtiṁ tapodhanaṁ*.[2] It was thus believed in those times that if a hermit lived a life of purity and *tapas*, his body would gradually become spiritualised, so that it would be very different in appearance from the bodies of ordinary men. The person would glow with beauty and supernatural light. Śarabhanga, purified through *tapas*, is lustrous like the gods.[3] Agastya looks bright as flame (*dīptatejasāṁ*).[4] The *tapasvi's* body thus becomes a fit expression of the exalted spirit within. He is also endowed with the power of conferring a boon as in the case of sage Chūli. The supernatural was regarded as quite natural in those days and the efficacy of *tapas* goes to prove this. These powers of *tapas* are referred to as *siddhis* in the Yogasūtras of Patañjali.

Types of ascetics

When Rāma visited Janasthāna, he was met with by the following types of ascetics who were organised into a great *vānaprasthagaṇa* or a community or guild of ascetics. They derive their names from their peculiar ascetic practices.[5]

(1) *Vaikhānasa*—This was the earliest name used to designate a hermit—from Vaikhānasa, the traditional author of the rule.[6]
(2) *Vālakhilyā*—Having the size of a thumb, dwarfish.
(3) *Samprakṣāla*—Keeping their utensils washed, not hoarding food for next meal time.
(4) *Marichipā*—Drinking flames.
(5) *Aśmakuttā*—Subsisting on raw food pounded with stones.
(6) *Patrāhārā*—Feeding on leaves.
(7) *Pañcataponvita*—Practising the five-fire penance by sitting amid four fires, the sun burning down upon the head as the fifth.

[1] I. 49. 17: Paritāṅgi dhumenāpi diptāmagniśikhāmiva durāgarṣāṁ diptāṁ sūryaprabhāmiva.
[2] I. 29. 12.
[3] III. 5. 4: devaprabhāvasya tapasā.
[4] III. 12. 22.
[5] III. 6. 2-3-4-15.
[6] *Gaut*. (3. 2), *Baudh*. (2. 11.14), and *Manu* (VI. 21) refer to the *Vaikhānasa-śāstra* which described the duties of the forest hermits. Medhatithi adds that the hermit has to learn other practices and conduct of living also from that book: *SBE*, XXV, p. 202.

(8) *Dantolūkhalin*—Using the teeth as a mortar, grinding grain to be eaten between the teeth.
(9) *Unmajjakā*—Plunging in water upto the neck.
(10) *Gātra-śayyā*—Having the limbs for their bed.
(11) *Aśayyā*—Using no bed for rest or sleep.
(12) *Anavakāsikā*—Having no leisure because of being always engaged in doing good.
(13) *Salilāhārā*—Subsisting on water.
(14) *Vāyu-bhakṣā*—Feeding only on the air.
(15) *Ākāśanilayā*—Living under the clouds, lodging under no roof.
(16) *Sthaṇḍila-śāyin*—Sleeping on the bare sacrificial ground.
(17) *Taponityāh*—Performing tapas, penance.
(18) *Urdhvavāsin*—Abiding at lofty altitudes.
(19) *Dānta*—Having self-control.
(20) *Ārdra-paṭa-vāṣas*—Constantly wearing wet clothes.
(21) *Sajapā*—Ever engaged in reciting mantras.

All these ascetics were in the *Vānaprastha* stage of life as their guild name indicates. They were adherents of the *Vaikhānasa-mārga*.[1] They are described as furnished with the grace that comes of spiritual energy and were firmly concentrated in Yoga.[2]

The belief that asceticism or a life of *tapas* can bring about great merit and pave the way to heaven prevailed. There are references to the attainment of Brahmaloka and bodily ascent to heaven through fierce *tapas*.[3] As pointed out earlier, the privilege of practising *tapas* was confined to the *dvijas*. A *śūdra* violating it could be punished even by death. The *Rāmāyaṇa* relates a story of the *Śūdra* Śaṁbuka who was killed by Rāma as he performed penance with a view to going to heaven with his earthly body.[4] This suggests that in spite of his severe penance, a *śūdra* was unfit for heaven. The epic declares: 'In the three yugas (*satya*, *treta* and *dvāpara*) a *śūdra* had no right to perform ascetic practices (*tapas*).'[5]

It may be argued that the position of the *śūdras* with their religious disabilities hardly does credit to Rāma who has been depicted

[1]II. 52. 71, also III. 5. 15: Muni Sārabhanga is described as Brāhmaṇbhuyiṣṭho Vānaprasthagaṇo mahān.
[2]III. 6. 6: Sarve brāhmyā śriyā yuktā dṛdhayogasamāhitāḥ:
[3]III. 5. 28; IV. 13. 19.
[4]VII. 76. 2.
[5]VII. 75. 25.

as the Perfect Man and God by Vālmiki. In his Rāma-Rājya, the ideal kingdom, even the lowliest should have been provided ample opportunities for normal and even higher aspirations.

Female Ascetics (*Tāpasis*)

According to the *Rāmāyaṇa*, the sphere of austerities was quite open to female aspirants. Some women took to ascetic life as a temporary measure with some definite object in view, on the realization of which they returned to their family fold. Diti, the wife of Kaśyapa, performed penance for the sake af a heroic son.[1] Anasūya, the wife of Atrī, is said to have practised austerities for several years. She was a pious *tāpasi* famous among the people for her work in relieving popular distress, famine, draughts, etc.[2] Wives sometimes joined their husbands in austerities. Viśvāmitra resorted to penance in company with his queen.[3] The wives of Sāgara practised penance along with their husbands and returned to their former mode of life after securing boons for progeny.[4] Umā, adopting a stern vow, carried on austerities to win Rudra as her husband.[5]

There were, however, other women who permanently embraced the ascetic life of *vanavāsa*, shunning all worldly attachments and never returning to household life. To this category belonged ascetics like Vedavati,[6] Śabari,[7] and Svayaṁprabhā.[8] They were known as *Tāpasis*[9] or *Śramaṇis.*[10] They wore deerskins, matted locks and bark garments,[11] kept their senses restrained,[12] practised righteousness, engaged in the welfare of all[13] and were endowed with spiritual lustre.[14] Śabari was ever engaged in pious observances.[15] By virtue of her devout meditation, it is said that she attained to holy regions

[1] I. 46. 2-3.
[2] II. 117. 11.
[3] I. 57. 2.
[4] I. 38. 5 also I. 38. 5-15.
[5] I. 35. 19.
[6] VII. 17. 2.
[7] III. 74. 7.
[8] IV. 50. 38.
[9] V. 15. 31.
[10] II. 38. 4.
[11] VII. 17. 2 also IV. 50. 38: Kṛṣṇacira jaṭādharaṁ (Vedavatiṁ).
[12] V. 15. 31: Niyatāmiva tāpasiṁ.
[13] IV. 51. 9-10: Tāpasi dharmacāriṇi sarvabhutahiteratāḥ.
[14] IV. 50-39: Tāpasi niyatāhāra jvalantīmiva tejasā.
[15] III. 73. 27: Tvāṁ (Śabri) tu dharmesthitā nityaṁ.

after she surrendered herself into fire.[1] Vedavati performed severe austerities so that her father's desire of getting her married with Viṣṇu might be realised.[2]

Women ascetics were required to perform the rites of hospitality upon guests who visited them. Vedavati performed the rites of hospitality for Rāvaṇa who met her in her hermitage in the Himālayas.[3]

The epic also narrates the story of Ahalyā, her act of adultery with Indra, as the result of which as punishment, she was forced to lead a life of severe penance. Gautama, cursed his wife for being a willing partner saying: 'You will lie here in the forest on a bed of ashes, unseen by anybody, living on air without food and should perform severe austerities. When Rāma, the son of Daśaratha will visit the forest you will be purified and by paying him homage as a guest you will regain your body.'[4] The story throws ample light on the practices of severe austeries and *prāyaśchit* (penance) to purify oneself for a moral lapse through a process of severe *tapas* by women.

Female ascetics, however, stood in danger of molestations at the hands of ruffians, as the episode of Vedavati's ravishment by Rāvaṇa clearly proves.[5] To worldly-minded men like Rāvana, the sight of lovely maidens like Vedavati, wasting their glorious youth in leading the ascetic mode of life, was nothing short of foolhardiness. They considered the hermit life to be suitable for the aged and senile people.[6]

Pativratā Ideal

One factor which definitely discouraged women taking to the ascetic life was the *Pativratā* ideal. Sītā was herself a worthy model in this respect. The epic depicts her as the highest type of a Pativratā, the ideal woman and wife, who prefers the hardships of *vanavāsa* to a life in the palace.[7] Vālmiki regards attachment to the

[1]II. 74. 32. 35.
[2]VII. 17 ff.
[3]VII. 17. 8.
[4]I. 84.
[5]VII. 17.
[6]VII. 17. 4-5.
[7]II. 27.9. When Sītā is deserted by Rāma she says according to Kālidās (*Raghuvaṁsa*, XIV. 66): Sāhaṁ tapaḥ sūryaniviṣṭadṛṣtir ūrdhvaṁ prasūteś

husband as the only ornament of the wife.[1] His *śuśruṣa* or attending to the personal comforts of the husband was to be her highest religion.[2] It is this *śuśruṣa* which is the best means of attaining salvation and not fasts, penances or worship of the deities.[3] According to Rāma, the wife who served not her husband, though engaged in religious rites and fasts, would fare badly in the next world, while a woman might obtain salvation (*svarga*) by serving her husband.[4] This idea is even carried in those days to great extremes. Anasūya maintained that women loving their husbands whether a saint or a sinner, poor or rich, wicked or licentious might obtain great merit.[5] The epic says that the wife, by thought, word and deed, should have only her husband's welfare at heart.[6] The wife who is dear and obedient and has conferred a son on her husband is a virtual fulfilment of the three objects of life—*dharma*, *artha* and *kāma*.[7] On the wife, indeed, along with the trinity depend also dutiful service, propagation of the family and good of the forefathers. The portrait of a model wife with her physical and moral perfections is presented before us by Vālmiki in the character of Sītā.

All these evidences go to prove that when the husband was considered the Deity for the wife and his service the best means to attain salvation, there was no need for her to resort to ascetic life. Indirectly the epic exalts the *Gṛhasthāśrama* and not *Saṁnyāśa*. And *Rāmāyaṇa* itself is an eloquent monument to the greatness of *Gṛhasthāśrama*.

caritum yatiṣye Bhūyo yathā me janānantarepi tvameva Bharatā na ca viprayogaḥ. She symoblises the highest and purest love which grows beyond the need of any love in return. Even today a good wife like Sītā prays for the same husband for seven lives. This shows how a hallowed tradition continues to be part of an Indian woman's life. Sītā is India idealised.

[1]I. 77. 27.

[2]II 24. 28.

[3]II. 24. 25.

[4]II. 24. 24.

[5]II. 117. 8-12.

[6]VII. 97. 15.

[7]II. 21. 57.

[8]In immensity, poetry and moral, Indian epic poetry, the *Rāmāyaṇa* and the *Mahābhārata*, is unrivalled and not even Greek epics can compare with it. M. William writes: 'In depicting scenes of domestic affection and expressing those universal feelings and emotions which belong to human nature in all time and in all places, Sanskrit epic poetry is unrivalled even by Greek Epics.' Raghavan, *Sanskrit Literature*, p, 20.

Vānaprasthāśrama

Many of the ascetics leading the life in the woods (*vanavāsa*) were accompanied by their wives. We properly call them hermits in the third stage (*vānaprastha*) engaged as they were in working out the truth of spirit in the seclusion of the forest retreats. The hermitages are described as reverberating with the sonorous recitals of Vedic hymns.[1] The *āśramites* spent their lives in *svādhyaya*, study and discussion of religion, philosophy and mythology.[2] Agnihotra and the different kinds of sacrifices as prescribed by the scriptures, accompanied with prayers or invocations and meditation formed the daily ritual.[3] The hermits, many of whom are called *munis* and *ṛiṣis*, have gathered the disciples around them and receiving the inquirer and seeker they are imparting them Vedic lore.[4] The epic is full of the sketches of such sages which dwell on the greatness of penance and the sublimity of a spiritual life.

In such environs of Vālmiki's hermitage we find that the pregnant Sītā banished by Rāma is welcomed and tenderly nursed by many female ascetics, evidently the wives of the resident sages, who resided there. Ascetics were attended upon by *tāpasis*. Śabari was a *paricārini* or attendant woman of the sages of Mātaṅgavan.[5] The sage Cūli was served in all humility by the Gandharvi Somadā.[6]

Sometimes we find female ascetics being waited upon by male attendants, as we find Indra serving Diti at all times by providing for her, kusa, faggots, water, fruits, roots and other things she wanted, and also by rubbing her person and removing her fatigue.[7]

There are instances of ascetics who courted wives. In most cases maidens were either bestowed upon them or maidens themselves sought to become their wives. Satyavati, the elder sister of the Kśatriya king Viśvāmitra, was given in marriage to Ṛicika.[8] King Triṇabindu's daughter was herself ready (*svayamudyatā*) to become the wife of sage Pulastya.[9] Sage Viśrava was wooed and won by

[1] III. 1. 6: brahmagoṣaninādítaṁ.
[2] VII. 2. 8; II. 54. 11. 12; II. 54. 34.
[3] III. 1. 6; III. 38. 4.
[4] VII. 49. 11.
[5] III. 73: 26: teṣām (munināṁ) dṛṣyate paricāriniśramaṇi śabari nāma.
[6] I. 33. 12-13.
[7] I. 46. 9-11.
[8] I.34. 7.
[9] VII. 2. 25.

the fugitive Rākṣasa chief Sumāli's daughter Kaikasi.[1] The hermit in the Pañcāpsaratirtha, the sage Maṇḍakarṇi, married the five Apsarās sent to lure him[2] and lived with them in revelries in a house built in the midst of the āśrama tank.[3] The Vaiśya ascetic, Andhamuni had begotten a son on a śūdra woman.[4]

We come across good many references of ascetic aberrations. These, together with the above account show that the hermits have not gone beyond their third stage of life into the last stage of *Saṁnyāsa*. They have still not risen above their routine obligations, exclusive loves, and become free to throw every remaining tie and to wander over the world in an extreme spiritual detachment.

Ascetic Aberrations

Two or more ascetics keeping connection with one female were condemned as bringing disgrace upon the ascetic order.[5] Adulterous ascetics could be severely punished by the ruling king. In the course of his dispute with Vāli, Rāma refers to the punishment of an unrighteous *Śramaṇa* by his ancestor Māndhāta.[6] Sexual aberration was indeed the most formidable obstacle in the path of ascetic's progress towards spirituality. We come across instances of sages, who befooled by witcheries of love,[7] became oblivions of their exalted station in life and went astray throwing to the winds the merit of their asceticism.

The story of Ṛṣyaśringa shows how he was so much engrossed in *svādhyāya* and *tapas* that he was ignorant (*anabhigña*) of the sensual pleasures arising from contact with women and how courtesans exerted all their feminine charms, seduced and enchained him so that a spell was cast over his mind and he accompanied them to Aṅga.[8] Indra, who always stood in great trepidation of the power of asceticism, struck precisely at this infirmity of the sages—their weakness for feminine charms—by sending out beautiful nymphs to dislodge them from their pedestal of ascetic merit. Viśvāmitra's allurement by Menakā is a classic instance of how *tapasvis* of

[1] VII. 9.
[2] III. 11. 18.
[3] III. 11. 15-19.
[4] II. 63. 50; II. 64. 32.
[5] III. 2. 11-12.
[6] IV. 18-33.
[7] I. 64. 1: lobhanaṁ kāmamohasamanvitam.
[8] I. 10.

seasoned penance when snared and blinded by the wiles of fair enchantresses, are swept away by a few moments of madness and passion, dissipating their spiritual achievement in pleasures of the flesh. It is only after the grievous error has long been committed that their eyes open out in heart rending anguish and repentance and they have to start afresh their ascetic career.[1] Perhaps it is never given to a mortal to be ever free from the desire of a woman!

The above account of the ascetic aberrations goes to prove that Kāma is the vital elan of the potent sex urge, very hard to suppress, much harder to eradicate. The ascetic morality of life-long abstinence even for seasoned sages—far less for the average man—is a virtue far from being a practical proposition. It can be rightly said that there was no ascetic without the latent erotic spark hidden within him![2]

The epic nowhere suggests that sex urge is unnatural and hence to be condemned. The manner in which the story of Ṛṣyaśringa referred to above points out that imposed celibacy was looked upon as abnormal and undesirable. The prudery or monkish austerity of sage Vibhāṇdaka had excluded women altogether from his *āśrama* unlike the majority of other *āśramas* mentioned in the epic. His son Ṛṣyaśringa's celibacy was jealously guarded under the vigil of his austere father. This came to be regarded by the people as the cause of draught and unfertility in the realm of Romāpada where the sage's āśrama was situated. The state thought it fit to corrupt Ṛṣyaśringa and the wily raids of accomplished light skirts from the Anga court led to the easy fall of Ṛṣyaśringa. This led to the marriage of the celibate youth to the Anga princess.[3] In other words the fertilization of the sexual impulse latent in the hermit youth which was unnaturally curbed led to the fertility of the kingdom itself. The examples of many ascetics courting maidens referred to earlier also suggest preference for conjugal life to that of asceticism.

Not only the enjoyment of sex was considered natural but even its disturbance was felt as especially inhuman. Pārvatī, united with her husband, cursed the gods for their intrusion upon her privacy.[4]

[1]cf. IV. 33. 57: maharṣayo dharmatapobhirāmah: kāmānukāmāḥ pratibaddhamohāḥ.

[2]I. 63. 3-14; I.64.

[3]I. 10 f.

[4]I. 66. 21.

Vālmiki pronounced a vehement curse on the fowler who shot at the pair of *Krauñcha* birds, who were just in the joys of pairing.[1] It is this act of the fowler which separated the two birds lost in the ecstasy of sex union which enrages the sage and the idea to portray the sufferings of Sītā separated from Rāma is born. The epic looks upon sex as a natural instinct, sex life as decent and conjugal union sacred.

Ascetic Merit

The ascetics were not free from human faults. Besides sexual slips, cursing was a common weakness amongst the sages who often lost their temper. Agastya, Vasiṣṭha, Gautama, Durvāsā, Viśvāmitra, Kaṇdu and others were all given to cursing people for breaches of good conduct. Especially the irascibility of Durvāsā is proverbial. Agastya's curse turns Yakṣi Tāraka into a terrible form.[2] Viśvāmitra cursing Raṁbhā turns her into a stone.[3] The hundred sons of Vasiṣṭha, engaged in austerities curse Triśaṅku to turn into a *cāṇḍāla*.[4] Viśvāmitra reduces Vasiṣṭha's sons to ashes by his curse.[5] If the sages could confer boons for good, they could also curse to make one's life miserable or bring it to extinction.

The efficacy of the curse depended on the asceticism and meritoriousness of the curser. But it has been emphasised time and again in the epic that cursing or bursting into rage tended to detract from one's accession of spiritual strength and gave a definite setback to one's efforts at self-discipline. Viśvāmitra realised the deterioration in his ascetic merit when he had cursed Raṁbhā.[6] Vedavati hesitated in pronouncing a curse on Rāvaṇa lest it should result in a loss of her *tapas*.[7] Sītā refrained from reducing Rāvana to ashes but for her husband's mandate and her ascetic observances.[8] The daughters of Kuśanābha, who were *tāpasis*, felt themselves capable to dislodge Vāyu from his place but refrained due to fear of losing their ascetic merit.[9] It was this very fear of loss of

[1] I. 2. 15.
[2] I. 25. 12-13.
[3] I. 64. 15.
[4] I. 58. 9-10.
[5] I. 59. 18: the above examples also indicate the power born of *tapas*.
[6] I. 64. 16.
[7] VII. 17. 31.
[8] V. 22. 20.
[9] I. 32. 20.

their ascetic merit that explained the reluctance of the sages to exterminate the Rākṣasas who constantly molested them and disturbed their sacrifices. 'It is true that by the power of these austerities we could at will slay these goblins, but we are unwilling to nullify the merit which has been earned by long exertion,' declared the ascetics of Daṇḍākāraṇya to Rāma.[1] The utterance of a curse was an act which neutralized the sanctity of him who pronounced it. For the hermit, his *tapas* was his sole and paramount wealth (*tapodhana*),[2] the one object of his legitimate pride (*tapaślāgya*).[3] Hence it was necessary for him to guard it with the utmost care and vigilance on his part. Vālmiki stresses the necessity of desisting from all iniquitous acts for the protection of the religious merit reaped by undergoing extreme mortification in penance.[4]

The Ideal Ascetic

The *Rāmāyaṇa* frequently dwells upon the ideal qualities to be cultivated by the ascetics. They should be self-controlled (*dānta*) and self-disciplined (*niyata*, *bhāvitātman*),[5] leading a life of sexual abstinence (*vijitendriyāḥ*).[6] They should be truthful, of excellent character (*śilavān*), of a pure spirit (*śuchi*), not addicted to the pleasures of life and ever studious of religion.[7] They were to be *nyastadaṇdas*, their vow being not to hurt anybody, by thought, word or deed, master of the temper (*jita-krodha*) and *jitendriya*, having subjugated their senses.[8] Above all they should be the embodiments of supreme altruism, ever engaged in the welfare of all creatures.[9] A typical instance of the extent to which the self-denial of ancient sages reached is furnished by the class of ascetics who, abstaining from every other kind of food subsisted solely on the froth of milk (*phenapaḥ*),[10] falling off from the udders of the cow after the calf had drunk it. It is said that this froth-drinking in preference to drinking the milk itself was inspired by a motive of

1III. 10. 13-14.
2VII. 2. 20.
3I. 4. 8.
4V. 51. 25.
5VI. 125. 31. 32.
6VII. 9. 39.
7VII. 3. 2.
8III. 1. 21.
9III. 1. 15: Sarvabhutahiterataḥ.
10VII. 23. 23.

charity viz. not to deprive the calf of its legitimate fare. When Rāma ordered Lakṣmaṇa to present Lava and Kuśa with gold coins and numerous other valuable presents for their excellent music performance, forthwith came their significant reply: 'We are dwellers of the forest and we live upon furits and roots. Living there what shall we do with gold and with coins?'[1] This was characteristic hall-mark of the hermit culture of those days.

Power of Asceticism

Patañjali in his *Yogasūtras* brought together and classified a series of ascetic practices and contemplative formulas that India had known from time immemorial.[2] The practices broadly called 'Yogic' were known in the esoteric circles of ascetics and mystics long before Patañjali. Discussing the psychic powers arising from the practice of Yoga-meditation he also mentions austerities (*tapas*) and incantations (*mantras*) as akin sources from which certain yogic powers or *siddhis* spring.[3] In the list of such *siddhis* are included: Knowledge of past and future, knowing what others are thinking, the attainment of various kinds of strength, control of hunger and thirst, control of the senses, perfection of the body and to have the fulfilment of any wish at will.[4] The epic affords many examples of the ṛṣis, munis and hermits who have through long and rigid practice of austerities or *tapas* have acquired many of these *siddhis*.

We have already made reference to how Rāvaṇa had by long and painful austerities obtained from Bṛahmā the boon that neither god nor demon should be able to deprive him of his life. Protected thus he became a terror to the world. In his pride, he had omitted to ask for protection against *man*.[5] The demon Virādha had by his austerities obtained the privilege of being proof against every kind of weapon. However, he met his fate at the hands of Rāma, who overcame him, not with weapons, but with his fists and flung him into a deep pit.[6] Not only these were conferred boons by gods to be powerful in strength but muni like Cūli performing Brāhmya *tapas* conferred upon Gandarbhi, an excellent son, named

[1]VII. 94. 20.
[2]Eliade, op. cit., p. 7.
[3]*YS.*, IV. 1. janmauṣadhiyantra tapaḥ samādhijāḥ siddhayaḥ.
[4]ibid, III, 16-48.
[5]I. 16. 4. 5.
[6]III. 3. 6.

Brahmadatta.[1] We find Viśvāmitra, conferring upon Rāma different weapons endowed with exceeding prowess.[2] Sages like Agastya, Bhārdvāja, Bhārgava, Vaisiṣṭha and Viśvāmitra were reputed for their marvellous capacity to bless or curse, make or mar the fortunes of men. Apart from this we refer to that mighty and miraculous power of asceticism which we distinctly call Yogic powers or *siddhis*.

We come across many examples in the epic, of ascetics who proved in their own experiences the virtue and power of asceticism. The rigorous self-discipline and self-abstinence which went in its practice endowed them with almost superhuman powers. Although poorly, emaciated, with their bodies covered with dust,[3] they could be recognised from a distance by a certain majesty that characterized them.[4] They are depicted as full of grace that is born of spiritual energy and endowed with spiritual intuition,[5] resembling the fire or the sun and as radiating lustre all around.[6] Even mundane power of a Kśatriya was deemed to be no match for the spiritual powers born of ascetic practices.[7]

Many were the *siddhis* achieved by them. They could know the intent of others[8] and were credited with intuitive vision, the outcome of their *tapas*,[9] by which they could divine unseen things in their supra-normal consciousness. The sage Gautama detects the crime of adultery committed by Indra with his wife Ahalyā, and cursed him so that he became impotent.[10] Through Yogic powers it was considered possible to be gifted with divine vision (*jñāna dṛṣti, jñāna cakṣu*). Vālmiki is said to have witnessed all the incidents in the life of Rāma, past, present and future before he composed the epic. He perceived the characters as each acted his or her part aided by his *dharma-virya*.[1] On seeing the unfortunate Sītā in a deserted condition, weeping near his *āśrama*, the revered sage divined the

[1]I. 33. 18.

[2]I, 27f.

[3]VI. 125-30: dinaṁ, kṛśaṁ, maladigdhāṅgaṁ karśitaṁ.

[4]III. 12-23.

[5]III. 6. 6: brāhmayā śriyāyuktāh: III. 1. 10: divyajñanopapannah.

[6]VI. 35. 18: pradipta eva pāvakah; VI. 35. 17: agnikalpaḥ; III. 1. 7: sūrya vaiśvānarābhaiḥ; III. 1. 16; VII. 51. 4.

[7]I. 56. 23.

[8]VII. 9. 19.

[9]VII. 49. 6: tapasā labdhacakṣusman.

[10]I. 84.

[11]I. 3. 4. 6. 7: tatsarvaṁ dharmaviṛyeṇa yathāvat sampraṣaśyati.

events leading to her banishment by his spiritual concentration.[1] In the assembly of Rāma, he refers to his age-long *tapas* and his discipline of life as unfailing factors which enabled him to measure the stainless character of Sītā.[2] Sage Bhārdvāja's asceticism enabled him to divine all the events during Rāma's exile in the forest.[3] Ṛishi Nishākara sees the coming of Rāma, who is separated from Sītā and divines the future events.[4] Sampati could divine by his *jñāna cakṣu* that the Vānaras would succeed in getting scent of Sītā.[5] Budha, on meeting King Ila, transformed into a female, was able to divine his precedents by his Yogic knowledge.[6] Nalakubera, by such powers was able to divine the ravishment of Raṁbhā by Rāvaṇa.[7] Viśvāmitra makes Triśaṅku bodily ascend heaven and when compelled by Indra to fall, makes him stay in the sky.[8] Bhārdvāja entertains Bharat and his forces lavishly at his *āśrama*. It was wonderful hospitality when the Maharṣi calls the Gāndharvas and serves his guests, the best of foods, drinks and entertainments.[9] Even a holy man is depicted as the magnificent magician and host treating the guests in the most royal and romantic manner!

The ṛṣis, munis and hermits have acquired through *tapas* many *siddhis*. Endowed with the halo of these powers, they are described variously as highly effulgent, flaming in ascetic energy, *mahātejāḥ*, *tapodhanāḥ*, *mahātapāḥ*, *tapomurti* etc. *Tapas* not only enhanced their physical and mental powers but they also became as powerful as gods. The gods are pleased with *ugram tapas* and confer boons on these *tapasvis*.

The survey of the culture of hermitages as obtained in the *Rāmāyaṇa* should not lead us to the impression that there was a sort of water-tight barrier between the city and hermitage. On the other hand sufficient intercourse existed between the two to enable the hermitages to exert their edifying influence over urban culture. 'Asceticism is indeed the foremost of things conducive to one's

[1] VII. 49. 8-14.
[2] VII. 96. 19-20.
[3] VI. 125. 9-16: sarvaṁmamaitadviditaṁ tapasā. VI. 127-7.
[4] IV. 62.
[5] IV. 58. 25-27.
[6] VII. 38. 20.
[7] VII. 26. 50 f.
[8] I. 13. 14. 20.
[9] II. 91 f.

welfare and all other worldly joys are mere illusions,'[1] declares the epic. This truth was realised in the evening of their lives by the celebrated kings of the age who, laying the reins of government in the hands of their heirs, courted ascetic life in the wilderness.[2] Even during their reigning career, kings visited *āśramas* and stayed there for some time in company of the pious munis.[3] King Yayāti is represented as associating himself with the holy sages of the forest after his downfall from heaven.[4] Vālmiki was a great friend of King Daśaratha.[5] Hermits used to be sumptuously fed at Daśratha's sacrifice.[6] Not only this but even invitations used to be extended to the principal hermit-settlements for participation in sacrificial festivals.[7] Rāma's life as a ruling monarch, as depicted in the Uttarkāṇḍa, was spent in active association with sages who frequently sought his hospitality at Ayodhyā.

We can have some glimpses of the spirit of cooperation which permeated the relations between the kings and hermits. The kings enquired about the well-being of the sages' penance, fire-worship and disciples.[8] For, being the protectors of the realm, the kings were responsible for the safe conduct of the rituals of the ascetics and such enquiries furnish a positive proof of their solicitude for the weal of the hermit order and of their tacit readiness to take up arms in defence of their interests. Rāma's life, not merely during his exile but also before and after it, is replete with instances of such help readily rendered. In return for this, the forest-dwellers habitually made enquiries about the army, the treasury, and the welfare of the king's subjects,[9] thereby showing that they were not wanting in interest about the material prosperity of the realm. Being the custodians of the spiritual heritage of the land, they were anxious to find out whether the kings were engaged in the proper maintenance of dharma by a righteous administration of the country.[10]

[1]VII. 84. 9: tapo hi paramaṁ śreyaḥ saṁmohamitaratsukhaṁ.

[2]cf. VII. 84. 10: sa nikṣiṣya sutaṁ jyesṭhaṁ paureṣu madhureṣvaraṁ tapa ugraṁ samātiṣthataṁ, I. 42-3.

[3]VII. 51. 3-5.

[4]II. 77. 10.

[5]VII. 47. 16-17.

[6]I. 14. 12.

[7]VII. 91. 2-3.

[8]I. 52. 4.

[9]I. 52. 9.

[10]I. 52. 7.

Their contribution to the welfare of the community was more silent yet no less valuable than that of the kings. Some of their hermitages were semi-religious educational institutions where the training of the young was fittingly taken up by these sages who living a sublime life of *tapas* themselves gave their best freely with open hearts. Although considered renouncers of the world, they poured forth disinterested love in the service of the forlorn and the afflicted, as nobly illustrated by what Vālmiki did for Sītā and her children. Some of these ṛṣis travelled from place to place, visiting kings and holding religious conferences at their court. They were honoured and respected by all.

The Four Āśramas

During the period of the *Rāmāyaṇa*, the four stages of life—āśramas were recognised.[1] The Upanayan ceremony introduced the young boy into the *Brahmacaryāśrama* which coincided with the student stage of the individual. This stage was followed by *Gṛhasthāśrama.* We have a portrayal of this stage of life with its love and longing blended with sex as it actually prevailed in the age,[2] which is quite in harmony with the role romance and love plays in human life. In the *Vānaprastha* stage, the retired householder lived an abstemious and self-denying life in the woods, engaged in the welfare of all creatures, receiving alms, performing sacrifices and devoted to the study of the Vedas. He lived under a tree, with restrained senses, subsisting on easily available roots and fruits.[3] We have also met the *tapasvis*, the ascetics and sages of the hermitages many of whom are in the *vānaprastha* stage of life.

As for the final *āśrama*, it must be noted that neither the word *saṁnyāsa* occurs in the *Rāmāyaṇa* nor *Saṁnyāsāśrama* described therein though we come across the words *bhikṣu* and *parivrājaka.* When Rāvaṇa came to abduct Sītā in Pañcavatī, he had disguised himself in the dress of a *parivrājaka.*[4] He is described as carrying an umbrella, a waterpot, and a *yaṣti* (stick) and wearing an orange

[1] II. 106. 22: caturnāmāśramāṇāṁ.

[2] Vyas, *Love and Longing in the Rāmāyaṇa*, *JOI.*, II. No. 2, pp. 105-117.

[3] V. 13-38.

[4] Dharma interprets the word *parivrājaka* to mean *Saṁnyasa* in III. 46.3; *Social life in the Rāmāyaṇa*, *JMS.*, XXVIII, 1937-38, pp. 80-81. Sircar takes him to be an itinerant monk-teacher, *Educational Ideas and Institutions in Ancient India*, p. 150.

coloured (*kāśāya*) cloth. He also had a tuft of hair (*sikhi*).[1] Should a *parivrājaka*, if he was a *saṁnyāsin*, have such paraphernalia? We also find that Hanumān, when sent by Sugrīva to meet Rāma and Lakṣmaṇa for the first time, renounces his monkey form and goes to meet them in the guise of a mendicant (*bhikṣu*).[2] It is thus not certain whether a *parivrājaka* or a *bhikṣu* was the same as a *saṁnyāsin*, or whether this final stage of life came after the *vānaprastha* or could be resorted to even earlier.

However, we have to remember that in the full-fledged scheme of *āśramas*, the *saṁnyāsi* 'goes forth' (*pravrājya*) leaving all—family, possessions, property, all earthly ties, every mundane desire. Abandoning truth and falsehood, pleasure and pain, the Vedas and the next, he seeks only the Ātman.[3] The initiary ritual prescribed for him implied a total rejection of the Vedas.[4] Even the *Mahābhārata* lays down that the *saṁnyāsi* should leave off the Vedic study and the sacred thread which marks his birth.[5] The *Rāmāyaṇa* depicts the *ṛṣis*, *munis* and hermits whose lives are completely saturated with Vedic rituals. The *saṁnyāsi*, 'casting off' everything, leads an unsocial, resourceless and wandering life and is concerned solely with his spiritual welfare. The *ṛṣis* and *munis*, as pointed out earlier, though acknowledged renouncers of the world and custodians of the spiritual heritage of the land, were equally anxious about the maintenance of Dharma by the kings during their rule and the material prosperity of the realm. Their attitude was one of service to the society at large and the kings. The *saṁnyāsi*, on the other hand, lived solely for himself, shunning the society, seeking his own salvation. Hence it becomes difficult to state with certainty whether *Saṁnyāsa* as understood in the terms of the full-fledged āśrama scheme was known.

It appears from the epic that though it does not describe or mention *Saṁnyāsa* as the final stage of life, the four-fold scheme of *āśramas* was adhered to in all normal cases. Neglecting the duties of a particular *āśrama* fit for oneself and arbitrarily resorting to the life reserved for another *āśrama*, evoked the disapproval of sensible

[1] III. 46. 3.

[2] IV. 3. 2. 23.

[3] *AP. DS.*, II. 9. 21, 13.

[4] *Vaik DS.*, IV. 6-8; cf. Kane, op. cit., 954-961. Also *Saṁnyās Upanisads* cf. Deussen, *POU.*, p. 376.

[5] *Mbh.*, XII. 244 ff, 245 ff.

and wise men. *Rāma's* departure for the life of *vanavāsa* evoked criticism from many a person on the ground that the *vānaprastha* life was not suited to one of his age and position. The suggestion is clear that he should prepare for it living a full life of a *gṛhastha*. At Citrakūta, Bharat put the very question to Rāma, who had embraced the hermit's life in his very youth, as to how did he, well conversant as he was with Dharma, take recourse to the *vānaprastha* life, abandoning the *gṛhastha* stage.[1]

On this point the epic does not leave us in any doubt. The *gṛhasthāśrama* is acclaimed as the best of the four āśramas,[2] and the *Rāmāyaṇa* itself is an epic par excellence of this stage of Āryan life. Its motive is said to be inculcation of the virtues of the householder's life as the primary means of encompassing one's spiritual welfare. The special eulogy bestowed upon this *āśrama* by the *Rāmāyaṇa*, and indeed by all *Dharmaśāstras*, is due to the fact that the *gṛhastha* lent support to the other *āśramas* and made direct contributions to the weal of the individual as also the society. It is the most fitting vehicle for the satisfaction of all the obligations of life, individual as well as social.

Let us evaluate the position of asceticism in the Epics.

The *Mahābhārata* affords many examples of men and women engaged in austerities (*tapas*) which is not the sole privilege of ascetics. Even the kings and *asuras* practise austerities for variety of reasons but broadly either to gain power or some material end. Women are seen practising austerities for getting a husband. Some of them have taken to the life of *Naiṣṭhika Brahmacarya*. We find detailed descriptions of the *tapasvis* who have become immune to their environment and physical needs. Many of them are either in the *gṛhastha* or the *vānaprastha* stage. The *saṁnyāsa* mode of life is recognised and also described. *Tapas* as a moral force is also directed towards attainment of *mokṣa*. The rights and privileges of the ascetic life are confined to the twice-born (*dvijas*).

The epic eulogises *tapas*, its efficacy and its power. There is nothing superior to it. Its might enables a person to achieve great results. The ascetic through *tapas* acquires supernatural power which can be properly called Yogic. But such powers are accessible to women also if they are chaste. The institution of marriage is well established. Marriage is regarded as a social and religious duty

[1]II. 106. 23.
[2]II. 106. 22.

hence a necessity for every woman. The *Pativratā* ideal is upheld. It is emphasised again and again that chastity is the only penance a woman should perform and *gṛhasthāśrama* is the fittest stage to reach heaven. All these factors discouraged women from taking to ascetic life.

The epic discusses two parallell strands of thought: One favouring the path of renunciation (*nivritti mārga*) and the other of active participation as embodied in *gṛhasthāśrama* (*pravṛtti mārga*) and shows the preference for the latter. The whole epic emerges as the assertion of the heroic activism of the warrior against the world denial of the ascetic. If asceticism claimed that withdrawal from the world was the only way to salvation, the warrior class made the counter-claim that death on the battlefield also led to heaven. The epic further seeks to resolve the conflict between the two paths of *Nivṛtti* and *Pravṛtti* by emphasising the fair aims of life and striking a proper balance between them. The first three, *artha*, *kāma* and *dharma* should be so guided that they lead to the ultimate end of human life, *mokṣa*. It is this integrated view that the epic unfolds. But the process necessarily involves the gradual ethical evolution of man's personality till he attains *mokṣa*, through *gṛhasthāśrama*.

In this ethical evolution of man, the *Gītā* forms the integral part of the epic, with its *activist* teachings. It disfavours the ascetic life and recommends a life of moderation which avoids extremes of self-indulgence and self-restraint. It also makes the ideal of world-negation as a part of active life, *gṛhasthāśrama*. Emphasising the *pravṛtti mārga*, it speaks of Yoga as the means by which one can attain purity of heart which is most essential for proper human relations to be effected and maintained. This state of mind is to be attained through steady practice (*abhyāsa*) and the implementation of dispassion (*vairāgya*) or disinterestedness (*anāsakti*). The *Gītā* goes into details of day-to-day life and makes Yoga as an attitude, which if cultivated, brings a living contact with God. At the same time, Yoga does not imply a remote, silent or uplifted life. It is life as it is, a struggle, a battlefield.

To Indian religions and social thought the *Gītā* makes a special contribution by way of three concepts. These are the ideal of *Sthitaprajña* or the person of equable mind, the doctrine of *Niṣkāmakarma* or action without personal desire or attachment, and the principle of *Lokasaṁgraha* or welfare of the world towards which all actions should be directed. These three concepts are blended together in the ideal of the *Karma Yoga*—of selfless action in this world for the benefit of this world. Not *Saṁnyāsa* but active, self-less participation in the activities of the world becomes a gospel of supreme importance in the *Gītā*.

The *Rāmāyaṇa*, while narrating the movingly tender love-story of Rāma and Sītā in all its vicissitudes, also depicts the ascetic culture of the hermitages wherein the *munis*, *ṛṣis* and hermits reside, engaged in the study of Vedic lore and performing the Vedic rituals. We also have a picture of their life of tapas in its aspects of abstinence, mortification, meditation and self-discipline aimed at self-purification and emancipation of the soul. Most of them have achieved miraculous and wonderful powers or *siddhis* as the result of their *tapas*. They could bless or curse, make or mar man's fortune or make his life miserable. Not only the Āryans—men and women but Rāksasas and Yakṣas practise auterities for various ends: power, progeny, happiness, wisdom and purification, material or spiritual welfare. We come across many types of ascetics who derive their names from their peculiar ascetic practices. They are required to tread the path of righteousness and observe purity of conduct. The ascetics or *tapasvis* most of whom are designated as *ṛṣis*, *munis* and sages, though leading a life of *vanavāsa*, are accompained by their wives. They are thus in the *vānaprastha* stage. They are not free from aberrations, physical and moral. But at the same time they realise that these are obstacles in their path of self-discipline and spiritual progress.

Though female ascetics existed, they were in a minority. One factor which militated against women taking to ascetic life was the *Pativratā* ideal of which Sītā was the fittest model. The epic declares that the wife should consider her husband as a deity and his *śuśruṣā* was her highest religion. Religious rites and fasts etc. were secondary. Thus when she could attain salvation serving the husband as a *Pativratā*, there was absolutely no need for her to take to ascetic life.

The epic recognises the four *āśramas* and expects every one to live through the stages in their strict order. Any breach thereof was met with disapproval. With regard to *Saṁnyāsa*, the epic is silent for it neither mentions it or depicts it as a mode of life-stage. All the while we meet the *ṛṣis*, *munis* and hermits who are *vānaprasthas*. They are still living the Vedic mode of life, and thought. Though leading a secluded life, they still continue to take interest in the maintenance of Dharma by the kings and welfare of the people, unlike the *Saṁnyāsi* who lives an unsocial resourceless and wandering life, seeking his own salvation. Some of the hermits definitely show a preference for the conjugal life over the ascetic. The epic looks upon sex as a natural instinct; sex-life as clean and sacred. Naturally there is an exaltation of *Gṛhasthāśrama* as the highest ideal wherein the righteous *gṛhastha* can fulfil all individual and social obligations.

In fine, it is the *Gṛhasthāśrama* which is upheld in the epic as the pivot round which all the aims of life revolve. It is also an essential stage to attain *samatva* which enables a man to walk *evenly* among the beauties and perils of the world. The attainment makes his journey towards the final aim of *mokṣa* easy. It is the best and only stage which prepares a man to serve the society and to work for the benefit of this world.

Chapter 9

Asceticism in the Arthaśāstra

The science of polity, in ancient India, was known by various names, *Daṇḍanīti*, *Nītiśāstra*, *Rājnīti*, *Rājdharma* and *Arthaśāstra* and dealt not only with the political theories and the actual organisation of administrative machinery, but also various matters connected with state and society. Kautilya's *Arthaśāstra*, which systematizes the essentials of Indian statecraft known at the time it was written, has gradually come to be regarded as the standard work, a masterly and comprehensive treatise on the subject. As Panikkar asserts, 'the influence of the *Arthaśāstra*, on the political thinking of India from that time is something which no one can deny.'[1]

Indian tradition is unanimous in holding the *Arthaśāstra*, this famous work on polity, as the work of Kautilya. The work repeatedly ascribes itself to Kautilya or Vishnugupta, also styled Chāṇakya, who is reported to have been the Prime Minister of Chandragupta Maurya, who overthrew the Nandās. While the Brāhmanical sources like Viśākhadatta's *Mudrārākṣasam* regard Chāṇakya rather than Chandragupta, as the chief actor in the great drama which ended in the extermination of the Nandās, the Buddhist and Jaina sources confirm as to the close association of the Brāhmin Chāṇakya as his guide and leader in all the stupendous enterprise of empire building. However, with ragard to the date of the work, the views of various scholars very considerably ranging from the Pre-Buddhist times[2] to a much later date.[3] Its exact date is still a matter of discussion. In view of the suspicion of the later editing, the authenticity of the attribution of Kautilya is often rejected. In any case, in the light of all the evidence it must be admitted that the *Arthaśāstra* seems to be a Mauryan document. It refers to Mauryan times and the author was a contemporary of Chandragupta Maurya.

[1]Panikkar, *The Determining Periods of Indian History*, p. 6.

[2]Shamasastri, *Kautilya Arthaśāstra*, Introduction, p. xviii.

[3]For summary of all the views see *The Age of Imperial Unity*, pp. 285-287. Also Thapar, *Aśoka and the Decline of the Mauryas*, pp. 218-225.

The great importance of the work lies in the fact that Kautilya, as an exponent of the art of the government, the duties of kings, ministers and officials and the methods of diplomacy, gives with great skill, a detailed picture touching almost all the aspects of the state activity and the state of society of the time. At the same time, in the long line of sacred Sanskrit texts, where everything is considered with respect to *dharma*, this is the only text which while claiming *dharma* as the ultimate goal, has no illusions about society. It discusses practically everything with extra-ordinary frankness. Moreover, it confirms and extends much of what we learn from certain observations of the Greek writer, Megasthenes, who as it is well-known, spent considerable time in India as the Syrian king Seleucus Nikator at the Court of Chandragupta Maurya.

Varṇāśrama-dharma

Kautilya calls *dharma* 'the eternal truth holding its way over the world,'[1] and accepts the triple Vedas—Rig, Sām and Yajur Veda as the social basis which determined the respective duties of the four *Varṇas* and the four stages (*āśramas*) of life.[2] The elaborate rules about the *dharma* of the *āśramas* are described as under:

'The duty of a householder (*Gṛhastha*) is earning livelihood by his own profession, getting married, rearing up a family, gifts to gods, ancestors, guests and servants and the eating of the remainder.

That of a student (*Brahmacārin*) is learning the Vedas, fire-worship, ablution, living by begging and devotion to his teacher.

That of a forest-recluse (*Vānaprastha*) is observance of chastity, sleeping on the bare ground, keeping twisted locks, wearing deer-skin, fire-worship, ablution, worship of gods, ancestors and guests and living upon food-stuffs procurable in forests.

That of an ascetic retired from the world (*Parivrājaka*) is complete control of the organs of sense, abstaining from all kinds work, disowning money, keeping away from society, begging in many places, dwelling in forests and purity both internal and external.'[3]

This account fully corroborates the respective duties of the four *āśramas* found in the Brāhmanical religious texts. These *āśramas* were introduced or more correctly 'formulated' during the Brāhmaṇa

[1] I. 3. 17: trayyābhirakṣito lokaḥ prasidati na sidati.

[2] I. 3. 4: es trayidharmacaturnāṁ varṇāmaśramāṇāṁ.

[3] I. 3. 9-12.

age.[1] They were already a familiar institution during the time of Pāṇini.[2] It is of particular significance that Kautilya enumerates the duties of a *Gṛhastha* first and that of a *Brahmacāri* afterwards though the *āśrama* of the *Brahmacāri* precedes that of *Gṛhastha.*

Kautilya further points out that the virtues which should be cultivated in common to all the four *āśramas* are harmlessness, truthfulness, purity, freedom from jealousy, abstinence from cruelty and forgiveness.[3] Special emphasis is placed on the observance of one's duty which leads one to *svarga* and infinite bliss. When it is violated, the world, it is said, will come to an end, owing to the confusion of castes and duties. Hence it is the responsibility of the king to see that the people do not swerve from their duties.[4]

Emphasis on the Artha

'Wealth and wealth alone, is important, inasmuch as charity and desire depend upon wealth for their realization,' says Kautilya.[5] This shows that Kautilya assigned a high place to *artha* as against *dharma* and *kāma.* According to him, the major aim of polity is four-fold viz., 'to make acquisitions, to keep them secure to improve them and to distribute among the deserving the profits of improvement.'[6] This clearly shows that the edifice of the state is built upon a secure material basis and the state activity is centered round the material objective, the creation of wealth. Where the material values occupy a prominent place in the social mind and where the state firmly lays down its policy towards the advancement of such a worldly objective, it is but natural that ascetic institutions which are opposed to the material values should be relegated to the background. The *Arthaśāstra* clearly reflects its hostile attitude towards asceticism and renunciation of worldly life. No doubt the state should promote *dharma* but Kautilya wants it also to regulate the age and conditions under which one might renounce the world.

Reaction against Asceticism

The scheme of the four *āśramas* was designed to give wide scope

[1] Radhakrishnan, *IP.*, I, p. 132.

[2] Agrawala, *India as known to Pāṇini*, p. 81.

[3] I. 3, 13.

[4] I. 3. 14-16.

[5] I. 7. 6-7: artha eva pradhānaḥ arthamūlau hi dharmakāmāviti.

[6] I. 4. 3: alabdhalabhārtha labdha parirakṣni rakṣitavivardhini vriddhasya tirthe pratipādani ca.

to individuals in the choice of a vocation in life which was best suited to their intellectual capacity and mental inclinations. It was not necessary that one should strictly follow the four stages one after another. Though this might be regarded as a normal procedure by the orthodox section and one that was largely followed in practice, still the choice was left to every individual who was not forced, either to lead a householder's life or to renounce it against his will. But on the whole the different stages very well reflect the different ideals which inspired society.

This voluntary system worked well so long as there was no preponderING attraction for an ascetic life, for the neglect of household duties on the part of a large section disturbs the economy of society. The great wave of renuciation which may be regarded both as the cause and effect of the rise of heterodox sects like Jainism and Buddhism was a menace to orthodox Āryan society and to the *Varṇāśrama-dharma* upon which it was based. Its integrity was threatened by the growth of various ascetic orders and brotherhood, based upon renunciation of the world and social obligations. Their pessimistic teachings made men forget their social duties and family responsibilities. In many cases husbands left their wives and wives forsook their husbands. Domestic ties were often broken and women or children made destitute and homeless.[1] Marriage was viewed as a burden. As a result, poverty and indigence increased. The state had to face the problem of maintaining the deserted and the destitute. Rules were, therefore, clearly laid down as to who could embrace asceticism and certain restrictions were placed on those embracing the ascetic life. Kautilya does not at all approve of a premature renunciation of the world and the duties of domestic life without the formal sanction of the legal authorities and without making provision for son and wife. He says: 'When, without making provision for the maintenance of his wife and sons, any person embraces asceticism, he shall be punished with the first amercement.'[2] At what stage he must do so is also stated: 'Whoever has passed the age of copulation may become an ascetic after distributing the properties of his own acquisition among his sons, otherwise he will be punished.'[3] The claims of society and family

[1] *Therigatha* gives us many instances of women refusing to marry or rear children or of being left destitute because of the desertion of husbands.

[2] II. 1. 29.

[3] II. 1. 30-31.

life must be first satisfied. Kautilya is well aware that wide-spread and indiscriminate renunciation interferes with economic production. Accordingly he goes to the length of banning the entry into villages such unlicensed ascetics as a disintegrating factor in rural society. He says: 'No ascetic sect other than the Brāhmanical forest-hermit (*Vānaprastha*) shall find entrance into the villages of the kingdom.'[1] All heretical sects from the villages were excluded. Their entry. it was feared, may cause distrubance in the economic activities of the villagers.[2] Another check on the growth of ascetic institution was the punishment to any person who converted a woman to asceticism (*pravrājayataḥ*).[3] The security of domestic life was thus safeguarded. The state also took effective steps to prevent indiscriminate mendicacy. Men or women suspected of having recently joined any of the orders were caught by the police or by the officers of the *Nāvādhyakṣa* at the ferries.[4] Members of the non-Brāhmanical orders were also excluded from villages and were not allowed to organise Saṅghas and Āśrāms in villages.[5] Not only this, the dwellings of heretical monks (*pāṣaṇḍa*) like those of the lower castes (*cāṇḍālas*) were to be outside the royal cities.[6] Adultery with a nun (*pravrajitā*) was made punishable with a fine; the nun who submitted herself had also to pay a similar fine.[7] The necessity of such a measure suggests that there must have been some cases of adultery with a nun or her being involved in such affairs. Even though women joined the order of nuns, it was not often possible for them to maintain rigid chastity as expected of them. They sometimes misbehaved and disturbed social ethics. This also may be another reason why a woman was not allowed to take to ascetic life and even her conversion by any person was a punishable offence. No doubt the security of the family life and stability of society were the main motives against women embracing asceticism.

Uses of Asceticism

There is no doubt that during the time of Kautilya, the ascetics who renounced the world for developing spiritual life, formed an

[1]II. 1. 32: Vānaprasthadānyaḥ pravajitbhāvaḥ.
[2]II. 1. 34: Karmavighnāṁ kuryuḥ.
[3]II. 1. 29.
[4]II. 28. 20.
[5]II. 1. 33: na ca tatrārāmā vihārāthaṁ va sātāsyuḥ.
[6]II. 4. 23.
[7]IV. 13. 36.

unique feature in Indian society. The Greek writers have left an interesting account of some of these ascetics whom they actually met. *Arthaśāstra* reflects the state of society of Kautilya's times and his concern to stem wide-spread and indiscriminate renunciation. Kautilya did not want that *Dharma* be allowed to exert too great strain on society. *Dharma*, according to him, must be realised through *Artha*. *Dharma* and *Mokṣa* were no doubt worthy ideals but they should follow after *Artha* and *Kāma* are satisfied. Such was Kautilya's concept of polity within the framework of which the individual had to find fulfilment and social institutions had their justification. Kautilya predicted that asceticism not only transform the people into a contemplative society but also undermine its necessary material foundation, as economically asceticism was not productive. It is not surprising, therefore, that he values asceticism primarily for its usefulness in espionage and intelligence activities:

(1) The king was advised to create spies under the guise of a recluse (*udāsthita*), an ascetic practising austerities (*tāpasa*) and a mendicant woman (*bhikṣuki*).[1]

(2) A woman-spy under the guise of an ascetic (*parivrājikā*) and highly esteemed in the harem of the king may allure each prime minister (*mahāmātra*) one after another saying: 'The queen is enamoured of thee and has made arrangements for thy entrance into her chamber; besides this, there is also the certainty of large acquisition of wealth.' If they discarded the proposal, they were pure.[2]

(3) Spies in the grab of ascetics were employed for detection of youths of criminal tendency.[3]

(4) A mendicant woman (*bhikṣuki*) having captured the wife of a seditious minister by administering such medicines as excite the feelings of love, may through that wife contrive to poison the minister.[4]

(5) A spy disguised as an ascetic, may apply to a lover such medical ointments as are declared to be capable of captivising the beloved woman and as are adulterated with poison; and then he may disappear. Other spies may ascribe the incident to an enemy's action.[5]

[1]I. 11. 12.
[2]I. 10. 7-8.
[3]IV. 5.
[4]V. 1. 19.
[5]XI. 1. 40-41.

(6) An ascetic with shaved hair (*muṇḍa*) or braided hair (*jatilo*) and living in the cave of a mountain, may pretend to be four hundred years old followed by a number of disciples, halt in the vicinity of the capital city of the enemy. He employs strategic means in order to capture a fortress, sows the seeds of dissension and entices enemy kings by secret contrivances.[1]

It is clear from the above instances that Kautilya was not otherwise interested in asceticism except for spies disguised as ascetics, as people in the garb of ascetics could have access to all stratas of society. This is also indicative of the fact that the people considered those belongings to ascetic orders as honest.

Light on the Ājīvikas

The *Arthaśāstra* throws some light on the Ājīvikas during the Mauryan period. The Ājīvika seems frequently to have been an astrologer or fortune teller. *Nakkhatta Jātaka*[2] tells the story of an Ājīvika regularly dependent on a certain family for support (*Kūlūpaka*), who was consulted about the most propitious date for a wedding after the preliminary preparations had already been made and who caused it to be postponed in annoyance. A similar *Kūlūpaka* Ājīvika was attached to the court of King Bindusāra and he correctly prophesied Asoka's greatness.[3]

In the *Arthaśāstra* the Ājīvikas are mentioned once. The householder who feeds *Sākyas*, Ājīvikas or other heretical monks (*vṛṣal*) at *Śrāddha* feasts or ancestral ceremonies is to be fined a hundred *paṇas*.[4] The Sākyas are the Buddhists. The Ājīvikas is mentioned here with the Buddhist as the leading representative of the heretical orders. He is still a significant force in the community, for he, not the *Nirgantha* comes second in the list. The latter is presumably included in the general group of heretical monks of other sects. The reason behind the prohibition on the householder feeding the mendicants seems to be the same which prompted Kautilya ban their entry into villages. They were not given any chance to come into contact with the people under any pretext for fear that they may disturb the economic activities of the people. Thus Kautilya dis-

[1]XIII. 2.

[2]*Jātakas*, i. p. 257.

[3]*Mahāvamsa*, Comm. i. p. 190; *Divyvadan*, pp. 370 ff.

[4]XII. 20. 16: Sakyajivakādi vṛṣal pravajitān devapitṛ kāryeṣu bhojayataḥ satyodaṇḍaḥ.

couraged monastic propaganda with a view to prevent disruption of rural society.

In spite of the fact that Kautilya does not take kindly to asceticism, it is interesting to note that there is a reference to the help given to the Ājīvikas and Nirganthas in Aśokan edicts. In two caves in the Barbara Hill, there are two inscriptions which record the gift of two cave temples to the Ājīvikas by Aśoka in the twelfth year after his coronation.

Foreign References to the Ascetic Institution

It is at this time that we have the impressions recorded by the Greek and the Romans in their writings on India.

Alexander's invasion of India in 327 BC brought for the first time the direct Greek knowledge of India to the banks of the Sutlej. Alexander was accompanied by some of the eminent men of science and letters of his times and he caused the whole of India to be described by men well acquainted with it.[1] They wrote invaluable memoirs which are believed to be lost but they furnished ample material to subsequent writers: Diodorus (100 BC to AD 100), Plutārch (50 BC), Strabo, the Roman historian (60 BC to AD 19), Curtis (AD 100), Arrian (AD 200) and Pliny (AD 23).

Others who described India in their works even before these writers were Herodotus (484-431 BC), Ktesias (398 BC) and Megāsthenes, who was the ambassador of the Graeco-Persian King Seleukos at the court of Chandragupta, (*Sandrokyptos*, as the Greeks called him) from 311 to 302 BC. Most of the Greek writers who primarily dealt with Alexander's Indian campaign have also left valuable descriptions of some aspects of India's economic conditions and social life in those days. It must be, however, noted that the personal acquaintance of Alexander and his companions with India was limited to the North—upto the Indus and its tributaries. Megasthenes in his capacity of the ambassador naturally came to see more of the country during his nine years stay and has furnished a reliable picture of Indian life, customs and institutions as he saw it.

In a treatise on India written by Ktesias, the Knidian (about 400 BC), he relates many wonderful stories about India, with which the author had been entertained while resident for 17 years in Persia as physician to the Royal family.

[1]cf. McCrindle, *Ancient India as described in Classical Literature*, p. 1.

Herodotus (484-431 BC) knew something of the countries from Scythia to Abyssinia and from India to the Pillars of Hercules. But his knowledge of India was meagre and most vague. He knew that it was one of the remotest provinces of the Persian Empire towards the East, but of its extent and exact position he had no proper conception.[1] In his work the *Historica* (III, 100), he was the first to refer to 'a class of people which neither killed anything that had life, nor saw anything, nor did they have houses. But they lived upon herbs and a grain that grew spontaneously. This they gathered and ate after boiling it.' This is a good account of the life of the forest-dwelling hermits of India who used wild rice (*nivara*) as their staple food.

Amongst the many unusual objects and institutions which attracted the attention of these foreigners, the ascetic philosophers *Brāhman, Buddhist as well as Jainas* and their peculiar ways were of special interest. The Greeks called them *Gymnosophists* and appreciative stories af their wisdom travelled to Greece with descriptions of their endurance and some of the curious penances to which they subjected themselves. According ta Strabo: 'The ascetic sages who were held in the very highest honour by both the people and their rulers, lived on austere life, often in communities. They studied self-control, spent much of their time in serious discourses and in imparting wisdom to others teaching that the best doctrine was that which removed pleasure and grief from the mind.' (Strabo, XV. II. 65).

The Graeco-Roman world was aware of this peculiar Indian attitude and the ascetic practices of the Indian sages, through its interest in Indian philosophers is attested by Tertullian who in a work (Apol. XL. 11) refers to 'Brāhmanas or naked Indian philosophers (*gymnosophists*), dwellers of the forest and exiled from life.' Obviously the allusion is to the ascetics and Brāhmanas in their third and fourth *āśrama*. Some Greek historians also claim that a great lawgiver named Lycurgus had come as far as India and talked with these naked philosophers (*gymnosophists*) who had 'neither home nor academies.'[2]

It is narrated in the *Life of Socrates* by Aristoxenus of Toranto (3rd century BC) that the great Greek philosopher was once introduced to an Indian who had come to Athens. The Indian asked

[1]cf. McCrindle, *Ancient India as described in Classical Literature*, p. 1.
[2]Barr, *The Will of Zeus*, p. 56.

what was the object of his philosophical studies. Socrates answered that he was engaged in the study of human life; at which the Indian had a good laugh and is said to have rejoined: 'It is impossible to acquire knowledge of things human, when divine things are ignored.'[1] The reply of the Indian is in perfect agreement with what we read in the Upaniṣad: 'The Universe is made known through the Ātman.'[2]

It is for this reason that Indian philosophy pays greater attention to the inner world of man than to the outer world. The external world is to be known through the inner world, inward realization. It is the self-realization which is of supreme importance which is the *sādhanā* aspect of Indian culture.

Brunton records how this perpetual quest for self-realization has come from the Vedic seers down to Maharṣi Raman in our own times and how this hallowed tradition will still continue till man continues to seek happiness. In an interview with him, the Maharṣi poses this eternal problem:

> 'As you are, so is the world. Without understanding yourself, what is the use of trying to understand the world? First find out the truth behind yourself; then you will be in a better position to understand the truth behind the world, of which yourself is a part.'[3]

Besides this supreme search for truth, everything else is of no consequence. The Maharṣi continues:

> 'The greatest kings and statesmen try to rule others when in their heart of hearts they know that they cannot rule themselves. Yet the greatest power is at the command of the man who has penetrated to his inmost depth. There are men of giant intellects who spend their lives gathering knowledge about many things. Ask these men, if they have solved the mystery of man, if they have conquered themselves, and they will hang their heads in shame. What is the use of knowing about everything else when you do not know who you are? Men avoid this enquiry into the true self, but what else is there so worthy to be undertaken?'[4]

[1]Aristoxenus Tarentinus vita Socrates, Frag. 31 in Miller, *Fragmenta Historicorum Graecorum*, II, p. 281. cf. Heras, *Mystic Teachings of the Haridasas of Karnatak*, Introduction, pp. xxxii-xxxiii.

[2]*Bṛhad. Up.*, I. 4. 7: Sarvasya yadayamātmānen hyetatsarvaṁ veda *Chand. Up.*, III. 14. 1-4; Sarvaṁ khalu idam brahmā ātma antar hṛdaye tad brahmā.

[3]Brunton, *A Search in Secret India*, p. 146.

[4]ibid, p. 160.

The Maharṣi points out that the realization of truth is the same for all. Unless and until a man embarks upon this quest of the true self, doubt and uncertainty will follow his footsteps throughout life. The Maharṣi shows the way out to achieve 'happiness untainted with sorrow.' His message is:

'The true self is imperishable; therefore, when a man finds it, he finds a happiness which does not come to an end...know first that 'I' and then you shall know the truth.' 'To know all except the knower is but ignorance.'[1]

The Greek accounts of Alexander's invasion reveal that the Greeks were very much impressed by the Indian ascetics whom they first saw at Takṣaśilā. Alexander was after them out of curiosity which they won't respect. As they did not care themselves to come to see Alexander, he sent to them his friend, Onesikritus, who reports that he saw fifteen ascetics about ten miles from the city, given to meditation in the sun. When told that the Yavana king was anxious to learn their wisdom, one of them bluntly answered that 'no one coming in the bravery of European clothes (cavalry cloak and broad-brimmed hat and top-boots, such as the Macedonians wore) could learn their wisdom. To do that, he must strip himself naked and learn to sit on the hot stones beside them.' (Strabo, XV. II. 63).

Aristobulus in his book states that 'he saw at Takṣaśilā two of these ascetics, one with a shaven head and the other with long hair, while both had their groups of disciples. When they went to the market place, crowds flocked to them for counsel. They had the privilege of taking without payment whatever they wanted that was offered for sale.'[2]

The leader of these ascetics is named by the Greeks Dandamis (Daṇḍī-svāmi)? who didn't even care to see Alexander on pain of death and sent his reply in a singularly spiritual vein as follows: 'God alone is the object of my homage. Alexander is not God since he must taste of death. I have no fear or favour to ask. What Alexander can offer is utterly useless. The things that I prize are these leaves which are my house, these blooming plants which supply me dainty food. Having nothing which requires guarding, I have tranquil slumber, whereas had I gold to guard, that would banish sleep. The Brāhmans neither love gold nor fear death.

[1]Brunton, *A Search in Secret India*, pp. 146-158.
[2]ibid, XV. II. 61.

Death means that one will be delivered from his ill-assorted companion, the body.' (Megasthenes. Frags. LIV, LV).

These words were characteristic of the higher mind of India and gave expression to its innate spirituality which considered material splendour and worldly pleasures as subordinate to the spiritual. The Saṁnyāsi gave up everything and sought only God. The ascetic Dandamis emerges out of his conversation with Alexander's men as an ambassador of ancient India's spiritual wisdom. It is recorded that when Alexander heard the curt and pithy remarks of this sage, he wished the more to see such a man, because he 'who had subdued many nations was overcome by an old naked ascetic.'[1]

The Greek historians in their references to Indian philosophy confined themselves to asceticism alone. Megasthenes mentions two kinds of ascetics—*Brachmanes* and *Garmanes* (Frag. XLI). Strabo also refers to them (XV. 1.59). The Brachmanes as is clear must be Brāhmins while Garmanes, are *Śramaṇa* or *Samaṇa* who are mentioned as *Samaṇa-Brāhmaṇa* by Aśoka in his inscriptions (RE. III and XIII) as people worthy of respect from all classes.

The term Śramaṇa as used by Megasthenes was then most probably a general term for all ascetics—the casteless, homeless, wandering group of religious men, as is evident from the Aśokan inscriptions. The compound expression *Śramaṇa-Brāhmaṇa* used therein denotes the two different representatives of intellectual and spiritual life in those times—the Brāhmins and the *Śramaṇas*.[2] They formed together in ancient India What Radhakrishnan says that 'natural elite,' which better than all the rest represents the soul of the entire people, its great ideals, its strong emotions and its essential tendency and to which the whole community looks as their example.'[3]

Megasthenes described the Brāhmins of the times who were small in number and first in rank and he calls them philosophers. The period of studentship is counted for 37 years. As householders they live in ease and security, decked in muslin. They eat meat but not that of animals employed in labour. (Frag. 59) They resided in a grove in front of the city within a moderate sized enclosure. They lived in simple style and lay on pallots of straw and deer skins. They abstained from sexual pleasure and occupied their time in

[1]McCrindle, op. cit., p. 129.
[2]Patañjali, II. 4. 12-Yeśāṁ ca virodha ity asya avakāśaḥ.
[3]*Hindu View of Life*, p. 92.

listening to discourse and instructing willing hearers. The Brāhmins did not practise asceticism for life but to a certain period after which they entered into worldly life and married, but they took care not to communicate the knowledge of philosophy to their wives lest they should desert them (Frag. XLI).

As to Sarmanes (*Śramaṇas*) those who were held in most honour were Hylobioi or forest-dwellers (*vānaprasthas*). They subsisted on leaves and wild fruits, wore garments from the bark of trees and abstained from wine and contact with women. They practised asceticism at greater length and underwent active toil by enduring physical suffering. They remained motionless for the whole day in one posture. This strict penance was also mentioned by Aristobolus (Strabo, XV.1.61) and Onesikritus (Strabo, XV.1.63).

Besides the *Brāhmaṇas* and *Śramaṇas*, Strabo mentions a third class of philosophers whom he calls the Pramnai (Prāmānikās)?[1] who were 'fond of arguments and ridiculed the Brāhmins who studied Physiology and Astronomy as fools and imposters.' (XV. 1.70).

A fourth class of philosophers was called Gymnetai who were naked ascetics and lived generally in the open air practising endurance for 37 years. (Strabo, XV.1-70). The reference probably pertains to the *Acelakas* or the Jaina monks who used to remain naked. The Greeks called them 'Gymnosophists,' the naked philosophers.

Arrian mentions the singular fact that 'the sophists (or philosophers) could be from any caste.' This suggests that the life of a *saṁnyāsi* was open to all castes and that there was no caste in the life spiritual. However, there are two opposite views on the subject: One holds that it was the privilege of the Brāhmins and second, that it was extended to the twice born (*dvijas*).[2] As far as the *Smṛti* texts are concerned, a *Śūdra* could not become a *Saṁnyāsin*. The medieval works fully support this view.[3]

Strabo narrates the story of an embassy sent by Porus to the court of Alexander. 'With this embassy,' he says, 'There was one who burnt himself at Athens, what some say they do in hard

[1]Mookerji identifies these *Pramnai* with *Pramanikas*. *Ancient India*, p. 157, but in the context *Sramanai* suits better. cf. Dutt, *EBM*., p. 98.

[2]Kane has summarised these views: *HDS*., II, pt. II, pp. 942-44.

[3]*Mbh*., XII, 63, 11-14, XIII. 27, *Ram*., VII. 76. 1-8, 75, 25. Also Kane, ibid, p. 944.

circumstances as he had done...for according to the customs of the country, to avoid evil circumstances, to get relief from anxieties and sufferings from a mundane existence, went to the pyre laughing, nude and annointed. He leaped into the fire and perished.' The following words were inscribed on his sepulchre, 'Here lies Zarmanes Xeganam, an Indian from Bargyaza,[1] according to the custom of the country of the Indians.' (Strabo, XV.1.73) Artemidorous, the Greek traveller and Geographer (100 BC) and author of the *Periplus of the Erythraean Sea* also makes a reference to this event.

Now the name *Zarmanes*—Śramaṇa referred to by Strabo in this passage leads us to believe that the monk was either a *Buddhist* or a *Jaina*. But it seems clear that the monk mentioned must not have been a Buddhist. Firstly, because suicide chiefly by burning is against the tenets of Buddhism. Secondly, he is said to have been *nude*, a practice which is not followed by the Buddhists. In all probability, therefore, the reference is meant to indicate a Digamber Jaina, the word *Śramaṇa* being used alike by the Buddhists as well as the Jainas. It may be noted that religious suicide was common among the Jainas.[2] According to Strabo (XV.1), Alexander invited Kalanos as a guest to his court, where he fell ill at Pasargade and decided on death on a pyre erected by his own wish, despite the opposition of the king. In spite of a certain interest evinced by Alexander in the Indian Gymnosophists, it is surprising that we have no records of any intellectual discourse he might have had with Kalanos during the latter's stay for several years at the court upto the time of his self-immolation.

According to Arrian (Frag. XI of *Indika*), the sophists akin to the philosophers of Megasthenes held the supreme place of dignity and honour. They were under no necessity of doing any bodily labour or of contributing from their own produce. No other work was required of them except to offer sacrifice to the gods on behalf of the state. The fact that women were allowed to associate themselves with the men as ascetics was also noted by Nearchus (Frag. 7) and Strabo (XV.C.716). The practice, however, is forbidden in the *Arthaśāstra*.[3]

It is interesting to note that Megasthenes (Strabo, XV.1.59) had

[1]Baryagaza has been identified with modern Broach in Gujarat, suggesting a commercial link between India and the outside world.

[2]cf. Chapter 7, on Jainism.

[3]*BK.*, II. 1. 48.

noted that Brāhmanas even from the time of conception, were under the care of learned men and lived for 37 years as philosophers before becoming householders. But he says nothing of the distinctive teachings of the *Sarmanes* or *Śramanas*. Their most distinguished members were the Hylobioi (*Vānaprastha*), the forest-dwellers who lived on the bark of trees. (Frag. XLI) Megasthenes apparently fails to distinguish Brāhminism from Buddhism, as this was not a Buddhist practice. His description that 'they lived in the forests on leaves of trees and wild fruits and wore garments made from the bark of the trees, and that they abstained from sexual intercourse and wine (Frag. 60) applies to the *Naishṭhika Brahmacārīs*, those who prefer to remain as students through life without marrying. The *Naiṣṭhika Brahmacarya* was a fairly ancient institution and a form of asceticism earliest known and practised. References to this ideal being followed are afforded by the accounts of Hieun Tsang[1] and Yuan Chwang.[2] This indicates that the rate of *Naiṣṭhika Brahmacārīs* who devoted themselves to lifelong studentship and celibacy in quest of learning and the truth was not extinct in India even in the seventh century AD.

Of these Sages of the forest or *Vānaprasthas*, Megasthenes writes: 'these ascetics were indifferent to the good or evil that happens to man; that all being, in their opinion is dreamlike illusion; that they regard the world as created and perishable; and believe that God who has created it pervades it completely.' (Frag. XLI.59): This seems to be quite a good description of the pantheism of the Upaniṣads.

It is also to be considered that the Indians did not take very seriously Alexander's campaign in a land so far from his own. A representative Indian, a detached ascetic Kalanos by name, gave expression to the Indian attitude towards Alexander's invasion by a homely illustration. He trod on a piece of dried up hide of which, as he pressed on one end, the other ends would fly up. This was intended to show that Alexander should control his empire from its centre and not wander away to its distant extremities, and that it was futile that he should waste his energies in his campaigns in regions so remote from the centre of his own empire.[3]

[1] Mookerji, *Education in Ancient India*, p. 506.
[2] Altekar, *Education in Ancient India*, pp. 114-115.
[3] cf. Mookerji, op. cit., p. 134.

There is another version of the story as reported by Arrian (VII.1.6).

It is reported that when these ascetics saw Alexander and his army, they said nothing but stamped the ground with their feet. When Alexander's interpreter asked what this action meant they replied:

'O King Alexander, each man possesses just so much of the earth as this on which we stand. You being a man like other men, save that you are full of activity and relentless are roaming over all this earth from your home, troubled yourself and troubling others. But not so long hence you will die and will possess just so much of the earth as suffices for your burial.'[1]

The reply brings out vividly the mortality of men and even empires. It proved prophetic particularly in the case of Alexander with reference to India. His campaign was just an episode to be obliterated with the cruel passage of time. Even the last vestige of his campaign was wiped out!

Summing up, it can be stated that the Greek and Roman accounts indicate the antiquity of the beliefs and practices of the ascetics of ancient India. But the Greek writers failed to notice the distinction between Brāhmanism, Buddhism and Jainism. They, of course, were attracted by certain practices which the ascetics observed. Alexander's experience of these ascetics reveal their great power of self-torture, self-denial and their deeper wisdom.

Summing Up

The various restrictions and conditions to embracing asceticism in respect of both the sexes clearly show that the *Arthaśāstra* looks upon the ascetic institution with disfavour. It also reflects the social mind, which is fully aware of the anti-social and disintegrating influence of asceticism especially on the realisation and protection of the *Artha* ideal of the society. It views *Dharma* and *Mokṣa* as worthy ideals but not before the due claims of both *Artha* and *Kāma* are satisfied. Thus asceticism ignores these latter claims is disapproved. Which also explains why *Gṛhasthāśrama* is given the first preference.

The lax social discipline consequent upon the pessimistic teachings of some of the *Parivrājaka* teachers had a disastrous effect on

[1]cf. Barr, *The Will of Zeus*, p. 430.

the society. Men left their wives and children. Wives left the protection of their husbands. Marriage was looked upon as a burden. As a result, poverty and indigence became greater. The state was confronted with the problem of maintaining the destitute and hence the Mauryan rulers interfered with the activity of the monastic orders. Indiscriminate mendicancy was forbidden and men were punished for leaving wives and children destitute with a view to join the order or seducing women into ascetic types of living. The state made stringent laws preventing men from joining orders without providing for their families. The monastic propaganda was excluded from villages. The state was empowered by circumstances to interfere even in religious matters. Hence thinking in terms of the state and its ends, Kautilya conceived the policy as the framework within which the individual found fulfilment and all institutions had their justification. He valued asceticism primarily for its usefulness in espionage and intelligence activities.

It was during this period that India was invaded by Alexander. Some of the Greeks who had accompanied him actually met some Indian ascetics of the time. The impressions recorded by these Greek writers throw much light on the strange practices and beliefs of the ascetics of ancient India. These accounts also bear ample testimony to the ascetics,' great power of self-torture, self-denial and their deeper wisdom.

Chapter 10

Asceticism in the Law Books

In the whole range of Sanskrit literature, *Dharma* is one of the few words with a comprehensive meaning. It is a word that means variously: Sacred law, duty, justice and religious merit.[1] It meant law in a broad sense. In ordinary usage it has a wider meaning as it includes the customs and practices of any caste and community. Hence the special manuals of the sacred law are called *Dharma Śāstras* or law books; they fall under the category of Smṛti literature i.e. traditional records. These law-books have governed and moulded the life and evolution of the Hindu community from age to age.

The earliest of the law-givers, Gautama declared the Vedas as the source of *Dharma*.[2] So did Baudhāyana and Āpastamba. But Manu made a departure and mentioned the Vedas as one of the sources of *Dharma*. Veda is the first source, tradition is the second and usages of virtuous men, the third source.[3] Yājñavalkya agreed with Manu,[4] but stressed on the secular aspect of law. No distinction was made between the two in early codes; every action of human life was clothed with some religious aspect. Hence from cradle to the grave, the life of man was a series of religious duties.

Manifold are the subjects that have been included in the *Dharma-śāstras*. The *Dharma-sūtras* of Gautama, Baudhāyana, Āpastamba and Vasiṣṭha and the law book of Manu deal with subjects[5] pertaining to man's whole life. As their very name suggests, their main emphasis is on *Dharma*. By *Dharma*, the writers of law books meant: 'Not a creed or religion but a mode of life or a code of conduct, which regulated a man's work and activities, as a member of society and as an individual and was intended to bring about the

[1]Shakuntala Rao Shāstri, *Women in the Sacred Laws*, p. 13.

[2]*Gaut.*, 1. 1. 2.

[3]*Manu.*, 11. 6 Vedokhilo dharmamūlaṁ smṛti śileca tadvidaṁ ācāraiścaiva sadhunāṁ ātmanas tuśtirva ca: *Manu.*, II. 6.

[4]*Yaj.*, I. 7.

[5]Kane, enumerates the list of subjects in *HDS.*, II, Pt. I, p. 1-2.

gradual development of a man and to enable him to reach what was deemed to be the goal of human existence.'[1] *Dharma* stood for right conduct and denoted any act which could give heavenly bliss and ultimate liberation to the human soul. It thus required a man to cultivate certain moral qualities on an individual level and as a member of society.

The basis for cultivating these qualities is found in the doctrine of the goals or ends of human existence (*puruṣārtha*). From very ancient times they are said to be four: *dharma*, *artha* (economic interests), *kāma* (satisfaction of sexual, emotional and artistic life), and *mokṣa* (liberation of the spirit).[2] The last is said to be the supreme end and the most valuable. It presupposes a higher life which demands discipline both of the body and mind. The whole teaching of *Dharmaśāstras* points out that all higher life requires the subjection of lower aims to aims of higher life.[3] Mokṣa, therefore, becomes an end to be attained only by the few and the vast majority can only place it as an ideal to be attained in the most distant future.

We have already seen that the society in the Epic period was based upon the *varṇāśramadharma*. The *varṇas* deal with the problem of social grades based upon birth and occupation, while the *āśramas* refer to the four consecutive stages of life viz. *Brahmacarya* (studentship), *Gārhasthya* (family life), *Vānaprastha* (forest hermit) and *Saṁnyāsa* (renunciation). The list of subjects under the *Dharmaśāstras* also reveal that the society at that time was based upon the *varṇāśramadharma* and that the four *āśramas* were recognised though there was a slight difference in the nomenclature and in their sequence.

Āśramas

According to Āpastamba, there are four *āśramas*: the stage of householder (*gārhasthya*), (studying in) the teacher's house (*ācaryakulaṁ*), stage of being a *muni* (*maunaṁ*) and that of being a forest-dweller (*vānaprastha*).[4] That here *mauna* stands for the *āśrama* of *Saṁnyāsa* is clear from Āpastamba's words: *atha parivrajakaḥ*

[1]Kane, enumerates the list of subjects in *HDS.*, II, Pt. I, p. 3.
[2]*Mbh.*, V. 124, 34-38.
[3]Kane, ibid, p. 7.
[4]*Ap.*, II. 9. 21. 1. also q.b. Sankara on *Vedāntasūtra*, III, 4. 47.

where he employs the word *parivrāj* to indicate *mauna*.[1] Āpastamba places the householder's stage first among *āśramas* probably on account of the importance of that stage to all other *āśramas*. Why he should mention the stage of *vānaprastha* last is not clear. The reason seems to be, as we shall see in the sequel, that the difference between the last two orders was very slight and almost a technical one.

Gautama enumerates the four *āśramas* thus: *Brahmacarya*, *Gṛhasthya*, *Bhikṣu* and *Vaikhānasa*.[2] *Vaikhānasa* stands for *Vanaprastha*. Here also Gautama speaks of *Bhikṣu* before *Vaikhānasa* as done by Āpastamba and Hardatta[3] explains this departure from the usual sequence of āśrama as due to the words: *prāg-uttamād traya āśraminaḥ*.[4] (persons belonging to the three āśramas) except the last may constitute a *pariṣad* i.e. to exclude Vaikhānasa from the *pariṣad*, he is mentioned last. Traditionally, the stage of *Bhikṣu*, one who begs for his livelihood, comes last after *Vānaprastha*.

According to Vasiṣṭha the four *āśramas* are those of: *Brahmacāri*, *Gṛhastha*, *Vānaprastha* and *Parivrājaka*.[5] He also employs the word *Yati* to denote a person in the fourth āśrama.[6]

Baudhāyana names the four *āśramas* in the same order as Vasiṣṭha[7] and gives the interesting information that *asura* Kapila, son of Prahlāda, who was in rivalry with the gods, made the distinctions which a wise man should pay no heed.[8] What Baudhāyana means appears to be that there is really one *āśrama* namely that of the householder and that Kapila devised the scheme of four āśramas so that those who become *vānaprasthas* and *pativrājakas* would perform no *yajñas* and thereby the gods would lose the offerings they received from men and become less powerful. It is clear that Baudhāyana prefers the stage of *Gṛhastha* to those of *Vānaprastha* and *Parivrājaka*.

The theory of Manu[9] about the four *āśramas* takes into view the ascending order of the four stages, with *Saṁnyāsa* as the last. He

[1] *Ap.*, II. 9. 21. 7.
[2] *Gaut.*, III. 2.
[3] Hardatta on *Gaut.*, III. 2.
[4] *Gaut.*, 28. 47.
[5] *Vas.*, VII. 1-2.
[6] ibid, XI. 34.
[7] *Baudh.*, II. 6. 17.
[8] ibid, II. 6. 29-31.
[9] *Manu.*, IV. 1, V. 169; VI. 1-2, VI. 33.

takes the span of human life as one hundred years (*śatāyur vai puruṣaḥ*). The first part of man's life is *brahmacarya* in which he learns at his teacher's place and after he has finished his study, in the second part of his life he marries and becomes a *gṛhastha*, discharges his debts to his ancestors by begetting sons and to the gods by performing *yajñas*. When he sees that his head has grey hair and that there are wrinkles on his body he retires to the forest. He becomes a *vānaprastha*. After spending the third part of his life in the forest for sometime he spends the rest of his life as a *saṁnyāsi*. Similar rules are found in many other *Smṛitis*.

Manu speaks of the four āśramas,[1] the last being called *Yati* by him and also *Saṁnyāsa*.[2] It would thus be seen that a person who belongs to the last *āśrama* is variously called *parivrāt* or *parivrājaka*, (one who wanders from place to place), *bhikṣu* (one who begs for livelihood), *muni* (one who ponders over the mysteries of life and death), or *yati* (one who controls his senses). These words suggest the various traits of the man who undertakes the fourth *āśrama*. According to Manu, only Brāhmans were entitled to enter the fourth *āśrama* of *Saṁnyāsa*,[3] as a rule. There is a clear evidence to this in *Vaikhānasadharmapraśna*[4] which follows Manu and says: The Brahmaṇas have four *āśramas*, the Kṣatriyas three and the Vaiśyas only two. The Śūdras were only entitled to *Gṛhasthāśrama*. However it appears that the privilege of embracing *Saṁnyāsa* was extended to the twice-born in the times of *Smṛitis*.[5] The salient features and duties of ascetics are set out by the law-givers.[6]

Vaikhānasa

Vaikhānasa means *Vānaprastha* in the Sūtras.[7] Hence the employment of the word *Vaikhānasa* for *Vānaprastha* by the law books needs some explanation.

In the *Anukramaṇi* one hundred *Vaikhānas* are said to have been

[1] *Manu.*, VI. 87.
[2] ibid, VI. 96.
[3] ibid, VI. 97.
[4] I. 10-13, IX. 8: Brāhmansyāśramaşcatvāraḥ Kşatriyādyatrayaḥ Vaiśyadau tadāśraminşcatvāro Bŗahmacārī, Gṛhastha Vānapŗastho Bhikşu iti.
[5] *Manu.*, V. 137; VI. 87.
[6] *Gaut.*, III. 10-24; *Ap.*, III. 9. 21, 7-20; *Baudh.*, II. 6. 21-27; II. 10. 18, 1.27; *Vas.*, IX. 12. 1-19; *Manu.*, VI. 33-86; *Yaj.*, III. 56-66; *Vaikh.*, IX. 9; *Visnu.*, 96.
[7] Kane, op. cit., p. 418.

the seers of the Ṛgveda.[1] Especially a Vāmra Vaikhānasa is specifically mentioned as a seer.[2] The *Taittirīya Āraṇyaka* connects the word *Vaikhānasa* with the nails (*nakhas*) of *Prajāpati.*[3] It appears that in ancient times there was some work called *Vaikhānasaśāstra* which treated of the rules of forest hermits. Gautama uses this word *Vaikhānasa* for *Vānaprastha*. Baudhāyana defines a *Vānaprastha* as one who follows the practices laid down in *Vaikhānasaśāstra.*[4] Manu describes the *Vānaprastha* as abiding by the views (*mata*) of *Vaikhānasa*. Medhatithi explains that *Vaikhānasa* is a *śāstra* in which the duties of the forest hermit are expounded.[5] We have already met the *Vaikhānasa* as forest-hermits in the epic period.[6] It thus appears that the two words *Vaikhānsa* and *Vānaprastha* were identical.

Characteristics of the last Two Āśramas

We have seen that though Vasiṣṭha and Baudhāyana follow the traditional sequence of the *āśramas*, Gautama and Āpastamba make a slight change in the the sequence. They have mentioned *Mauna* or *Parivrājya* after studentship and family life and then the hermit life.[7] This does not necessarily mean than the *Āśrama* sequence was not settled in the society. The peculiar enumeration is due to the fact that there is a great similarity between the characteristics of the last two āśramas as analysed below.

	Vānaprastha	*Parivrājaka* or *Bhikṣu*
(1)	He was a Dvijāti, who had undergone the Upanayana ceremony.	He was a Dvijāti, who had undergone the Upanayana ceremony.
(2)	He lived in the forest and was not allowed to come to the village.[8] He would	He used to wander from place to place and was not allowed to stay in a village for more

[1] *ṚV.*, IX. 66.
[2] *ṚV.*, X. 99.
[3] *TA.*, I. 23.
[4] *Baudh., Dh. S.*, II. 6. 19.
[5] *Manu*. (VI-21), refers to the institutes of Vaikhānasas when he prescribes rules for hermits of the forest. Medhatithi comments: vaikhānasaṁ nāma sāśtraṁ yatravānapṛastha dharmāvihitasteṣāṁ mate sthitaḥ.
[6] cf. Chapter 8 *Mbh.*, and *Ram.*
[7] *Gaut.*, I. 3.2. *Ap.*, I. 9. 21. 1.
[8] *Gaut.*, I. 3. 26, 33; *Vas.*, IX. 2; *Ap.*, II. 9. 22. 1. 8. 9; *Baudh.*, II. 6. 11. 15.

stay there alone or in the company of his wife.[2]

than two nights,[1] only in the rains he was allowed to stay in one place,[3] on the outskirts of a village, in a temple, in a deserted house or under a tree. Usually his abode was the forest.[4]

(3) He used to practice penance and was celibate.[5]

He was celibate and used to stay alone[6] and had no possession.[7]

(4) He used to eat only fruit and roots[8] and meat.[9]

He used to eat food procured by begging.[10]

(5) He used to grow his hair (*Jatila*).[12]

Usually he was clean shaved[11] but some law-givers allowed him an option to grow his hair.[13]

(6) He used to wear bark garments or the antelope-skin.[14]

He either used to wear a cast out rug just sufficient to cover his lower limbs or[15] he could even dispense with clothing.[16]

(7) He used to worship Agni.[17]

He did not worship Agni but spent his time in meditation.[18]

(8) He was a worshipper of the gods, Pitṛs, supernatural beings and particularly

He was absolved from making offerings to gods or men, and discontinued performance of all

[1]*Gaut*., I. 3. 21; *Ap*., II. 9. 21, 10; *Vas*., X 2. 12; *Baudh*., II. 6. 11. 17.
[2]*Ap*., II. 9. 22; *Baudh*., II. 6. 11. 15.
[3]*Gaut* , I. 3. 13; *Baudh*., II 12. 11. 20.
[4]*Vas*., X. 15; *Baudh*., II. 6. 11. 17.
[5]*Gaut*., I. 3 26; *Vas*., IX 6; *Ap*., II. 9. 21. 19; *Baudh*., II. 6. 11. 15.
[6]*Gaut*., I. 3. 12; *Vas*., X. 28; *Ap*., II. 9. 21. 8; *Baudh*., II. 6. 11. 16.
[7]*Gaut*., I. 3. 11; *Vas*., X. 6.
[8]*Gaut*., I. 3. 26; *Vas*., IX 4; *Ap*., II. 9. 22. 10; *Baudh*., II. 6. 11. 15.
[9]*Gaut*., I 3. 31; *Baudh*., II. 6, 11, 15.
[10]*Gaut*., I. 3. 14; *Vas*., X. 5. 6; *Ap*., II. 9. 21. 10.
[11]*Gaut*., I. 3. 34; *Vas*., IX. 1; *Baudh*., II. 6. 11. 15.
[12]*Vas*., X. 6.
[13]*Gaut*., I. 3. 22; *Baudh*., II. 6. 11. 18.
[14]*Gaut*., I. 3. 34; *Vas*., IX. 1; *Baudh*., II. 6. 11. 15.
[15]*Gaut*., I. 3. 18. 19; *Vas*., X. 9; *Baudh*., II. 6. 11. 19.
[16]*Ap*., II. 9. 21. 11-12.
[17]*Gaut*., I. 3. 27; *Vas*., IX. 10; *Ap*. II. 9. 22. 7-8. 12-21; *Baudh*., II. 6. 11. 15.
[18]*Vas*., X. 5. 14; *Ap*., II. 9. 21. 10.

the guests,[1] because he could only give and not receive.[3]	ceremonial observances.[2]
(9) He took only sixteen monthfuls of food while eating.[5]	He took only eight mouthfuls of food while eating.[4] Some say that he used to wear (*Yajñopavīta*) the sacred thread.[6] Some are of opinion that he should beg only at seven houses, avoiding the food given by a Sūdra.[7] He used to sleep on a stone-slab.[8] The majority opined that he should give up the Vedas.[9]

It will be noticed from the above that the duties and regulations prescribed for the third *āśrama* of *Vānaprastha* are practically the same as those for the last *āśrama* of *Saṁnyāsin*, *Parivrājaka* or *Bhikṣu*. For example, the rules laid down in Manu for foresthermits (*vānaprastha*) are almost the same as those for *Parivrājakas*.[10] *Āpastamba* employs the same words twice in delineating the characteristics of both.[11] The order of hermits gradually passes over into that of *Saṁnyāsins*. Both have to observe celibacy and restraint of senses, both have to regulate the intake and quality of food, both have to contemplate on the passages of the Upaniṣads and strive for the knowledge of Brāhman. There were no doubt some differences. The *Vānaprastha* could be accompanied by his wife at least in the beginning. A *Saṁnyāsīn* could not do so. A *Vānaprastha* had to keep fires, perform the daily and other *Yajñas* at least in the

[1] *Gaut.*, I. 3. 29-30; *Vas.* IX. 7; *Baudh.*, II. 6. 11. 15.
[2] *Vas.*, IX. 8; *Ap.*, II. 9. 22. 11.
[3] *Ap.*, II. 21. 11.
[4] *Vas.*, VI. 29; *Ap.*, II. 4. 9. 13.
[5] *Vas.*, VI. 29; *Ap.*, II. 4. 9. 13.
[6] *Vas.*, X. 31.
[7] *Vas.*, X. 7. 31.
[8] ibid, X. 11.
[9] *Ap.*, II. 9. 21, 13; *Baudh.*, II. 6. 11. 26.
[10] Vasiṣṭha says he must not give up studying the Veda because by doing so he will be reckoned as a Ṣūdra (X. 4); Gautama does not say anything either way.
[11] *Manu.*, VI. 25-29; VI. 38, 43, 44. *Ap.*, II. 9. 21. 10 and 20.

beginning; whereas the *Saṁnyāsin* gave up his fires. The *Vānaprastha* had to concentrate upon *tapas*, upon inuring himself to privations, severe austerities and self-mortification while the *Saṁnyāsin* was concerned primarily with *saṅyama* (restraint or quienscence of senses) and contemplation of the highest Reality.[1] Owing to the great similarity and virtual fusion of the two āśramas, the stage of *Vānaprastha* came to be gradually ignored and passed from the householder's life directly to the life of *Saṁnyāsa*.[2] The *Dharmasūtras* bear the impress of this process as can be seen in the remarks of a commentator on Baudhāyana when he says that the *ācārya* (Bāudhayana) should be asked why he describes the two orders of *Vānaprastha* and *Saṁnyāsa* as distinct.[3]

When we talk of the four *āśramas* it is to be borne in mind that the scheme represented the ideal rather than the real. Its chief merit lay in the fact that it tells an individual what his spiritual goal is, how he is to order his life and what preparations are required to attain that goal. But the cycle was not obligatory at all. The great majority never went beyond the two first stages; many passed away in the *vānprastha* stage. Only the rare few made the last extreme venture and took to the life of the wandering recluse. The writers of the law books were ever conscious of this fact as we find that on the whole their tendency is to glorify the status of a *Gṛhastha* and push into the background the two *āśramas* of *Vānaprastha* and *Saṁnyāsa*. They realised that for the majority, *Gṛhasthāśrama* was proper and desirable, and was a natural stage of life. Hence they exalt *Gṛhasthāśrama* in no uncertain terms.

Gṛhasthāśrama Praised

Gautama[4] and Baudhāyana[5] state that there is really one āśrama—that of a *Gṛhastha* and that the other āśramas are inferior to it. To quote a passage from Gautama[6]: 'But the venerable teacher (*Ācāryaḥ*) prescribes one order only, because the order of the householder is explicitly prescribed in the Vedas.' Baudhāyana

[1]Sankara, *Vedantasūtra*, III. 4. 20.

[2]Kane., op. cit., II. pt. I, p. 929.

[3]Govindaswami on *Baudh.*, III. 3. 14-17: Vānaprasthasaṁnyāsabhedaḥ kirmarthamacāryakṛta ityasāveva praṣtavyaḥ.

[4]*Gaut.*, III. 1. & 35.

[5]*Baudh.*, II. 6. 29ff.

[6]*Gaut.*, II. 36.

says that *āśramas* other than *gṛhasthāśrama* do not beget offspring and quotes Vedic passages[1] in support: 'May we, O Agni, attain immortality through progeny!' And further: 'A Brāhmaṇa when born is born involved in three debts viz. he owes *brahmacarya* to the sages, sacrifice to the gods and progeny to the *pitṛs*.' Baudhāyana categorically asserts that the various ascetic orders were created by asura king Kapila and a brāhmaṇa on being born owes the debt of a son to his ancestors. Baudhāyana obviously does not favour asceticism as according to him the obligations of a domestic life and to the society can only be properly discharged in *gṛhasthāśrama*. It is the source of other *āśramas*.[2] He considers *Saṁnyasa* as violating Vedic injunctions and assigns its non-Āryan origin to Kapila.

The *Gṛhasthāśrama* not only is upheld as the source of other *āśramas* but it is also the highest *āśramas*. Says Manu: 'As all creatures depend upon air for life, so do the men of all other *āśramas* depend on the householder. The state of the householder is the highest, as it is the householder who maintains the people of the three other *āśramas* by daily supply of food and instruction.'[3] A similar view is expressed by Vasiṣṭha: 'It is the householder who offers sacrifice, it is he who practices austerities; so the state of the householder excels among the four *āśramas*. As all streams and rivers seek shelter in the sea, so the people of all *āśramas* seek shelter with the householder. As all creatures need the mother's protection for their life, so all almsmen live under the householder's protection.'[4] Vasiṣṭha does not stop here by assigning the *gṛhasthāśrama* the highest place amongst the four *āśramas* but makes it the place from which one can reach even heaven. He further says: 'The Brāhmaṇa who bathes daily, has his sacred thread on him always, studies the Vedas every day, does not accept food from degraded people, has intercourse with his wife according to season, offers sacrifice according to the prescribed rites, does not miss heaven.'[5] He seems to suggest that when one can reach heaven through *Gṛhasthāśrama*, one need not take to *Saṁnyāsa*. His partiality to *Gṛhasthāśrama* can only be understood in this light. Later on Viṣṇu echoes a similar view: 'It is the householder who

[1] *Baudh.*, II. 6. 2. 29ff; *ṚV.*, V. 4. 10; *Tatt. Sam.*, I. 4. 46. 1; VI. 3. 10. 5.
[2] *Baudh.*, III. 3.
[3] *Manu.*, III. 77.80; VI. 87, 89, 90.
[4] *Vas.*, VIII. 14-16.
[5] ibid, VIII. XVII. 17.

offers sacrifice, it is he who practices austerities, it is he who gives, therefore the man in the state of the householder is the highest of all. The Ṛṣis, the elders, the gods, other creatures, guests and kindred are protected by him and so the householder is the highest.'[1]

From the above it can be seen that though the law givers prescribe certain rules and regulations about the four *āśramas* including the *Vānaprastha* and *Saṁnyāsa*, they praise the *Gṛhasthāśrama* as the highest. It is so excellent so as to lead one even to heaven.

Controversy over Renunciation

Amongst the law givers, it is Baudhāyana who depicts a detailed procedure of becoming a *Saṁnyāsin.*[2] The central ideas of the ceremony are the renunciation of all worldly ties, contempt of the world and all earthly riches, a life of *ahiṁsā* and contemplation on and realisation of the Absolute Brahman. It is of particular interest that he is hesitant to recommend renunciation. He states his own opinion that the sages prescribe *Saṁnyāsa* after the 70th year.[3] According to him it was the asura Kapila who in his rivalry with the gods, made these distinctions to which 'a wise man should pay no heed.'[4] This indicates that he did not favour renunciation as in his view there was only one *āśrama*, that of the householder.

Manu lays a particular emphasis that a man should pass through each and all the four stages and that he should become a forest-hermit only after completing the householder's life.[5] *Jābāla Upaniṣad* laid down that even from the *Brahmacarya stage*, one could become a *Vānaprastha.*[6] But according to *Vedāntasūtra*, a man cannot take *Saṁnyāsa* immediately after *Brahmacarya.*[7] Manu is the prime supporter of this view.[8] He says: 'When the householder notices his wrinkles and greyness and sees his child's child, then he should retire to the forest.'[9] The reason behind such an injunction

[1] *Viśnu*, lix. 28-29.
[2] *Baudh.*, II. 10. 11-30; cf. *Vaikh. Dh.*, IX. 6.8; For summary see Kane, op. cit., pp. 954-961.
[3] *Baudh*, II. 10. 5.
[4] ibid, II. 6. 29-31.
[5] *Manu.*, VI. 1.
[6] *Jabalopaniṣad*, 4.
[7] III. 4. 40.
[8] *Manu.*, IV. 1; VI. 1. 33-37, 87.88.
[9] ibid, VI. 2.

was that the person who was entitled to the life of the *Vānaprastha* was only one who had abandoned all longing for the objects of sense. It is not easy to tear oneself away from the family, when once one has entered it. He must be in a position to sever all worldly ties, give up all mundane desires. When one feels by experience that one could whole-heartedly and successfully devote oneself to spiritual pursuits, then alone one has to renounce the world completely and become a *Saṁnyāsin.* It is for this reason that Manu prescribes *Saṁnyāsa* when a son is born to one's son. If one waits till this happens in the case of the youngest son, the occasion for *Saṁnyāsa* will never arise.

A controversy also emerged on the issue whether this sequence of *āśramas* was obligatory or whether after the initial study of the Vedas, the Brahmacāri could straightway become an ascetic. The *Jābāla Upaniṣad* makes the choice optional. It says: 'When the period of Brahmacarya is ended, he becomes a *Gṛhastha*; after he has been a *Gṛhastha*, he becomes a *Vānaprastha*; after he has been a *Vānaprastha*, let him wander about as a *Parivrājaka.* Or, if in the alternative, one passes into the last stage, from *Brahmacarya*, or from *Gārhasthya*, or *Vānaprasthya* (in every case), one goes to the world of Brāhman.'[1] Gautama[2] and Vasiṣṭha[3] also concede the choice as a matter of opinion. This reflects the inroad made by the pessimistic view of life which disturbed the balance in favour of renunciation. But when Buddhism and Jainism established their orders of monks, accepting even young men, regardless of caste or creed, there was a reaction in the Brāhmanical tradition which first emphasised the sequence as obligatory and later exalted the *gṛhasth-āśrama.* Āpastamba, after examining all the views, says that, although some ascetics may gain heaven through their austerities, still this is no reason to place one order above the other.[4] Manu frowns upon any tendency to pass over *gṛhasthāśrama* in favour of a premature withdrawal from social responsibility: 'The man who seeks final liberation without having studied the Vedas, without having begotten sons, and without having performed sacrifices, sinks downwards.'[5] Manu is convinced about the most exacting

[1]*Jabala.*, 4.
[2]*Gaut.*, III. 1.
[2]*Vas.*, VII. 1. 3; II. 9. 24-15.
[4]*Ap.*, II. 9. 24. 15.
[5]*Manu.*, VI. 35-37.

discipline the *gṛhastha* has to confront.[1] He is not only against any individual skipping *gṛhasthāśrama*, he does not also think it necessary that the *gṛhastha* should retire to the forest even in his old age. He can continue to reside in his own house, under the protection of his son, practising austerities even in the thick of life and meditating on that which is good for his soul.[2]

To understand this attitude of Manu's code in trying to dissuade the *gṛhastha* from a formal renunciation of the world, we have to take note of the time when the present version of Manu's code was compiled, when Buddhism had made the order of monks more popular and more accessible to all castes of all ages and even to women. The old orthodox Brāhmanical order was restricted to the Brāhmins only. Hence the Brāhmanical legislators held up the ancient ideals with a view to stop the senseless rush to the ascetic orders, of men and women not prepared for them by a necessary course of discipline and restraint. They repeatedly insisted on the cultivation of the genuine ascetic attitude even at home, as distinguished from the formal entrance into the order. In the last analysis, it is *Dharma* which is most emphasised by them. As Vasiṣṭha says: 'Practise *Dharma* and not *Adharma*. Speak the truth and not untruth. Look far ahead, not near. Look at what is the highest, not at what is not the highest.'[3] He adds that avoiding egoism, pride, jealousy and anger is the *Dharma* of all *Āśramas* alike.[4] It will give, Manu avers, satisfaction to the inner self.[5]

It appears that Āpastamba was a rebel against the old order. About him Shakuntala Rao Shastri writes: 'Āpastamba plays the part of a reformer, discarding the old order as being unfit for the new. He considers himself a child of the Kali Age; the liberal rules of the past were suitable only for the older generation as they were gifted with superior merit. They are not fit for the degenerate public of his times and hence new rules are necessary.'[6] She then goes on to say how he frames rules to limit the freedom of women, to lessen the undue importance of a son, to discourage from remarrying to reject sons of all kinds as legal heirs to the property.

1 *Manu.*, IV. 1-8.
2 *Manu.*, IV. 257-58.
3 *Vas.*, XXX.
4 ibid, X. 30.
5 *Manu.*, IV. 1. 61.
6 op. cit., p. 49.

Against such a background we can appreciate Āpastamba's remarks that 'No ṛṣis are born in the Kali Yuga.'[1]

Altekar opines that the 'early Dharmasūtra writers regarded renunciation as a positively anti-Vedic custom'[2] and in support quotes Āpastamba. Hiriyana's[3] view is that Āpastamba[4] and Jaimini[5] contend that *Saṁnyāsa* or renunciation unlike *Gṛhasthya* or the state of a householder is no part of the normal scheme of Āryan life. In the light of the evidence quoted above from the law givers in praise of and exalting *gṛhasthāśrama*, it is difficult to disagree with the views of Altekar and Hiriyana.

We have already seen how Kautilya makes *Artha* as the predominant basis of his polity and looks upon asceticism with disfavour, regards it as anti-social and believes that it disintegrates society. The law givers by praising *gṛhasthāśrama* and exalting it, want to ensure the social basis on an equally sure foundation by making the family life strong and enduring.

Summing Up

The *Dharmasūtras* though they enumerated the rules and regulations of the four *āśramas* amongst other subjects, praised *Gṛhasthāśrama* as the most excellent and the highest *āśrama*. Not only they looked upon renunciation as an anti-Vedic custom but also regarded it outside the normal scheme of Āryan life. They emphasised that each individual was expected to pass normally through the four stages and that he should perform the duties prescribed for each of the *āśramas*. Such an attitude on the part of the law-givers arose from the conditions of the times. The aftermath of Buddhism and Jainism saw the popularity of the monastic ideal. There was an indiscriminate admission of men into the ascetic order without the natural gradation through the preceding stages. This was likely to draw into that order many undesirables who by their imperfect discipline were not yet fitted to be there. The law-givers felt that this influx of immature persons into the order of homeless wanderers would tend to produce a general deteriotion in the health of the society and disturb the economic foundation of the whole social

[1] *Ap.*, I. 2, 5, 4.
[2] *The Position of Women in Hindu Civilisation*, p. 424.
[3] *Popular Essays in Indian Philosophy*, p. 36.
[4] *Ap.*, II. IX.
[5] *Vedānta Sūtra*, III. IV. 17.

structure. They, therefore, insisted upon people passing from order to order in regular sequence, sought to press it home that the householder was the basis and support that held up the entire social frame. They sought to ensure that admission to *Saṁnyāsa* be conditioned on adequate preparation through learning and discipline. They therefore, laid down severe punishments by way of penances for those who failed to keep up the standard of purity of the three stages of *brahmacārins*, *vānaprastha* and *saṁnyāsins*. They also pointed out it was not indispensable for an individual to enter formally into the ascetic order, and that the highest realization was possible even if one stayed at home, living a detached and righteous life according to Vedic injunctions.

Chapter 11

Impact of Asceticism on Indian Civilisation

The foregoing pages reveal that asceticism was a persistent feature in the religious life and thought of ancient India. Our enquiry also indicates that through its long evolution, not only it had taken on new shades of meaning from time to time but also there were periods, which were marked by its rise and decline, favour as well as disfavour. From the analysis of the reasons of motives leading to the ascetic life, two facts stand out prominently. Firstly, asceticism was a way of life confined to the comparatively few people. The masses were never suited to it as it required a high form of mentality and conduct. Secondly, there never was a time when it was universally acclaimed in total disregard of one's social obligations. On the other hand Indian life respected a harmonious blending of religion, profession and material pleasure.

It is impertinent to state here that life to most men was not a vale of tears from which to escape at all costs. This has to be asserted with a view to assess the impact of asceticism dispassionately down the ages. For misconceptions about India as well as the inner motives or drives of its culture abound. It is a sad fact that not only the foreigners but even Indian scholars are not free from this error. Glorification of the past is another prominent characteristic of Indian writers. That Indian civilisation was great, needs no proving by anyone today. There is no necessity to proclaim from the housetops that the Indians had achieved this or that in the ancient past. And yet it is customary for some Indians to say that India has much to teach the West. The truth is that Indian thought has a great deal to teach the Indians and that they themselves stand in more urgent need of that teaching than do their brethren of the West. Thus it becomes rather imperative for the Indians to have the strength of maturity to see their own faults or shortcomings and correct them, if possible or tolerate them if inevitable.

Asceticism Exaggerated

The foremost misconception is the fashion to take an unduly exaggerated view of asceticism as an institution and interpret ancient India's religion in terms of asceticism. Says Oman: 'It is the ascetic profession that time out of mind has been of pre-eminent dignity in the eyes of the Indian people.'[1] And again: 'That the *only* possible state of a religious (holy) life is one involving asceticism.'[2] These statements contain only a partial truth. That asceticism has contributed largely to the religious and philosophical thoughts of India, as this study goes to prove, cannot be denied. That withdrawal from the world (*saṁnyāsa*) as the supreme aim of earthly existence and toward self realisation is also recognised and recommended. And yet to assign it the most predominant place in Indian thought is an exaggeration which needs to be avoided. Renunciation was undoubtedly considered a noble ideal; but it represented the final stage of life after the fulfilment of man's social duties. It was always emphasised that no one should accept *saṁnyāsa* without having discharged one's responsibilities as a *brahmachāri*, *gṛhastha* and *vanaprastha*. Also emphasised was *vairāgya* as an essential precedent to *saṁnyāsa*. If the *saṁnyāsī* was more honoured than anyone else it was due to his being looked upon as having achieved the highest end. This has led superficial observers to the conclusion that India believes in renunciation and not action.

It deserves a special mention that if India has revered the seers and saints, mystics and ascetics, it has also adored the rulers and statesmen, poets and philosophers, heroes and men of valour. Rāma and Kriṣṇa, Parasurām and Droṇācārya, Chandragupta and Chāṇakya, Aśoka and Harṣa, Vyās and Patañjali, Kālidas and Bhavabhūti have been the great personalities whose names still invoke admiration and reverence from the Indian people. World makers and world forsakers alike adorn the annals of our ancient past. If the ascetic ideal claimed special regard of some, it was also condemned by others. And it was due to such different reactions of different individuals at different times that the institution of asceticism became a complex one. Some emphasised its spiritual aspect while others associated it with other-worldliness, Māyā or pessimism.

[1]Oman, *The Mystics, Ascetics and Saints of India*, pp. 271-272.
[2]ibid.

Superior Spirituality

Deussen[1] attributes the emergence of asceticism to the high metaphysical capacity of the Indian people. It is generally believed that renunciation of the world in quest of a spiritual life is the badge of superiority of Indian culture.[2] Some western scholars struck by the metaphysical bent of the Indian mind have given currency to the myth that the Indians look upon the world as an illusion and that in thought and spirit they are aloof from the realms of activity. Absorbed in the contemplation of the Absolute, what matters most to them are the things of the spirit. It was Swami Vivekananda who declared: 'India has a mission in the world to fulfil—the mission of spiritualising the human race.'[3] It is thus pointed out that the spiritualisation of the human race is the inner theme of Indian history. This has led even a modern historian to say: 'In India there is an attitude towards life and an approach to the needs of the present situation in the world as a whole,' and exhorted her 'to go on giving the world *Indian* examples of the spiritual fight that makes man human.'[4] Such a view highlights not only the spiritual basis of the Indian culture but also suggests its superiority.

That the essence of Indian culture has in her spirituality is discernible in the oft-quoted expression—India's *spiritual* culture. Śri Aurobindo regards intense spirituality as the most distinguishing mark of the Indian civilisation. According to him the whole root of difference between Indian and European culture springs from the 'spiritual aim' of Indian civilisation. 'A spiritual aspiration was the governing force of this culture, its core of thought, its ruling passion.'[5] That spirituality is the basis of Indian life and thought is also emphasised by Radhakrishnan. He writes: 'Philosophy in India is essentially spiritual . . . . The spiritual motive dominates life in India.'[6] In his view the dominant character of the Indian mind is its spiritual tendency. He says: 'Spiritual experiences is the foundation of India's rich cultural history.'[7] Such views have won us many an advocate from the West who have spoken of

[1] *POU.*, p. 65.
[2] Roy, *Extract From the Fragments of A Prisoner's Diary*, p. 239.
[3] Dutt, *The Culture of India as envisaged* by Sri Aurobindo, foreword, p. 9.
[4] Toynbee, *One World and India*, pp. 41, 63.
[5] Aurobindo, *The Foundations of Indian Culture*, pp. 137-138.
[6] Radhakrishnan, *IP.*, I, p. 24.
[7] ibid. p. 41.

India's spiritual legacy which though flattering to our ego have given rise to some lop-sided conclusions.

Firstly to hold that spirituality as the sole characteristic of Indian culture is to ignore the pursuit of material prosperity as a worthy ideal for a great civilization. *Artha* and *Kāma* subsisted alongside of an ideal of *Mokṣa*, *Saṁnyāsa* (renunciation) and *Aparigraha* (non-acquisition). *Gṛhasthāśrama* received if not a higher status certainly occupied as respectable a position as *Saṁnyāsa.* Liberation was to be attained as a result of a full life of *dharma*, *artha* and *kāma.* And *kāma* included physical and artistic enjoyment of life and appreciation of music, dance, poetry and art.

Our Indian thinkers and students of culture have not been oblivious to the dangers of regarding Indian culture as superior to other cultures and to guard against the over-emphasis of the spirituality of Indian culture, Aurobindo and Radhakrishnan themselves caution us now and then. Aurobindo rightly points out: 'Spirituality is not the monopoly of India, however, it may hide submerged in intellectualism or in other concealing veils, it is a necessary part of human nature.' But he asserts that the difference between other cultures and the culture of India is between spirituality made the leading motive and determining power of both the inner and the outer life.[1] Putting the same view in its correct perspective, Azad observes: 'The characteristic of Indian thought is that it has paid greater attention to the inner world of man than to the outer world.'[2] The inherent dangers of such an attitude of spiritual excess was not without its disadvantages. Radhakrishnan pertinently observes: 'In the East, the exaggerated respect for spiritual life has issued an indifference to those material conditions, in which alone the spiritual intentions can be carried out. As a result, the Eastern spirituality became pertrified in dead forms which are effete and corrupting.'[3] To appreciate the truth behind this statement, we have to consider the conditions that existed in India as the consequence of the blind pursuit of asceticism and the cult of *Saṁnyāsa.*

In the post-Upaniṣadic times there was a confusion made in certain groups between *Saṁnyāsa* and *Tyāga*. *Tyāga* which stood for renunciation of desire and egoistic attachment (*vairāgya*) was

[1]Sri Aurobindo, op. cit., p. 14.
[2]*Indian Inheritance*, I, pp. 164-165.
[3]*East and West in Religion*, p. 68.

mistaken for renunciation of life and work (*Saṁnyāsa*). This brought about total withdrawal from the earthly interests—mentally and physically. The mandate of the *Īśa Upaniṣad*, 'verily wish to live out thy hundred years' span of life doing works in the world,'[1] was forgotten. Contemplation and action are not irreconciliable opposites as Vedantic thought has explained to us over and over again. They find their harmony in action without attachment, in enjoyment without desire: '*tyaktena bhuñjīthā*.'[2] The Upaniṣads also tell us: 'Awake! Arise! Stop not till you Reach the Goal.'[3] The message finds its practical demonstration in the Gītā when Kriṣṇa said again and again to Arjuna: 'Gird up your loins, pick up your weapons and engage in the fight . . . . Action is superior to inaction.'[4] It is not the fight *away from* the world but the fight *in* the world and against the life's odds that the Gītā upholds. It is not a renunciation from action but a renunciation in action: *Karmaphala-saṁnyāsa*. This truly Indian point of view should dismiss the charge that Indians in thought and spirit are indifferent to the world and its affairs and are mere onlookers.

Other-worldliness and Māyā

The misunderstanding of Indian religion in terms of asceticism and too much emphasis on the spirituality behind it has given rise to the view that India's is a religion of pessimism and creates a feeling of despair and otherworldliness in the minds of its votaries. No doubt the doctrine of Māyā looking upon the world as an illusion, arose from the cult of *Saṁnyāsa* as also the other-worldliness which characterises some of the Hindu sects. But this is a fairly later growth which ignores the fundamental principles of India's religious and philosophical thought. There is also some truth in the charge of other-worldliness when we consider a section of preachers who sang of the human body as a polluted thing and of human existence as a calamity to be overcome. This was due to the central conception of the ascetic life or the monastic system that the complete abstinence from all sexual intercourse was meritorious and essential for the total withdrawal from the world. The body

[1] *Isa.*, 2: Kurvanneveha karmāṇi jijiviṣechatani samāḥ.

[2] ibid.

[3] *Kathā. Up.*, Uttiṣṭhata jāgṛata prāpya varānnibodhata.

[4] *BG.*, III, 8: Niyataṁ kuru karma tvaṁ karma jyāyo hyakarmaṇaḥ Śarirayātrapi ca te na prasidhyedakarmaṇaḥ.

came to be despised. Chastity was regarded as the ideal state. It was the absolute suppression of the whole sensual side of man's nature, a perpetual struggle against all carnal impulses and all that stimulates desire. It was an inevitable consequence of the ascetic life here.

But this ascetic creed despising the human body does not truly represent Indian thought. On the other hand our ancient scriptures not only look upon the human body as a means to the attainment of the final end but also consider it as an abode of the supreme deity: *Ye puruṣe brahmaviduḥ te viduḥ parameṣthinaṁ.*[1] The human body is called the city of the gods (*devānāṁpuḥ*).[2] It is considered so holy that it is likened to the *āśrama* of the seven *ṛṣis* (*sapta ṛṣayah*).[3] How beautiful is this description of the human body!

The ancient Indians did not have an indifferent attitude towards life. The Vedas not only set a hundred years as the norm of human life but pray for a full and complete life.[4] The *Ishopaniṣad* calls upon man to 'perform action here and desire to live a hundred years.'[5] The Upaniṣad reminds us at the same time that all worldly things are alive with God and that they should be enjoyed without attachment: *tyaktena bhunjīthā*. There is no need to be blind to the material world. It is a deep and disinterested acceptance of it and a joyful recognition that no part of it may be refused. The *Taittirīya Upaniṣad* enjoins: '*Bhootyai na pramaditavyam*'—'Swerve not from the path of worldly prosperity.'[6] This means: do not be other-worldly too early and before your time. Do not turn your face away from the conflicts of this world and do not be engrossed in vague imaginings and speculations into things which may ignore the problems of tomorrow and the day after. 'This world is the most beloved of all: *ayaṁ lokaḥ priyatamaḥ*, says the *Ātharvaveda*, addressing a diseased man, 'Die not before decrepit age.'[7] It is true

[1]*AV.*, X, 7. 17.

[2]*AV.*, X. 2: aṣṭācakrā navadvārā devānāmpuḥ ayodhyā tasyāṁ hiraṇyayaḥ kośahsvargo jyotiṣāvṛtaḥ tasmin hiraṇyaye kośe tryare tripratiṣṭhite tasmin yadyakṣmātmanvat tad vai brahmavido viduḥ.

[3]*YV.*, IV., IV. S.S.: sapta ṛṣayaḥ pratihitāḥ śarīre sapta rakṣanti sadama pramādaṁ saptapaḥ svapato lokamiyuḥ tatra jāgṛto svapna jau satrasadau ca devau.

[4]*ṚV.*, VII. 66-16; *YV.*, 36-25; *AV.*, XIX. 63-60; *ṚV.*, I. 89. 9.

[5]*Īsa.*, 2.

[6]*TU.*, I. 11.

[7]*AV.*, V. 30. 17.

that the Upaniṣads encourage a renunciatory spirit on the ground that knowledge of the soul can be obtained by retiring from the world of actions, but not on the ground that the whole manifold world is an illusion.

The mistaken idea of the other worldliness arose from a false reading of the theory of Māyā—an erroneous belief that the world is a mere illusion. Indeed, the noblest exponent of Māyā, Śankarācārya, never said that the world of the senses is an illusion—to the senses. He did proclaim the relativity of knowledge and the illusory nature of sensation—experience. He also proclaimed that the human mind and senses are not the last or only arbiters of Truth; that Time, Space, Matter and God Himself are not, in Absolute Truth. What they appear to be to the mind and the senses; that the Absolute Truth must be realised through means beyond the intellect; and that the means to such realisation is enlightenment throuth Yoga. What he meant in essence was that the world has no reality apart from God, which is very different from saying that the world has no reality. What is illusory is not the world but the false meaning that has been attached to Māyā, that is responsible for a pessimistic outlook of life.[1] The narrow ascetic denies the material world, while the matter of fact materialist denies the spirit, forgetful of the fact that the true Truth includes and transcends both,'[2] says Aurobindo. It is due to this ignorance that some Western critic exaggerate and overstress the other-worldliness of Indian culture.

To the doctrine of Māyā, the Gītā furnishes a corrective. It says that not only is the world a reality for us but disinterested action in the worldly life is the key to get happiness and salvation. It advises that one need not despair and give up worldly pursuits nor desire to die to get release. It is in this world, in living a life of moderation and doing one's duties without attachment that one can learn the art of living a balanced life. One must identify oneself completely with *Sat* and *Chit* i.e. whatever is good and true. If one does so, one will surely acquire the third quality of *Ānanda* or joy. This is not pessimism but optimism of a superior kind, based not on some favour coming from outside but from the inner, robust and

[1]Sarvavyavahārāṇāmeva prāk brahmātmavijñanāt satyatvopatteḥ, svanpnavyavahārasya prāk prabhodhāt prāk prabodhāt saṁsāritvābhigamaḥ (*SB.*, II. 1. 14; IV. 1. 3). dehātmapratyayo yadvat pramāṇatven kalpitaḥ laukikaṁ tadvadevedaṁ pramāṇaṁ tvātmaniscayāt (*SB.*, I-4).

[2]op. cit., p. 26.

rational faith, that whatever bitterness of misfortunes one may experience in doing one's duties, it is a part of one's life and will ultimately bring one joy and happiness. The Gītā also points out that true *Saṁnyāsa* does not consist *merely* in retiring from the world but in subduing it to the purpose of the soul. *Pravṛtti* and *Nivṛtti* need not be two different paths opposed to each other. On the other hand, the former should be a preparation for the latter.

Pessimism

Pessimism is necessarily linked with otherworldliness and Māyā and inter-related as a distinct aspect of Indian asceticism. A common charge levelled against the Indians is that their view of life is essentially pessimistic. Observes Radhakrishnan: 'Almost every critic of Indian philosophy and culture harps on its pessimism.'[1] Pessimism is so much exaggerated that it is taken as pervading the entire range of Indian thought. As one critic states: 'Pessimism infects the whole physical and intellectual life of India and that the Indian philosophers have never been able to paint any positive picture of bliss.'[2]

It has to be pointed out, however, that Indian philosophy has various thought processes. It is not true that all Indian philosophers emphasise the importance of pessimism. Among them are thinkers like the Lokāyatas and the Buddha who propagate the importance of life for the sake of living. They give a positive philosophy of life, requiring every man to live a full life and not to escape from it.

Some scholars hold that the cause of Indian pessimism is environmental. Their attempt often stretches beyond reasonable limit in wanton disregard of the fact of Indian history. Especially, they overplay the factor of climate so much that it assumes a misconception of a grave nature.

A special mention should be made in this regard to Montesquieu who goes to prove that the Indians are next to good—for—nothing people for which climate is solely responsible, He observes: 'The Indians are naturally a pusillanimous people; even the children of Europeans born in India lose the courage peculiar to their own climate . . . . The heat of the climate may be so excessive as to deprive the body of all vigour and strength. Then the faintness is communicated to the mind; there is no curiosity, no enterprise, no

[1]Radhakrishnan, *IP.*, I, p. 40.
[2]Ronaldshay, q. b. Radhakrishnan, ibid.

generosity of sentiment; the inclinations are all passive; indolence constitutes the utmost happiness; scarcely any punishment is so severe as mental enjoyment.'[1] This charge of Montesquieu derogatorily dubs the Indian people as effiminate, indolent and feeble, lacking in manliness and smacks of a strong political bias. Such a prejudicial view also indicates a niggardly acquaintance with India's past, a deliberate indifference to the many-sided richness and depth of her achievements. Neither history nor literature justifies this description of the Indian people.

Aurobindo summing up the many-sided character of India's vast past and panorama writers: 'India has not only had the long roll of her great saints, sages, thinkers, religious founders, poets, creators, scientists, scholars, legists; she has had her great rulers, administrators, soldiers, conquerors, heroes, men with the strong active will, the mind that plans and the seeing force that builds.'[2] The story of ancient India is one of material prosperity and grandeur, valour and venture. The spirit of adventure which led to the building up of magnificiant empires and the setting up of prosperous colonies across the seas is hard to reconcile with an ascetic and merely negative frame of mind.

Better still, by way of a contrast to the erroneous view of Montesquieu, Durant represents India in its real perspective. His view, which serves a befitting reply, is worth quoting. He writes: 'Nothing should more deeply shame the modern student than the recency and inadequacy of his acquaintance with India. Here is a vast peninsula of nearly two million square miles; two third as large as the United States and twenty times the size of Great Britain; 320 million souls, more than in all North and South America combined or one fifth of the population of the earth (the reference is obviously to the undivided India); an impressive continuity of development and civilisation from Mohenjodaro, 2900 BC or earlier, to Gandhi, Raman and Tagore; faiths compassing every stage from barbarous idolatory to the most subtle and spiritual pantheon; philosophers playing a thousand variations on one monastic theme from the Upaniṣads eight centuries before Christ to Shankara, eight centuries after him; scientists developing astronomy three thousand years ago and winning Nobel prizes in our own time; a democratic constitution of untraceable antiquity in the villages and

[1]Montesquieu, *The Spirit of Laws*, I, p. 294.
[2]Sri Aurobindo, op. cit., p. 211.

wise and beneficient rulers like Aśoka and Akbar in the capitals, ministrels singing great epics almost as old as Homer and poets holding world audience today; artists raising gigantic temples for Hindu gods from Tibet to Ceylon and from Cambodia to Java or carving perfect palaces by the score of Mogul Kings and Queens—that is the India that patient scholarship is now opening up, to that Western mind which only yesterday thought civilisation an exclusively European thing.'[1] And all this by the born, tired, lazy, unenergetic, weak, passive and incurious Indians!

The temperamental tendency to look upon the dark side of things with regard to Indian pessimism is more assumed than proved. No one can be a pessimist when life is joyous and hopeful. And it can be said in all fairness that the people of India had, on the whole, their share of the natural joys of life, which was full of optimism. The Vedic age was an age of the appreciation of the good things of life and of strenuous effort to secure them. There was a vigorous pursuit of material life and the desire for prosperity. To live a full life with material blessings was a worthy ideal. Even in the times of the Upaniṣads when the philosophical trait of the Indian mind asserts itself, we find that the reputed teachers like Yājñavalkya were married men and desired material goods. When asked by King Janaka whether he desired wealth and cattle or victory in debate, he said he wanted both.[2] The sages preached, no doubt, detachment from life but it would be wrong to say, therefore, that they would impose their gloomy views upon all the people of the land. The average Indian, though he paid homage to them and respected their ideals, did not find life a wretched existence; rather he was willing to accept the world as he found it and to extract what happiness he could from it.

About the sadness of life in India, an Indian scholar writes: 'There is a certain sadness in Indian life which is unmistakable. The villager finds rest from his daily toil mostly in listening to the sufferings of Rāma, weeping with Sītā and exulting in the victory of Rāma over Rāvana.'[3] This does not prove the sadness of Indian life. If the villager weeps with the suffering Rāma and Sītā, it is as much a tribute to his capacity to identify himself with the epic characters

[1]Durant, Will, *Our Oriental Heritage*, p. 391.

[2]*Bṛhad. Ar. Up.*, IV. I, 1.

[3]Wadia, Art: 'The Philosophical Outlook in India and Europe' in Radhakrishnan *Comparative Studies in Philosophy*, p. 99.

as the power of the poet to evoke wide sympathy and wring out tear and joy from the human heart. On the contrary, there runs through the epics a dominant note which urges man to make his mundane life full and opulent, to fill it with colour and beauty and enjoyment. The heroic side of this idea 'is stamped in strong relief over the epic and the classical literature.'[1] The scheme of the four *āśramas* and the emphasis on *Artha* and *Kāma* among the four objectives of life suggest too that man should live a full and whole life and not starve any of its aspect. The appreciation of art, architecture, literature, music and dance all found their due place in Indian life which should prove that it emphasised the good things of life. The ideals of life that the great secular literature of India presents have no relation to pessimism.

It now remains to consider pessimism as a philosophy of life. The Upaniṣads constantly insisted that salvation was won by the knowledge of Brahman—Ātman and all else was merely preliminary. Transmigration and Karma brought about a sense of defeatism with the result that all action and existence were looked upon as a positive evil. The ascetic philosopher felt the worthlessness of the phenomenal world as contrasted with the changeless bliss of the Ātman. The futility of the world and the evil of activity logically involved renunciation of the world and a life of meditation. Pessimism was the inevitable result of these factors at work. Viewed thus, Indian pessimism can be understood as related to the great doctrine of Brahman, Karma and transmigration.[2]

The pessimistic view of life implies not merely dissatisfaction with what is or exists but whether existence is fundamentally and essentially evil and worthless. Such a theory is found in Indian thought. According to Dasgupta: 'There is an inherent pessimism in most systems of Indian thought which considers that normally we are all under the evil influence of false knowledge and are all gliding on the downward path of sins and afflictions.' He continues: 'They also consider all attachments lead to bondage and slavery to passions and thereby lead us away from the path ot liberation.'[3] But Indian pessimism is only initial and not final. Life is desire and desire is pain and only where both are at an end, is the craving of the soul at rest. Out of such a situation the Upaniṣads show a way

[1]Sri Aurobindo, op. cit., p. 27.
[2]cf. Chapter 3, pp. 80-87.
[3]*HIP*, II, p. 414.

out in the ideal of detachment or *Vairāgya* which seeks freedom from all passion and desire through self-knowlegde leading to *mokṣa*. This is not pessimism if the immense spiritual possibility resulting from it is considered. The *Upaniṣads* regard *mokṣa* not as a hypothetical state to be attained after death but as a realizable one in this life. They declare: 'When all the desires that the heart harbours are gone, man becomes immortal and reaches Brāhmana *here*.'[1] And the Gītā shows the way towards the attainment of the blissful supreme state through *Karmaphalasaṁnyāsa*.[2]

The Buddha's teaching laid heavy stress on the sorrow and annihilation of *tṛṣṇā* (craving). This is misconstrued as pessimistic. The misery of *saṁsāra* is most real. Life as it is commonly led is marred by sorrow and suffering. It is not pessimism to confront man with the truth of suffering, with the problem of his destiny, of decay and death and of the suffering inherent in all the things which he tries to cling desperately. The Buddha believes that religion is something to be lived and not merely to be studied or discussed. He believes in the application of religion to life and conduct so that it becomes a second nature. He shows man a distinct and positive path out of suffering. His Eight-fold-path admirably sums up practical duties and obligations of religious life. He admits the possibility of attaining peace here and now whereby man instead of being the victim of misery becomes its victor. The Nirvāṇa which is to be won 'by the heroic spirit of moral self-conquest and calm wisdom is a state of ineffable calm and joy, open to all.'[3] If the Buddha paints a deeply moving picture of life, he sees also the way to a better life. He is neither a hopeless pessimist nor a superficial optimist.

It is noteworthy that for all the severity of the discipline of the Jaina ascetic, the Jaina scriptures contain numerous passages which mention the quiet inner happiness of the homeless life—the great sense of relief, of freedom, which comes with the abandonment of family ties. The life of asceticism is not looked upon as weakly giving way before the sorrows of the world but as a great spiritual struggle to be looked upon with courage and resolution like that of a soldier.[4]

[1] *Bṛhad. Up.*, IV. 4.7; *Katha Up.*, VI. 14.

[2] *BG*., II. 51; IV. 20, Eliade prefers the term *phalatṛṣṇāvairāgya*: *Images and Symbol* , p. 68.

[3] Aurobindo, *Foundation of Indian Culture*, p. 84.

[4] *Sources of Indian Tradition*, p. 66.

In the midst of popular notions and misunderstandings about pessimism in particular and Buddhism and Hinduism in general, it is notable of a Westerner to tell us that 'the tenets of Hinduism and Buddhism are neither annihilistic nor negative but positive as *nirvāṇa* is tranquility, not negation, a state of indifference but of understanding and acceptance.'[1] In our own times, this is a presentation of a refreshingly correct perspective of Hinduism and Buddhism with their emphasis on wholeness of life and the importance of training not only the intellect and the body but also 'the inner mind of the subconsciousness.' To this may be added Basham's correct estimate of ancient India that 'her people enjoyed life passionately delighting both in the things of the senses and the things of the spirit.'[2]

On the whole we might conclude that Indian religious thought was a mixture of both pessimism and optimism. Pessimism was there but all philosophers were not pessimists. The various *bhakti* movements that arose were optimistic and greatly enriched the religious life of India. The belief in a personal God, in His Love and grace and in the possibility of personal contact with Him helped Indians to live a life of real joy and peace. *Bhakti* has been a source of deep spiritual feeling and it succeeded to break the force of pessimism. The *āśrama dharma* and the four *puruṣārthas*—*artha*, *kāma*, *dharma* and *mokṣa* alongwith various sacraments (*saṁskāras*) which covered man's life from the cradle to the grave and led to the full-fledged growth of man's personality, would also serve as a corrective against the popular misconception that the ancient Indians always thought in terms of fatalism, pessimism and asceticism. Indian outlook on life has never been one of complete negation or denial.

Having cleared the ground by referring to some of the chief objections urged against Indian culture and the ascetic institution, let us now turn to the impact of asceticism on the civilisation of ancient India.

Social and Religious Aspects

In the times of the Upaniṣads, as discussed earlier, the mystic

[1]Horace Alexander, *Consider India: An Essay in Values*, pp. 1-26. How the Gītā, the Vedas and the Dhammapada affect the lives of Indian today and may one day affect that of the world form the thesis of this book.

[2]Basham, *The Wonder that was India*, p. 9.

thinkers in their search for truth lived in a dream of eternity, renounced the world and became solitary recluses in wild forests or on mountain heights contemplating the splendour of Life Divine. They did not come forward to mix with the people with a view to improve their spiritual condition. The Upaniṣadic seers were more concerned with their own salvation and were approachable by only a few of the intelligentsia to whom the subtle philosophy of *Brahman—Ātman* could make its appeal. The Upaniṣadic philosophy was not sufficient to fulfil the moral or religious needs of the masses. The Upaniṣadic philosophers were not concerned with common people or mundane matters. Instead of seeking to remedy the society of its ills, they were repelled by the sorrows and injustices in the world. Their otherworldly aspiration took no notice of the deterioration in society. As a result, the people continued to live in misery. To what extent the lower strata of society suffered is vividly described in the *Kūṭadanta Sutta.*[1]

The orthodox Brāhmanic tradition recognised the ideal of *Saṁnyāsa* (renunciation) but did not encourage too many people to take to it. This tradition also insisted that man should first pass through the earlier stages of life and thus excluded the majority, which consisted of the fourth caste. The Brāhmin ascetic orders depended on birth and were open to the Brāhmins only. Jainism, Buddhism and Lokāyatas revolted against this rigid Brāhmanic tradition. Not only this, Jainism and Buddhism removed the restrictions of caste and sex and opened the gates of monastic life to all. The general masses, who were eager to know about this life and had been prevented from knowing it, therefore, welcomed Jainism and Buddhism. Monastic life came to be admired and the orders of monks and nuns increased.[2]

The compassionate life of the Buddha drew many followers to the way of life he propagated. The Buddhists founded a large number of big monasteries and the best and the ablest men and women became monks and nuns. Society was the poorer and weaker for it. The great kingdom of Magadha was so full of monasteries that it came to be called Bihar, the land of *Vihāras* or monasteries. The Jaina and Buddhist monasteries provided an opportunity even for those who merely wanted to escape the responsibilities of life although ethically and intellectually they were unfit to lead the life

[1]cf. Chapter 5, pp. 127 ff; *DOB.*, p. 180.
[2]cf. Chapter 6, pp. 145 ff.

of the monk. Many who were frustrated in life and living in misery also found a shelter in monastic life. As a result corruption entered monasteries and they became a burden upon society which deteriorated economically and morally.

In the *Mahābhārata* we come across a group of mendicants (*munimuṇḍāḥ*) who did not believe in a fixed abode, subsisted only on alms and were constantly on move from one place to another. These ascetics used to visit kings and other people in distress and rendered them help or advice. The miserable received soothing words from them in times of troubles and calamity. They contributed a great deal to improve the lot of the people.[1]

Both the epics, the *Rāmāyaṇa* and the *Mahābhārata* refer to many hermitages in the seclusion of the forests where the *riṣis* and ascetic teachers lived. The hermitages of Kanva, Vasiṣṭha and Viśvāmitra were great centres of learning where the students congregated. These *āśramas* kept alive the bright fires of learning and spiritual thought. Young men of noble birth sought education at these sacred shrines of learning. Those tired of the world and the old went there for peace. These centres of culture were cherished by the rulers of the land who treated the members of the hermitages with respect and consideration. The sages who were in charge of the training of the young gave them their very best. They were looked upon as the custodians of the spiritual heritage of the land. The sages, besides contributing to the welfare of the community also evinced keen interest in the proper maintenance of *dharma* by a righteous administration of the country by the kings. They served the lonely and the lost, the forlorn and the afflicted as illustrated by Vālmiki's care of Sītā and her children. Some of these ṛiṣis travelled from place to place, visiting kings and holding religious conferences at their court.[2]

The aftermath of Buddhism and Jainism saw the popularity of the monastic life. There was an indiscriminate admission of men and women into the ascetic orders. Men forgot, their social duties and family responsibilities. In many cases they left their wives and often wives left their husbands. Domestic ties were broken and women and children made destitute and homeless. Marriage was viewed as a burden. Poverty and misery of life increased. The state had to face the problem of maintaining the deserted and the destitute.

[1]cf. Chapter 8., *Mbh.*, see pp. 217-20
[2]cf. Chapter 8., *Ram.*, pp. 274-75.

There was another problem which the state was confronted with. The proselytizing sects had multiplied and disturbed the social and religious life of the people. The growth of ascetic orders was a great burden on the livelihood of the people. Kautilya utilised the agency of the state to reduce the incidence of a life of asceticism on the social energy of manhood and womanhood of his times. He forbade the practice of abandoning domestic life and made it a rule that only old men could become ascetics and only after making adequate provisions for their dependants and getting sanction from the *dharmasthas*. He laid down that women should not be converted to a life of renunciation and those who committed this crime were punished. The youth, if they showed a leaning towards a life of *saṁnyāsa*, while their services were required for the preservation of society and the state, were also punished. The movements of ascetic institutions were regulated and their incidence for maintenance on the honest and industrious population was reduced. Kautilya valued asceticism primarily for its usefulness in espionage and intelligence activities.[1]

The law-givers found that there was an influx of undesirable persons into the stage of *saṁnyāsa* who were not fitted for such a life. They felt that their admission into the ascetic order without the natural gradation through the first three stages was bound to produce a general deterioration in society and disturb its economic foundation. They, therefore, insisted upon people passing from all the stages. A premature life of asceticism was viewed as anti-social. They also preached that the householder was the basis and support which held up the entire society. They praised *Gṛhasthāśrama* as the most excellent and the highest *āśrama*.[2] They sought to ensure that admission to *saṁnyāsa* be conditioned on adequate preparation through learning and discipline. They, therefore, laid down severe punishments by way of penances for those who failed to keep up the standard of purity of the three stages of *brahmacarya*, *vānaprastha* and *saṁnyāsa*.

Intellectual Aspect

In the intellectual life of the people, the wandering scholars (*parivrājakas*) and forest-dwellers (hermits, *vānaprasthas*) both Brāhmin and non-Brāhmin who represented asceticism played a prominent

[1]cf. Chapter, 9, pp. 286-87.
[2]cf. Chapter, 10, pp. 305-10.

role as religious teachers of ancient India. From the Vedic times the institution of *Naiṣṭhika Brahmacārīs* was fairly known. There were many, of both the sexes, who remained life-long celibates and applied themselves to learning. In their quest of the Brahma-realisation they led a mendicant life of renunciation, carrying enlightenment wherever they went. They practised Brahmacarya not only as an aspect of austerity but owing to its detachment from life, also as an opportunity for the persistent pursuit of knowledge and imparting religious instruction to those who were willing to listen to them.

The Buddhist and Jaina literature assign an important part to the *śramaṇa*, who is often mentioned as an important personage. He was a religious teacher whose function was intellectual guidance and spiritual instruction. A characteristic feature of the religious life of India in this period was the number and variety of ascetic groups of *Śramaṇas* and *Brāhmaṇas*, all *Parivrājakas*, followers of different *Ditthis* (*Darśanas* or *systems*), Khantis (*Kṣānti*), Beliefs (*Ṛcis*), aims and organisations (*Nissāya—āśraya*).[1] According to Jaina source, every religious order of the *śamaṇas* was a travelling school. The furtherance of the course of truth and knowledge in all branches of learning by open discussions was a remarkable feature of their educational and cultural activities.[2] The *Aṅguttara Nikāya* mentions a number of religious and philosophical sects of hermits and wanderers.[3] While the *Śṛtis* call them *Carakas* literally 'Wanderers,' the *Smṛtis* call them *Parivrājakas*, some of whom had their group of disciples. A characteristic of the Wanderer was his love of philosophical discussion and disputation. Many of such, singly or in groups, wandered through the country, holding discussions at noted centres of learning and spreading education. The philosophical discussions were held at the courts of kings like Janaka, in the *Panchāla Parishad* or in *Saṅthāgāras* or *Samyappa-vādaka-śāla*, as the Pāli texts call them or *sabhās* as the Smṛtis call them. Evidence of actual places where such public philosophical discussions were held is ample in Pālī literature.

[1]*Udanam*, pp. 66-67.

[2]*Brihatkalpa Bhāsya*, 4, 5179; 5431 *Vya*, *Bha.*, 1. p. 57 af; cf. Jain, *Social Life in the Jaina Literature*, p. 174.

[3]See Chapter 6 pp. 140-49 For a typical description of the Parivrajakas, see *Udumbarika—Sihanadsutta. Dighā Nikāya*, III, pp. 36ff.

The *Parivrājakas*, except during the rainy season wandered throughout the country expounding their doctrines, meeting new teachers and learning from them, disputing with them and thus winning the allegiance of the people and rulers alike. These discussions often resulted in conversions and borrowings as between their different sects and schools. These wandering scholars were responsible for a wide-spread movement to encourage speculation for its own sake and to repudiate sacerdotalism, authority and tradition if they were not compatible with their rationalism.[1]

These discussions afforded a good scope to the proselytizing tendencies of the *Bhikkus* of the *Saṁgha* who spread the message of the Buddha far and wide. Even the story of the Buddha's life is largely a tale of the numerous conversions of leaders of non-Buddhist systems brought about by him. Jainism also likewise borrowed largely of the *Acelakas* and *Ājīvikas* who can truly be called their ancestors.

It was these wandering teachers belonging to different sects who were primarily responsible for giving the unity of outlook and temper which in spite of local differences characterises to this day the mentality of the village folk from one part of the country to another, their fortitude and the philosophical approach to life. The demands of life in ancient India were comparatively few and were easily satisfied. Even when the peasant did not suffer from lack of food, he was content to speculate upon the mysteries of fate. The rustic here has in some sense a philosophy of life and can talk of fate and circumstances with a detachment and insight which is often surprising. This quality of resignation and tolerance in his mental make up is all the more so in view of the almost universal lack of literacy in India. The question arises: Whence comes this culture of the mind?

Toward this the wandering teacher and mendicant played a big part. It was their function to bring the teachings of religion and morality within the reach of the average villager. Their tales compensated to a large extent for their lack of a literary education. Philosophy was translated into myth and religion embodied in the

[1]Havell observes: 'Among the Wanderers, *a fraternity of mendicant sophists* open to all classes within the Āryan pale, the greatest freedom of thought prevailed, and in the public debating halls of *Āryavarta* Brāhmanical doctrines were controverted as freely as those of the orthodox Christian churches are at popular resorts of the present day in Europe.' *Aryan Rule in India*, p. 50.

actions of men. Morality was turned into the form of legends and rural life was thus enriched by the wisdom of generations. Havell narrates how during the Gupta age the *sādhus* and *saṁnyāsis* carried the epics, especially the *Mahābhārata* throughout the length and breadth of the country which gave abundant material for a system of popular education, as the *bhikkus* of the Saṅgha formerly spread the message of the Buddha.[1] The epic tales of valour and romance, legends of wisdom and morality, aimed to delight, amuse and educate the people, also served as a code of life, a philosophy of social and ethical relations, touching many human problems. The *Sādhus* and *Saṁnyāsis* made the Epics and the Purāṇas a living force to guide the people in their day-to-day life. Not only they were both poets and historians as story tellers but also custodians of local tradition and faith, whose stories were woven round the religious experience and expectations of the people. It is in this manner that the teachings of Hinduism permeated the masses, the characters and the incidents of Hindu mythology became common currency in the social and intellectual intercourse of the people.

How the religo-intellectual activities of these wanderers affected deeply and widely the life of the people can be gathered from the writings of the Chinese monk, Hiuen-Tsang, (who followed Fa-Hian) who visited India between AD 629-645. Hiuen-Tsang gives high praise to the wandering *bhikkus* or *sādhus*, men deeply versed in antique wisdom and possessing the culture accumulated by constant travel, who, though sometimes belonging to wealthy families, were content to live a life of poverty apart from the world unmoved by honour or reproach. 'For them there is honour in knowing truth and no disgrace in being destitute.'[2] No fatigue was too great when an opportunity offered them of gaining knowledge or of using their own for helping others. Those who were famed for their wisdom were treated with the highest respect; but not even the honours which kings could bestow tempted them to forsake the path of knowledge.

However, the greatest gift of monastic life to ancient India was the educational benefits provided through the monasteries. The Chinese pilgrims Fa-Hian and Hiuen-Tsang found monasticism flourishing in the North India and the great monasteries with their thousands of learned and studious monks exercised a powerful

[1]Havell, ibid, p. 157.

[2]Watter's translation, I, p. 162.

influence. Amongst them, renowed for its university was Nālaṅda, which was the centre of Mahāyāna Buddhism.

Hiuen-Tsang has much to say about educational matters, both with regard to popular instruction and the higher learning of the Buddhist monasteries. Brāhmana and Buddhist teachers vied with each other in devotion to their duties. The brethren of the Sangha often met together to sharpen their wits in intellectual contests and to promote the moral aims of their order. Learning was not the monopoly of the Buddhist monks or Brāhmins. 'A man who delighted in wisdom could study diligently at home and be a monk or layman as he pleased.'[1]

Ethical Aspect

Asceticism contributed as well to the ethical code of Brāhmanism, Buddhism and Jainism.

The Saṁnyāsis as described in the Vedic literature had to adopt the ten vows as personal conduct while embracing *saṁnyāsa.*[2] The major five vows were:

1. Abstention from injuring living beings (*ahiṁsā*)
2. Truthfulness (*satya*)
3. Abstention from appropriating the property of others (*asteya*)
4. Continence (*brahmacarya*)
5. Liberality

The five minor vows were:

6. Abstention from anger
7. Obedience towards the Guru
8. Avoidance of rashness
9. Cleanliness
10. Purity in eating.

The *saṁnyāsi* served as a model from which the Jains and Buddhists borrowed many important practices and institutions of ascetic life. The five Buddhist vows are identical with those of the Jaina ascetics:[3]

1. Not to destroy life (*ahiṁsā*)
2. Not to lie (*sunrita*)
3. Not to take that what is not given (*asteya*)
4. To abstain from sexual intercourse (*brahmacarya*)

[1]Watter's translation, I, p. 162.

[2]*Baudh. DS.*, II, 10. 18.

[3]Rhys Davids, *Buddhism*, pp. 139, 160.

5. To renounce all interest in worldly things (*aparigraha*)

These vows were binding on every *Bhikkhu* or *Samaṇa*. To the former they were known as *pañkśīla* and to the latter as *pañca mahāvvayas*. The observance of these became the basis of every field of the Jaina and Buddhist monastic conduct. In the course of time they became binding on every Jaina or Buddhist follower.

The *Yogasūtras* of Patañjali borrows these and they form the *Yamas* or abstention in his *Yoga* system. The *Yamas* consist of five self-restraints or disciplinary practices described as:

1. Non-injury (*ahiṁsā*)
2. Truthfulness (*satya*)
3. Non-theft (*asteya*)
4. Continence (*brahmacarya*)
5. Frugal living (*aparigraha*)

The *Niyamas* which were also borrowed from ascetic rules are five:

1. *Śoucha* (bodily and mental purity)
2. *Santoṣa* (contentment)
3. *Tapas* (ascetic practices)
4. *Swādhyāya* (study of the sciences and philosophy)
5. *Iśwar Pranidhāna* (total dedication to God)[1]

The *yamas* and *niyamas* were already a part of the personal conduct of the *saṁnyāsi* or the *bhikkhu* or the *samaṇa, muni*. Now they became the rules of personal conduct to be observed by the Yoga aspirants, who are advised to give up the desire to injure anybody or to lie or to steal or to be sensual or greedy and even in the *thought* of injury to another. The *yamas* and *niyamas* are expected to be observed in all circumstances and at all times. Patañjali emphasises that progress in Yoga depends upon goodness in personal character and in social relations. This brings about a complete change in the aspirant's attitude towards the outer world and toward himself, in short, to ethics and morality in the widest sense. Aided by the *yamas* and *niyamas*, the aspirant was ensured with social and individual stability. They were necessary for the full physical and moral development of his personality.

This impact permeated many layers of society which provided for men and families dedicated to religion and philosophy the study and practice of Yoga. Those who actually practised it and regarded

[1]*YS.*, II. 29, 32.

it as the most important part of their lives both in personal practice and in social application, not only enriched and strengthened their inner life but also served others in promotion of human happiness.

The moral qualities like *Ahiṁsā*, *Satya*, *Asteya*, *Aparigraha* and *Brahmacarya* formed the ethical foundation of the Brahmanical Buddhist and Jaina monachism and part of their ascetic philosophy. As social ethics they became a part of their respective religious systems.

Other Aspects

Asceticism tended to keep before man's eyes a higher ideal, a life of purity and self-restraint. The ascetic practised the spiritual way of life as a matter of voluntary undertaking. His life and action were an ever-present reminder to the people that man could know the path of true happiness when he came to recognise spiritual values and realised that material prosperity was not the be-all and end-all of life. As a result, a number of ideas came to be held by the people which had a certain influence over their minds down the ages, viz. the vanity of the world, the supremacy of the spiritual life and the nobility of asceticism. Men have believed that the man who gave up everything for God was a true saint. Union with Him has been the spiritual ideal of the people. In India where poverty is conspicuous, asceticism with its emphasis on voluntary poverty helped to some extent reduce the impact of poverty on the life of a common man. It made poverty somewhat tolerable and vicissitudes of life acceptable with patience, and certain amount of resignation.

It will, therefore, be no exaggeration to suggest that asceticism of ancient India had its impact on social, religious, intellectual and ethical life of the people. Ancient Indian literature, as we have seen is replete with evidences to this effect. There is no doubt, therefore, that asceticism had a varied impact on the entire culture of India.

Bibliography

Indus Valley Civilisation

Chanda, R.P., *Survival of the Prehistoric Civilisation of the Indus Valley* (Memoirs of the Archaeological Survey of India No. 41), Calcutta, 1929.

Dikshit, K.N., *Prehistoric Civilisation of the Indus Valley*, Madras, 1939.

Heras, H., *Studies in Proto-Indo-Mediterranean Culture*, Vol. 1, Bombay, 1953.

——, *Minkan*, Bombay, 1947.

Mackay, Ernest, *The Indus Civilisation*, London, 1935.

——, *Early Indus Civilisation*, London, 1948.

——, *Further Excavations at Mohenjodaro*, 2 Vols., Delhi, 1937-38.

Marshall, John, *Mohenjodaro and the Indus Civilisation*, 3 Vols., London, 1931.

Nath, Raj Mohan, *A Clue to the Indus Valley Scripts and Civilisation*, Calcutta, 1959.

Vats, M.S., *Excavations at Harappa*, 2 Vols., Delhi, 1940.

Wheeler, Mortimer, *The Indus Civilisation*, Supplementary Volume to *CHI*., London, 1953.

Vedic Literature

Advaita Ashrama, *Minor Upanishads*, Almora, 1938.

Agrawala, V.S., *Sparks from the Vedic Fire*, Varanasi, 1962.

——, *Veda Vidya* (Hindi), Agra, 1959.

Aiyar, K. Narayanaswamy, *Thirty Minor Upaniṣads*, Madras, 1914.

Bhargava, P.L., *India in the Vedic Age*, Lucknow, 1956.

Bloomfield, M., *Hymns of the Atharvaveda*, *SBE*., XLII, Oxford, 1897.

——, *Religion of the Vedas*, New York, 1908.

Bose, A.C., *The Call of the Vedas*, Bombay, 1954.

Coomaraswamy, A.K., *A New Approach to the Vedas*, London, 1933.

Das, A.C., *Rigvedic India*, Culcutta, 1927.

Deussen Paul, Tr. A.S. Geden, *Philosophy of the Upanishads*, Edinburgh, 1908.

Deshmukh, P.S., *The Origin and Development of Religion in Vedic Literature*, Bombay, 1933.

Diwakar, R.R., *Upanishads, in Story and Dialogue*, Bombay, 1961.

Eggeling, J., tr., *Śatapatha Brāhmana*, 5 Vols. *SBE.*, Vols. XII, XXVI, XLI, XLIII, XLIV, London, 1882-85, 1894-97, 1900.

Gajendragadkar, K.V., *Neo-Upanishadic Philosophy*, Bombay, 1959.

Ghate, V.S., *Lectures on Rigveda*, Poona, 1926.

Gough, A.A., *The Philosophy of the Upaniṣhads*, London, 1903.

Griffith, R.T.H., tr., *Hymns of the Rigveda*, 2 Vols., Benares, 1896-97.

——, tr., *Hymns of the Atharvaveda*, 2 Vols., Benares, 1895-96.

——, tr., *Hymns of the Samaveda*, Benares, 1907.

——, tr., *White Yajurveda*, text and popular comm., Benares, 1899.

Griswold, H.D., *The Religion of the Rigveda*, London, 1923.

Haug, Martin, *Aitareya Brāhmaṇa*, 2 Vols., Bombay, 1863.

Hiriyanna, M., tr., *Vedāntasāra of Sadananda*, Poona, 1929.

Hume, R.E., tr., *The Thirteen Principal Upanishads*, London, 1921, Madras, 1958.

Karamblekar, V.W., *The Atharvavedic Civilisation*, Nagpur, 1959.

Keith, A.B., *The Religion and Philosophy of the Vedas and Upanishads*, 2 Vols., Cambridge, Mass., 1925.

——, tr., *Taittirīya Saṁhitā*, 2 Vols., Cambridge, Mass., 1914.

——, tr., *Rigveda Brāhmaṇas: Aitareya and Kauśītakī*, Cambridge, Mass., 1920.

——, tr., *The Sāṅkhyāyana Āraṇyaka*, London, 1908, reprint, New Delhi, 1975.

——, tr., *The Aitareya Āraṇyaka*, London, 1909.

Macdonell, A.A., *Vedic Mythology*, Strassburg, 1898.

Macdonald, K.S., *The Brāhmaṇas of the Vedas*, Madras, 1896.

Madhavananda, Swami, *Vedānta Paribhāṣā of Dharmaraja Adhvarindra*, Calcutta.

Majumdar, R.C., ed., *The Vedic Age*, Bombay, 1952.

Manikar, T.G., *Mysticism in the Rigveda*, Bombay, 1962.

Max Müller, F., *The Upanisads*, *SBE.*, Vol. XV, Oxford, 1900.

——, *Rigveda Samhita*, 4 Vols., London, 1890-92.

Mitra, Rajendra, ed., *The Taittīriya Āraṇyaka of Black Yajurveda with the Comm. of Sāyaṇācārya*, Calcutta, 1872.

Mitra and Cowell, *The Twelve Principal Upanishads*, Vol. III, Madras, 1932.
Nikhilananda, Swami, tr., *The Upanishads*, London, 1963.
Parab, B.A., *The Miraculous and Mysterious in Vedic Literature*, Bombay, 1952.
Radhakrishnan, S., *The Philosophy of the Upanishads*, London, 1924.
——, *The Principal Upanishads*, London, 1953.
——, *The Brahma Sutra*, London, 1960.
Rajagopalachari, C., *The Upanishads*, Delhi, 1949.
Ranade, R.D., *A Constructive Survey of Upanishadic Philosophy*, Poona, 1926.
Rawson, J.N., *The Katha Upanishad*, Calcutta, 1934.
Renou, Louis, *Vedic India*, Calcutta, 1957.
Roer, E., *The Twelve Principal Upanishads*, 2 Vols., Madras, 1931.
Roth and Whitney, ed., *Atharvaveda Saṁhitā*, Berlin, 1896.
Schrader, F. Otto, *The Minor Upanishads*, Vol. 1, Madras, 1912.
Shende, N.J., *The Foundations of the Atharvanic Religion*, Mysore.
——, *The Religion and Philosophy of the Atharvaveda*, Poona, 1952.
Thibaüt, G., *The Vedānta Sūtra*, *SBE.*, Vol. XLVIII, Oxford, 1904.
Whitney, W.D., *Atharvaveda Saṁhitā*, 2 Vols., *HOS.*, VII-VIII, Cambridge, Mass., 1905.
Wilson, H.H., tr., *Rigveda*, 6 Vols. Vol. I, Poona, 1946; II-VI, Bangalore, 1925-28.

Buddhism

Bapat, P.V., ed., *2500 Years of Buddhism*, New Delhi, 1959.
Bhagwat, Durga, *Early Buddhist Jurisprudence*, Poona, n.d.
Burtt, E.A., *The Teachings of the Compassionate Buddha*, New York, 1955.
Chalmers, R., tr., *Majjhima Nikāya* (Further Dialogues of the Buddha), 2 Vols., London, 1926-27.
——, tr., *Sūtta-Nipāta* (Buddha's Teachings), London, 1932.
Conze, Edward, *Buddhist Meditation*, London, 1956.
——, tr., *Buddhist Scriptures*, London, 1959.
——, *Buddhist Texts Through the Ages*, New York, 1954.
——, *Buddhism—Its Essence and Development*, London, n.d.
——, *Buddhist Thought in India*, London, 1962.
Coomaraswamy, A.K., *Buddha and the Gospel of Buddhism*, London, 1928, reprint, New Delhi, 1972.
Cowel and Neil, *Divyāvadāna*, Cambridge, 1886.

Cowel and Neil, *Buddhacarita of Aśvaghosha*, Oxford, 1893.
Dahlke, Paul, tr., Bhikkhu Silacara, *Buddhist Essays*, London, 1908.
Davids, C.A.F. Rhys, *Buddhism: Its History and Literature*, New York, 1896.
——, *Buddhism*, London, n.d.
——, *Buddhist India*, London, 1903.
——, *Outlines of Buddhism*, London, 1934.
Davids, T.W. Rhys, and C.A.F., tr., *Dialogues of the Buddha*, Pt. I, II, III, London, 1899-1921.
——, tr., *The Book of Kindred Sayings*, 5 Vols., *Samyutta Nikāya*, London, 1917-30.
——tr., *Psalms of the Early Buddhists—Sisters and Brothers*, 2 Vols., London, 1909, 1913.
Davids, T.W. Rhys, and Oldenberg, H., tr., *Vinaya Texts*, 3 Vols., *SBE.*, Vols. XIII, XVII, XX, Oxford, 1881-82-85.
Davids, T.W. Rhys, and Carpenter, ed., *Sumangalavilāsini* (of Buddhaghosha), *PTS.*, London, 1886-1932, Comm. to *Dīgha Nikāya*, 3 Vols.
Diwakar, R.R., *Bhagawan Buddha*, Bombay, 1960.
Dutt, Sukumar, *Early Buddhist Monachism*, Bombay, 1960.
——, *The Buddha and Five After-Centuries*, London, 1957.
——, *Buddhist Monks and Monasteries of India*, London, 1962.
Dutt, Nalinaksha, *Early Monastic Buddhism*, 2 Vols., Calcutta, 1941-45.
Elliot, Charles, *Hinduism and Buddhism*, 2 Vols., London, 1921, 1962.
Fausboll, V., *The Jātakas*, 7 Vols., London, 1877-97.
Gard, R.A. ed., *Buddhism*, New York, 1963.
Gehman, H.S., tr., *Pettavattu*, *PTS.*, London, 1942.
Horner, I.B., *Women Under Primitive Buddhism*, London, 1930.
Keith, A.B., *Buddhist Philosophy in India and Ceylon*, Oxford, 1923.
Kern, H., *Manual of Indian Buddhism*, Strassburg, 1896.
Law, B.C., *A History of Pali Literature*, 2 Vols., London, 1933.
Leou, Freer, ed., *Saṁyutta Nikāya*, 6 Vols., *PTS.*, London, 1884-1904.
Lokur, N.S., tr., *Buddhacaritam of Asvaghosh*, Belgaum, 1912.
Müller Max, tr., *Dhammapada*, *Sutta-Nipāta*, *SBE.*, Vol. X, Oxford, 1898.
——, *Buddhist Suttas*, *SBE.*, Vol. XI, Oxford, 1881.
Monier Williams, M., *Buddhism*, London, 1889.

Narasu, P.L., *The Essence of Buddhism*, Bombay, 1948.
Oldenberg, H., tr. W. Hoey, *Buddha: His Life, Doctrine and Order*, London, 1882.
Pande, G.C., *Studies in the Origin of Buddhism*, Allahabad, 1957.
Poussin and Thomas, ed., *Mahāniddesa*, 2 Vols., *PTS.*, London, 1916-17.
Radhakrishnan, S., tr., *The Dhammapada*, London, 1950.
——, *Gautama the Buddha*, Bombay, 1945.
Smith, F.H., *The Buddhist Way of Life*, London, 1951.
Thomas, E.J., *History of Buddhist Thought*, London, 1963.
Vaidya, P.L., ed., *Lalita-Vistara*, Darbhanga, 1958.
Warren, H.C., *Buddhism in Translation*, Cambridge, Mass., 1896.
Woodward and Hare, *The Book of the Gradual Sayings*, 5 Vols., *PTS.*, London, 1932-36.
Zurcher, E., *Buddhism*, London, 1962.

Jainism

Abhayadeva, Comm., *Bhagavai*, Bombay, 1921.
——, *Ovavāiya*, Surat, 1949.
——, *Samvāyaṅga*, Ahmedabad, 1938.
——, *Rāyapaseniya*, Ahmedabad, 1949.
——, *Thānaṅga*, 3 Pts., Bombay, 1937.
Abhyankar, K.V., ed., *Dasaveyāliya*, Ahmedabad, 1938.
Acharya, Kundakunda, *Panchastikaya Gatha*, Bombay, 1904.
Basham, A.L., *History and Doctrines of the Ajīvikas: A Vanished Indian Religion*, London, 1951.
Bhadrabahu, N., *Āvassaya (Āvaśyaka)*, with Haribhadra and Malayagiri's Comm., Bombay, 1916, 1928.
——, *Āyāranga* (Ācāranga Sutra), with Silanka's Comm., Surat, 1935.
——, *Suyagadaṅga*, with Silanka's Comm., Bombay, 1917.
Bloomfield, M., tr., *Pārśvānāthacarita*, Baltimore, 1919.
Bühler, J.G. tr., J.A.S. Burgess, *The Indian Sect of the Jains*, London, 1903.
Choudhary, G.C., *Political History of Northern India from Jaina Sources*, c. 650 AD to 1300 AD, Amritsar, 1954.
Deo, S.B., *The History of Jaina Monachism*, Poona, 1955.
——, *Jaina Monastic Jurisprudence*, Poona, 1960.
Jacobi, H., *Jaina Sutras* (*Ācāranga Sutra; Kalpa Sutra*), *SBE.*, Vol. XXII, Oxford, 1894.

Jacobi, H., *The Uttarādhyayanasutra and the Sutrakritanga Sutra, SBE.*, Vol. XLV, Oxford, 1895.

Jain, J.C., *Life in Ancient India as Depicted in the Jaina Canons*, Bombay, 1947.

——, *History of Prakrit Literature*, Varanasi, 1961.

Jaini, Jagmanderlal, *Outlines of Jainism*, Cambridge, 1916, 1940.

Kapadia, H.R., *A History of the Canonical Literature of the Jains*, Bombay, 1941.

Law, B.C., *Mahavira: His Life and Teachings*, London, 1937.

Mehta, Mohanlal, *Outlines of Jaina Philosophy*, Bangalore, 1954.

——, *Jaina Psychology*, Amritsar, 1957.

Nahar and Ghosh, *An Epitome of Jainism*, Calcutta, 1917.

Sanghavi, Pt. Sukhlalji, ed., *Tattvārthasūtra*, Benares, 1966.

Schubring, Walther, tr., Wolfgang Beurlen, *The Doctrine of the Jains*, Delhi, 1962.

Shah, C.J., *Jainism in Northern India*, 800 BC–AD 526, London, 1932.

Stevenson, S., *The Heart of Jainism*, London, 1915, reprint, New Delhi, 1970.

Sundara, Samaya, Comm., *Kappasutta, Kalpalatā-Vyākhyā*, Surat.

Tatia, Nathmal, *Studies in Jaina Philosophy*, Benares, 1951.

Upadhye, A.N., ed., *Bṛhatkalpa Kosa* of Harisena, Bombay, 1943.

——, *Pravacanasara* of Sri Kundakundacarya, Bombay, 1935.

Vaidya, N.V., ed., *Nayadhammakahao* with Abhayadeva's Comm., Bombay, 1940.

——, *Mūlācāra* of Vaṭṭakera, 2 Pts., Bombay, 1980.

Vaidya, P.L., ed., *Antagadadasao*, with Abhayadeva's Comm., Poona, 1932.

——, *Uvasagadasao*, with Abhayadeva's Comm., Poona, 1930.

——, *Dasāsuyakkhandha*, Lahore, 1936.

——, *Dravyasrayakavya*, *BSS.*, LXIX, Bombay, 1915.

Vijaya, Ratna-Prabha, *Sramana Bhagavan Mahavira*, 5 Vols., Ahmedabad, 1948.

The Epics

Mahābhārata

Bhandarkar Oriental Research Institute, *The Mahabharata*, critical editions by different authors, 19 Vols., Poona, 1933-66.

Dutt, M.N., tr., *The Mahabharata*, 3 Vols., Calcutta, 1895-1901.

Hopkins, E.W., *The Great Epic of India: Its Character and Origin*, New York, 1902.

Iyer, V.V., *Notes of a Study of the Preliminary Chapters of the Mahabharata*, Madras, 1922.
Rajagopalachari, C., *Mahabharata*, Bombay, 1962.
Roy, P.C., tr., *The Mahabharata*, 12 Vols, Calcutta, n.d. revised edition, New Delhi, 1970-76.
Sukthankar, V.S., *Critical Studies of the Mahabharata*, Vol. I, Poona, 1944.
——, *On the Meaning of Mahabharata*, Bombay, 1957.
Vaidya, C.V., *The Mahabharata*—A Criticism, Bombay, 1905.
——, *Epic India*, Bombay, 1933.

The Bhagavad Gītā

Avinasananda, *Gītā Letters*, Bombay, 1954.
Bhave, Vinoba, *Talks on the Gita*, Benares, 1959.
Desai, Mahadev, tr., *The Gita According to Gandhi*, Ahmedabad, 1956.
Divetia, H.V., *Art of Life in Bhagavad Gita*, Bombay, 1960.
Edgerton, Franklin, tr., *The Bhagavad Gita*, Cambridge, Mass., 1944.
Hill, W.D.P., tr., *The Bhagavadgita*, London, 1928.
Juan, Mascaro, *The Bhagavad Gita*, Middlesex, 1962.
Munshi, K.M., *Bhagavad Gita and Modern Life*, Bombay, 1960.
Prabhavananda, Swami and Isherwood Christopher, tr., *The Song of God: Bhagavad Gita*, London, 1960.
Prem, Kishen, *The Yoga of the Bhagavad Gita*, London, 1938.
Purohitswami, *The Geeta*, London, 1965.
Radhakrishnan, S., tr., *The Bhagavadgita*, London, 1958.
Rajagopalachari, C., *Bhagavad Gita*, Bombay, 1964.
Ranade, R.D., *The Bhagavadgita as a Philosophy of God-realisation*, Bombay, 1965.
Roy, S.C., *The Bhagavad Gita and Modern Scholarship*, London, 1941.
Telang, K.T., tr., *The Bhagavadgita*, *SBE.*, Vol. VIII, Oxford, 1908.
Tilak, B.G., *Gita Rahasya*, 2 Vols., Poona, 1935-36.
Wadiyar, Sri Jaya Chamaraja, *The Gita and Indian Culture*, Madras, 1963.

The Rāmāyaṇa

Dutt, M.N., *The Ramayana*.
Griffith, R.T.H., tr., in verse, *The Ramayana of Valmiki*, Benares, 1895.

Rajagopalachari, C., *Ramayana*, Bombay, 1962.
Vaidya, C.V., *The Riddle of the Ramayana*, London, 1906.
Sharma, Vasudeva, ed., *Ramayana*, Bombay, 1915.
Shastri, H.P., tr., *The Ramayana of Valmiki*, 3 Vols., London, 1952, 1957-59.

The Arthaśāstra

Bandopadhyaya, M.C., *Kautilya: An Exposition of His Social Ideal and Political Theory*, Calcutta, 1927.
Jolly, J., *Arthasastra of Kautilya* (Text), 2 Vols., Lahore, 1923-24.
Kangle, R.P., *The Kautilya Arthaśāstra*, 3 Vols., Bombay, 1960, 1963, 1965.
Krishna Rao, M.V., *Studies in Kautilya*, Delhi.
Law, N.N., *Studies in Ancient Hindu Polity* (based on the Arthasastra of Kautilya), London, 1914.
Ramaswamy, T.N., *Essentials of Indian Statecraft* (Kautilya's Arthasastra for Contemporary readers), Bombay, 1962.

The Law-books

Apte, V.M., *Social and Religious Life in the Grihya Sutras*, Ahmedabad, 1939.
Banerji, S.C., *Dharmasutras*, Calcutta, 1962.
Bühler, G., tr., *The Sacred Laws of the Aryas*, *SBE.*, Vols. II, XIV, Oxford, 1879, 1882.
Bühler, G., *The Laws of Manu*, *SBE.*, Vol. XXV, Oxford, 1886.
Caland, W., ed., *Vaikhānasasmārtasūtram* (The Domestic and Sacred Laws of the Vaikhanasa School belonging to the Black Yoga), Calcutta, 1929.
Hopkins, E.W., tr., *The Ordinances of Manu*, London, 1891, reprint, New Delhi, 1971.
Jha, Ganganatha, ed. and tr., *Manu Smrti:* The Laws of Manu with the Bhasya of Medhatithi, 9 Vols., Calcutta, 1920-26.
Jolly, Julius, *Hindu Law and Custom*, Calcutta, 1928.
——, *The Minor Law-Books*, Oxford, 1889.
——, *The Institutes of Vishnu*, *SBE.*, Vol., VII, Oxford, 1880.
Kane, P.V., *History of Dharamaśāstras*, Vol. I, Poona, 1930, Vol. II., Pt. I and II, Poona, 1941, Vol. III, Poona, 1946.
Oldenberg, H., *The Grihyasutras*, *SBE.*, Vols. XXIX, XXX, Oxford, 1886-92.
Rangachari, K., *Vaikhānasa Dharma Sūtra*, Madras, 1930.

Shastri, Shakuntala Rao, *Women in the Sacred Laws*, Bombay, 1959.

General

Adam, Leonard, *Primitive Art*, London, 1963.
Agard, Roy, *The Still Mind*, London, 1961.
Agehananda Bharati, *The Ochre Robe*, London, 1961.
Agrawala, V.S., *India as Known to Panini*, Lucknow, 1953.
Akhilananda, Swami, *Mental Health and Hindu Psychology*, London, 1952.
——, *Hindu Psychology*, London, 1947.
Albig, William, *Modern Public Opinion*, New York, Toronto, London, 1956.
Alexander, Horace, *Consider India* – An Essay in Values, Bombay, 1961.
Allen Grant, *The Evolution of the Idea of God*, London, 1931.
Altekar, A.S., *Education in Ancient India*, Benares, 1934.
——, *The Position of Women in Hindu Civilisation*, Benares, 1956.
Arnold, Edwin, *The Light of Asia*, London, 1945.
Athavale, Sadashiva, *Carvaka—Itihas Ani Tatva jnana*, Marathi, Vai, 1958.
Atmananda, Swami, *Sri Sankara's Teachings in His Own Words*, Bombay, 1960.
Aurobindo, Sri, *Hymns to the Mystic Fire*, Pondicherry, 1946.
——, *The Foundations of Indian Culture*, New York, 1953.
——, *The Life Divine*, Calcutta, 1947.
Bain, *Sociology: Introductory Readings*, Chicago, 1962.
Baldeva Misra, Pandit, ed., *Yogasutram* with the Yogapradipika Comm., Benares, 1931.
Ballantyne, J.R., *The Sankhya Aphorisms of Kapila*, London, 1885.
Benerji, R.D., *Prehistoric Ancient and Hindu India*, Calcutta, 1934.
Bankey Bihari, *Sufis, Mystics and Yogis of India*, Bombay, 1962.
Barnett, L.D., *Antiquities of India*, London, 1913.
Barr, Stringfellow, *The Will of Zeus*, London, 1961.
Barth, A., *The Religions of India*, London, 1921.
Barua, B.M., *A History of Pre-Buddhistic Philosophy*, Calcutta, 1921.
Basak, Radhagovinda, *Asokan Inscriptions*, Calcutta, 1959.
Basham, A.L., *The Wonder that was India*, London, 1954.
Belvalkar S.K. and Ranade R.D., *History of Indian Philosophy*, Vol. II, Poona, 1927, reprint, New Delhi, 1975.
Bernard, Theos, *Hindu Philosophy*, Bombay, 1957.

Berard, FR., *Indian Mind*, Mangalore, 1962.
Besant, Annie, *Mysticism*, London, 1914.
Bhandarkar, D.R., *Vaishnavism, Saivism and Minor Religious Systems*, Strassburg, 1913.
——, *Some Aspects of Ancient Indian Culture*, Madras, 1950.
Bhattacharya, Sachidananda, *Select Asokan Epigraphs*, Calcutta, 1960.
Bouquet, A.C., *Comparative Religion*, London, 1945, 1962.
——, *Sacred Books of the World*, London, 1959.
Brahma, N.K., *Philosophy of Hindu Sadhana*, London, 1932.
Brandon, S.G.F., *Man and His Destiny in the Great Religions*, Manchester, 1962.
Brooks, C.E.P., *Climate through the Ages*, London, 1926.
Brunton, Paul, *The Secret Path*, London, 1959.
——, *The Hidden Teaching Beyond Yoga*, New York, 1941.
——, *Indian Philosophy and Modern Culture*, London, 1951.
——, *A Search in Sacred India*, London.
——, *The Inner Reality*, London, 1962.
——, *The Quest of the Overself*, London, 1959.
——, *Spiritual Crisis of Man*, London, 1960.
——, *The Wisdom of the Overself*, London, 1961.
Buckle, H.T., *Introduction to the History of Civilisation*, Vol. I, New York, 1913.
Byles, Marie, B., *The Lotus and the Spinning Wheel*, London, 1963.
Cave, Sydney, *Living Religions of the East*, London, 1952.
Chaitanya, Krishna, *A New History of Sanskrit Literature*, Bombay, 1962.
Chakraborty, Chandra, *The Racial History of India*, Calcutta, n.d.
Chattopadhyaya, Debi Prasad, *Lokayata*, Delhi, 1959.
Childe, V. Gordon, *Man Makes Himself*, New York, 1951.
——, *New Light on the Most Ancient East*, London, 1934.
Choudhari, Haridas, and Spiegalberg Frederic, ed., *The Integral Philosophy of Shri Aurobindo*, London, 1960.
Colledge, Eric, *The Mediaeval Mystics of England*, London, 1962.
Coomaraswamy, A.K., *Dance of Shiva*, London, 1918, reprint, New Delhi, 1975.
——, *Hinduism and Buddhism*, New York, 1943, reprint, New Delhi, 1975.
Cultural Heritage of India, 4 vols., Ramakrishna Mission, Calcutta 1937-56.

Coster, G., *Yoga and Western Psychology*, London, 1957.

Cowell, E.B. and Gough, A.E., tr., *Sarvadarsanasamgraha of Madhava*, London, 1914.

Dasgupta, Surendranath, *A History of Indian Philosophy*, 5 Vols. London, 1922-23, 1957.

——, *A Study of Patanjali*, Calcutta, 1920.

——, *Philosophical Essays*, Calcutta, 1941.

——, *Yoga as Philosophy and Religion*, London, 1924.

——, *Hindu Mysticism*, Chicago, 1927.

——, *Indian Idealism*, Cambridge, 1962.

Dowson, J., *A Classical Dictionary of Hindu Mythology and Religion*, London, 1928, reprint, New Delhi, 1973.

Drekmeier, Charles, *Kingship and Community in India*, Bombay, 1962.

Durant, Will, *The Mansions of Philosophy*, London, 1929.

——, *Our Oriental Heritage*, New York, 1954.

Dutt, C.C., *The Culture of India as Envisaged by Sri Aurobindo*, Bombay, 1960.

Edgerton, Franklin, *The Beginnings of Indian Philosophy*, London, 1965.

Edwards, Michael, *A History of India*, London, 1961.

Eliade, Mircea, tr., Willard R. Trask, *Yoga: Immortality and Freedom*, London, 1958.

——, ed. and Kitagawa, J.M., *The History of Religions*, Chicago, 1959.

——, tr., Willard R. Trask, *The Myth of the Eternal Return*, London, n.d.

——, tr., Mariet Philip, *Images and Symbols*, London, 1961.

——, tr., Mariet Philip, *Myth and Reality*, London, 1964.

——, tr., Rosemary Sheed, *Patterns in Comparative Religion*, London, 1958.

Ellsworth, Huntington, *Civilization and Climate*, London, 1915.

Erich, Fromm, *The Art of Loving*, London, 1962.

Fairservis, W.A., *The Origins of Oriental Civilization*, New York, 1959.

Farquhar, J.N., *The Crown of Hinduism*, London, 1930, reprint, New Delhi, 1971.

——, *Outlines of the Religious Literature of India*, London, 1920.

——, *A Primer of Hinduism*, Madras, 1911.

Frankfort, Wilson and Jacobsen, *Before Philosophy*, London, 1954.

Fuchs, Stephen, *The Origin of Man and His Culture*, Bombay, 1963.
Gambhirananda, Swami, *History of the Ramakrishna Math and Mission*, Calcutta, 1957.
Garrett, G.T., ed., *The Legacy of India*, Oxford, 1937.
Ghosal, H.R., *An Outline History of the Indian People*, Delhi, 1962.
Ghurye, G.S., *Indian Sadhus*, Bombay, 1953.
——, *Culture and Society*, Bombay, 1947.
Gibbon, Edward, *The Decline and Fall of the Roman Empire*, 3 Vols., American Edition.
Giles, H.A., *The Travels of Fa-Hien*, Cambridge, 1923.
Gokhale, B.G., *Indian Thought Through the Ages*, Bombay, 1961.
Gonda, J., *Ancient Indian Ojas, Latin Augos and the Indo-European Nouns in es-os*, Utrecht, 1952.
Gordon, D.H., *The Pre-historic Background of Indian Culture*, Bombay, 1958.
Grant, Allen, *The Evolution of the Idea of God*, London, 1931.
Gundry, D.W., *Religions*, London, 1958.
Hadfield, J.A., *Psychology and Morals*, London, 1923.
Havell, E.B., *The History of Aryan Rule in India*, London, 1948.
——, *A Short History of India*, London, 1924.
Hazra, R.C., *Studies in the Puranic Records on Hindu Rites and Customs*, Dacca, 1940.
Heimann, Betty, *Indian and Western Philosophy*, London, 1937.
Hiriyana, M., *The Essentials of Indian Philosophy*, London, 1956.
——, *Outlines of Indian Philosophy*, London, 1932.
——, *Popular Essays in Indian Philosophy*, Mysore, 1952.
Honigberger, J.M., *Thirtyfive Years in the East*, London, 1852.
Hopkins, E.W., *The Religions of India*, Vol. I, New York, 1895.
——, *Ethics of India*, London, 1924.
Howells, George, *The Soul of India*, London, 1913.
Hrozny, Bedrich, tr., Jindrich Prochazka, *Ancient History of Western Asia, India and Greek*, New York, 1953.
Hussain, Abid, *The National Character of India*, Bombay, 1956.
Huxley, Julian, *Religion Without Revelation*, London, 1957.
Inge, W.R. *at el.*, ed., *Comparative Studies in Philosophy*, Presented in honour of Radhakrishnan, London, 1951.
Iyer, C.P.R., *Pen Portraits, Essays and Addresses*, Bombay, 1948.
Jacolliot and Others, *Mystics and Magicians of India*, Calcutta, 1953.
Jacquetta, Hawkes and Leonard, Woolley, *History of Mankind*, Vol. I, London, 1963.

James, E.O., *Primitive Religion*, London, 1957.
James, William, *The Varieties of Religious Experience*, London, 1915.
Javadekar, A.G., *Approach to Reality*, Baroda, 1957.
Jha, Ganganatha, *The Philosophical Discipline*, Kamala lectures, Calcutta, 1928.
Johnson, R.C., *A Religious Outlook for Modern Man*, London, 1963.
Jones, Rufus, M., *New Studies in Mystical Religion*, London, 1928.
Kabir, Humayun, *Our Heritage*, Bombay, 1946.
Kaegi, Adolf, tr., Arrowsmith, R., *Life in Ancient India*, Calcutta, 1950.
Kale and Gurjar, tr., *Bhartṛhari's Nitiśataka and Vairāgyaśataka*, Bombay, 1898.
Karmarkar, A.P., *The Haridasas of Karnataka*, Dharwar, 1939.
Kaviraj, A.C., *Charaka Samhita*, Vol. I, Calcutta, 1956.
Keith, A.B., *History of Sanskrit Literature*, Oxford, 1928.
Koestler, Arthur, *The Lotus and the Robot*, London, 1960.
Kosambi, D.D., *An Introduction to the Study of Indian History*, Bombay, 1956.
——, *Myth and Reality*, Bombay, 1962.
Kraemer, Hendrik, *World Cultures and World Religions*, London, 1960.
Law, B.C., *India as Described in Early Texts of Buddhism and Jainism*, London, 1941.
Leckey, W.E.H., *History of European Morals*, 2 Vols., London, 1905.
Legge, James, *A Record of Buddhist Kingdoms Being an Account by the Chinese monk Fa-Hien*, Oxford, 1886.
Leuba, J.H., *The Psychology of Religious Mysticism*, London, 1929.
Liebman, Joshua Loth, *Peace of Mind*, New York, 1955.
Lissner, Ivar, tr., J. Maxwell Brownjohn, *The Living Past*, London, 1957.
Livingstone, R.W., ed., *The Legacy of Greece*, London, 1951.
Lowie, R.H., *Primitive Religion*, London, 1960.
Luniya, B.N., *Evolution of Indian Culture*, Agra, 1960.
Macdonell, A.A., *History of Sanskrit Literature*, Delhi, 1958, reprint, New Delhi, 1972.
——, *Lectures on Comparative Religion*, Calcutta, 1925.
Macfie, J.M., *Myth and Legends of India*, Edinburgh, 1924.
Maciver, R.M., *Society*.

Macnicol, Nicol, *The Living Religions of the Indian People*, London, 1934.

Mahadevan, T.M.P., *Outlines of Hinduism*, Bombay, 1960.

Majumdar, Raychaudhari and Datta, *An Advanced History of India*, London, 1961.

Majumdar, R.C., *The Classical Accounts of India*, Calcutta, 1960.

——, and Pusalker, A.D., ed., *The Age of Imperial Unity*, Bombay, 1960.

Malinowski, B., ed. Phythis M. Kaberry, *The Dynamics of Culture*, London, 1945.

——, *A Scientific Theory of Culture and Other Essays*, Chapel Hill, 1944.

Marshall, Anne, *Hunting the Guru in India*, London, 1963.

Masson-Oursel, Paul, *Ancient India and Indian Civilisation*, London, 1951.

McCrindle, J.W., *Ancient India as Described by Megasthenes and Arrian*, London, 1877.

——, *The Invasion of India by Alexander the Great*, London, 1893.

——, *Ancient India as Described in Classical Literature*, London, 1901.

McKenzie, John, *Hindu Ethics*, London, 1922, reprint, New Delhi, 1971.

Mehta, Ratilal, N., *Pre-Buddhist India*, Bombay, 1939.

Merton, Thomas, *Seeds of Contemplation*, New York, 1956.

——, *Waters of Silence*, London, 1950.

——, *The Silent Life*, London, 1957.

Mitra, Sisirkumar, *The Vision of India*, Bombay, 1949.

Mookerji, Radha Kumud, *Hindu Civilisation*, 2 Vol., Bombay, 1957.

——, *Glimpses of Ancient India*, Bombay, 1961.

——, *Ancient India*, Allahabad, 1956.

Motwani, Kewal, *India: A Synthesis of Culture*, Bombay, 1947.

Muir, J., *Original Sanskrit Texts*, 5 Vols., London, 1868-73.

Mukerjee, Radha Kamal, *The Culture and Art of India*, London, 1959.

Müller, F. Max, *What Can India Teach Us?* London, 1882, reprint, New Delhi, 1961.

——, *A History of Ancient Sanskrit Literature*, Allahabad, 1926.

——, *Lectures on Origin and Growth of Religion*, Varanasi, 1964.

——, *The Six Systems of Indian Philosophy*, London, 1899.

Munshi, K.M., *Foundations of Indian Culture*, Bombay, 1962.

Murphy, John, *The Origins and History of Religions*, Manchester, 1952.
Nair, B.N., *The Dynamic Brahmin*, Bombay, 1959.
Nikhilananda, Swami, *Self-Knowledge* (Shankaracarya's Atmabodha), New York, 1946.
Nilakanta Sastri, K.A., ed., *A Comprehensive History of India*, Vol., II, Calcutta, 1957.
Oldenberg, H., *Ancient India, Its Language and Religions*, Calcutta, 1962.
Oman, J.C., *The Mystics, Ascetics and Saints of India*, London, 1903.
——, *Cults, Customs and Superstitions of India*, London, 1908.
——, *Indian Life: Religious and Social*, London, 1889.
Otto, Rudolf, tr., Bertha L. Bracey Richendra C. Payne, *Mysticism East and West*, New York, 1959.
——, tr. John W. Harvey, *The Idea of the Holy*, London, 1936.
——, tr., Brian Lunn, *Religious Essays*, London, 1937.
Ouspensky, P.D., *In Search of the Miraculous*, London, 1950.
Pai, D.A., *Monograph on the Religious Sects in India*, Bombay, 1928.
Panikkar, K.M., *A Survey of Indian History*, Bombay, 1947.
——, *The Foundations of New India*, London, 1963.
Parrinder, Geoffrey, *Upanishads, Gita and Bible*, London, 1962.
Payne, E.A., *The Saktas*, Calcutta, 1933.
Philips, C.H., ed., *Historians of India, Pakistan and Ceylon*, London, 1961.
Piggott, Stuart, *Prehistoric India*, Harmondsworth, 1950.
Potdar, K.R., *Sacrifice in the Rigveda*, Bombay, 1953.
Powys, J.C., *Meaning of Culture*, London, 1930.
Prabhavananad, Swami, *The Spiritual Heritage of India*, London, 1962.
Prabhu, Pandharinath, *Hindu Social Organisation*, Bombay, 1958.
Puntambekar, S.V., *An Introduction to Indian Citizenship and Civilisation*, Vol. II.
Puri, Baij Nath, *Indian History—A Review*, Bombay, 1960.
——, *India as described by Early Greek Writers*, Allahabad, 1939.
——, *India in the time of Patañjali*, Bombay, 1957.
Radhakrishnan, S., *East and West in Religion*, London, 1949.
——, *Indian Philosophy*, 2 Vols., London, 1923-27.
——, *Occasional Speeches and Writings*, 3 Vols., Delhi, 1952-59.

Radhakrishnan, S., *The Hindu View of Life*, London, 1954.
——, *An Idealist View of Life*, London, 1932.
——, ed., *A Source Book of Indian Philosophy.*
——, *The Brahmasutras*, London, 1960.
——, *Religion and Society*, London, 1947.
——, Muirhead, ed., *Contemporary Indian Philosophy*, London, 1936.
——, and Raju, P.T., ed., *The Concept of Man*, London, 1960.
Raghavan, V., *Sanskrit Literature*, Delhi, 1961.
Raghavananda, *Parmarthasara* of Sri Adi Sesha, *TSS.*, Trivandrum, 1911.
Raikar, Y.A., *Indian History: A Study in Dynamics*, Baroda, 1960.
Raja, C. Kunhan, *Survey of Sanskrit Literature*, Bombay, 1962.
Rajagopalachari, C., *Our Culture*, Bombay, 1963.
Ranade, R.D., *Indian Mysticism: Mysticism in Maharashtra*, Poona, 1933.
Rangacharya, V., *History of Pre-musalman India*, Vol. I, Madras, 1929.
Rapson, E.J., *Cambridge History of India*, Vol. 1 and 4, London, 1922.
Rawlinson, H.G., ed., Seligman, C.G., *India: A Short Cultural History*, London, 1937.
Renou, Louis, ed., *Hinduism*, New York, 1963.
Riencourt, Amaury De, *The Soul of India*, New York, 1960.
Ronaldshay, *India—A Bird's Eye-view*, London, 1924.
Roy, M.N., *Crime and Karma, Cats and Women*, Calcutta, 1957.
——, *The Historical Role of Islam*, Calcutta, 1958.
Russell, Bertrand, *Mysticism and Logic*, London, 1953.
Rutledge, Dan Denys, *In Search of a Yogi*, London, 1962.
Sampurnananda, *Evolution of the Hindu Pantheon*, Bombay, 1963.
——, *Vratyakanda*, Madras, 1956.
Sankalia, H.D., *The University of Nalanda*, Madras, 1934.
Sankaranarayana, P., *Values in History*, Bombay, 1962.
Sarkar, S.C., *Educational Ideas and Institutions in Ancient India*, Patna, 1928.
——, *Some Aspects of the Earliest Social History of India*, London, 1928.
Sarma, N.A., *Woman and Society*, Baroda, 1947.
Sastri, K.A. Nilakanta, *A History of South India*, Madras, 1955.
Sastri, K.S.R., *The Evolution of Indian Mysticism*, n.d. n.p.

Sastri, S.M., *Cunningham's Ancient Geography of India*, Calcutta, 1924.
Sastri, Dakshinaranjan, *A Short History of Indian Materialism, Sensationalism, Hedonism*, Calcutta, 1930.
Schweitzer, Albert, *Civilisation and Ethics*, London, 1961.
——, *Indian Thought and Its Development*, London, 1936, 1957.
Sen, K.M., *Hinduism*, London, 1961.
Sharma, Har Dutt, *Contributions to the History of Brahmanical Asceticism* (Saṃnyās), Poona, 1939.
Sharma, Chandradhar, *A Critical Survey of Indian Philosophy*, London, 1960.
Sidhanta, N.K., *The Heroic Age of India*, London, 1928, reprint, New Delhi, 1975.
Singer, Milton, *Traditional India: Structure and Change*, Philadelphia, 1959.
Sinha, Jadunath, *History of Indian Philosophy*, Vol. I, Calcutta, 1956.
Sircar, D.C., *Inscriptions of Asoka*, Delhi, 1957.
——, *Studies in the Geography of Ancient and Medieval India*, Delhi, 1960.
Slater, T.E., *The Higher Hinduism in Relation to Christianity*, London, 1903.
Smith, Vincent, *Oxford History of India*, London, 1958.
Sorokin, P.A., *Social and Cultural Dynamics*, Vol. I, New York, 1937.
——, *Sane Sex Order*, Bombay, 1961.
——, *The Reconstruction of Humanity*, Bombay, 1958.
Spencer, Sydney, *Mysticism in World Religion*, Harmondsworth, 1963.
Srinivasachari, P.N., *Mystics and Mysticism*, Madras, 1951.
Subbarao, B., *The Personality of India*, Baroda, 1956.
Tagore, Rabindranath, *Sadhana: The Realisation of Life*, London.
——, *Gitanjali.*
Teape, W.M., *The Secret Lore of India*, Cambridge, 1932.
Thapar, Romila, *Asoka and the Decline of the Mauryas*, London, 1961.
Thomas, P., *Incredible India*, Bombay, 1966.
——, *Hindu Religion, Customs and Manners*, Bombay, n.d.
——, *Epics, Myths and Legends of India*, Bombay, n.d.
Tomlin, E.W.F., *Great Philosophers of the East*, London, 1959.
Toynbee, Alfred, *One World and India*, Delhi, 1960.

Tripathi, R.S., *History of Ancient India*, Delhi, 1960.
Underhill, Evelyn, *Essentials of Mysticism*, London, 1920.
——, *Mysticism*, London, 1931.
Upadhyaya, B.S., *India in Kalidas*, Allahabad, 1947.
Urquhart, W.S., *Pantheism and the Value of Life*, London, 1919.
Vasu, S.C., *An Introduction to the Yoga Philosophy*, Allahabad, 1926, reprint, New Delhi, 1976.
Venkateswara, S.V., *Indian Culture Through the Ages*, 2 Vols. London, 1932.
Vivekananda, Swami, *The Complete Works*, Mayavati, Almora, 1932.
——, *Rajayoga*, London, New York, Bombay, 1897.
Vora, D.P., *Evolution of Morals in the Epics*, Bombay, 1959.
Walker, K., *The Conscious Mind*, London, 1962.
Walters, John, *Mind Unshaken*, London, 1961.
Watters, Thomas, ed., T.W. Rhys Davids and S.W. Bushell, *On Yuan Chwang's Travels in India*, 2 Vols. New Delhi, 1973.
Weber, A., *History of Indian Literature*, Varanasi.
Weber, Max, *The Religion of India*, Illinois.
Wheeler, J.T., *Ancient and Hindu India*, Calcutta, 1961.
Wilcken, Ulrich, tr., G.C., Richards, *Alexander the Great*, London, 1932.
Williams, Monier, *Brahmanism and Buddhism*, London, 1887, 1891.
——, *Indian Wisdom*, London, 1875.
Wilson, H.H., *Sketch of the Religious Sects of the Hindus*, Calcutta, 1846, London, 1861.
Winternitz, M., *Some Problems of Indian Literature*, Calcutta, 1925.
——, *A History of Indian Literature*, 2 Vols., Calcutta, 1927, 1933, reprint, New Delhi, 1972.
Wood, Ernest, *Yoga*, London, 1959.
Woods, J.H., *The Yoga-System of Patanjali*, Cambridge, Mass., 1914.
Yale, John, ed., *What Vedanta Means to me*, London, 1961.
Yatiswaranda, Swami, *Adventures in Vedanta*, London, 1961.
Zacharias, O.C.D., *An Outline of Hinduism*, Alwaye, 1956.
Zaehner, R.C., *Hinduism*, London, 1962.
——, *Hindu and Muslim Mysticism*, London, 1960.
Zimmer, H.R., *Hindu Medicine*, Baltimore, 1948.
Zimmer, Heinrich, *Philosophers of India*, New York, 1957.
Zimmer, Heinrich, *Myths and Symbols in Indian Art and Civilisation*, New York, 1946.

Articles, Journals and Periodicals

Agrawala, V.S., Nāsadīya Sūkta, *Bharati*, No. 6, pt. II, 1962-63, pp. 1-11.

——, Words Notes on the Divyāvadāna, *Bharati*, No. 6, pt. II, 1962-63, pp. 47-75.

Altekar, A.S., The Asrama System, *Prof. Ghurye Felicitation*, Vol., 1954, pp. 183-94.

Anderson, Rock Paintings of Singhanpur, *JBORS.*, 1918, pp. 298-306.

Barua, Benimadhab, The Ajivikas: a short history of their Religion and Philosophy, *JDL.*, II, 1920, pp. 1-80.

Bhagvat, Durga, Origin of Indian Monachism, *JBU.*, Vol. VIII, Pt. 2, September, 1939, pp. 104-30.

Bhandarkar, D.R., Ajivikas, *IA.*, XLI, 1912, pp. 286-90.

Bhattacharya, V.C., An aspect of the Samavidhāna Brāhmaṇa, *Our Heritage*, Vol. VI, pp. 55-81.

Bloomfield, M., On False Ascetics and Nuns in Hindu Fiction, *JAOS.*, XLIV, 1924, pp. 202-42.

Carnac, J.H.R., On Stone Implements from the NWP of India *JASB.*, 1883, pp. 221-24.

Chanda, Sind Five Thousand Years Ago, *Modern Review*, Vol. LII, August, 1932, pp. 151-60.

Chattopadhyaya, B K., Philosophy of the Upanishads, *Journal of the Bihar Research Society*, Vol. XLIV, Pts. III-IV, 1958, pp. 129-36.

Cockburn, John, Cave Drawings in the Kaimur Range, *JRAS.*, 1899, pp. 89-97. *JASB.*, 1883, pp. 56-64. *JASB.*, 1907, pp. 467ff.

Davids, C.A.F., Rhys, Asceticism (Buddhist) *ERE.*, Vol. II, pp. 69-70.

Dutta, Churamani, The Bhagavadgita—A Representative Hindu Scripture, *Bharati*, No. 8. Pt. I, 1964-65, pp. 103-14.

Edgerton, Franklin, The Philosophical Materials of the Atharva-veda, *Studies in the honour of Maurice Bloomfield*, 1920, pp. 117-35.

——, The Upanishads: What do they teach and why, *JAOS.*, 49, 1929, pp. 97-121.

Edgerton, Franklin, The Meaning of Samkhya and Yoga, *American Journal of Philosopy*, 45, 1924, pp. 1-46.

——, Dominant Ideas in the Formation of Indian Culture, *JAOS.*, 62, 1942, pp. 151-56.

Farquhar, J.N., The Organisation of the Samnyasis of the Vedanta, *JRAS.*, 1925, pp. 479-86.

Fawcett, Rock Cravings in the Edakad Cave, *IA.*, 1901, pp. 413-21.

Gajendragadkar, S.N., The Roving Mendicants in the Mahabharata and Their Teaching, *JASB.*, Vol. 30, Pt. I, 1955, pp. 43-51.

Garbe, R., Yoga, *ERE.*, Vol. XII, pp. 831-33.

Geden, A.S., Asceticism (Hindu), *ERE.*, Vol. II, pp. 87-96.

Ghoshal, Rules for Ascetics in Jainism, Buddhism and Hinduism, *JA.*, Vol. I, No. IV, 1936, pp. 67-81.

Hariharan, K.V., Some Thoughts on Protohistory, *JBU.*, XXV, Pt. I (July, 1956), pp. 12-18.

Heras, H., The Plastic Representation of God Amongst the Proto-Indians, Sardesai, Comm., Vol., 1938.

Hoernle, AFR, Ajivikas, *ERE.*, I, pp. 259-68.

Hopkins, E.W., Yoga Technique in the Great Epic, *JAOS.*, XXII, 1901, pp. 333-79.

Jain, The Jaina References in the Buddhist Literature, *IHQ.*, Vol. II, p. 698.

——, The Practice of the Earlier Tirthankars, *AIOC.*, XIX, 19th Session, II, pp. 75-81.

Keny, L.B., Buddha Ani Nirashavad (Marathi), *Sadhana*, May, 24, 1956, pp. 29-32.

Kosambi, D.D., Urvasi and Pururavas, *JRAS.*, Bombay Branch, Vol. 27, 1951, pp. 1-30.

Law, B.C., Gautama Buddha and the Paribrajakas, *JRASB.*, n.s. XXI, 1925.

——, Influence of the Five Heretical Teachers on Jainism and Buddhism, *JRASB.*, n.s. XV, 1919, pp. 123-36.

——, A Short Account of the Wandering Teachers at the Time of the Buddha, *JRASB.*, n.s. XIV, 1918, pp. 399-406.

Macculloch, J.A., Austerities, *ERE.*, Vol. II, pp. 225-35.

Macdonell, A.A., Vedic Religion, *ERE.*, Vol. XII, pp. 601-18.

Mitra, Kalipada, Magic and Miracle in Jaina Literature, *IHQ.*, XV. 2, 1939, pp. 175-82.

Raj Narain, Psychic Powers in Hindu Shastras, *Aryan Path*, 1937, pp. 209-300.

Rao, S.R., New Light on Indus Valley Civilisation, *Indian Cultural Review*, No. 3-4, 1960, pp. 19-29.

Silberrad, C.A., Rock Drawings in the Banda District, *JASB.*, Vol. III, 1907, pp. 567-68.

Van Troy, J., The Origin of Asceticism and of the Asrama Dharma, *Bharati*, VIII, Pt. I, 1964-65, pp. 1-26.

Vyas, S.N., Love and Longing in the Ramayana, *JOI.*, Vol. II, 1952-53, pp. 105-17.

——, Belief in Omens in the Ramayana Age, loc. cit., pp. 23-29.

——, Karma and Transmigration in the Ramayana, loc. cit., pp. 23-29.

——, Polygamy and Polyandry as depicted by Valmiki, loc. cit., pp. 221-31.

——, The Valmikian Concept of an Ideal Wife, loc. cit., pp. 303-10.

——, The Caste-System in the Ramayana Age, *JOI.*, Vol. III, 1953-54, pp. 72-83.

——, The Culture of Hermitages in the Ramayana, loc. cit., pp. 227-35, 315-27.

——, The Aryan Way of Life in the Ramayana, *JOI.*, Vol. V, 1955-56, pp. 135-39.

——, Religious Beliefs in the Ramayana, *JOI.*, Vol. VII, 1957-58, pp. 125-34.

Wadia, The Philosophical Outlook in India and Europe, *Comparative Studies in Philosophy Presented in Honour of Radhakrishnan's Sixtieth Birthday*, 1951, pp. 87-103.

Wadiyar, Jaya Chamaraja, Is Indian Philosophy Applicable to Modern Living? *Sunday Standard*, June, 25, 1961.

Dictionaries, Encyclopaedias, Indexes

Apte, V.S., *Sanskrit-English Dictionary.*

Bloomfield, M., *A Vedic Concordance.*

Davids, T.W. Rhys and William Stede, ed., *Pali English Dictionary*, reprint, New Delhi, 1975.

Deb, R.K., *Shabdakalpadrum*, 5 Vols.

Dikshitar, V.R.R., *The Purana Index*, Vol. I.

Encyclopaedia Britannica.

Jacob, G.A., *A Concordance to the Principal Upanishads and Bhagavadgita*, Delhi.

Hastings, James, *Encyclopaedia of Religion and Ethics*, 13 Vols.

Keith, A.B. and A.A. Macdonell, *Vedic Index*, 2 Vols.

Macdonell, A.A., *Sanskrit English Dictionary.*

Maharaj, Ratnachandraji, *Ardha-Magadhi Dictionary*, 5 Vols.

Malalasekera, *Dictionary of Pali Proper Names*, 2 Vols.

Monier Williams, *English Sanskrit Dictionary.*

Rice, E.P., *The Mahabharata Analysis and Index.*
Seligman, Edwin, *Encyclopaedia of Social Sciences.*
Sorenson, S., *An Index to the Names in the Mahabharata.*
Tandon, Yashpal, *A Concordance of Purana Contents.*
Visvabandhu, *A Complete Alphabetic Index of all the Words in the Atharvaveda.*
Webster's Dictionary.

Index